ACOMA GRAMMAR AND TEXTS

ACOMA GRAMMAR AND TEXTS

BY

WICK R. MILLER

UNIVERSITY OF CALIFORNIA PRESS
BERKELEY AND LOS ANGELES
1965

UNIVERSITY OF CALIFORNIA PUBLICATIONS IN LINGUISTICS

Advisory Editors: W. E. Bull, C. D. Chrétien, M. B. Emeneau, M. R. Haas,
Harry Hoijer, D. L. Olmsted, R. P. Stockwell
Volume 40

Approved for publication September 27, 1963
Issued June 30, 1965
Price, $5.00

University of California Press
Berkeley and Los Angeles
California

Cambridge University Press
London, England

Manufactured in the United States of America

CONTENTS

[v]

TEXTS

INTRODUCTION

The Indian pueblo of Acoma is located in New Mexico, about sixty miles west of Albuquerque. The pueblo was built on a mesa top to offer protection from the Navajo and Apache. Today most of the Acomas live in the nearby farming colonies of Acomita and McCarties, and return to Acoma only for special occasions. Only a few of the older people live permanently at Acoma. There are approximately two thousand Acoma Indians, and virtually all of them are native speakers of Acoma.

Acoma belongs to the Keres language family, which includes also six other closely related languages or dialects. Laguna, a Keres pueblo located a few miles to the east, is Acoma's closest neighbor. Laguna and Acoma are mutually intelligible. The other five Keres pueblos are located in the Rio Grande Valley to the east and north. Cochiti is the most northern of the Keres pueblos, and it differs more from Acoma than any other Keres language. Cochiti and Acoma are mutually intelligible only if the speakers have had considerable opportunity to hear each other's language. There is a gradual transition in the Keres language family from Cochiti in the north to Acoma in the west (see Davis, 1959).

Keres is not known to be related to any other language group. Sapir placed Keres in the Hokan-Siouan stock, but evidence is still lacking.

There are three other language families represented in the pueblo area, namely Zuñi, Tanoan, and Uto-Aztecan. Zuñi is spoken at the single pueblo of the same name in western New Mexico. The Tanoan languages are spoken at a number of pueblos in the Rio Grande Valley and form a more diversified family than Keres. Uto-Aztecan is represented by the Hopi language, spoken at a number of pueblos in northeastern Arizona.

Acoma has been in contact with other pueblo groups for some time, probably at least since the beginning of the pueblo era, some fifteen hundred to two thousand years ago. There has been much cultural borrowing but surprisingly little linguistic borrowing. Acoma has been in contact with Spanish for over three centuries and has borrowed more from that language than from neighboring pueblo languages (Miller, 1959b,

1960). On the other hand, the more recent contact with English in the past one hundred years has resulted in very little borrowing.

There are a few monolingual Acomas, most of whom are older women. Spanish is spoken by a few of the older people, but the language is seldom used today, and apparently it was never as common at Acoma as it was in the Rio Grande pueblos. The majority of the Acomas have been to the Indian Service schools and speak English. What eventual effect English will have on the native language remains to be seen, but it can be predicted that it will be considerable. In 1949 none of the first grade children at Acomita Day School spoke English when they entered school. Today a few of the first graders already speak some English, but Acoma is still their first language. (See Fox, 1959, for an excellent account of language use and function at Cochiti; the situation at Acoma is probably similar to that at Cochiti, except for the position of Spanish.)

The pueblo area is ethnographically one of the best known areas in North America north of Mexico. Linguistically, it is one of the least known, and Keres is the least known of the four pueblo language families. The first serious linguistic work was done by Boas (1923, 1925, 1928). Spencer (1946) attempted to present a phonemic analysis which would account for all the dialects. Unfortunately, many important phonemic distinctions are ignored. The only thorough treatment of a Keres language has been done by Davis (in press).

My field work was done entirely in the San Francisco Bay Area from 1956 to 1959, under grants from the University Patent Fund and the Department of Linguistics, University of California at Berkeley. Most of the field work was done with Anne Hansen, an Acoma speaker who was then about thirty-five years old. Tape-recorded texts were obtianed from Mrs. Hansen, as well as from other Acoma speakers living in or visiting the San Francisco Bay Area: Andrew Lewis, Margaret Lim, Bell Lewis, Mary Histia (brother and sisters of Mrs. Hansen), George Garcia, Mary Valley, and her daughter Ruth Valley. All of the texts were transcribed with the help of Mrs. Hansen, and all of the grammatical notes were obtained from Mrs. Hansen. The phonemic analysis is based on material from Mrs. Hansen and Mrs. Lim.

The grammar is a revision of my dissertation submitted to the Graduate Division of the University of California in partial satisfaction of the requirements for the degree of Doctor of Philosophy in 1962. Grateful thanks are due to the members of the committee, Mary R. Haas, Murray B. Emeneau, and Francis J. Whitfield, for their suggestions and patience; to my wife for her patience; and to the Acoma speakers, whose willing coöperation made this grammar possible.

BIBLIOGRAPHY

Boas, Franz
    1923.   "A Keresan Text," International Journal of American Linguis-
             tics, Vol. 2, pp. 171-180.
    1925.   Keresan Texts. American Ethnological Society Publications,
             Vol. 8, Pt. 2.
    1928.   Keresan Texts. American Ethnological Society Publications,
             Vol. 8, Pt. 1.

Davis, Irvine
    1959.   "Linguistic Clues to Northern Rio Grande Prehistory," El
             Palacio, Vol. 66, pp. 73-84.
             The Language of Santa Ana Pueblo. Bureau of American
             Ethnology, Bulletin (in press).

Fox, J. R.
    1959.   "A Note on Cochiti Linguistics," in Charles H. Lange, Cochiti,
             A New Mexico Pueblo, Past and Present, Austin: University
             of Texas Press, Appendix No. 44, pp. 557-572.

Gatschet, Albert S.
    1876.   Zwölf Sprachen aus dem Südwestern Nordamerikas (Pueblo-
             und Apache-Mundarten; Tonto, Tonkawa, Digger, Utah). Wei-
             mar: Hermann Böhlau. [Quéres und Acoma, pp. 60-62.]
    1879.   "Seven Linguistic Stocks of Western Indian Dialects," Report
             upon United States Geographical Surveys West of the One Hun-
             dreth Meridan, Vol. 7, pp. 403-486. Washington.

Gunn, John M.
    1917.   Schat-Chen, History, Traditions and Narratives of the Queres
             Indians of Laguna and Acoma, Albuquerque, N. M.: Albright
             and Anderson.

Menaul, John
    1882.   Laguna Indian Translation of McGufefyf's [sic] New First
             Eclectic Reader. Laguna, New Mexico.

Mickey, Barbara H.
    1956.   "Acoma Kinship Terms," Southwestern Journal of Anthropology,
             Vol. 12, pp. 249-256.

[3]

Miller, Wick R.
  1959a.   "Some Notes on Acoma Kinship Terminology," Southwestern
           Journal of Anthropology, Vol. 15, pp. 179-184.
  1959b.   "Spanish Loanwords in Acoma: I," International Journal of
           American Linguistics, Vol. 25, pp. 147-153.
  1960.   "Spanish Loanwords in Acoma: II," International Journal of
           American Linguistics, Vol. 26, pp. 41-49.

Miller, Wick R., and Irvine Davis
  1963.   "Proto-Keresan Phonology," International Journal of American
           Linguistics, Vol. 29, pp. 310-330.

Newman, Stanley S.
  1954.   "American Indian Linguistics in the Southwest," American
           Anthropologist, Vol. 56, pp. 626-644.

Spencer, Robert F.
  1946.   "The Phonemes of Keresan," International Journal of Ameri-
           can Linguistics, Vol. 12, pp. 229-236.
  1947.   "Spanish Loanwords in Keresan," Southwestern Journal of
           Anthropology, Vol. 3, pp. 130-146.

Stirling, Matthew W.
  1942.   Origin Myth of Acoma and other Records. Bureau of Ameri-
           can Ethnology, Bulletin 135, pp. 1-123.

Toomey, T. N.
  1914.   Grammatical and Lexical Notes on the Keres Language.
           Hervas Laboratories of American Linguistics, Bulletin 5.

White, Leslie A.
  1932.   The Acoma Indians. Bureau of American Ethnology, Annual
           Report 47, 1929-1930.
  1943.   New Material from Acoma. Bureau of American Ethnology,
           Bulletin 136, pp. 303-359.
  1944a.   "Notes on the Ethnology of the Keres," Papers of the Michi-
           gan Academy of Science, Arts, and Letters, Vol. 30, pp. 557-
           568.
  1944b.   "A Ceremonial Vocabulary among the Pueblos," International
           Journal of American Linguistics, Vol. 10, pp. 161-167.
  1945.   "Notes on the Ethnozoology of the Keresan Pueblo Indians,"
           Papers of the Michigan Academy of Science, Arts, and Letters,
           Vol. 31, pp. 223-243.

GRAMMAR

100. PHONOLOGY

110. Phonemes

The phonemes of Acoma are divided into three groups—consonants, vowels, and tonal accents:

CONSONANTS

	plain					glottalized				
	Labial	Dental	Palatal	Retroflex	Velar	Labial	Dental	Palatal	Retroflex	Velar
OBSTRUENTS										
OCCLUSIVES										
Stops										
unaspirated	b	d	dy		g					
aspirated	p	t	ty		k	ṗ	t́	t́y		ḱ
Affricates										
unaspirated		z	ž	ẓ						
aspirated		c	č	c̣			ć	č́	ć̣		
SIBILANTS		s	š	ṣ			ś	š́	ṣ́		
SONORANTS										
Nasals	m	n				ḿ	ń			
Semivowels and flaps	w	r	y			ẃ	ŕ	ẏ		

MANNER CONSONANTS   ʔ and h

VOWELS

i   ə   u

e

a

*

[7]

* in the chart represents length which is handled orthographically as a doubling of the preceding vowel.

TONAL ACCENTS

High (´), Falling (ˆ), and Glottal (ˀ)

(Juncture and terminal contours are given in Section 140)

120. Distribution[1]

121. Every word has at least one tonal accent. The domain of the accent is the syllable, and for convenience the diacritic is written over the first vowel.

The high accent is unrestricted in its distribution:

ḱú 'woman'	sái 'all'
múši 'soap'	šína 'louse'
báani 'sash'	díní 'above'
dáwáa 'good'	sḱúrúuná 'peas'
zíibái 'he is sleeping'	mayú 'song leader'
šisáwá 'six times'	sídyá 'I touched it'

The falling accent is normally restricted to nonfinal syllables with vowel clusters:

sêeča 'I am warm'	sîuní 'I know him'
dyâana 'four'	ḱâakaaťi 'plaza'
híyâani 'road'	

A syllable with a single vowel may have the falling accent if the following syllable has a plain sonorant, is final, and has the high accent:[2]

gûní 'he knows him'	dyâwá 'early'
zuḱâwá 'willow'	ˀisdûwá 'arrow'

The falling accent is found in final position in two monowyllabic words:

čâi 'last'	râi 'king'

---

[1]Some of the distributional statements are deferred until the morphophonemics is treated.

[2]The contrast between the falling and high accents with single vowels was found rather late. Since I did not recheck all my field notes with reference to this contrast, forms written with the high accent in this environment may, in some instances, be misrecordings. All the forms listed in Section 121, however, were checked.

The glottal accent is restricted to syllables that have vowel clusters:

séeča 'my tooth'   čuudá 'plums'
y̓aisé 'fine hailstones'   síyuuce 'I took him'
búuřaika 'butterfly'   ʔadáuši 'cooking pot'
cíy̓aicu 'it stopped raining'   wášuuzá 'it fits him'

Words that have the glottal accent in final position are not common.
Most such words are either monosyllabic, are baby talk words, or are
probably from baby talk:

báabáa 'grandparent, grand-   žíižii 'sibling of the opposite
   child of the opposite sex'   sex'
búibii 'insect' (baby talk)   ʔədə́ə 'hot'
wée 'that one'   də́i 'here'

The first accent normally falls on the first or second syllable. Most
of the exceptions are either loanwords or else have accent ablaut (see
Sections 210, ‖ 19 and ‖ 22):

ʔarawagéki 'Albuquerque'   ʔarawagú 'apricot'
ʔayuná 'Lent'   sahusé 'San José'
sakisdâana 'sexton'   k̓apišə́ní 'at night'

Contrary to the general rule there are a few words that have no accent: ku 'or', n̓ə 'down', si 'back' and ṣa 'in both directions'. These
words are usually phonologically affixed to the preceding or following
word (see Sections 741 and 750).

Some forms of {-záaN} 'to talk' have an optionally unaccented initial
syllable (see Section 210, ‖ 7.8). This sometimes results in a word with
no accent: sgâaʔacikuya ~ skaaʔacikuya 'I said to them'.

122. The syllable has the shape (C)CV(V). Most of the consonant
clusters consist of /s/ plus a stop:

sbúuná 'pottery'   spáati 'mocking bird'
w̓iispi 'cigarette'   sdák̓aci 'tangled hair'
ʔúčastáan̓i 'walking cane'   sustá 'I took water'
ʔúusdyúuci 'drum'   g̓uistyaṣa 'knot'
ʔésgá 'rawhide'   skúuy̓u 'giant'
sk̓áašu 'fish'

Nasal plus plain stop clusters in noninitial syllables are found in a
few words. Only single vowels are found before these clusters. All such
words are loanwords or probable loanwords:

kumbâari 'godfather'   sárámpi (name of a Kachina
sántu 'saint'   dancer)
mendâana 'window'   ʔíntyu 'Indian'
wánku 'bank'   mánki 'monkey'

The remaining consonant clusters form no pattern. The examples given are exhaustive:

/sč/, sč- an allomorph of the distributive dubitative prefix (see
    Section 233), sčâuʔu 'they dwell'

/nč/, ránču 'ranch'; kumánči 'Comanches'

/ns/, pinsibâari 'Principal' (a pueblo officer); ransîisku 'Francisco';
    sawaransîisku 'San Francisco'; sawururénsu 'San Lorenzo'

/ny/, nyáanyáa 'to nurse' (baby talk)

/hy/, hyêesta 'feast day'

/sw/, swêera 'sweater'

/gr/, hisugrístu 'Christ'

Any vowel except length may be the first member of a vowel cluster, but only /i/, /u/, and length may be the second member. The clusters are:

....	iu	ii
ei	eu	ee
ai	au	aa
ui	....	uu
əi	....	əə

The only real gap is /ə/ + /u/. The other two gaps are, in effect, filled by /i/ and /u/ + length. Examples:

cíukúmi 'string'	mîiça 'hummingbird'
séibé 'I am a liar'	hárámeuṣa 'tortilla'
péeça 'jack rabbit'	gaibé 'he is a liar'
háu 'who'	táaskáná 'potsherds'
k̓ûisdyáma 'smoke hole'	kúuku 'winter'
b̓óiníišu 'by the west side'	nəəćə 'rubber'

Vowel clusters are not found before the first accent. There are a few exceptions, resulting from irregular morphophonemic changes: ṣaayániya 'we were talking' (see Section 210, ‖ 7.9).

123. There are certain restrictions in the distribution of consonants and of consonant-plus-vowel sequences.

123.1 Retroflex consonants and palatal stops are not found before front vowels. In reality the contrast between dental and palatal stops is neutralized in this environment, and these stops are identified with the dentals for morphophonemic reasons (see Sections 210, ‖ 12, and 221) rather than with the palatals, which would be phonetically more realistic (see Section 131).

123.2. Unaspirated occlusives are not found in unaccented syllables that are after the last accented syllable. In other unaccented syllables unaspirated occlusives are found only if (1) the following vowel is short, (2) the following syllable is accented, and (3) the initial consonant of the following syllable is a glottalized occlusive, glottalized sonorant, or glottal stop. This distributional fact is associated with the morphophonemic change described in Section 210, ‖ 29. The few forms that do not fit this formulation, all in a particular morphophonemic environment, are discussed in ‖ 29.

123.3. The sequence /ye/ is found in a small number of forms:

śáuyéeca 'I made up my mind'

yêenisi 'Friday'

yêetu 'mesquite bean'

The sequence /yi/ is found only in forms that undergo a morphophonemic process described in Section 210, ‖ 1.7:

ʔúwâaneeyi 'the hunt'   ʔáačáwáiyí 'stick race'

/y̓/ is not found before front vowels.

The sequence /wu/ is found only in: sawururénsu 'San Lorenzo'. /w̓u/ does not occur.

123.4. Normally, the glottal stop in medial position is preceded and followed by the same vowel; or, if preceded by the length vowel, is preceded and followed by syllables that have the same initial vowel:

ya ʔáaná 'skunk brush'   húu ʔúuka 'dove'

ti ʔišáaci 'I am strong'   sámá ʔákə 'my daughter'

śâayaa ʔáńa 'we allowed it'   y̓áa ʔa 'reeds'

șa ʔâu ʔu 'our home'   ya ʔái 'sand'

śípəenai ʔi 'I put it in'   náwâa ʔai 'adult'

The few examples of nonidentical vowels before and after glottal stop are morphophonemically irregular and are given in Section 210, ‖ 14.

The glottal stop is not found between two single unaccented vowels after the last accented syllable, nor between a single accented vowel and a single unaccented vowel. The glottal stop is rare between two single accented vowels.

The sequences /ʔiu/ and /ʔui/ are not found in initial position, and in medial position vary freely with /y̓uu/ and /w̓ii/ (see Section 210, ‖ 16). It would be possible to analyse initial /y̓uu/ and /w̓ii/ as /ʔiu/ and /ʔui/ (see Section 135), but then we would find that while initial /y̓uu/ and /w̓ii/ did not occur, /y̓u/, /w̓i/, /yuu/, and /wii/ did.

123.5. /h/ is found in morpheme medial position only in:

bíhí 'female in-law'   yâihiya (a woman's name)

báhá 'bread'   kuháy̓a 'bear'

sahusé 'San José'   máuhárúuci (a kiva name)

ʔáahíiná (name of a Koshari   nahâaya 'day before yester-

    dance)   day'

gúuhúuca 'he howled'   sgúhima 'I believed'

/h/ is found in morpheme initial and word medial position in a few restricted morphophonemic environments (see Section 210, ‖5.4, ‖18.2):

    hiihiika 'he is grinning'   háuhause 'I am yawning'
    šahâami ~ šâami 'my tobacco'

123.6. Initial /r/ is found only in Spanish loanwords:

    rîiku 'rich'   risdûuna 'ribbon'
    rûuku 'crazy'   rûuniši 'Monday'
    rusá 'prayer'   rusâayu 'silver beads'

Initial /ř/ is found in one word, řeuřeubášǎ, the name of a Kachina dancer. It is probably borrowed from an eastern Keres dialect.

123.7. /č/ and /č̓/ are not found before /e/. /č̓/ is almost always found before /a/, but there are a few words with other vowels:

    č̓ə́dígá 'sparrow hawk'
    šúuč̓uuci 'I volunteered'
    č̓ubáýa 'build the fire!'

/ž/ is found in four Spanish loanwords:

    žîinu 'curly'   kužûuna 'mattress'
    kužîinu 'pig'   matažîina 'Matachina'

The phoneme is also found in one non-Spanish word: žíizii 'sibling of the opposite sex'. The word is probably taken from baby talk (see Miller 1959a).

130. Phonetics

Acoma is a lenis language. This feature is characteristic in the speech of Acomas whether speaking Acoma or English. The principal objection to my pronunciation of Acoma was that I spoke with too much force.

131. Obstruents. The glottalization of obstruents is light and follows the consonant. The glottalized occlusives and sibilants are phonetically identical with the unaspirated occlusives and plain sibilants except for the feature of glottalization. The aspiration of the aspirated occlusives is light.

The affricates have two phonetic components, a stop component plus a homorganic sibilant component. The sibilant following the dental affricates is [s]. In other affricates the sibilant component is phonetically identical with the corresponding sibilant phoneme. The sibilant component appears to be slightly voiced at the termination of its production when the affricate is unaspirated. It is voiceless in other affricates.

The labial stops are bilabial and show no detectable positional allophonic variation:

bíyá 'tilted'   wâabə́ni 'abalone shell'
piici 'deer hide'   pákura 'salamander'

The dental occlusives are clearly dental. The affricates show little
or no variation in position. The stops are usually palatalized before
front vowels and appear to be phonetically identical to palatal stops (note
that palatal stops are not found before front vowels; Section 123.1). The
dental sibilants are followed by a theta offglide. The /ṡ/ is difficult to
distinguish from the /s/ because the glottalization is imbedded in the
theta offglide:

dâani 'squash'   tâama 'five'
tée?e 'far'   t́ákaci 'it is square'
t́îiça 'spring'   zêeni 'language'
cína 'turkey'   ćúku 'twins'
séepe 'I went to bite it'   séepe 'we bit it'

The palatal stops are articulated with the flat of the tongue just behind the alveolar ridge, and are similar in position to the 't' of 'tune'
as pronounced in some Oklahoma dialects of English. The palatal affricates and sibilants, similar in position to English /č/ and /š/, are
fronted before front vowels and slightly retroflexed before /ə/ and /u/.
When retroflexed, the contact is still made with the blade of the tongue,
thus maintaining the contrast between palatal and retroflex consonants:

dyáamí 'eagle'   háatyani 'yucca'
záat́yau 'plains'   žîinu 'curly'
čámi 'three'   čə́ná 'river'
ḱúučíni 'yellow'   čánanaci 'cloth'
šáaḱu 'pipe'   kašéená 'albino'
šídiita 'star'   šúta 'crow'

Retroflex consonants are slightly backed before /u/ and /a/, slightly
fronted before /ə/. The contact is made with the tip of the tongue, the
position of articulation being similar to that of English 't' in 'true'. The
sibilant element is not as marked for the retroflex affricates as for the
other affricates, probably because there are no contrasting retroflex
stops:

ẓáici 'rabbit club'   ẓə́apəšíšə 'small piece'
ẓúusa 'brittle bush'   ċûukača 'did you see it?'
kəċáana 'you said it'   ṣâaḱaaku 'frost'
ẓə́ci 'raw'   ṣ́aaci 'it is torn'

The range of the velar stops is slightly greater and the position is
slightly more backed than in English. They are fronted before front
vowels and backed before /u/:

géesu 'cheese'
gúuci 'firewood'
kə́əci 'antelope'
pikíḱi 'bat'

gánami 'beans'
kúuku 'winter'
ḱúuti 'mountain'
ḱáyámá 'chipmunk'

132. Sonorants. A sonorant is lengthened when it is preceded by a single accented vowel.

Glottalization is medial for lengthened glottalized sonorants, initial elsewhere. Glottalization is especially light in initial position, and it is difficult to distinguish glottalized sonorants from plain sonorants in this position.

The flap phonemes are single dental flaps, much like medial 'r' in Spanish.

The dental nasals are palatalized before front vowels, before consonants (other than /k/) plus front vowels, and before /ty/ and /č/:

sîuní 'I know him'
mandêeki 'lard'
ʔíntyu 'Indian'

népišugú 'it will be night'
pinsibâari 'Principal'
ránču 'ranch'

The /ny/ of nyáanyáa 'to nurse' (baby talk) is phonetically identical with the /n/ before a front vowel. The alternative to setting up a cluster would be to set up two phonemes, /n/ and /ñ/, which would hardly ever contrast. /n/ is a velar nasal before /k/: wánku 'bank'; mánki 'monkey'.

Examples of the sonorants follow:

múši 'soap'
nə́əti 'prairie dog'
wái 'there'
hérérégá 'tadpole'
yaʔái 'sand'

músu 'a kind of plant'
ńə́əwá 'loose'
wái 'today'
búuŕáika 'butterfly'
yagə́çəni 'rib'

133. Sibilant clusters. The sibilant in sibilant clusters varies betwen a palatal and retroflex sibilant. It is retroflex before labial and velar stops plus /a/, /u/, or /ə/; elsewhere it is palatal. In the following examples the sibilant under consideration is written phonetically and underlined:

špíníní 'dwarf corn'
ýáasbá 'dough'
yúcispə́tini 'backbone'
náašt́émi 'starry eyes'
máaštu 'silver fox'
šdyáici 'it is muddy'
wíištyəgə́ńi 'beads'
ʔíšḱé 'the one'
sgúzúẃa 'tadpole'
ščâuʔu 'they dwell'

hîušbéẏu 'cry baby'
ʔúuspúrúuná 'chicken pox'
číišdiini 'honey'
wíišdáańi 'container'
št́ə́əci 'it is straight'
ʔúušdyúuci 'drum'
súuškiici 'I am brave'
ʔíška 'one'
skəzə́əná 'crumbs'

The retroflex sibilant sometimes varies freely with the palatal sibilant, but the reverse never occurs.

The palatal and retroflex sibilants (as well as the other four sibilants) contrast in prevocalic position: ?ašáni 'a step'; ?aṣáni 'wheat'. In the sibilant clusters, however, the sibilant contrasts are neutralized, and 's' is written, for example, ?ískế 'the one'; ?íska 'one'.

134. Vowel quality. Most of the vowel allophony can be described by a sliding allophony between two positions:[3] /i/ <u>high</u> to <u>lower-high</u> front unrounded; /ə/ high to <u>higher-mid</u> central or back unrounded; /u/ <u>high</u> to <u>higher-mid</u> back rounded; /e/ <u>higher-low</u> to <u>mid</u> front unrounded; /a/ <u>low</u> to <u>lower-mid</u> front unrounded. The first position is approached if the vowel is (1) accented, (2) part of a vowel cluster (with some exceptions, noted below), (3) phonetically voiced (see Section 136), and/or (4) nonfinal. The second position is approached if these conditions do not obtain. By various combinations of these conditions, various points between the two positions can be reached. In addition, there is a certain amount of free variation, so that it would be unrealistic to state the exact phonetic quality for any given environment.

There are certain allophonic variations crosscutting this scheme that apply to particular vowels. /u/ is lower after labials and in the vowel clusters /au/ and /eu/. In the cluster /eu/ the first vowel is higher than normal and the second vowel lower than normal so that both vowels are at about the same tongue height.

The vowel /ə/ has allophonic variations conditioned by the preceding consonant. The consonants are placed in four groups that condition allophones from central to back, in the order: (1) labials, (2) other consonants not listed, (3) palatal affricates and sibilants, and (4) retroflex consonants. The onset of /ə/ is slightly labialized after labial consonants, giving the effect of a diphthong.

135. Vowel clusters and vowel quantity. Vowel clusters are a little more than twice as long as single vowels. Vowel clusters have little variation in vowel length. A final single vowel is shorter than other single vowels.

In vowel clusters ending with /i/ or /u/ the second vowel is about twice as long as the first. There is never any question about the vocalic character of the second vowel. The length vowel is realized as a continuation of the first vowel.

---

[3]The phonetic terms are used as defined by Block and Trager, Outline of Linguistic Analysis, Special Publications of the Linguistic Society of America (1942), p. 22.

In the clusters /iu/ and /ui/ the first vowel often loses its vocalic character after certain consonants: a velar stop plus /ui/ can be phonetically a labialized velar plus [i·]; a dental nasal plus /iu/ is always a palatalized nasal plus [u·] (cf. the treatment of /n/ before front vowels and in the cluster /ny/, Section 132); /ʔiu/ can be phonetically [ʔyu·]; and /ʔui/ can be phonetically [ʔwi·]:

    [gʷi·] in: gúičaapə 'he crossed over'

    [k̇ʷi·] in: s̓âuk̇ui 'my wife'

    [ñu·] in: ñíukúičánigú 'it will be divided'

    [ʔyu·] in: siʔíuyá 'I killed them'

    [ʔwi·] in: s̓uʔúičaapə 'we crossed over'

The contrast between /ʔiu/ and /ẏuu/ and between /ʔui/ and /ẅii/ (found in medial position only, Section 123.4) is very slight and can disappear entirely (Section 210, ‖ 16).

The contrast between dental stop plus /iu/ and palatal stop plus /uu/ is not very great, but the two sequences never fall together. In the first sequence the palatal element between the stop and [u] is slightly longer and always maintains something of its vocalic character: díukača 'the other one saw him' (obviative); dyúukača 'he saw him'.

The vowels in /v́y/ and /v́w/ (where /v́/ represents any vowel except /i/ and /u/ respectively) sometimes sound like the vowel clusters /v́iy/ and /v́uw/, since the sonorant is lengthened in this position (Section 132). The distinction between the two types is manifested by the fact that the second vowel in the phonemic cluster is always long and clearly vocalic:

    gúyá 'he killed him'   gúiyâut̓uwi 'he threw a rock'

    síwíiz̓ə̇əca 'he aimed'   zíuwáica 'he scratched him'

136. Devoicing. Vowels and plain sonorants of final unaccented syllables are devoiced or have a devoiced termination under certain conditions. A vowel can be devoiced if it is final or followed by a devoiced syllable (as defined below) and comes after the last accented syllable; the devoicing is in part conditioned and in part in free variation. If the preceding consonant is a plain occlusive (always an aspirated occlusive, see Section 123.2) or /h/ the vowel is devoiced. If the preceding consonant is a plain sonorant or glottal stop the vowel may be voiced, devoiced, or terminally devoiced; if the vowel is devoiced the sonorant may be voiced, devoiced, or terminally devoiced. If the preceding consonant is glottalized the vowel may be voiced or terminally devoiced. A devoiced syllable is defined as consisting of a voiceless obstruent or devoiced plain sonorant plus a devoiced vowel.

In the following examples the vowel is underlined if it is optionally devoiced or terminally devoiced; capitalized if it is always devoiced, that is, when final or followed by a devoiced syllable:

čápIpIcI	'it is spotted'	sgúhIma	'I believed'
gáẉicI	'seeds'	kápAcIšI	'thick'
zítyApI	'it is wooded'	zítyApIIma	'forest'
kawâayu	'horse'	sḱaašU	'fish'
yûusI	'God'	báaṣU	'straw'
síukAčA	'I see him'	sîuḱusIcA	'I limp'
sínani	'skin'	kuhâaru	'curd'
sénâaʔašI	'my arch'	kusêeʔe	'his hair'
zíyúucEEʔe	'they took him'		

A devoiced vowel after an aspirated occlusive is little more than pro-
longed aspiration with the proper vowel coloring. Two or more such
syllables at the end of a word sound like a final consonant cluster. A
final devoiced high vowel after a plain sibilant is usually realized as a
long sibilant with front articulation before /i/, unrounded and backed
articulation before /ə/, rounded and backed articulation before /u/.

A short unaccented vowel that does not come after the last accent is
optionally devoiced if it is preceded and followed by plain obstruents:

kə̣zâaná	'your eye'	ṣíukačáṅa	'we saw him'
kaṣâiti	'summer'	sacə̣kání	'when I smoked'

137. Accents. The accents consist of pitch, stress, and glottal features.
The feature of pitch is more important than the other features. The stress
differences and pitch intervals are less than in English.

If a word has more than one accent, each succeeding accented syllable
starts at a lower pitch. The difference in pitch is slightly greater if the
intervening consonant is an obstruent than if it is a sonorant. The accented syllables may be equally stressed, or the last accented syllable
may have a slightly louder stress than the others. An unaccented initial
syllable, if voiced, has a mid or high-mid level pitch, not much lower
than the pitch of the accented syllables; such a syllable is unstressed.
All other unaccented voiced syllables have a low pitch, are at the same
pitch, and are unstressed. The difference between the highest and lowest
pitch of a word is about a minor third.

The high accent on single vowels is usually realized as a high pitch
with a slight fall if (1) the following syllable is unaccented and starts
with a glottalized sonorant, or (2) the following syllable is short, accented, has an initial plain sonorant, and is followed by a glottalized consonant: dyáṇi 'deer'; húwáḱa 'cloud' (the accent under consideration is
underlined). In these environments the high accent has the same pitch
contour as that of the falling accent on short vowels. Since there is no
contrast between the two accents in these environments, the phonetically

falling pitch is analyzed as a high pitch to yield neater phonemic and morphophonemic statements (Sections 121; 210, ‖28). In all other environments the high accent is a high level pitch.

The falling and glottal accents with vowel clusters are phonetically similar, and the similarities are especially marked when the speakers are not carefully articulating the words for my benefit. In addition, the speaker that I worked with most made less of a phonetic distinction between the two accents than other speakers and was not aware of the contrast between the two types of accents in Acoma in spite of minimal pairs that she gave me. As a result, there are probably many misrecordings of these accents, misrecordings in both directions. Some days I would hear only glottal accents, on other days only falling accents. Both accents have a falling pitch. If the following syllable is accented, the first two-thirds of the vowel nucleus has a level pitch, and the fall occurs abruptly during the last third. After the fall there is a short rearticulation of the vowel for the falling accent; a short rearticulation preceded by a light glottal catch or glottal stricture for the glottal accent. If the following syllable is unaccented, the fall starts with the onset of the vowel nucleus and continues to the end of the syllable; if the following syllable is devoiced (as defined in Section 136), the termination of the fall is devoiced. In this environment the vowel is not rearticulated for the falling accent; the vowel is rearticulated with or without glottal stricture or a glottal catch or the glottal accent. The pitch range of the fall is greater for both accents when an unaccented syllable follows.

The falling accent on single vowels is realized as a slight falling pitch, just below the pitch level of the following accent.

140. Juncture and Terminal Contours

Little time was spent with the speaker in working out junctural and intonational phenomena. Only the plus juncture has been reasonably well delimited.

141. The plus juncture, indicated by space or by /+/ if greater specificity is desired, marks off phonological words. There is a close, but not perfect, correlation between the phonological and grammatical word.

Many of the phonetic features that define plus juncture have been anticipated in Section 130. That is, the position within the word governs allophonic variations of pitch and stress of accents, vowel quantity, and devoicing of vowels. The word-final devoiced vowels are the best single marker of plus juncture, but they are not infallible markers because ini-

tial syllables sometimes contain voiceless vowels. The following paragraph gives additional phonetic features that reflect the presence of plus
juncture.

In a sequence of two words the first accent in the second word is
slightly lower in pitch than the first accent of the first word, but slightly
higher than the second or following accents of the first word; it can be
seen that this phenomenon can be a criterion only when the first word
has more than one accent. A final accented vowel ends with a slight
aspiration. There is often a short pause, about half the length of a single
vowel, between words; the final vowel sometimes continues during this
period giving, phonetically, half long vowels.

Several of the features that mark plus juncture are optional. Others
are operative when certain phonological sequences are found. And some
indicate that a plus juncture is present but do not indicate exactly where
it is. This can give rise to ambiguous situations. Such is the case with
the following two words, which occur in a tape-recorded text: ṣ́aráncuši
sǝdeʔéku 'we went to our ranch', lit. 'our-ranch we-went'. The last two
vowels of the first word and the first vowel of the second were devoiced.
There was no pause between the words. The pitch of the accented syllable of the second words was lower than the pitch of the first accent
of the first word, but higher than the pitch of the second accent. The
second syllable of the first word had a slightly stronger stress than the
first syllable. By using only phonological evidence and by listening only
to the forms that occur on the tape (that is, not asking the speaker for
repetitions of the same forms), it is impossible to tell if the forms are
to be written ṣaráncu+šisǝdeʔéku, ṣaráncuši+sǝdeʔéku, or ṣaráncušisǝ+
deʔéku. If there had been a slight pause between the words or if the
first vowel of the second word had been voiced, there would have been
no problem. According to some schools of thought, this sort of phenomenon would force us to either set up an additional phoneme or arbitrarily
to make a rule that in such situations the juncture will always be written
after the last voiceless vowel. A far more practical and methodologically
defensible solution is to use grammatical evidence and to consider repetitions of the forms as being phonemically identical.

The plus juncture is found within grammatical words before certain
suffixes and auxiliaries. Such forms are unmarked in the grammar except in the section of the morphophonemics that deals specifically with
plus juncture (Section 210, ‖ 24).

142. Several punctuation marks are used in the chapter on syntax and
in the texts, some of which have little or no phonological, or even grammatical, foundation. The primary justification for their use is convenience.

These punctuation marks are: quotation marks (". . ."), comma (,), period (.), and question mark (?).

The beginning of a quotation starts out at a high pitch level, often with considerable glottal constriction, and drops down to normal level without glottal constriction after the first few syllables. This feature is used by Acomas in speaking both Acoma and English. The quotation mark is used to mark both the beginning and end of a quote, even though there is no phonetic marking of the end.

The use of the period and comma is probably based on a feel for Acoma phonology and syntax, along with a certain amount of interference from English. There appears to be no phonological marking for questions, and the use of the question mark is based solely on semantic considerations.

200. MORPHOPHONEMICS

Hockett has used the term morphophonemics for that which "subsumes every phase of the phonemic shape of morphemes: the typical shapes of alternants, the types of alternations, which elicit one alternant or another of those morphemes which appear in more than one shape."[1] This usage is consistent with the view, held by many linguists, that language consists of two levels or structures: phonological and grammatical. Morphophonemics, then, is a system that serves as a bridge between the two, and is, of course, applicable only when the two levels do not display a one to one relationship.

In this grammar, alternations are divided into two groups, morphophonemic and allomorphic.[2] The division, made to facilitate the presentation of the linguistic material, is not based on any theoretical principles. It is arbitrary and no attempt is made to define it in any rigorous fashion. In general, alternations that are not limited to, and definable by, specific morphemes are treated under morphophonemics. Alternations that must be defined in terms of individual morphemes and have little bearing on the morphophonemic alternations are treated under allomorphy. In Acoma these two kinds of alternations are not distinct, and it is sometimes convenient to include alternations of specific morphemes in the morphophonemics. The morphophonemics is treated in Sections 210 and 220. The pronominal prefixes and plural sufix enter into several different constructions described in several different places in the grammar; therefore the allomorphy of these affixes is pulled together and described in one place (Sections 230 and 240). The remaining allomorphy is treated in the course of the grammatical description (Sections 400-700).

---

[1]Charles F. Hockett, "Peiping Morphophonemics," Language 26. 63-85 (1950).

[2]This division is similar to, but not identical with, that which Hockett calls phonemically and morphemically conditioned alternations (A Course in Modern Linguistics, New York: The Macmillan Company [1958], p. 281).

The morphophonemic alternations are described by setting up basic forms and applying a series of morphophonemic rules. The rules are ordered; that is, the first rule must be applied before the second, and so on. This is the method used by Bloomfield[3] and is outlined briefly by Lounsbury.[4] A form to which no morphophonemic rules have yet been applied is defined as a basic form, and is written morphophonemically. A form that has not had all the applicable morphophonemic rules applied is defined as a morphophonemic form. Thus, by definition, a basic form is always a morphophonemic form, but a morphophonemic form is not always a basic form.

Basic forms consist of phonemes and morphophonemes.[5] The morphophonemes, set up to account for some common alternations, mark which forms undergo certain alternations, alternations defined in terms of the morphophonemic[6] and/or morphological environment. It would be possible to extend the use of morphophonemes by setting up a morphophoneme for every alternation that is not automatic. But by so doing it would not be clear which alternations are productive, which alternations are limited to a small number of forms that could and should be listed, and which alternations could be described by a common pattern in most constructions but are irregular in a few constructions. Other common alternations are accounted for by setting up basic forms with nonoccurring phonemic sequences. This procedure is essentially the same as setting up morphophonemes. Nonoccurring phonemic sequences could just as easily have been used in place of most of the morphophonemes, and vice versa.

A few morphemes are not set up with any basic form and thus must always be written morphemically. These are the number prefixes (‖ 7),[7] the reduplicative and length morphemes (‖ 18), and certain thematic pre-

---

[3]"Menomini Morphophonemics," Travaux du Cèrcle Linguistique de Prague 8. 105-115 (1939).

[4]Oneida Verb Morphology, Yale University Publications in Anthropology 48 (1953).

[5]A phoneme in a basic form is not the same construct or unit as a phoneme in a phonemic form, though the two are obviously related. Alternatively, basic forms could be defined as consisting wholly of morphophonemes. There would then be two types of morphophonemes: those that define alternations, and those that are coterminous with phonemes. The two sets of statements are equivalent; they differ only in terminology.

[6]In this context, "phonological" rather than "morphophonemic" is often used in the older literature, e.g. Morris Swadesh and Charles Voegelin, "A Problem in Phonological Alternation," Language 15. 1-10 (1939). These two terms are used interchangeably in this grammar.

[7]See Section 203 for an explanation of the symbols in parentheses.

fixes (‖5). The pronominal prefixes (Section 230) can contain up to three morphemes, and the morpheme complex is treated, morphophonemically, as one morpheme. A morphophonemic sequence that is not considered part of a basic form is set up as an empty morph. Empty morphs are found between certain pronominal prefixes and themes (Section 230) and certain roots and one of the continuative suffixes (Section 441.1).

Within the morphophonemic framework that has been outlined it can be stated that if a morpheme has more than one basic form, those basic forms are allomorphs of that morpheme. Occasionally the term is applied when a morpheme has only one basic form.

201. Lounsbury has noted that a morphophonemic interpretation "cannot be said to represent a previous state of the language."[8] This is because the rules correspond to phonetic changes that have occurred at different historical periods and some of the rules correspond to analogical changes, not phonemic changes. Another factor, not mentioned by Lounsbury, is that phonemic changes are reflected in the morphophonemics only if the morpheme boundaries happen to be in the right place; for example, the change in Acoma of palatal stops to dental before front vowels is reflected morphophonemically only if there is a morpheme boundary between the consonant and the vowel (see ‖12). By placing the rules in an ordered sequence it is sometimes possible to separate out different chronological layers of change. Morphophonemic, or internal, evidence for historical change is, of course, never as solid as comparative evidence. Nevertheless, it is useful in supplying additional evidence, and when internal and comparative evidence do not agree, there is a problem worth investigating. When the method of morpheme alternants is used, the problem is never brought out. And while the internally reconstructed forms do not reflect a single period of time, the same can be said of reconstructions based on the comparative method; the only difference is that the time span is greater for the internally reconstructed forms.

In the presentation of the morphophonemic rules, the internal and external evidence is compared in footnotes when such comparisons are interesting.[9] A general survey of the problem is given in Section 220 when the distribution of the morphophonemes is discussed. The Keres languages are closely related, so many of the morphophonemic rules reflect Pre-

---

[8]Op. cit.

[9]The Santa Ana material by Davis and Proto-Keres material by Miller and Davis (see bibliography) is used as the basis for the comparisons.

Keres changes. For the most part rules ‖1 through ‖20 reflect this earlier period, and ‖21 through ‖30 reflect changes peculiar to Acoma. A few of the rules seem to be out of order from the historical point of view, and some rules reflect changes that took place at about the time of the breakup of Proto-Keres and hence are difficult to identify as Pre- or Post-Keres. Most of the early rules must take the morphemic environment into account, and therefore it is clear that analogical changes have modified the phonetic changes. Santa Ana has similar, but not identical, morphophonemic rules that reflect this period. It is difficult, and it may even prove impossible, to sort out those analogical changes that took place in Pre-Keres and those that took place in the separate Keres languages. The analogical changes that affect the later rules are easier to locate, and in a few instances they can be inferred from the morphophonemic rules. The comparative evidence sometimes corroborates the internal evidence.

202. The following morphophonemes have been set up:

Final morphophonemic consonants: N, M, $\overline{\text{M}}$, W, Ẃ, B, G^W, Y, D, SD, Ṣ, Z, S (see ‖1)

Replacive morphophoneme: ‖ ~ ‖ (see ‖2)

Harmonic vowel morphophoneme: ‖V‖ (see ‖15)

Morphophonemic accent: ‖ ` ‖ (see ‖3)

Variable length morphophoneme: ‖ : ‖ (see ‖13, 20)

Primary coarticulation morphophonemes: j, q, ' (see ‖11)

Secondary coarticulation morphophonemes: J, J̄, Q, A (see ‖10)

Accent ablaut: ‖(´)‖ (see ‖19)

Accent ablaut with length: ‖(´´)‖ (see ‖19)

The phoneme /ž/, found in very few words (Section 123.7), never undergoes any alternations and never is the result of an alternation. Every other phoneme is included in the morphophonemic system, and either undergoes alternations and/or is the result of alternations. A few phonemes are never or are rarely found in basic forms and thus are normally the result of morphophonemic changes. These phonemes are discussed in Section 220.

203. The following symbols are used:

/. . ./   to indicate phonemic material

‖. . .‖   to indicate a morphophonemic form

{. . .}   to indicate a morpheme

Reference is made to a particular rule by a numeral preceded by the morphophonemic double bar; thus ‖10 indicates morphophonemic rule no. 10. A basic form can be distinguished from other morphophonemic forms by placing a zero after the double bar: ‖. . .‖0. Morphophonemic

forms that have had certain rules applied can be distinguished in a similar fashion: ‖ . . . ‖ 10 indicates that all the rules up to and including
‖ 10 have been applied, but ‖ 11 and following rules have not yet been
applied. Some or all of these symbols are omitted when the context is
clear. When it is not convenient to order certain rules in respect to
each other they are grouped together as a number of subrules of one
rule. Subrules are symbolized by a decimal point followed by a number;
thus ‖ 7.3 indicates subrule no. 3 of morphophonemic rule no. 7. A zero
in the subrule position is used for the introductory remarks of a rule,
never for a subrule as such; thus ‖ 7.0 indicates the introduction of rule
no. 7. An 's' in the subrule position is used in a similar manner to
indicate a summary of the rule: ‖ 7.s.

In giving some of the morphophonemic rules, reference is made to
themes and stems. These terms are defined in Section 300. Additional
terms are necessary. Thematic syllable refers to the vocalic nucleus of
the first syllable of the theme; the rule will indicate whether preceding
coarticulation morphophonemes which may be present are to be considered
part of the syllable. Stem syllable is defined in the same way with reference to the stem. Thematic and stem syllables never have an initial consonant. Initial vowel refers to a vowel that is the first phoneme in a suffix or a thematic syllable, excluding any coarticulation morphophoneme
that may precede.

A long vowel refers to a vowel cluster with length as the second member of the cluster. A vowel cluster is restricted to mean a vowel cluster
with ‖i‖ or ‖u‖ as the second member of the cluster. A long syllable
refers to a long vowel or vowel cluster. A variable length vowel refers
to a vowel along with a following ‖:‖ (but "variable length" refers only
to the morphophoneme ‖:‖, as listed in Section 202).

210. Ordered Rules

‖ 1.0 When a suffix with an initial vowel is added to a form, a consonant
usually appears before the suffix, a consonant that is not found in the un-
suffixed form: gúukača 'he saw him', gúukačáńa 'they saw him'. It might
appear from this example that the /ń/ can be considered part of the suffix. But it turns out that such consonants can most easily be accounted
for by setting up the preceding morphemes with final morphophonemic
consonants, since the same consonants are normally found with the same
morphemes whenever an initial vowel suffix follows. However, it is also
necessary to specify which suffix follows because some final morphopho-

nemic consonants have different realizations before different suffixes. In
addition, some of the suffixes have allomorphs the choice of which is determined by the preceding final morphophonemic consonant. These final
morphophonemic consonants are found entirely with verb roots and verb
suffixes.

The initial vowel suffixes are:

    {-qədyəəZ} dual suffix, Section 433

    {-qeeD} plural suffix, Sections 240 and 433

    {-qiṢ} completive suffix, Section 442.7

    {-qeeY} motion suffix, Section 442.3

    {-ʿíʔiD} benefactive suffix, Section 411

    {-(ʿ)í} a subordinative suffix, Section 762, ‖ 19

    {-iku} Section 442.8

    {-iši} a subordinative suffix, Section 761

    {-iguyaN} a continuative suffix, Section 441.3

    {-u} Sections 442.9, 764

Suffixes that do not typically begin with a vowel but have some allomorphs
that do, are:

    {-ńáaťaN} habitual suffix, Section 442.2

    {=itaaN} a continuative suffix, Section 441.1

    {=áayaN} a continuative suffix, Section 441.2

Not considered here are the inceptive suffix {-iẓaadyaaN} (Section 442.4),
which typically begins with a vowel, and the subordinative suffix {-ṣa}
(Section 763), which has allomorphs that begin with vowels, since there
are too few examples of these suffixes in diagnostic environments.

The reader is forewarned that the resulting forms often undergo further morphophonemic changes. The consonant may be glottalized (‖ 11,
30) or aspirated (‖ 11, 29); there may be accent changes (‖ 21, 28).

  ‖ 1.1   N > n and ʔN > ń when followed by:

      ‖-qədyəəZ‖ allomorph of {-qədyəəZ}

      ‖-qaaD‖ allomorph of {-qeeD}

      ‖-qiṢ‖ allomorph of {-qiṢ}

      ‖-qeeY‖ allomorph of {-qeeY}

      ‖-ʿíʔiD‖ allomorph of {-ʿíʔiD}

      ‖-(ʿ)í‖ allomorph of {-(ʿ)í}

      ‖-iku‖ allomorph of {-iku}

      ‖-iši‖ allomorph of {-iši}

      ‖-iguyaN‖ allomorph of {-iguyaN}

      ‖-u‖ allomorph of {-u}

      ‖-qáayaN‖ allomorph of {=áayaN}

Elsewhere N is dropped and ʔN > ʔV (see ‖ 15).

Examples of the preceding morphemes after -úukačaN 'to see';
-úsúmé?estaaN 'to learn, study'; -ú:wagəN 'to dress'; -Jugûu?N 'to be
pregnant':

‖-qədyəəZ‖: síukačáńətyə 'we (dual) saw them'; zísúméestaańətyə
'they (dual) taught him'

‖-qaaD‖: síukačáńa 'we (plural) saw him'; suwáẃagśńa 'we (plural)
got dressed'

‖-qiṢ‖: ?úukačáńi 'mirror'; gáusúméestaańi 'he has him trained'

‖-qeeY‖: súsúméestaańe 'I am on my way to school'

‖-ʼíʔiD‖: síẃakəní 'I dressed him for her'

‖-(ˊ)íʼ‖: susuméestáaní 'when I was in school'; súẃágśní 'when I
got dressed'

‖-iku‖: káisuméestaaniku 'they would learn'

‖-iši‖: káisuméestaaniši 'students'; cigûuńiši 'her pregnancy'

‖-iguyaN‖: síukačanikuya 'I am seeing him'

‖-u‖: skúẃakənu 'when one dresses'

‖-qáayaN‖: súẃagəńáaya 'I am getting dressed'

Elsewhere:

síukača 'I saw him', final position

níukačagú 'he will see him', auxiliary {gú}

síuẃakəsə 'I (continuously) wear his clothes', suffix ‖-sə∅‖

síuẃakəńáaťa 'I wear it (every day)', suffix ‖-ńáaťaN‖

cigûu?u 'she is pregnant', final position

The sequence -cv́ʔvN (where 'c' = a plain consonant and 'v' = a short
vowel) becomes -cv́vN before ‖-qədyəəZ‖, ‖-qeeD‖, and ‖-qiṢ‖.[10] Six
forms have this sequence: -bé?eN 'to tell'; -ʼúkaazá?aN 'to announce';
-úikaašá?aN 'to support (supply livelihood)'; -udíišá?aN 'to feed';
-pəkadá?aN 'to use up'; -ńazá?aN 'to be healthy':

‖-qaaD‖: síupééńa 'we (plural) told him'; sídiišáańa 'we fed him';
sépakaťáańa 'we used it up' (see ‖17)

‖-qiṢ‖: ćiupééńi 'the notice was given'; sáńaćáańi 'I am healthy'

Contrast:

‖-ʼíʔiD‖: síwiikaašáaní 'I supported her for him' (see ‖23)

‖-(ˊ)íʼ‖: síube?éní 'when I told him'; sidíišá?ání 'when I fed him'
(see ‖19, ‖23)

Final position: síubé 'I told him'; sidíišá 'I fed him' (see ‖23,
‖25)

---

[10] The rule can probably be stated more generally: the change takes place before
suffixes with an initial ‖q‖. The suffix ‖-qeeY‖, however, has not been recorded
with these roots.

-béʔN sporadically becomes -péeN in other environments: kúipéetita 'he is lying' from ‖-péeN-ẓaN=itaaN‖ (cf. kúibéeça 'he lied').

-úiḱaašáʔaN becomes -úiḱaašáu in final position: síwiiḱaašáu 'I am supporting him'

The form -áayúunáʔaN 'to move' undergoes the same accent changes described above, but the preceding consonant, basically glottalized, is usually unchanged. In a few forms, however, the consonant is deglottalized when followed by an initial vowel suffix that does not have ‖q‖: sáayúunaʔání 'when I moved'. The change is probably optional and is clearly analogical. When the plural suffix ‖-qaaD‖ is added, the /-náa-/ is cptionally dropped by haplology; the singular is then distinguished from the plural by a difference in accent: káayúuná 'he moved'; káayúuna ~ káayúunáaña 'they moved'.

The verb forming suffix {-zaN} (Section 621) plus the completive suffix {-qiṢ} irregularly yields ‖-ziṢ‖: ćíušiici 'it has been borrowed'; ćíicitamaci 'it has been turned over'; cf. síušiizáña 'we (plural) borrowed it from him'; síicitamazáña 'we (plural) turned it over'.

‖1.2 M > m and ʔM > m̉ when followed by:

    ‖-qədyəəZ‖ allomorph of {-qədyəəZ}
    ‖-qeeD‖ allomorph of {-qeeD}
    ‖-qiṢ‖ allomorph of {-qiṢ}
    ‖-qeeY‖ allomorph of {-qeeY}
    ‖-ʿíʔiD‖ varying freely with ‖-qíʔiD‖ allomorphs of {-ʿíʔiD}
    ‖-(ʹ)í‖ varying freely with ‖-(ʹ)qí‖ allomorphs of {-(ʹ)í}
    ‖-iku‖ allomorph of {-iku}
    ‖-iši‖ allomorph of {-iši}
    ‖-iguyaN‖ allomorph of {-iguyaN}
    ‖-a‖ allomorph of {-u}

Elsewhere M is dropped; ʔM > ʔV in final position, and elsewhere ʔM > ʔV varying freely with zero.

Examples of the preceding morphemes after úudíM 'to plant'; -áamáwáistíM 'to wash hands'; -uîšuwiM 'to put on shoes'; -naiʔM 'enclosed' (suffix, Section 442.5):

    ‖-qədyəəZ‖: sáudím̉ətyə 'we (dual) planted'; sípənaim̉ətyə 'we (dual) put it in'
    ‖-qeeD‖: sáudím̉e 'we (plural) planted'; sípənaim̉e 'we (plural) put it in'
    ‖-qiṢ‖: ʔamáwáistím̉i 'sink'; ʔúudím̉i 'to plant'
    ‖-qeeY‖: sáudím̉e 'I went to plant' (homophonous with the plural)
    {-ʿíʔiD}: síušuwimí 'I put shoes on him for her'; síudim̉í 'I planted it for him' (see ‖22)

{-(´)í}: sáaṁáwáistímí ~ sáaṁáwáistími 'when I washed my hands'

‖-iši‖: ḱaudímiši 'that is how one plants'; zâaʔapənaiṁiši 'that
  she had sent them through'

‖-a‖: sáaṁáwáistíṁa 'when I washed my hands'; záazíi sdípənaiṁi
  'I didn't put it in'

Elsewhere:

sáaṁáwáistí 'I washed my hands', final position

sáaṁáwáistísə 'I am washing my hands', suffix ‖-səɸ‖

ṅáudiisí 'I will plant', auxiliary {gú}

sípənaiʔi 'I put it in', final position

sípənaisə 'I am putting it in', suffix ‖-səɸ‖

sîuwáćinaiʔisə 'I am going visiting', suffix ‖-səɸ‖

{-iku} and {-iguyaN} are attested after ‖M‖ in only two forms.
gâaʔaṣumiku 'they (dual) would be (in a place)' is formed from the theme
‖-âaʔaB‖ 'to be located' (dual of the auxiliary {gáa}, Section 461.6). The
element /-ṣu-/ is unidentified but is presumed to be morphophonemically
‖-ṣuM-‖. síuťâanikuya ~ síuťâamikuya 'I am practicing' is formed from
‖-úuťâaN‖ ~ ‖-úuťâaM‖ 'to test, try'.

‖1.3 M̄ > m when followed by:

  ‖-ədyəəZ‖ allomorph of {-qədyəəZ}

  ‖-eeD‖ allomorph of {-qeeD}

  ‖-iṢ‖ allomorph of {-qiṢ}

  ‖-eeY‖ allomorph of {-qeeY}

  ‖-ʿíʔiD‖ allomorph of {-ʿíʔiD}

  ‖-(´)í‖ allomorph of {-(´)í}

Elsewhere M̄ is dropped.[11]

Examples of the preceding morphemes after -ûuyauskaM̄ 'to plaster';
-úukaM̄ 'to dye':

  ‖-ədyəəZ‖: sâuyauskamətyə 'we (dual) plastered'

  ‖-eeD‖: sâuyauskame 'we (plural) plastered'; sáukame 'we (plural)
    dyed it'

  ‖-iṢ‖: ćîuyauskamí 'it has been plastered'; ʔúukáṁi 'dye' (see
    ‖30); ćîukami 'it has been dyed'

  ‖-eeY‖: sâuyauskame 'I went to plaster' (homophonous with the
    plural)

  ‖-ʿíʔiD‖: sîuyauskamí 'I plastered for him'

  ‖-(´)í‖: sáuyáuskámí 'when I plastered'

---

[11]In this and following subrules of ‖1, "elsewhere" does not include a following
initial vowel suffix that does not appear in the list immediately above. Such suffixes are unattested. In most cases the form can be deduced by the general pattern.

Elsewhere:

    śâuyauska 'I plastered', final position

    śâuyauskasə 'I am plastering', suffix -səɸ

    ńaukagú 'he will plaster it', auxiliary {gú}

‖ 1.4 W > w when followed by:

       ‖-aaD‖ allomorph of {-qeeD}

       ‖-iȘ‖ varying freely with ‖-qiȘ‖ allomorphs of {-qiȘ}

       ‖-eeY‖ varying freely with ‖-qeeY‖ allomorphs of {-qeeY}

       ‖-'í?iD‖ allomorph of {-'í?iD}

       ‖-(´)í‖ allomorph of {-(´)í}

       ‖-itaaN‖ allomorph of {=itaaN}

W > b when followed by ‖-ədyəəZ‖ allomorph of {-qədyəəZ}

W > u when followed by ‖-guyaN‖ allomorph of {-iguyaN}

W > g varying freely with n when followed by ‖-u‖ allomorph of {-u}

Elsewhere W is dropped.

    Examples of the preceding morphemes after -áaťaW 'to open';
-áaḿáakúyaW 'to take a handful'; -úbeW 'to eat':

    ‖-ədyəəZ‖: śeeťapətyə 'we (dual) opened his'

    ‖-aaD‖: śeeťawa 'we (plural) opened his'

    {-qiȘ}: ?úpewi 'to eat'; ćaḿáakúýawi ~ ćaḿáakúýáwi 'a handful
       was taken'

    ‖-qeeY}: śeeťawe 'I went to open his'; sáaḿáakúýawe ~
       sáaḿáakúýáẃe 'I went to take a handful'

    ‖-'í?iD‖: śípewí 'I ate it for him'

    ‖-(´)í‖: śeeťáwí 'when I opened his'

    ‖-guyaN‖: śeeťaukuya 'I am opening his'

    ‖-u‖: záazíi sdyáaťanu 'I didn't open his'

    ‖-itaaN‖: śeeťawita 'I have been opening his'

Elsewhere:

    śeeťa 'I opened his', final position

    núpegú 'he will eat', auxiliary {gú}

There are a few irregular developments of W + -guyaN:

    subéukuya 'I am eating' (loss of first accent, regular by ‖22)

    síwádyâińawakuyańáaťa 'I find them all the time', -JuýâińaW 'to
       find it' (śee ‖8 for ẏ > dy)

    ?W is set up for three forms: -áińa?W 'to lap up, lick, taste';
-'ińáa?W 'to stick out, peer out'; -dâa?W 'to cover'. No general rule
can be stated for ?W, because it behaves slightly differently in each
form; but its development is analogous to ?N, ?M and ?B. /ṁ/ rather
than /ẇ/ is found in some forms, because of the interchange of W and
M (see ‖1.14):

{-qədyəəZ}: káiṅapətyə 'they (dual) lapped it up'; kiṅáamətyə 'they
(dual) looked out' (see ‖ 26); síidâamə 'we (dual) covered him'

{-qeeD}: káiṅawa 'they (plural) lapped it up'; kaʔáaṅáame 'they
(plural) looked out'; síidâame 'we (plural) covered him'

{-qiṢ}: cáiṅáwi 'it has been tasted'; wíiṅámi 'glass'; cíudâami 'it
has been covered'

{-qeeY}: káiṅáwe 'he went to lap it up'

{- 'íʔiD}: sêiṅawí 'I tasted his (pudding) for him'; síudâamí 'I
covered him for her'

{-(´)í}: káiṅáwí 'when he lapped it up'; kiṅáawí 'when he looked
out'; síidáamí 'when I covered him'

{-iguyaN}: káiṅâukuya 'he is lapping it up'

{-u}: záazíi skáiṅanu ~ záazíi skáiṅaku 'I didn't lick it'

Elsewhere:

káiṅâuʔu ~ káiṅa 'he lapped it up', final position

kiṅáu 'he looked out', final position

kiṅáasə 'it is sticking out', suffix ‖-sə∅‖

síidâuʔu 'I covered him', final position

síidáasə 'I am covering him', suffix ‖-sə∅‖

‖1.5 Ẃ is only found in the sequence aẂ. The Ẃ is replaced by M
before {-qədyəəZ} and {-qeeD} (cf. ‖1.14) and by W before other initial
vowel suffixes, including ‖-itaaN‖ allomorph of {=itaaN}; rules ‖1.2 and
‖1.4 apply. Elsewhere aẂ normally becomes áu, sometimes á.

Examples of the preceding morphemes after -ukûuyaẂ 'to thread a
needle'; -úudâakaadyaẂ 'to uncover':

‖-qədyəəZ‖: sikûuyámətyə 'we (dual) threaded a needle';
síudâakaadyámə 'we (dual) uncovered it'

‖-qeeD‖: sikûuyáme 'we (plural) threaded a needle'; síudâakaadyáme
'we (plural) uncovered it'

‖-iṢ‖: cîukuuyawi 'it is threaded'

‖-qeeY‖: sikûuyawe 'I went to thread it'

‖- 'íʔiD‖: sîukuuyawí 'I threaded a needle for her'

‖-(´)í‖: síudáakaadyáwí 'when I uncovered it'

‖-u‖: záazíi stikûuyanu 'I didn't thread a needle'

‖-itaaN‖: sikûuyawita 'I am threading a needle'

Elsewhere (cf. ‖3 and ‖4 for other changes):

sikûuyáu 'I threaded a needle', final

sikûuyasə 'I am threading a needle', suffix ‖-sə∅‖

ṅikûuyáusí 'I will thread a needle', auxiliary {gú}

síudâaakaadyáu 'I uncovered it', final

síudâaakaatyauku 'I am uncovering it', suffix ‖-Gᵂ‖

síudâakaatyausə 'I am uncovering it', suffix ‖-sə∅‖

‖1.6   B and G^W > b, and ?B > ?Vb (see ‖15 for ‖V‖) before:

     ‖-ədyəəZ‖ allomorph of {-qədyəəZ}

     ‖-eeD‖ allomorph of {-qeeD}

     ‖-iṢ‖ allomorph of {-qiṢ}

     ‖-eeY‖ allomorph of {-qeeY}

     ‖-ʹíʔiD‖ allomorph of {- ʹíʔiD}

     ‖-(ʹ)í‖ allomorph of {-(ʹ)í}

     ‖-iši‖ allomorph of {-iši}

     ‖-iguyaN‖ allomorph of {-iguyaN}

     ‖-itaaN‖ allomorph of {⁼itaaN}

B and G^W > g, and ?B > ?ug before ‖-u‖ varying freely with ‖-unu‖, allomorph of {-u}.

Elsewhere B is dropped, G^W > gu, and ?B > ?u.

Examples of the preceding morphemes after -úudyúB 'to find out'; -aʔáčəB 'to be enclosed'; -awáiG^W 'to fight'; -G^W repetitive suffix (Section 442.1); -ŝâaʔB 'to urinate'; -âaʔB 'to give, take a light object':

     ‖-ədyəəZ‖: śéeťapətyə 'we (dual) kept opening his'; kiŝâaʔapətyə 'they (dual) urinated'

     ‖-eeD‖: śéeťape 'we (plural) kept opening his'; kaʔâašaaʔape 'they (plural) urinated'

     ‖-iṢ‖: ćíudyúpi 'it was found out'; ćáwáipi 'war'

     ‖-eeY‖: śéeťape 'I went to keep opening his'; gúwíišâaʔape 'he went to urinate'

     ‖-ʹíʔiD‖: śéeťapí 'I kept opening it for him'; ŝêeʔeepí 'I gave it to him for her'

     ‖-(ʹ)í‖: kaʔáudyúpi 'when he found out'; sawáipi 'when I fought'

     ‖-iši‖: gaʔáčupiši 'the one enclosed'

     ‖-iguyaN‖: kiŝâaʔapikuya 'he is urinating'

     {-u}: záazíi sdâaʔaaku 'I didn't give it to him'; sgayâaʔaakunu 'when one gave it to them'

     ‖-itaaN‖: kaʔáudyúpita 'he is finding out'

Elsewhere:

     gaʔáčə 'he is enclosed', final position

     ńiičəgú 'he will be enclosed', final position

     kiŝâuʔu 'he urinated' (see ‖14)

     nišâuʔugú 'he will urinate'

     kawáiku 'he fought'

     kawáikugú 'he will fight'

Many of the forms with B, G^W, and ?B are slightly irregular. The final vowel of -âaʔB 'to give, take a light object' is lengthened before initial vowel suffixes (see above examples); and ?B > ?au before ‖-guyaN‖

allomorph of {-iguyaN}: saýâaʔaukuya 'I am taking it'.

In -àaG^W 'to bite' G^W > p̓ where b is expected; otherwise G^W develops normally in this morpheme:

   ‖-eeD‖: śéep̓e 'we (plural) bit it'

   ‖-eeY‖: séep̓e 'I went to bite it'

   ‖-iguyaN‖: sêep̓ikuya 'I am biting it'

   ‖-unu‖: záazíi sgáakunu 'I didn't bite it'

   gáaku 'he bit it', final position

-awáiG^W 'to fight' is sometimes interpreted as -awáiN plus the repetitive suffix -G^W:

   saẃâiṅa 'we fought'

   saẃáipe 'we are fighting' and 'we fought'

   saẃáiku 'I am fighting' and 'I fought'

-awáiN is used only when a vowel initial suffix follows, that is, *saẃái 'I fought' does not occur.

-úudyúB 'to find out' becomes -úudyu in final position: kaʔáutyu 'he found out'.

  ‖1.7   Y is dropped before:

      ‖-dyəəZ‖ allomorph of {-qədyəəZ}

      ‖-ʔVVD‖ allomorph of {-qeeD} (see ‖15 for ‖V‖)

Y > y before:

      ‖-iṢ‖ allomorph of {-qiṢ}

      ‖-ʻíʔiD‖ allomorph of {-ʻíʔiD}

      ‖-(ʻ)í‖ allomorph of {-(ʻ)í}

      ‖-iši‖ allomorph of {-iši}

      ‖-u‖ allomorph of {-u}

      ‖-qáat̓aN‖ allomorph of {-ṅáat̓aN}

The vowel ‖u‖ in the sequence ‖uY‖ > ‖ui‖ before the above suffixes; this change also applies when Y varies with M (see ‖1.14).
Elsewhere Y is dropped.

Examples of the preceding morphemes after -qeeY motion suffix (Section 442.3); -âačawaiY 'to run a foot or stick race'; -ut̓aikuY 'to take a basket along':

   ‖-dyəəZ‖: śíut̓âaneetyə 'we (dual) visited him'; sut̓áikuityə 'we (dual) took a basket along'

   ‖-ʔVVD‖: śíut̓âaneeʔe 'we (plural) visited him'; śâačawaiʔi 'we (plural) had a stick race'; suwa̓t̓aikuiʔi 'we (plural) took it along'

   ‖-iṢ‖: číut̓áaneeyi 'he has been visited'; ʔáačáwáiyí 'stick race'

   ‖-ʻíʔiD‖: śêečawaiyí 'I ran for him'; śit̓áikuiyí 'I took a basket along for him'

   ‖-(ʻ)í‖: síut̓áanéeyí 'when I visited him'; sut̓áikúiyí 'when I took a basket along'

‖-iši‖: śâačawaiyiši 'the race that I ran'

‖-u‖: záazíi skuťaikuiyu 'I didn't take a basket along'

‖-qáaťaN‖: sâuťâaneeýáaťa 'I am checking'

Elsewhere:

síuťaane 'I visited him', final position

ńeýáaťâaneesí 'I will visit him', auxiliary {gú}

śâačawai 'I ran a stick race', final position

suťaiku 'I took a basket along', final position

-íibâiY 'to sleep' becomes -íibáʔa before a suffix with an initial consonant other than ‖-dyəəZ‖ and ‖-ʔVVD‖: zíibáatu 'he went to sleep' (see ‖23); ćeebâiʔi 'they are sleeping'; zíibái 'he is sleeping' (see ‖28). ‖-guyaN‖ allomorph of {-iguyaN} is used with this stem: síibáakuya 'I am sleepy'.

‖1.8   D is dropped before ‖-dyəəZ‖ allomorph of {-qədyəəZ}.

D > d before:

         ‖-aaD‖ allomorph of {-qeeD}

         ‖-iṢ‖ allomorph of {-qiṢ}

         ‖-eeY‖ allomorph of {-qeeY}

         ‖-ʹíʔiD‖ allomorph of {-ʹíʔiD}

         ‖-(ʹ)íʹ‖ allomorph of {-(ʹ)íʹ}

         ‖-iku‖ allomorph of {-iku}

         ‖-iši‖ allomorph of {-iši}

         ‖-iguyaN‖ allomorph of {-iguyaN}

         ‖-qáaťaN‖ allomorph of {-ńáaťaN}

         ‖-qáayaN‖ allomorph of {=áayaN}

D > dy before ‖-a‖ allomorph of {-u}

Elsewhere D is dropped.

Examples of the preceding morphemes after -umínaaD 'to speak to'; -qeeD plural suffix (Sections 240 and 433); -učáyúmaaD 'to get tired'; -úwáaguD 'to hide it'; -ʹíʔiD benefactive suffix (Section 411):

‖-dyəəZ‖: śimínaatyə 'we (dual) spoke to him'; śîucuucańiityə 'we (dual) moved it for him'

‖-aaD‖: śimínaata 'we (plural) spoke to him'; śîucuucańiita 'we (plural) moved it for him'

‖-iṢ‖: ćîumínaati 'it has been spoken of'

‖-eeY‖: śimínaate 'I am on my way to speak to him'

‖-ʹíʔiD‖: śîumínaatí 'I spoke to him for her'

‖-(ʹ)íʹ‖: śimínáati 'when I spoke to him'; ziʔíukačańáati 'when they saw them'

‖-iku‖: zíyúuceeʔeetiku 'they would take it'

‖-iši‖: zâaʔapeetiši 'that they had eaten them'

‖-iguyaN‖: simíńaatikuya 'I am speaking to him'

‖-a‖: gúukačáńaatya 'if they saw it'

‖-qáaťaN‖: skučáyúmaťáaťa 'I am getting tired' (see ‖24, 25)

‖-qáayaN‖: suwáagutáaya 'I am hiding it'

Elsewhere:

  simíńa 'I spoke to him' (see ‖30), final position

  síucuucaní 'I moved it for him' (see ‖23, 25), final position

  gúukačáńa 'they saw it', final position

  níukačáńagúusa 'they will see it', auxiliary {gú}

‖dya‖ is the normal development of ‖D‖ plus the suffix ‖-a‖. In addition, ‖dyanu, diidya, gu‖ are found:

  ka?âatee?etyanu 'if they bring'

  záazíi sdimíńaaku 'I didn't speak to him'

  stídyáaku 'when one catches it'

  kuwámasawáatiitya 'one cooks'

  The allomorph ‖-ńáaťaN‖, rather than ‖-qáaťaN‖, is used after {-qeeD} plural suffix and {-'í?iD} benefactive suffix: sáyasťiipeeńáaťa 'we would winnow'; síumáacitaaníńáaťa 'I would help her'.

  ‖1.9 SD > šaN before {-qədyəəZ} (cf. ‖1.14) and rule ‖1.1 applies. SD > sd before:

          ‖-aaD‖ allomorph of {-qeeD}

          ‖-iṢ‖ allomorph of {-qiṢ}

          ‖-eeY‖ allomorph of {-qeeY}

          ‖-'í?iD‖ allomorph of {-'í?iD}

          ‖-(´)í‖ allomorph of {-(´)í}

SD > d before:

          ‖-iguyaN‖ allomorph of {-iguyaN}

          ‖-qáaťaN‖ allomorph of {-ńáaťaN}

          ‖-qitaaN‖ allomorph of {⁼itaaN}

          ‖-qáayaN‖ allomorph of {⁼áayaN}

Elsewhere SD > ša.

  Examples of the preceding morphemes after -úwâameeSD 'to put up a tent, to make shade'; -údyuSD 'to cover'; -u:ťaaSD 'to hang up'; -áSD 'to step':

  {-qədyəəZ}: suwâameešáńətyə 'we (dual) put up a tent'; guťáašáńətyə 'they (dual) hung it up'

  ‖-aaD‖: suwawâameesta 'we (plural) put up a tent'; guťáasta 'they (plural) hung it up'

  ‖-iṢ‖: číwâameesti 'the tent has been put up'

  ‖-eeY‖: suwâameeste 'I went to put up a tent'

  ‖-'í?iD‖: síwâameestí 'I made shade for him'

‖-(ˊ)í‖: síuťáasti 'when I hung it up'

‖-iguyaN‖: sátikuya 'I am taking a step'

‖-qáaťaN‖: súdyúťáaťa 'I keep putting on a cover' (see ‖21)

‖-qitaaN‖: súdyúťita 'I am covering myself'

‖-qáayaN‖: súdyúťáaya 'I am covering myself'; siuťaaťáaya 'I am hanging up clothes'

Elsewhere:

suẃâaḿeeša 'I put up a tent', final position

nuẃâaḿeešagú 'he will put up a tent, auxiliary {gú}

SD plus the suffix {-u} has been recorded as -šanu, -daadya, and -šaadyanu. There are not enough examples to determine the common pattern:

záazíi sguẃâaḿeešanu 'I didn't put up a tent'

sťyaʔátyušaatyanu 'everyone would be covered'

kaʔáišataatya 'it was spread'

‖1.10 Ṣ > ṣ (see ‖12) before:

‖-adyəəZ‖ allomorph of {-qədyəəZ}

‖-iiD‖ allomorph of {-qeeD}

‖-(ˊ)í‖ allomorph of {-(ˊ)í}

‖-iku‖ allomorph of {-iku}

‖-i‖ allomorph of {-iši}

‖-a‖ allomorph of {-u}

Elsewhere Ṣ is dropped.

Examples of the preceding morphemes after -ûuḿeeḱuḿeṢ 'to watch'; -qiṢ completive suffix (Section 442.7):

‖-adyəəZ‖: sîuḿeeḱuḿeṣatyə 'we (dual) are watching him'; sidyáatiṣatyə 'we (dual) are holding him'

‖-iiD‖: sîuḿeeḱuḿeši 'we (plural) are watching him'; sidyáatiši 'we (plural) are holding him'

‖-(ˊ)í‖: síuḿeeḱúḿéši 'while I was watching him'

‖-iku‖: ḱáudyaʔátišiku 'one would hold it'

‖-i‖: gáadyaẓáñiši 'something that is carved' ({-udyáaẓaN + -qiṢ + -iši}, see Section 761)

‖-a‖: záazíi sgûuḿeeḱuḿeṣa 'I didn't watch him'

Elsewhere:

sîuḿeeḱuḿe 'I am watching him', final position

sîuḿeeḱumeñáaťa 'I always watch him', suffix {-ñáaťaN} (unglottalized -m-, irregular)

‖1.11 Z > z before:

‖-iṢ‖ allomorph of {-qiṢ}

‖-(ˊ)í‖ allomorph of {-(ˊ)í}

‖-iku‖ allomorph of {-iku}

‖-iši‖ allomorph of {-iši}

Z > g before ‖-a‖ allomorph of {-u}

Elsewhere Z is dropped.

Z is found only in -qədyəəZ dual suffix (Section 433) and -áwâičaiZ, -áwâičaaZ 'to be hot' (liquid):

‖-iṢ‖: gáwáičáizíši 'while it was still hot' ({-qiṢ + -(´)í})

‖-(´)í‖: gúukačáṅədyə́əci 'when they (dual) saw it'; gáwáičáaci 'when it was hot'

‖-iku‖: kuwîistityaaṅətyəəciku 'they (dual) would count'

‖-iši‖: gûukačáṅətyəəciši 'so that they (dual) could see'

‖-a‖: záazíi čúubúuzáṅətyəəka 'they (dual) were not afraid'

Elsewhere:

gúukačáṅətyə 'they (dual) saw him', final position

ṅíukačáṅətyəṣúuʔu 'we (dual) will see him', auxiliary {gú}

dyâiʔipeetawáṅətyəṅáaťa 'they (dual) always made them (plural) cry', suffix ‖-ṅáaťaN‖

gáwâiča 'it is hot'

If no ambiguities result, the syllable ‖-dyəə-‖ may be dropped from the dual suffix when an initial vowel suffix does not follow. That is, the second syllable of a disyllabic allomorph may be dropped in this environment, except when the allomorph -ədyəəZ follows ‖ə∅‖ (see ‖1.13) or the allomorph -adyəəZ follows ‖Ṣ‖:

ṅíukačáṅəṣúuʔu, ṅíukačáṅətyəṣúuʔu 'we (dual) will see him'

ṣíukačáṅə, ṣíukačáṅətyə 'we (dual) saw him'

ṣâuẏatapə, ṣâuẏatapətyə 'we (dual) ate'

ṣêepə, ṣêepətyə 'we (dual) bit it'

The syllable /-tyə/ is the only mark of the dual for those forms that do not show this variation:

suťáikuityə 'we (dual) took a basket along' (-uťáikuY 'to take a basket along', ‖1.7)

gûucímətyə 'they (dual) love him'; cf. gûucímə 'she loves him' (see ‖1.13)

sgûuméekuṁeṣatyə 'they (dual) are watching me'; cf. záazíi sgûuméekuṁeṣa 'I didn't watch him' (see ‖1.10)

‖1.12 Ṣ > s before ‖-aaD‖ allomorph of {-qeeD}; this is lost in final position. Ṣ is found only in -úʔuṢ plural form of the auxiliary {gú} (Section 461.1) and -waizáṁaṢ 'to go to war':

ṅíukačáṅaṣúusa 'we (plural) will see him'

sťawâawaizáṁasa 'they had wars, went to fight'

gûuwaizáṁa 'he went to war', final position

‖ 1.13   A few verb roots and verb suffixes do not end in a final morphophonemic consonant, and ∅ is written in such cases. (Omission of an overt mark indicates that the status of the final morphophonemic consonant is unknown.) In such forms the final vowel is lost before:

‖ -ədyəəZ ‖ allomorph of {-ədyəəZ}
‖ -eeD ‖ allomorph of {-qeeD}
‖ -iṢ ‖ allomorph of {-qiṢ}
‖ - ʼíʔiD ‖ allomorph of {- ʼíʔiD}
‖ -(ʼ)í ‖ allomorph of {-(ʼ)í}
‖ -iku ‖ allomorph of {-iku}
‖ -iši ‖ allomorph of {-iši}
‖ -qjáaťaN ‖ allomorph of {-ńáaťaN}

Examples of the preceding morphemes after -sə∅ repetitive suffix (Section 442.1); -qéeyu∅ 'to go (dual)'; - ʼúusťu∅ 'to die'; -áizéeṣa∅ 'to dream'; -áayúma∅ 'to know how':

‖ -ədyəəZ ‖: śíukáasətyə 'we (dual) are shelling corn'; káayúmətyə 'they (dual) know how'

‖ -eeD ‖: śíukáase 'we (plural) are shelling corn'; káayúme 'they (plural) know how'

‖ -iṢ ‖: kúusťi 'he was dead'

‖ - ʼíʔiD ‖: śíukáasí 'I am shelling corn for him'

‖ -(ʼ)í ‖: śíukáasi 'when I was shelling corn'; ćéeyí 'when they (dual) went'; kúusťi 'when he died'

‖ -iku ‖: ćêeyiku 'they would go'

‖ -iši ‖: ćêeyiši 'how they had gone'

‖ -qjáaťaN ‖: kúusťáaťa 'he is dying'; gáizéešáaťa 'he is dreaming'

{-iši} is also represented by the allomorphs ‖ -ši ‖ and ‖ -aiši ‖: gumə́sə̣ši 'that which comes out' (suffixes {-sə∅} and {-iši}); záipaṣaišiḿée 'as though they were chasing them' ({-áipaṣa∅ + -iši- + -ḿée}).

‖ 1.14   There are some variations in the final morphophonemic consonants and final morphophonemic sequences. The variations are of three kinds: (1) mandatory variation definable by the morphophonemic consonant and the following suffix; (2) free variation between certain morphophonemic consonants, definable by the morphophonemic consonants involved; and (3) free variation between morphophonemic consonants in certain morphemes that must be listed or specially marked.

The first kind of variation has been built into the preceding subrules, for example, SD > šaN before the dual suffix and the subrule for N applies; Ẃ > M before certain suffixes and > W before other suffixes.

The second kind of variation is nonreversible. A statement of the form "A ~ B" is to be interpreted as "all A's can vary freely with B, but not all B's can vary with A." The first and second type of variation often converge so that the variation is mandatory before certain suffixes, optional before others. The second type of variation is the subject of the next several paragraphs.

W, Ẃ, and Y ~ M. However the W in -úuḱáyaW 'to wipe, rub' varies with M̄:

> -áyaceeW 'to whitewash' + {-qiṢ}: ćáyaceewi ~ ćáyaceemi 'it was whitewashed'
>
> -úuḱáyaW(M̄) 'to wipe' + {-qeeD}: śíuḱáyawa ~ śíuḱáyame 'we wiped it'
>
> -uk̂uuyaẂ 'to thread a needle' + {-qiṢ}: ćîukuuyawi ~ ćîukuuyáẃi (see ‖1.4) ~ ćîukuuyámi 'it is threaded'
>
> -áawiiY 'to throw' + {-qeeD}: ṣâawiiʔi ~ ṣâawiimi 'we threw it' (see Section 241)

SD ~ šaN (examples with -úwâameeSD):

> {-qeeD}: suẃaẃâameesta ~ suẃaẃâameešáńa 'we (plural) put up a tent'
>
> {-qiṢ}: ćíwâameesti ~ ćíwâameešáńi 'it has been put up'
>
> {-qeeY}: suẃâameeste ~ suẃâameešáńe 'I went to put up a tent'
>
> {-ʿíʔiD}: śíwâameestí ~ śíwâameešaní 'I made shade for him'
>
> {-(ʹ)í̱}: suẃáameesti ~ suẃáameešání 'when I put up a tent'

The sequence ‖aaM‖ ~ ‖aaN‖. This variation does not apply to forms with M that are the result of variations of other morphophonemic consonants:

> -úuťaaM 'to practice' + {-iguyaN}: síuťâamikuya ~ síuťâanikuya 'I practiced every day'
>
> -ú:yáaM 'to butcher' + {-qiṢ}: ćíuyâami ~ ćíuyáani 'it was butchered'

The third kind of variation, which must be defined by the individual morpheme rather than by the morphophonemic content of the morpheme, is marked as follows: if a final morphophonemic consonant varies freely with another morphophonemic consonant or morphophonemic sequence, the variant morphophoneme(s) are placed in parentheses. Thus -ugáwidyaaD(N) indicates that -ugáwidyaaD ~ -ugáwidyaaN; -ánamaD(čaN) indicates that -ánamaD ~ -ánamačaN. If a final morphophonemic sequence varies with another morphophonemic sequence, both sequences are placed in parentheses. Thus -úsť(íʔiD)(ičaN) indicates that -úsťíʔiD ~ -úsťičaN. The variations described here are in addition to the variations described above. Thus -âaćawaiY(N) indicates that -âaćawaiY ~ -âaćawaiM ~ -âaćawaiN.

Most occurrences of D vary with čaN: -ánamaD(čaN) 'to sit down'; -úmasawaaD(čaN) 'to stew food'; -úẃaisť(aN)(iD)(ičaN) 'to dish up food'.

Most roots that end with no final morphophonemic consonant ($\emptyset$) vary with forms that have a final morphophonemic consonant. The evidence seems to indicate that the variation is not completely free, but that certain variations are mandatory when certain suffixes follow. Some examples are: -áayúm̓(a$\emptyset$)(aṢ)(iṢ) 'to know how'; -ûučím̓ə$\emptyset$(Ṣ) 'to love'; -âaweeM(pe$\emptyset$) 'to winnow'; -úuḱéesi$\emptyset$(N)(Ṣ) 'to be jealous'; -ínáu(da$\emptyset$)(daN)(ti̓uD) 'to finish'.

Two forms have variants with an extra syllable -m̓eN: -áasbanašúM(m̓eN)(waN) 'to wash hair'; -áanúM(m̓eN)($\emptyset$) 'to take a bath'. The second variant is usually used before an initial vowel suffix; only the first variant is used elsewhere: ka?áaspanašúm̓áńa 'they washed their hair'; ka?áaspanašú 'she washed her hair'; ćáanum̓éńi 'it has been bathed'; ka?áanú 'he took a bath'.

There is no pattern to the remaining variations. Some examples are: -čáaSD(z̧aSD)(z̧aN) 'to listen'; -âačawaiY(N) 'to run a stick race'; -ugáwidyaaD(N) 'to thresh grain'; -ûučiG^W(t̓aaN) 'to punish'; -'úkaaz(á?aN)(íM) 'to announce'; -úudíM(M̄) 'to plant'; -úušiyaW(N) 'to beat in a contest'; -t̓a?aD(dyəM) 'to stand up'.

‖1.s   The application of ‖1 is restated in tabular form. Table 1 shows the development of the final morphophonemic consonants before initial vowel suffixes. Table 2 lists the allomorphs of the suffixes. Table 3 gives the development of the final morphophonemic consonants and the allomorphs of suffixes that do not typically begin with a vowel. No attempt is made to include all the details described in ‖1.

‖2   A replacive morphophoneme ‖⁼‖ is set up before some allomorphs of the continuative suffixes {⁼itaaN} (Section 441.1) and {⁼áayaN}, some empty morphs (Section 441.1), and the suffix {⁼áikuY} (Section 452), to account for the loss of the final vowel of the preceding form:

> ‖⁼itaaN‖ allomorph of {⁼itaaN}
> ‖⁼qitaaN‖ allomorph of {⁼itaaN}
> ‖⁼etaaN‖ allomorph of {⁼itaaN}
> ‖⁼é?etaaN‖ allomorph of {⁼itaaN}
> ‖⁼áayaN‖ allomorph of {⁼áayaN}
> ‖⁼jáayaN‖ allomorph of {⁼áayaN}
> ‖⁼qíit̓-‖ empty morph
> ‖⁼qiit̓-‖ empty morph
> ‖⁼ic-‖ empty morph
> ‖⁼áikuY‖ allomorph of {⁼áikuY}

Examples:

> ‖⁼itaaN‖: siušanawita 'I am shearing him'; cf. siušanawa 'I sheared him'

‖⁼etaaN‖: kaʔâušeeʔeta 'he is asking for permission'; cf. kaʔâušaaʔa
  'he asked for permission' (see ‖14)

‖⁼qííṭ-‖: séẏastíiṭita 'I am canning'; cf. séẏasta 'I canned'

A long or accented vowel before the morphophoneme shows alternative
treatments. There are not enough examples to formulate a general rule:

  šíizúwiita 'I am paying him'; -íizúwaaN 'to pay'

  sugáẇitita 'I am threshing grain'; -ugáwidyaaN 'to thresh grain'

  sáusiita 'I am getting some water'; -séeN 'to get water'

An additional syllable is lost when ‖⁼itaaN‖ is added to -únúunaaʔaN:
suñûunita 'I am getting ashamed'. Cf. -ûušaaʔaN 'to ask for permission',
given above.

‖3.0 Before certain suffixes and auxiliaries the glottal accent replaces
any accent that may be found on final syllables, and short vowels are
lengthened.

‖3.1 This change takes place (1) in periphrastic constructions with the
auxiliary {gú} (Section 470) and (2) before the suffix {-saa} (Section 652.1).
The change only takes place, however, if the final syllable is accented:

  néinúusťuziigú 'he will put the fire out'; -áinúusťizíM 'to put the
    fire out'

  ṅikûuyausí 'I will thread a needle'; cf. šikûuyáu 'I threaded a needle'

  hâaniisa 'the east side'; cf. hâaní 'eastern part'

The auxiliary {gú} that conditions this change and the changed morpheme
are separated by a pronominal prefix (see Section 461). The change does
not take place in nonperiphrastic constructions with {gú}: ʔámúugú 'he
loves her' (Section 632.6).

‖3.2 The accent change is found before the auxiliary {zá} (Section
461.8) and the suffixes {-méʔe} (Section 647), {-zéeši} (Section 653.2),
and {pədá} (Section 654.6), but only with certain forms. These forms
are marked with the morphophonemic accent ‖`‖:

  ‖-qúudì‖: k̂úudíizá 'it is mountainous'; k̂úudíimé 'Cochiti Indian';
    k̂úuti 'mountain'

  ‖múšì‖: múšíizá 'it is sudsy'; múši 'soap'

  ‖báasù‖: báasúumé 'Mexicans'; báasu 'Mexico'

  ‖yúuwì‖: yúuẇíizéeši 'the side part'; yúuẇi 'along, beside'

  ‖hác̀ə‖: hác̀əəpədá 'just a little bit'; hác̀əsái 'how many days?'

Contrast:

  ʔúurazá 'it is gold'

  díiwimé 'Santo Domingo Indian'

  náyáazéeši 'the underneath part', from ‖náyáa‖

  ťúuhámapədá 'just any old time'

TABLE 1

Final Morphophonemic Consonants

	-qədyeeZ	-qeeD	-qiṢ	-qeeY	-ʔʔiD	-(')í	-iku	-iši	-iguyaN	-u	final; before a consonant
N	n	n	n	n	n	n	n	n	n	n	∅
ʔN						ń		ń			ʔV
M, M̄	m	m	m	m	m	m	m	m	m	m	∅
ʔM	ḿ	ḿ	ḿ	ḿ	ḿ	ḿ	m	ḿ	m	ḿ	ʔV
W	b	w	w	w	w	w			u	g, n	∅
(a)Ẃ	m	m									áu
B	b	b	b	b	b	b		b	b	g	∅
Gʷ									b		gu
ʔB	ʔVb	ʔVb		ʔVb	ʔVb				ʔVb	ʔVg	ʔu
Y	∅	∅	y	y	y	y	y	y	y	y	∅
D	∅	d	d	d	d	d	d	d	d	dy	∅
SD	šan	sd	sd	sd	sd	sd		d	d		ša
Ṣ	ṣ	ṣ	sd	sd	sd	ṣ	ṣ	ṣ	ṣ	ṣ	∅
Z			z	z	z	z	z	z	z	g	∅
S	s	s									∅

TABLE 2

Initial Vowel Suffixes

N, Nˀ	Zeeʸpeb-	ɊeeD-	-qiṢ	-qeeY	-ˀíʔiD	-(ˀ)í	-iku	-iši	-iguyaN	-u
M, ʔM	Zeeʸpeb-	Ɋaa D-	-qiṢ	-qeeY	-ˀíʔiD	-(ˀ)í	-iku	-iši	-iguyaN	-u
M̄	Zeeʸpeb-	Ɋee D-	-qiṢ	-qeeY	-ˀíʔiD, -qiˀʔiD	-(ˀ)í, -(ˀ)qí	-iku	-iši	-iguyaN	-a
	Zeeʸpe-	-eeD	-iṢ	-eeY	-ˀíʔiD	-(ˀ)í		-iši		
W	Zeeʸpe-	-aaD	-iṢ, -qiṢ	-eeY, -qeeY	-ˀíʔiD, -ˀíʔiD	-(ˀ)í			- guyaN	-u
Ẉ	Zeeʸpeb-	Ɋee D-	-qiṢ	-qeeY						
B, Gʷ, Bˀ	Zeeʸpe-	-eeD	-iṢ	-eeY	-ˀíʔiD	-(ˀ)í		-iši	-iguyaN	-u, -unu
Y	Zeeʸp-	ʔVVD	-iṢ	-eeY	-ˀíʔiD	-(ˀ)í		-iši		-u
D	Zeeʸpe-	-aaD	-iṢ	-eeY	-ˀíʔiD	-(ˀ)í	-iku	-iši	-iguyaN	-a
SD	Zeeʸpeb-	-aaD	-iṢ	-eeY	-ˀíʔiD	-(ˀ)í	-iku	-iši	-iguyaN	
Ṣ	adyap-	-iiD			-(ˀ)í		-iku	-i		-a
Z		-aaD			-(ˀ)í		-iku	-iši		-a
S					-(ˀ)í		-iku	-iši		
∅	Zeeʸpe-	-eeD	-iṢ	- ' ' iD	-ˀíʔiD	-(ˀ)í	-iku	-iši		-nu

TABLE 3

Final Morphophonemic Consonants
and Other Suffixes

	-náataN	⁼itaaN	⁼áayaN
N			-n-qáayaN
W, Ẃ		-w-itaaN	
B, Gᵂ		-b-itaaN	
Y	-y-qáataN		
D	-d-qáataN		-d-qáayaN
SD	-d-qáataN	-d-qitaaN	-d-qáayaN
∅	-qjáataN		

{mə́ədì} has the allomorph ‖mə́ədɛ̀‖ before {zá}, ‖mə́ədì‖ elsewhere: mə́ədéezá 'it is a boy'; mə́əti 'boy'.

‖4   A short accented vowel or sequence of -áu (< ‖aẂ‖, see ‖1.5) becomes unaccented before the repetitive suffixes {-sə∅} and {-Gᵂ} (Section 442.1):

‖-ušûwíM(N)‖: sušúwìsə 'I am putting on shoes' (see ‖30); sušúwìku 'I am putting on shoes'; sušûwí 'I put on shoes'

‖-útisdyuwíM‖: kútistyuwiku 'it is sticky'; kútistyuwí 'it is stuck'

‖-ə́dyazíM‖: sə́tyacisə 'I kept stopping'; sə́tyazí 'I stopped'

Contrast:

‖-úukáaM‖: síukáasə 'I am shelling corn'

‖-úutáaM‖: síutáaku 'I am trying it'

Occasionally -sə∅ is realized simply by the accent change:

síudâakaatyau ~ síudâakaatyausə 'I am uncovering it'; síudâakaadyáu 'I uncovered it'

cítistyuwi 'it is sticking to it'; sítistyuwí 'I stuck it on'

A short unaccented vowel is (optionally?) lengthened in some stems before -Gᵂ:

‖-ûučaN‖: síukúičǎaku 'I am dividing it up'; gáaẏâačaape 'they keep giving some of it away' (plural suffix -eeD); sîukúičasə 'I am dividing it up'; cf. sîukúičáɲa 'we divided it up' (plural suffix -qaaD)

‖-úisdyaN‖: síwíistyaaku 'I keep making a knot'; cf. síwíisdyání 'when I made a knot' (suffix {-(´)í})

‖5.0   This rule describes the changes that take place when a thematic prefix is added to a stem syllable. The stem syllables that are set up are: ‖uu, u, u:, ui, a, aa, ai, au, áa, ii‖. The stem syllable listed as ‖áa‖ is to be read as ‖áa ~ a‖ and is found only before a glottalized sonorant. The three stem syllables ‖aa, ai, au‖ develop in identical fashion and are indicated by aV in stating the rules; note that V is not the morphophoneme ‖V‖ described in ‖15. The most common stem syllables are ‖uu‖, ‖u‖, and ‖ii‖. Many ‖ii‖ stems have alternates with ‖uu‖, ‖ai‖, ‖awii‖, or other types, and it is often difficult to identify this stem syllable.

Most of the thematic prefixes have an initial coarticulation morphophoneme, and some of the prefixes consist solely of such a morphophoneme. The morphophonemic changes produced by these morphophonemes are described in ‖10, 11, 13.

There are a number of accent changes that take place when thematic prefixes are added. The changes are accounted for in ‖5.1, 6, 20, 22, 28. In addition there is an apparent change that is the result of the convention of writing the accent over the first vowel of the syllable (see Section 121). When two syllables, one accented and one unaccented, are joined to form one syllable, the accent is unchanged but is sometimes placed over a different vowel because the first vowel of the new syllable is not always the first vowel of the old accented syllable. Note, however, that the variable length morphophoneme ‖:‖, which is not a vowel but can carry an accent, is exempted from this convention.

Examples are given in three forms: basic form, morphophonemic form after the application of ‖5, and phonemic form. The theme is a bound form, and it is therefore necessary to add a pronominal prefix in listing the phonemic form.

‖5.1   If both the thematic prefix and stem syllables are accented, the accent of the stem syllable is lost. The variable length morphophoneme in the stem syllable ‖u:‖ is lost, and any accent that occurs with ‖:‖ is usually shifted to the following syllable. This subrule applies to the following prefixes:

- ʽúu-	reflexive, ‖5.2
- ʽáʔi-	by mouth, ‖5.2
- ʽáʔ-	second active prefix, ‖5.3

Examples are given in ‖5.2 and ‖5.3.

‖5.2   The following thematic prefixes replace the stem syllable:

first set

- ʽúu-	reflexive
- ʽáʔi-	by mouth

first set (continued)

- -ʼi-   by body
- -qja-   dispersional
- -Auu-   external possessive

second set

- -Jaýa-   intransitive prefix
- -qjaʔa-   passive
- -ʼáaýa-   collective plural

The replacement by the first set is identical for all stem syllables. ‖-ʼi-‖ glottalizes a following sonorant, and the resulting form sometimes undergoes the accent change described in ‖22. Examples:

- -ʼúu-ûuráćizaN > -ʼúuráćiza: kúuráćica 'he banged himself'
- -ʼúu-uↄ̂ćayuzaN > -ʼúuↄ̂ćayuza: kúućáýuca 'he shot himself' (see ‖30)
- -ʼúu-uↄ̂mətizaN > -ʼúumətiza: kúumətica 'he killed himself'
- -ʼúu-ubáyaN > -ʼúubáya: súubáýa 'I burned myself'
- -ʼáʔi-úustúẃizaN >-ʼáʔistúẃiza: sáistúẃica 'I pointed with my lips' (see ‖23)
- -ʼi-úunə́əzaN > -ʼíńə́əza: kińə́əca 'he became rigid' (see ‖22)
- -ʼi-úuḱúduzaN > -ʼíḱúduza: kiḱútuca 'he bunched up into a ball'
- -ʼi-uↄ̂ḱusizaN > -ʼiↄ̂ḱusiza: kiḱúsica 'he curled up'
- -qja-úuḱúduzaN-qiṢ > -qjáḱúduzi: ćaḱútuci 'there are a whole bunch of lumps' (see ‖22)
- -qja-uↄ̂ćayuzaN-qiṢ > -qjaↄ̂ćayuzi: ćaćáýuci 'it was all shot up' (see ‖20, 30)
- -qja-úńadyumeN-qiṢ > -qjáńadyumen-qi: ćáńatyuméńi 'it has been suffered from'
- -Auu-uↄ̂ćayuzaN-qiṢ > -Auuↄ̂ćayuzi: gâućayuci 'his has a bullet hole'
- -Auu-âzəkaN-qiṢ > -Aûuzəkan-qi: śûuçəkáńi 'mine (e.g., cigarette) has been smoked'

The second syllable of the second set of prefixes is lengthened before a long stem syllable. The vowel may be lengthened before ‖u:‖, and ‖ii‖ may be replaced by ‖ai‖; these variations are probably free. Examples:

- -Jaýa-úušíizaN > -Jaýáašíiza: śeýáašíica 'I borrowed'
- -Jaýa-úćayawaN > -Jaýáćayawa: śeýáćayawa 'I got mad'
- -Jaýa-âaćawaiY > -Jaýâaćawai: zaýâaćawai 'he took part in a stick race'
- -qjaʔa-úušíizaN > -qjaʔáašíiza: sḱaʔáašíica 'it was borrowed from me'
- -qjaʔa-uↄ̂mayanikuyaN-qaaD > -qjaʔaↄ̂mayanikuyan-qaa: sḱaʔamáyanikuyáńa 'I was made fun of'

-qjaʔa-úːwageN-qaaD > -qjaʔaaːwagən-qaa: sǩaʔáawagéńa 'my clothes
    have been worn'

-qjaʔa-učáwaN-qaaD > -qjaʔačáwan-qaa: sǩaʔačáwáńa 'it was stolen
    from me'

-qjaʔa-íișaťâawaN-qaaD > -qjaʔáișaťâawan-qaa: sǩaʔáișaťâawáńa 'I
    was fattened up'

-ʿáaẏa-úćayawaN-qaaD > -ʿáaẏáćayawan-qaa: sáaẏáćayawáńa 'we (in
    a group) argued'

-ʿáaẏa-íizúwaaN-qaaD > -ʿáaẏáazúwaan-qaa: káaẏáazúwaańa 'they
    (in a group) paid'

‖5.3 The middle voice prefix ‖-Qa-‖ is added to long stem syllables
and the short stem syllable ‖u‖. The second active prefix ‖-ʿáʔ-‖ is
added primarily to ‖uu‖ stems, but also to a few ‖ii‖ stems. ‖-Qa-‖
is added to ‖u‖ stems with no morphophonemic change. The development
of the prefixes with long stem syllables is shown diagrammatically:

stem vowel:	uu	aV	ii
plus ‖-Qa-‖:	Qau	QaV	Qai
plus ‖-ʿáʔ-‖:	ʿáʔu		ʿáʔi

Examples:

-Qa-ûpəẓaN > -Qâupəẓa: kaʔâupəça 'he shook himself'

-Qa-úunə̀əẓaN > -Qáunə̀əẓa: kaʔáunə̀əca 'he pulled himself (e.g.,
    his own hair)'

-Qa-ûumúŕaẓaN > -Qâumúŕaẓa: sâumúŕaca 'something of mine got
    dented'

-Qa-áišaSD > -Qáišaša: sáišaša 'I spread out bedding'

-Qa-îiťaaN > -Qâiťaa: kaʔâiťa 'he stepped on himself'

-ʿáʔ-ûumúŕaẓaN > -ʿáʔumúŕaẓa: sáumúŕaca 'I dented it (see ‖23)

-ʿáʔ-íiskⁱ̂ə̀ʔəẓaiM > -ʿáʔiskⁱ̂ə̀ʔəẓai: káiskⁱ̂ə̀ʔəçai 'he turned it
    around'

‖5.4 The morphophonemic changes found with the possessive prefix
{-qa-} are similar to those found with the prefixes discussed in ‖5.3.
The main difference is that the possessive prefix can be added to almost
all stem syllables, including noun stems that can begin with a consonant.
In addition, there are many irregular forms.

‖-qa-‖ is usually added without change to noun stems with an initial
consonant:

-qa-páńaci > -qapáńaci: ǩapáńaci 'his lungs'; cf. páńaci 'lungs'

-qa-dúwímiši > -qadúwímiši: sadúwímiši 'my socks'; cf. dúwímiši
    'socks'

‖-qa-‖ plus ‖ʔ‖ and ‖h‖ may result in the loss of the manner consonant,
provided that the resulting stem syllable is one of those listed in ‖5.0.
(See examples under ‖-qa-‖ plus stem syllables, below.)

‖-qa-‖ replaces a folloiwng short stem syllable:

-qa-úćayuwaN-qiṢ > -qáćayuwan-qi: śáćayawáṅi 'I am mad'

-qa-áSD-qiṢ > -qášan-qi: ḱášáṅi 'he stepped and left footprints'

-qa-ʔúwíizíṁi > -qáwíizíṁi: śáwíizíṁi 'my cradle board'; ʔúwíizíṁi
'cradle board'

‖-qa-‖ added to long stem syllables gives the results shown in the
diagram:

stem vowel:	uu	ui	aV	áa
plus ‖-qa-‖	qau	qai ~ qau	qaV	qa (~ qáa?)

Examples:

-qa-ûuṁišuṁéewaN-qiṢ > -qâuṁišuṁéewan-qi: ḱâuṁišuṁéewáṅi 'he
moistened the ground'

-qa-úišaẓaN(M)-qiṢ > -qáišaẓan-qi ~ -qáušaẓan-qi: śáišaẓáṅi ~
śáušaẓáṅi 'I am wearing pants'

-qa-áaťaW-iṢ > -qáaťaw-i: śáaťawi 'I have it opened'

-qa-áayáť-iṢ > -qayáť-i: ḱayáťi 'he has it all smeared'

-qa-húućíṅi > -qáućíṅi: śáućíṅi 'my kilts'; cf. húućíṅi 'kilts'

-qa-hâaṁi > -qâaṁi: śâaṁi 'my tobacco'; cf. hâaṁi 'tobacco'

-qa-ʔ-úišaẓaN(M)-qiṢ-(´) > -qáišaẓan-qi-(´): ḱáišaẓáṅi 'his pants';
cf. ẃíišaẓáṅi 'pants' (see ‖16)

-qa-ʔ-áigayaŴ-qiṢ-(´) > -qáigayam-qi-(´): śáigáyáṁi 'my brakes';
cf. ʔáigáyáṁi 'brakes'

The loss of an initial manner consonant of a noun stem is optional, and
alternate forms occur: śâaṁi ~ śahâaṁi 'my tobacco'. The glottal stop
is almost always dropped from infinitive-derived nouns (Section 643). The
last two examples above come in this category.

The possessive prefix has an accented allomorph ‖-qá-‖ which is
found with a few nouns that have an initial plain sonorant:

-qá-náći: śánáći 'my food'; náći 'food'

-qá-mə́ədi: śámə́əti 'my son'; mə́əti 'boy'

-qá-ẃaasťi: ḱáẃaasťi 'his young ones'; ẃaasťi 'little ones; young of
animals'

-qá-máʔágə: śámáʔákə 'my daughter'; magə́ 'small girl' (irregular
stem change)

A few nouns have irregular stem and possessive prefix formations:

-qáaťisdyúṁi: ḱáaťisdyúṁi 'his belt'; húuťisdyúṁi 'belt'

-qjéeska (~ -qa-hiïska): ćéeska (~ ḱahiïska) 'his knife'; hiïska
'knife'

-qáusdya: śáustya 'my bow'; husdyâaḱa 'bow'

The nouns ṅáisdíya 'father' and ṅâaya 'mother' take ‖-i-‖, allomorph
of the possessive prefix, when preceded by a first person prefix (see

Section 230): sináisdíya 'my father'; ti?ináisdíya 'I had a father (dubitative)'. The possessive prefix is ‖-qá-‖ before other pronominal prefixes and before the number prefixes regardless of the pronominal prefix; the initial sonorant of the stem is unglottalized: kánáisdíya 'his
father'; ta?ánáisdíya 'we (dual) had a father (dubitative)' (see ‖7.9).

‖5.5 Certain stem syllable changes are found after:

{tr-1}   first transitive prefix

{tr-2}   second transitive prefix

-J̄-   benefactive

-qj-   perfect

{tr-1} plus ‖uu‖ in stems that have the derivational suffix -zaN (Section 621) becomes ‖u:‖. {tr-1} is realized as zero before ‖u:‖ stems.
Elsewhere the prefix has the allomorph ‖-J‖. {tr-2} is realized as
zero before all stem syllables.

‖u:‖ and ‖ii‖ become ‖u: ~ uu:‖ and ‖ii ~ uu‖ respectively after
‖-qj-‖ and become ‖uu:‖ and ‖uu‖ respectively after {tr-2} and ‖-J̄-‖.
These stem syllables are unchanged after {tr-1}.

‖u‖ becomes ‖u ~ uu‖ after ‖-J̄-‖ and ‖-qj-‖ and becomes ‖uu‖
after {tr-2}. It is unchanged after {tr-1}.

The remaining stem syllables are unchanged. Many of them, however,
undergo vocalic changes described in ‖11.3 when they come after a palatalizing morphophoneme (j, J, J̄).

Examples:

-{tr-1}-ûupúku-zaN > -û:púkuza: kupúkuca 'she sprinkled it'

-{tr-1}-úusâaN > -Júusâa: zíusâ 'he approved of him'

-{tr-1}-u:ĉayu-zaN > -u:ĉayuza: gučáyuca 'he shot it'

-{tr-1}-u:daiskaaM(N) > -u:daiskaa: kudâiska 'he peeled it'

-{tr-1}-ubáyaN > -Jubáya: cibáya 'he burned her'

-{tr-1}-úišazaN(M) > -Júišaza: zíušaca 'she put his pants on him'

-{tr-1}-áasgǝN > -Jáasgǝ: séeskǝ 'I fried it'

-{tr-1}-íicitama-zaN > -Jíicitamaza: zíicitamaca 'he turned it over'

-{tr-2}-ûupúkuzaN > -ûupúkuza: gûupúkuca 'she sprinkled his'

-{tr-2}-u:ĉayuzaN > -uu:ĉayuza: gûučayuca 'he shot something of
    hers'

-{tr-2}-ubáyaN > -uubáya: gûupaya 'he burned hers' (see ‖6)

-{tr-2}-úišazaN(M) > -úišaza: gúišaca 'she wore his pants'

-{tr-2}-áasgǝN > -áasgǝ: séeskǝ 'I fried his'

-{tr-2}-íicitamazaN > -úucitamaza: gúucitamaca 'he turned hers
    over'

-J̄-úušíizaN-'í?iD > -J̄úušíizan-'í?i: síušíicaní 'I borrowed it for
    him'

-J̄-uˑdaisk̇aaM(N)-ʼíʔiD > -Juuˑdaisk̇aan-ʼíʔi: śiutaiskaaní 'I peeled it for him'

-J̄-íicitamazaN-ʼíʔiD > -J̄úucitamazan-ʼíʔi: śiucitamacaní 'I turned it over for him'

-qj-úuśíizaN-qiS̱ > -qjúuśíizi: ćíuśíici 'it has been borrowed'

-qj-úṅadyumeN-qiS̱ > -qjúṅadyumen-qi ~ -qjũuṅadyumen-qi: ćíṅatyuméṅi ~ ćĩuṅatyuméṅi 'it has been hurt'

-qj-úiśaẓaN(M)-qiS̱ > -qjúuśaẓan-qi: ćíuśaẓáṅi 'the pants have been worn'

-qj-íicitamazaN-qiS̱ > -qjíicitamazi ~ -qjúucitamazi: ćíicitamaci ~ ćíucitamaci 'it has been turned over'

‖5.6 The stem syllable ‖uu‖ becomes ‖uu ~ u‖ and the stem syllable ‖ii‖ becomes ‖i‖ after the first active prefix ‖-ʼ-‖. If the resulting thematic syllable is ‖u‖ or ‖i‖, a following plain sonorant is glottalized, and the form may then undergo an accent change described in ‖22 (cf. ‖-ʼi-‖, in ‖5.2). Examples:

- -ʼ-ũukudyaaN > -ʼũukudyaa ~ -ʼũkudyaa: kũukutya ~ kúkutya 'he gathered wood'
- -ʼ-ũuméẏuzaN > -ʼũméẏuza: suméẏuca 'I got bruised'
- -ʼ-íiṣáʼaaN > -ʼiṣáʼaa: kíṣáʼa 'he is fat'
- -ʼ-úyúutaaN > -ʼúyúutaa: kuẏúuta 'he sang'

Other stem syllables are unchanged:

- -ʼ-úiśaẓaN: kúiśaça 'he put pants on'
- -ʼ-áyaceeM: káẏace 'he whitewashed it'[12]
- -ʼ-áaẏáaʼéewizaN: káaẏáaʼéewica 'he stepped in mud'

‖5.s Not all of the morphophonemic changes involved in thematic prefixation are covered by the subrules of ‖5. A number of nonproductive prefixes are difficult to isolate for morphophonemic and semantic reasons. There are a number of stems that do not fit into the stem syllable classes given in ‖5.0. Many stems have different stem syllables after different prefixes so that it is often difficult or impossible to separate the prefix and the stem syllable. There are also many irregular prefix and stem combinations. All such phenomena are left for dictionary listing. In the remainder of the grammar, themes rather than stems will be treated as the basic unit wherever possible. When it is necessary to give the stems of such themes, the stem will be identified morphemically

---

[12]The glottalization of this form is not the result of the prefix; ‖-ʼ-‖ glottalizes sonorants only when the thematic syllable is short ‖u‖ or ‖i‖. The glottalization is the result of ‖30, as can be seen by káẏácéemí 'when he whitewashed it'. This form has the prefix ‖-ʼ-‖, but the conditions for the operation of ‖30 are not present.

only. Thus the stem underlying the themes -ə̓:sḱəD 'to drink', -ûusḱaD
'to drink someone else's drink', -JíisḱaD-aW(N) 'to give someone a drink'
is written {-sḱaD}; the regular stem underlying the themes -JáasgəN 'to
fry it', -J̄aasgəN-'í?iD 'to fry it for someone', -qjáasgəN-qiṢ 'to have
been fried' is written -áasgəN.

The application of ‖5 is summarized in table 4. The table gives the
thematic syllables that result from the combination of the thematic prefixes (vertical line) and the stem syllable (horizontal line). There are
several blanks in the table. A few of the blanks are probably due to lack
of data. Most of them, however, are probably real, but are of morphological rather than morphophonemic significance (see Sections 411-415).

‖6   If a long unaccented thematic syllable results through the operation
of ‖5, the accent of the following syllable is shifted to the thematic syllable.

In the examples that follow the stems are -ušûw⁑M(N) 'to wear shoes';
-usíusdyaN 'to rope, tie up'; -udyáazaN 'to write':

    ṡûušuwi 'mine (for example, my horse) is shod'; prefix -Auu-, ‖5.2
    ka?áusiustya 'he is tied up'; prefix -Qa-, ‖5.3
    ṡíusiustyaní 'I roped it for him'; prefix -J̄-, ‖5.5
    ṡíusiustya 'I roped his (for example, his horse)'; prefix {tr-2}, ‖5.5
    ćíutyaazáni 'it has been written'; prefix -qj-, ‖5.5

‖7.0   The dual and plural prefixes are so tightly fused to a following
theme that it is convenient to set up the prefixes in morphemic rather
than morphophonemic shape, {dl} and {pl}, and give a set of rules that
account for the morphophonemic shape of themes with prefixes included.
The morphophonemic shape of such themes is governed by one of the
following factors: (1) the thematic syllable and coarticulation morphophoneme, ‖7.1-3; (2) the thematic syllable excluding any coarticulation morphophoneme, ‖7.4-5; (3) the initial vowel excluding any coarticulation
morphophoneme, ‖7.6-8; or (4) the following thematic prefix, ‖7.9. Irregular forms are treated in ‖7.10. In stating the subrules ‖7.4-8, in which
the coarticulation morphophoneme is not a governing factor, the symbol
$\underline{X}$ is used to indicate a coarticulation morphophoneme that may be present.

The thematic syllable with a number prefix is usually expanded to two
syllables. The accent of the thematic syllable falls on the second syllable,
unless otherwise stated.

Examples are given in three forms: the morphophonemic form of the
theme after the application of rules preceding ‖7, the morphophonemic
form of the theme after the application of ‖7, and the phonemic form
with a pronominal prefix.

TABLE 4

Thematic Prefix and Stem Syllable

	uu	u:	u	ui	a	aV	áa	ii
‖5.2 -'úu-	'úu	'úu	'úu					
-'á?i-	'á?i	'í:						
-'i-	'i							
-qja-	qja	qja:						
-Auu-	Auu	Auu:	Auu		Auu			Auu
-Jaẏa-	Jaẏaa		Jaẏa			Jaẏa		
-qja?a-	qja?aa	qja?a: ~ qja?aa:	qja?a		qja?a	qja?aa	qja?a	qja?ai
-'áaẏa-	'áaẏaa		'áaẏa					'áaẏaa
‖5.3 -Qa-	Qau		Qau			QaV		Qai
-'á?-	'á?u	'á?u						'á?i
‖5.4 -qa-	qau		qa	qai ~ qau	qa	qaV	qa	
‖5.5 {tr-1}	u:, Juu	u:	Ju	Jui	Ja	JaV	Jáa ~ Ja	Jii
{tr-2}	uu	uu:	uu	ui	a	aV	a	uu
-J̄-	J̄uu	J̄uu:	J̄u ~ J̄uu	J̄ui	J̄a	J̄aV	J̄áa ~ J̄a	J̄uu
-qj-	qjuu	qju: ~ qjuu:	qju ~ qjuu	qjui	qja	qjaV	qjáa ~ qja	qjii ~ qjuu
‖5.6 -'-	'uu ~ 'u	'u:	'u	'ui	'a		'áa	'i

‖ 7.1   The following subrule applies to the thematic syllables ‖Ju‖
and ‖J̃u‖ that are followed by a sonorant:

   {dl} + Ju, J̃u > aʔa
   {pl} + Ju, J̃u > aẏa

Examples:

   {dl} + -Júyȧaka > -aʔáyȧaka: gaʔáyȧaka 'he burned them (dual)'
   {pl} + -Júyȧaka > -aẏáyȧaka: gaẏáyȧaka 'he burned them (plural)'
   {dl} + -J̃úwȧisṫan-ʿíʔi > -aʔáwȧisṫan-ʿíʔi: seʔéwȧisṫaní 'I dished
      up stew for them (dual)' (see ‖ 13)
   {pl} + -J̃úwȧisṫan-ʿíʔi > -aẏáwȧisṫan-ʿíʔi: seẏáwȧisṫaní 'I dished
      up stew for them (plural)'

   Cf. zíyȧaka 'he burned him'; śíwȧisṫaní 'I dished up stew for him'
   This rule also applies to three themes that have an obstruent after
the thematic syllable: -JučáwaN 'to blame someone'; -JúspȧawaN 'to
sprinkle (clothes)'; -JúpəkaawaN 'to chop wood'.   Examples:
   gaʔačáẇa 'he blamed them (dual)'; gaẏačáẇa 'he blamed them (plural)'
   seʔépəkaawa 'I chopped two pieces'; seẏápəkaawa 'I chopped a few
      pieces, one by one'

‖ 7.2   The following rule applies to the thematic syllables ‖Ju‖ and
‖J̃u‖ that are followed by an obstruent:

   {dl} + Ju, J̃u > âaʔa
   {pl} + Ju, J̃u > âiʔi

If the thematic syllable is accented, the accent is lost. If the thematic
syllable is unaccented, the accent on the following syllable is lost.
Examples:

   {dl} + -Jupánúusṫu > -âaʔapanúusṫu: gâaʔapanúusṫu 'they (dual) are
      thirsty'
   {pl} + -Jupánúusṫu > -âiʔipanúusṫu: gâiʔipanúusṫu 'they (plural) are
      thirsty'
   {dl} + -Júbənaiʔi > -âaʔabənaiʔi: gâaʔapənaiʔi 'he put them (dual)
      in'
   {pl} + -Júbənaiʔi > -âiʔibənaiʔi: gâiʔipənaiʔi 'he put them (plural)
      in'
   {dl} + -J̃utâaṅizan-ʿíʔi > -âaʔataaṅizan-ʿíʔi: sêeʔetaaṅicaní 'I
      worked for them (dual)'

   Cf. cipánúusṫu 'he is thirsty'; zípənaiʔi 'he put it in'; śitâaṅicaní
      'I worked for them'

   This rule also applies to one theme that has a sonorant after the
thematic syllable, -JumínaaD 'to speak to someone'; sêeʔemina 'I spoke
to them (dual)'; sêiʔimina 'I spoke to them (plural)'. Cf. śimíṅa 'I spoke
to him'.

Either this subrule or ‖ 7.1 applies, in free variation, to a few forms that have an obstruent after the thematic syllable: sgâaʔadyú ~ sgaʔádyú 'we (dual) are covered', theme -Júdyú.

The plural prefix is zero in a small group of classificatory verb themes (Section 451). This group consists of: -JúsťiD(čaN) 'to place a container of liquid'; -JúsdiiD(čaN) 'to place a sack of something'; -JútiD(čaN) 'to place a basket of something'. Examples:

    síšťiča 'I placed one container of liquid'

    sêeʔesťiča 'I placed two containers of liquid'

    síšťiča 'I placed several containers of liquid'

‖ 7.3   {dl} + Juu, Ĵuu > aʔau

         {pl} + Juu, Ĵuu > áawaa

Examples:

    {dl} + -Júusdyəgə > -aʔáusdyəgə: sgaʔáustyəkə 'he put beads on us (dual)'

    {pl} + -Júusdyəgə > -áawáasdyəgə: sgáawáastyəkə 'he put beads on us (plural)'

    {dl} + -Ĵúumáazan-'íʔi > -aʔáumáazan-'íʔi: seʔéumáacaní 'I helped them (dual)'

    {pl} + -Ĵúumáazan-'íʔi > -áawáamáazan-'íʔi: séewáamáacaní 'I helped them (plural)'

    Cf. skúistyəkə 'he put beads on me'; síumáacaní 'I helped him'

‖ 7.4   {dl} + Xui > uʔui

         {pl} + Xui > uwau

An initial coarticulation morphophoneme, represented in the rule by $\underline{X}$, is lost. Examples:

    {dl} + -úičaabə > -uʔúičaabə: guʔúičaapə 'they (dual) crossed over'

    {pl} + -úičaabə > -uwáučaabə: guwâučaapə 'they (plural) crossed over'

    {dl} + -qúiska > -uʔúiska: guʔúiska 'they (dual) have a bruise'

    {pl} + -qúiska > -uwáuska: guwáuska 'they (plural) have a bruise'

    Cf. gúičaapə 'he crossed over'; kúiska 'he has a bruise'

‖ 7.5 Forms with a variable length vowel have a number of treatments with the dual and plural prefixes. If one separates forms that have the high accent from forms that have the falling or glottal accent in the initial syllable, it is possible to construct rules that will account for all but six of the almost forty forms of this type that have been recorded with the number prefixes:

    High accent:

        {dl} + Xu: > uʔu:

        {pl} + Xu: > uwa

Falling or glottal accent:

    {dl} + Xu: > ûuʔu

    {pl} + Xu: > úwâa

In the second case, the accent of the thematic vowel or variable length morphophoneme is lost. It is possible that the rules do not represent productive morphophonemic processes, but are formulations that account for the few forms that happen to be in the corpus. Examples:

    {dl} + -ú:yáa > -uʔú:yáa: guʔúyá 'he slaughtered them (dual)'

    {pl} + -ú:yáa > -uẃáyáa: guẃáyá 'he slaughtered them (plural)'

    {dl} + -u:šanawa > -ûuʔušanawa: gûuʔušanawa 'he cut their (dual) hair'

    {pl} + -u:šanawa > -úwâašanawa: gúwâašanawa 'he cut their (plural) hair'

    {dl} + -ú:šiya > -ûuʔušiya: gûuʔušiya 'he beat them (dual)'

    {pl} + -ú:šiya > -úwâašiya: gúwâašiya 'he beat them (plural)'

    Cf. gúyá 'he slaughtered him'; kušánawa 'he cut his hair'; gúšiya 'he beat him'

The thematic syllable of -û:kasdyaN 'to invite someone' is replaced by ‖uu‖ after {dl}, and ‖7.6 applies; the form is regular after {pl}. The thematic syllable of -û:čiťuwaaN 'to drain something' and -ú:yáaniṢ 'to hate someone' is replaced by ‖uu‖ after both {dl} and {pl}, and ‖7.6 applies:

    sîukastya, siʔîukastya, síwáakastya 'I invited him, them (dual), them (plural)'

    sîučisťuwa, siʔîučisťuwa, siwâačisťuwa 'I drained it, them (dual), them (plural)'

    síuyáani, siʔíuyáani, siẃáayáani 'I hate him, them (dual), them (plural)'

The falling accent of the thematic syllable in -uîwiskəziṢ 'to have a scratch' (< -uîwiskə-zaN-qiṢ) is replaced by the high accent after {dl}, and the regular rule applies; the form is regular after {pl} (other derivations of the stem -uîwiskə-zaN 'to scratch' are regular). The high accent of the thematic syllable in -ú:čiskaiM 'to be full of water' is replaced by the falling accent after {dl}, and the regular rule applies; the form is regular after {pl}:

    sîuwiskəci, ṣuʔúwiskəci, ṣúwâaskəci 'I, we (dual), we (plural) have a scratch'

    síučiskai, ṣûuʔúčiskai, ṣuẃáčiskai 'I, we (dual), we (plural) are full of water' (see ‖21 for accent change in the dual)

The theme -uîseeńiši 'hair' combines irregularly with the number prefixes to give -ûuseêńiši (dual) and -úwaseêńiši (plural): kuseêńiši 'his hair'; gûusêeṅiši their (dual) hair'; gúw̃asêeṅiši 'their (plural) hair'.

‖ 7.6 {dl} + Xu > u?u

    {pl} + Xu > uw̃a

This rule applies to themes with an initial ‖u‖ that have not been treated in preceding subrules. Examples:

  {dl} + -ûum̃éeḱum̃e > -u?ûum̃éeḱum̃e: sgu?ûum̃éeḱum̃e 'he is watching us (dual)'

  {pl} + -ûum̃éeḱum̃e > -uw̃âam̃éeḱum̃e: sguw̃âam̃éeḱum̃e 'he is watching us (plural)'

  {dl} + -úwaasáa > -u?úwaasáa: sgu?úwaasá 'we (dual) are sick'

  {pl} + -úwaasáa > -uw̃áwaasáa: sguw̃áwaasá 'we (plural) are sick'

  {dl} + -qúwáw̃i > -u?úwáw̃i: gu?úwáw̃i 'their (dual) faces'

  {pl} + -qúwáw̃i > -u w̃áwáw̃i: guw̃áwáw̃i 'their (plural) faces'

  Cf. sgûum̃éeḱum̃e 'he is watching me'; sgúwaasá 'I am sick';

   ḱúwáw̃i 'his face'

The thematic syllable is shortened in -úukačaN 'to see someone' after {pl}; the formation with {dl} is regular: síukača 'I see him'; si?íukača 'I see them (dual)'; siw̃ákača 'I see them (plural)'.

The theme -úusa 'to be lazy' combines irregularly with the number prefixes to give -ûu?uusa (dual) and -ûuw̃aasa (plural): sgúusa 'I am lazy'; sgûu?uusa 'we (dual) are lazy'; sgûuw̃aasa 'we (plural) are lazy'.

‖ 7.7 {dl} + Xi, Xə > a?a (if the thematic syllable is short)

        > a?ai (if the thematic syllable is long; length is

         lost)

  {pl} + Xi, Xə > aýa

When the thematic syllable is short, the changes are identical with those described in ‖ 7.1 for ‖Ju‖ and ‖J̄u‖. Examples:

  {dl} + -Jíisée > -a?áisée: ga?áisé 'he filled two things with liquid'

  {pl} + -Jíisée > -aýáasée: gaýáasé 'he filled several things with liquid'

  {dl} + - ˈəəgáṅi > -a?âigáˈni: ga?âigáṅi 'they (dual) are blushing'

  {pl} + - ˈəəgáṅi > -aýâagáṅi: gaýâagáṅi 'they (plural) are blushing'

  {dl} + - ˈjiýúuspii > -a?aýúuspii: ga?aýúuspi 'their (dual) shoulders'

  {pl} + - ˈjiýúuspii > -aýaýúuspii: gaýaýúuspi 'their (plural) shoulders

  Cf. zíisé 'he filled it'; kəəgáṅi 'he is blushing; ciýúuspi 'his shoulder'

Four themes have irregular accent and length changes when {pl} is prefixed (the forms with {dl} are regular):

  -JíisazaN 'to name someone'; with {pl}, -áýasázaN

  -JíitaaN 'to step on something'; with {pl}, -aýatâaN

  -JíizaačuwaM(N) 'to wake up someone'; with {pl}, -áýazáačuwa

  -JíisḱadaW(N) 'to give someone a drink'; with {pl}, -áýasḱadaW(N)

Examples: ziicaačuwa, gaʔâicaačuwa, gáyazáačuwa 'he woke him, them (dual), them (plural)'.

‖ 7.8   {dl} + Xa > aʔa
           {pl} + Xa > aya

This rule applies to themes with an initial ‖ a ‖, except those treated in ‖ 7.9. Examples:

{dl} + -Jâanú > -aʔâanú: gaʔâanú 'she gave them (dual) a bath'
{pl} + -Jâanú > -ayâanú: gayâanú 'she gave them (plural) a bath'
{dl} + -'ásdíi > -aʔásdíi: saʔásdí 'our (dual) feet'
{pl} + -'ásdíi > -ayásdíi: sayásdí 'our (plural) feet'
{dl} + -qáusa > -aʔáusa: gaʔáusa 'they (dual) are slowpokes'
{pl} + -qáusa > -ayáusa: gayáusa 'they (plural) are slowpokes'
Cf. zâanú 'she gave him a bath'; sésdí 'my feet'; káusa 'he is a slow poke'

Themes that are formed by the passive prefix {-qjaʔa-} (‖ 5.2) lose the initial vowel and glottal stop after the number prefixes. Note that by the application of this rule the dual differs from the singular by the absence of the initial coarticulation morphophonemes. Examples with -qjaʔáašaazíM 'to be cut': skaʔáašaazí 'I was cut'; sgaʔáašaazí 'we (dual) were cut'; sgayáašaazí 'we (plural) were cut'.

The theme -JáaciguyaN 'to say to someone' has two alternates, in free variation, with the number prefixes. One set of alternates has an unaccented initial syllable, and the resulting forms have no accent (see Section 121). One alternate with {pl} is regular; the other alternate with {pl} and both alternates with {dl} are irregular and have shapes similar to themes with ‖ Ju ‖ described in ‖ 7.2: -âaʔaciguyaN ~ -aaʔaciguyaN (dual prefix); -ayáaciguyaN ~ -aiʔiciguyaN (plural prefix). Examples: séecikuya 'I said to him'; sêeʔecikuya ~ seeʔecikuya 'I said to them (dual)'; seyáacikuya ~ seiʔicikuya 'I have said to them (plural)'.

The theme -ánadiṢ '(corn) to get ripe' has the form -áyánadiṢ with the plural prefix (the dual is lacking): gánati 'it got ripe'; gáyánati 'they got ripe'.

{dl} and {pl} are not prefixed directly to the theme -qáazáaN 'could be heard, to be loud enough'. Instead, a new theme is used, -úukáazáaN, formed by prefixing the thematic syllable ‖ úu ‖ and the third person prefix ‖ g- ‖. {dl} and {pl} are prefixed to the resulting theme, and ‖ 7.6 applies: káazá 'he could be heard'; guʔúukáazá 'they (dual) could be heard'; guwáakáazá 'they (plural) could be heard'.

‖ 7.9 The development of the dual prefix plus forms with the thematic prefixes {-qa-} 'possessive' and {-Jaya-} 'intransitive' is regular, and ‖ 7.8 applies. The development of such themes with the plural prefix dif-

fers from other themes with an initial ‖a‖ and is treated in this subrule. There are four types of development:

    (1) {pl} + qa, Ja > áa

    (2) {pl} + qa > qa

    (3) {pl} + qa > a

    (4) {pl} + qa > áa

The accent of type 1 replaces any accent found with the thematic syllable.

Themes with {-Jaya-} use only type 1. Noun themes with {-qa-} use
types 1 and 2. Verb themes with {-qa-} use types 1, 2, and 3. Type 1,
however, is found only with short thematic syllables (the thematic syllable is always short with the thematic prefix {-Jaya-}). Aside from
these restrictions there is free variation between these three types.

When type 4 is used, the accent following the thematic syllable is
lost. This type is used with a small group of themes, all of which have
a short unaccented thematic syllable:

    -qadyáa 'domesticated animal'

    -qabáaṢ 'to have a fire going'

    -qasbéẓeN-qiṢ 'to have (for example, chili, beads) strung'

    -qasdyáċəzaN-qiṢ 'to have on a hat'

    -qasdyúwaaN-qiṢ 'to sweat'

    -qadyâwaN-qiṢ 'to have a splinter'

    -qašûwiM(N) 'to have on shoes'

    -qagáyaN 'to be stuck'

    -qadúwiM 'to have on socks'

In the examples that follow, a singular and plural form are given pho
nemically. The plural forms have, in addition to the plural prefix, the
harmonic plural suffix (see Section 241). Forms that contain {-Jaya-} are
identified; all others have {-qa-}.

    Type 1:

    ḱadyûuni 'her pottery'; gáadyûuniši 'their pottery'

    sáwáaméesti 'my tent'; ṣáawáaméestiši 'our tent'

    ḱawáaskəti 'he is ticklish'; gáawáaskətyaimiši 'they are ticklish'

    ḱámašáaci 'he is always hitting'; gáamašáaciši 'they are always
       hitting'

    sa?áapə 'my stuff is scattered'; ṣáa?áapəši 'our stuff is scattered'

    sáwíizími 'my cradle board'; ṣáawíizímiši 'our cradle board'

    seyáamáaca 'I helped'; ṣáayáamáazáña 'we helped', prefix {-Jaya-}

    zayâaċawai 'he took part in a stick race'; gáayâaċawai?i 'they took
       part in a stick race', prefix {-Jaya-}

Type 2:

ḱadyûuni 'her pottery'; ḱadyûuniši 'their pottery'

ḱáunádíisti 'his clothing'; ḱáunádíistiši 'their clothing'

ṣáigáḿi 'my trap'; ṣáigáḿiši 'our trap'

kəẑâinaaʔáńi 'you gambled'; kəĉâinaaʔáńiši 'you (plural) gambled'
 (see ‖ 11.4)

Type 3:

ṣáiši 'they are mine'; ṣáišíimí 'they are ours'

kəẑâinaaʔáńi 'you gambled'; kəẑâinaaʔáńiši 'you (plural) gambled'

ḱáapastyu 'he has a hair knot'; ǵáapastyumiši 'they have hair knots'

Type 4:

ṣadyá 'my pet'; ṣáatyaaši 'our pet'

ḱabá 'he has a fire going'; ǵáapaaši 'they have a fire going'

ṣasdyúwaańi 'I am sweating'; ṣáastyuwaańiši 'we are sweating'

ḱadyáwáńi 'he has a splinter'; ĝáatyawáńiši 'they have splinters'

The themes -qjéeska 'knife' (see ‖ 5.4) and -qjêeẓəəzaN-qiṢ 'to be persistent' contain the possessive prefix {-qa-}. They are unique in that they are the only forms with ‖ee‖ to take the number prefixes. The development iṣ: {dl} + qjee > jeʔee; {pl} + qjee > qjee. Examples: ćéeska 'his knife'; zeʔéeska 'their (dual) knife'; ćéeskaši 'their (plural) knife'.

The theme -JaẏáaciguyaN 'to be talking, gossiping' (prefix {-Jaẏa-}) has two alternates, in free variation, with {dl} and {pl}. One of the alternates with {pl} has a long unaccented initial syllable (see Section 122). (Cf. the similar treatment of the theme -JáaciguyaN 'to say to someone', ‖ 7.8; both themes are irregular derivations of the stem {-záaN}.) The first alternate with {dl} is regular; the remaining forms are suppletive: -aʔaẏáaciguyaN ~ -aʔawázáaniguyaN (dual), -aaẏáńiya ~ -áawázáaniguyaN-qaaD (plural). Examples: ṣeẏáacikuya 'I was talking'; ṣaʔaẏáacikuya ~ ṣaʔawázáanikuya 'we (dual) were talking'; ṣaaẏáńiya ~ ṣáawázáanikuyáńa 'we (plural) were talking'.

‖ 7.10 A number of intransitive verb themes have irregular formations with the dual and plural prefixes which must be listed. A few themes are regular with one of the prefixes or are similar to the formations described in ‖ 7.1-9. Some themes have regular alternates in addition to the irregular formations.

Unlike the regular formations, the number prefixes usually combine with the thematic syllable of the irregular themes to form one syllable. The thematic vowel is usually changed, and often a coarticulation morphophoneme is added or changed.

A number of themes undergo changes when the number prefixes are added. Sometimes the changes are so great that the themes can be considered suppletive. There is, however, no clear-cut difference between irregular and suppletive changes. Occasionally themes derived from the same stem undergo the same irregular changes, and this is indicated in the list. Normally, however, related themes are regular.

In the following list, alphabetized by gloss, three forms are given: unprefixed theme, theme with {dl}, and theme with {pl}, that is the singular, dual, and plural forms. The theme is written morphophonemically with the final morphophonemic consonant indicated and is followed by a phonemic form with a pronominal prefix. Only the singular form is translated. Roman numerals in parenthesis refer to pronominal prefix sets explained in Section 230.

to arrive:	-jaʔáćiN, seʔéći 'I arrived'
	-âaʔáćiN, ṣâaʔáći
	-jéedyuB, sǝdéetyu
to be big:	-'jíčǝ ~ -'jíšǝ, cíčǝ ~ cíšǝ 'it is big'
	-áičáa ~ -aʔâišáa, gáičáa ~ gaʔâišáa
	-áačáaṢ ~ -aẏâašáaṢ, gáačáa ~ gaẏâašáa
to be born:	-'jíẏaaN, cíyá 'he was born'
	-qáiyáaN, ḱáiyá
	-áidyáaN, gáidyá

The same changes are found with the derivation -'jíẏaaN-qiṢ 'to be alive'. Different changes are found with the derivation -'jíẏaaNiši:

	-'jíẏaaniši, cíyáaniši 'his soul, the life in him'
	-aʔáiyáaniši, gaʔáiyáaniši
	-qáiyáaniši, ḱáiyáaniši
to buy:	-JúnáadaN, śínáata 'I bought it'
	(dual, regular)
	-áanáadaN-qaaD, ṣáanáadána
to climb:	-óyaN, síẏa 'I climbed'
	-áayaN, ṣáaya
	-jéeyaN, sǝdéeya
to have it closed:	-qâaʔaʔa, śâaʔaʔa 'I have it closed' (III)
	-aʔâaʔa, ṣaʔâaʔa
	-qáaćiši, ṣáaćiši
to cry:	-'áatikuya, séetikuya 'I was crying'
	-qáatikuya, ṣáatikuya
	-qáata, ṣáata

to die:	-ʼúustu∅, kúustu 'he died'
	-aʔástu∅, gaʔástu
	(plural, unattested)
to drink:	-ə́:sk̓aD, síisk̓a 'I drank'
	-aʔásk̓aD, ṣaʔásk̓a
	-qáask̓aD-aaD, ṣ́áask̓ata
to dwell:	-Aâuʔu, ṣ̂âuʔu 'I live at, dwell' (II)
	-âaʔa, ṣ̂aaʔa (varying with regular dual)
	-âazəədya, ṣ̂aaçəətya
to eat:	-ʼúbeW, súpe 'I ate' (II)
	-âaʔabeW, ṣ̂aaʔape (dual and plural)
to be	
enclosed:	-aʔáčəB, gaʔáčə 'he is enclosed'
	-âaʔačəB, ĝaaʔačə
	-jeʔéčəB, zeʔóče
to enter:	-ú:bəN, síupə 'I went in'
	-âaʔabəN, ṣ̂aaʔapə
	-jéebəN, sədéepə
eyes, to	
be closed:	-ə́əč̓âiʔM ~ -ə́əč̓áiM, síič̓âiʔi ~ síič̓ái 'my eyes were
	closed'
	-qáič̓áiM, ṣ́áič̓ái
	-qjéeč̓aiʔM-iiD, sət̓éeč̓aiḿi
to fall in:	-ûuẓaʔabəN, sîuçaapə 'I fell in'
	-áuẓáabəN, ṣ́áuẓáapə
	-qjéeẓáabəN-iiD, sət̓éeẓáapəni
to fall off:	-ûuẓaʔača, sîuçaača 'I fell off'
	-áuẓáača, ṣ́áuẓáača
	(plural, unattested)
to be fat:	-ʼíṣát̓a∅, kíṣát̓a 'he is fat'
	-âiṣát̓a∅, ĝaiṣát̓a
	-aẏáaṣát̓a∅, gaẏáaṣát̓a
to finish:	-ʼjínáuda∅(N), cínáuta 'he finished'
	-qáináuda∅(N) ~ -qáináutíuda∅(N), k̓áináuta ~ k̓áináutíuta
	-qjéenáudi ~ -qjéenáutíuda∅(N), ćéenáuti ~ ćéenáutíuta
to be first:	-jíiẏâadyuwiiY, síiẏâatyuwi 'I am first'
	-qáiẏâadyuwiiY, ṣ́áiẏâatyuwi
	-qáiẏâadyuwi-mišiiD ~ -âiẓâadyuwiiY, ṣ́áiẏâatyuwimiši ~
	ṣ̂aiẓâatyuwi

to float:	-jidâaʔa, sidâaʔa 'I am floating'
	-áidâaʔa, ṣáidâaʔa
	(plural, unattested)
to fly:	- 'jíẏu∅(N), ćíẏu 'he flew'
	-qáiẏu, ḱaiẏu
	-âaẏu, gâaẏu
to go:	zúu-, zúuse 'I went' (see Section 632.7)
	-qjéeyu∅, sǝt́éeyu
	-jeʔéguY, sǝdeʔéku
to grow:	- 'ítûuníM, kitûuní 'he grew up'
	-áʔitûuníM, gáitûuní
	-Qáatuuní M, kaʔáatuuní (II)
to hear:	- 'akáaN, seká 'I heard it'
	(dual, regular)
	-âakáaN-iiD ~ -âakáaN-eeD, ṣâakáani ~ ṣâakáane
to be hungry:	-Júyámast́u∅, síyámast́u 'I am hungry'
	(dual, regular)
	-aʔíẓámast́u∅, ṣaʔíẓámast́u
to know how:	-û:sú, sîusú 'I know how, I am skilled'
	(dual, regular)
	-ûuʔusa, ṣûuʔusa
to leave:	-û:ḿǝN, sîuḿǝ 'I left'
	-ûuḿǝN, ṣûuḿǝ
	-jêeḿǝN, sǝdêeḿǝ
to listen:	-áačáaza, séečáaça 'I listened'
	(dual, regular)
	-qáačáaẓaSD-eeD, ṣáačáaçaste (varying with regular plural)
to be lost:	- 'áyawaaN, sáẏawa 'I am lost' (II)
	(dual formed with dual suffix)
	- 'aʔíẓawaaN, saʔíçawa
Cf. 'to lose', given in list below
to have luck:	-qáweeʔeṢ, ḱáweeʔe 'he had luck' (III)
	(dual, regular)
	-âiweeʔeṢ-iiD, gâiweeʔeši
to nurse:	-jíisdyaB(SD), zíistya 'he nursed'
	-qáisdyaB(SD), ḱaistya
	-qjéesdyaB(SD)-eeD, ćeestyape
to grow old:	- 'jíináwéetu∅, ćíináwéetu 'he has grown old'
	-qáináwéetu∅, ḱáináwéetu
	(plural, regular)

to pass by: -Júyádyu, s̓íyátyu 'I passed by'

-qáiyádyu, s̓áiyátyu

-áiẓádyu, s̓áiẓátyu

to be
pregnant: -JugûuʔN, cigûuʔu 'she is pregnant'

-áigûuʔN, gáigûuʔu

(plural, regular)

to release: -áat̓úwiiY, sáat̓úẃi 'I released it, let it go' (II)

(dual, regular)

-qáat̓úwiiY-ʔVVD, s̓áat̓úẃiim̓e

to rise:
(from sitting?) -ʼjípətеeʔedyə, cípəteeʔetyə 'he got up'

-qápətееʔepədyə, k̓ápətееʔepətyə

-qjépətееʔedyəM̄-eeD, ćépəteeʔetyəme

to rise:
(from lying?) -ʼjíipadyəM(N), cíipatyə 'he got up'

-qáipadyəM(N), k̓áipatyə

-qjéepadyəM(N)-iiD, ćeepatyəni

to say: -án̓aat̓aN, sén̓aat̓a 'I said it'

-qáan̓ikuya, s̓áan̓ikuya

-qáan̓a, s̓áan̓a

to sleep: -jíibáiY, zíibái 'he is sleeping'

-qáibáiY, k̓áibái

-qjéebáiY-ʔVVD, ćéebâiʔi

to speak up: -am̓áṣaN, sem̓áṣa 'I spoke up'

(dual, regular)

-âam̓aṣaN, s̓áam̓aṣa

to stand up: -ə:t̓aadyəM̄, gət̓áatyə 'he stood up'

-qáit̓aadyəM̄, k̓áit̓aatyə

-qjêet̓aadyəM̄-eeD, ćeet̓aatyəme

to be
standing: -ə́:čán̓iṢ, síičán̓i 'I am standing'

-áičán̓iṢ, s̓áičán̓i

-qjéečán̓iṢ-iiD, sət̓eečán̓iši

to step down: -ə:ˈdyaaN, síitya 'I stepped down'

-âaʔadyaaN, s̓aaʔatya

(plural, unattested)

to be strong: -Juš̓áaziṢ, síš̓aaci 'I am strong'

-áiš̓áaziṢ, s̓áiš̓aaci

-ay̓áaš̓aaziṢ ~ -ʼáaš̓aaziṢ, s̓ay̓áaš̓aaci ~ s̓áaš̓aaci (IV ~ II)

to be stuck: -qagáyaM, s̓agáya 'I am stuck' (III)

-âagáyaM, s̓âagáya

-âagayaN-iiD, s̓âakayani

to be talk- ative:	-(q)ázá²aN, ḱázá 'he is talkative'
	-ȧazá²aN, gȧazá
	-ȧazíẏa, gȧazíẏa
to throw:	-ȧawiiY, sȧawi 'I threw it' (II)
	(dual, regular)
	-qȧawiiY-²VVD, ṣȧawii²i
to throw away:	-átizuwiiY, sátiçuwi 'I threw it away' (II)
	(dual, regular)
	-âatizuwiiY-²VVD, ṣâatiçuwii²i
to wake up:	-'izáačúwaN(M), kizáačúẇa 'he woke up'
	-ȧizáačúwaN(M), gȧizáačúẇa
	-'ȧazáačúwaN(M), ḱȧazáačúẇa (II)
to be walking:	-âanazədeyaW, sêenaçəteya 'I am walking'
	-qjéeyáaN, səťéeyá
	-jé²egúyaN, sədȧegúẏa
to win:	-jíšiyaW, zíšiya 'he won'
	(dual, regular)
	-âašiyaW-aaD, gâašiyawa

A few themes that are not intransitive verbs can best be considered at this point:

to be a fast runner:	-Jíiyái, sgúiyái 'I am a fast runner' (static)
	-a²áyái, sga²áyái 'we are fast runners'
	-âidyái, sgâidyái 'we are fast runners'
to find:	-JuẏâiṅaW, ṡiẏâiṅa 'I found him' (transitive)
	(dual prefix, regular)
	-úwádyâiṅaW, síwádyâiṅa 'I found them'
to know:	-û:níM, sîuní 'I know him' (transitive)
	(dual prefix, regular)
	-âizuuníM, sêiçuuní 'I know them (plural)'
to lean:	-'jígúťa∅-iṢ, cígúťi 'it is leaning; it is a bridge' (impersonal
	-ȧigúťa∅-iṢ, gȧigúťi 'they are leaning'
	(plural, unattested)
to lie down:	-Jíikaiḋ, sḱúikai 'I am lying down'
	(dual, regular)
	-jûučai, sədîučai 'we are lying down'

The singular and dual are static themes; the plural is an intransitive theme (Section 410).

to look for: -JuyáibaaD(N), ziyáipa 'he looked for him' (transitive)
                (dual, regular)
                -úwátyáibaaD(N), gúwátyáipa 'he looked for them'

to lose: -JúyawaaN, síyawa 'I lost it; I told him to go' (transitive)
                (dual, regular)
                -aʔízawaaN, seʔícawa 'I told them to go'

to spend
the night: -Júyáaska, skúyáaska 'I spent the night' (static)
                (dual, regular)
                -âiyáaska, sgâiyáaska 'we spent the night'

to take: -JúyúuzeeY, síyúuce 'I took him' (transitive)
                -âaʔayuuzeeY, sêeʔeyuuce 'I took them'
                -áizúuzeeY, séizúuce 'I took them'

to tend: -JúyúugaiY, síyúukai 'I tended him' (transitive)
                -âaʔayuugaiY, sêeʔeyuukai 'I tended them'
                -áizúugaiY, séizúukai 'I tended them'

to wait for: -Júyûuk̇amiṢ, skúyûuk̇ami 'he waited for me' (transitive)
                -âaʔayuu k̇amiṢ, sgâaʔaguuk̇ami 'he waited for us'
                -âizûuk̇amiṢ, sgâizûuk̇ami 'he waited for us'

‖7.s   A synopsis of ‖7.1-9 is given in table 5. The initial morphophonemic sequence that is effected by the subrule is listed, followed by
the morphophonemic shape of the sequence that results after {dl} and
{pl} are prefixed. The accent of the resulting form is given only if it
is not predictable from the accent of the thematic syllable. The thematic syllables that have been recorded with the number prefixes for each
initial type are listed in the last column. The accents of the thematic
syllables are not listed except in the case of ‖u:‖, where the type of
accent conditions the shape of the resulting form.

‖8   A few stems that have ‖y‖ or ‖ẏ‖ as the first consonant of the
stem replace the consonant with ‖z̧‖, ‖dy‖, or ‖ty‖ when the plural
prefix precedes. The plural prefix is irregular with these forms (see
‖7.10). The changes may be grouped as follows:

	without {pl}	with {pl}
(1)	y	z̧
(2)	y	dy
(3)	ẏ	z̧
(4)	ẏ	dy
(5)	ẏ	ty

The following list of themes that undergo this change is complete:

TABLE 5

Number Prefixes and Thematic Syllable

Rule	Initial	Dual	Plural	Thematic Syllable
7.1	Ju, J̄u	aʔa	aẏa	Ju, J̄u + sonorant
7.2	Ju, J̄u	âaʔa	âiʔi	Ju, J̄u + obstruent
7.3	Juu, J̄uu	aʔau	áaẇaa	Juu, J̄uu
7.4	Xui	uʔui	uẇau	ui, qui, Aui
7.5	Xu:	uʔu:	uẇa	ú:, uʃ, ʻú:
	Xu:	ûuʔu	úwâa	û:, uʃ̂, ú:, uʃ̈
7.6	Xu	uʔu	uẇa	u, uu, Au, Auu, ʻu, qu, quu
7.7	Xi, Xə	aʔa(i)	aẏa	Jii, ʻji, jii, qji, qjii, ʻəə
7.8	Xa	aʔa	aẏa	a, aa, Ja, Jaa, J̄a, J̄aa, ʻa, ʻaa, jaa, ʻja, qaa, au, Jau, qau, Aau
7.9	qa, Ja	aʔa	(1) áa (2) qa (3) a (4) áa	qa, qaa, qai, qau, Ja ({-qa-} and {-Jaẏa-})

(1)   -Júyádyu, síyátyu 'I passed by'
       -áiẓádyu, ṣaiẓátyu 'we passed by'

       -JúyúuzeeY, síyúuce 'I took him with me'
       -áiẓúuzeeY, seiẓúuce 'I took them with me'

       -JúyúugaiY, síyúukai 'I tended him'
       -áiẓúugaiY, seiẓúukai 'I tended them'

       -Júyûuk̇amiṢ, síyûuk̇ami 'I waited for him'
       -âiẓûuk̇amiṢ, seiẓûuk̇ami 'I waited for them'

       -Júyáṁast́u∅, síyáṁast́u 'I am hungry'
       -aʔíẓáṁast́u∅, ṣaʔíẓáṁast́u 'we are hungry'

       -JúyawaaN, zíẏawa 'he lost it'
       -aʔíẓawaaN, gaʔíçawa 'he lost them'

       - ʻáyawaaN, sáẏawa 'I am lost'
       - ʻaʔíẓawaaN, saʔíçawa 'we are lost'

(2) -ʼjíyáaN, síyá 'I was born'
     -áidyáaN, s̩áidyá 'we were born'
     (The same change is found with -ʼjíyáaN-qiṢ 'to be alive';
     see ‖ 7.10)

     -Jíiyái, sgúiyái 'I am a fast runner'
     -âidyái, sgâidyái 'we are fast runners'

(3) -jíiy̆âadyuwiiY, síiy̆âatyuwi 'I am first'
     -âiz̩âadyuwiiY, s̩âiz̩âatyuwi 'we are first'

(4) -Juy̆âiṅaW, ziy̆âiṅa 'he found him'
     -úwádyâiṅaW, gúwádyâiṅa 'he found them'

(5) -Juy̆áibaaD(N), s̆kuy̆áipa 'he looked for me'
     -úwát̆y̆áibaaD(N), sgúwát̆y̆áipa

A number of other themes show somewhat similar irregularities:

     -Qáuy̆astíM, s̆áuy̆astí 'I washed one piece of clothing'
     -ʼûitéeʔestíM, sîutéeʔestí 'I washed several'

     -QâinaD-aN, s̆âinata 'I roasted a piece of meat'
     -ʼûit̆ainaD-aN, sîut̆ainata 'I roasted some meat'

     -qjúy̆ačəN-iṢ, c̆íy̆ačəni 'it is burned'
     -qjút̆ačəN-iṢ, c̆ítačəni 'they are burned'

     -ú:yáabəN, gúy̆áapə 'he went wading'
     -ûuz̩aʔabəN, gûuc̆aapə 'he fell in (water?)'

The members of each pair are certainly related, but not by any recur-
rent derivational pattern. The first two pairs are intransitive verb
themes; such forms take number affixes, but for subject, not for what
is here translated as the object. The themes of the third pair are impersonal themes; impersonal themes are not inflected for number, but
they may include a number prefix in derived forms (Section 415).

‖ 9.0 Some intransitive verb themes undergo a thematic syllable expansion, symbolized (TSE), when the plural suffix is added. The shape
of the expansion can usually be predicted by the morphophonemic shape
of the thematic syllable.
    Examples are given in three forms: basic form, morphophonemic
form after the application of ‖ 9, and phonemic form.
    ‖ 9.1 (TSE) + ʼu, ú > ʼúwá. The expanded syllable undergoes further
accent changes defined in ‖ 22. Examples:

(TSE) + -ʻúskúmeN-qaaD > -ʻúwáskúmen-qaa: suwáskúméńa 'we fell
in the water'

(TSE) + -ʻuʔíndyuẓaN-qaaD > -ʻúwáʔíndyuẓan-qaa: suwáʔíntyuẓáńa
'we made fools of ourselves, just like Indians'

(TSE) + -ʻutâańiẓaN-qaaD > -ʻúwátâańiẓan-qaaD: kúwatâańiẓáńa
'they worked'

Cf. súksúḿe 'I fell in the water'; suʔíntyuça 'I made a fool of
myself'; kutâańiça 'he worked'

The expansion is not found with -ʻúčaN 'to fall'; kúčáńa 'they fell';
cf. kúča 'he fell'

‖ 9.2 (TSE) + ʻúu > ʻúuwáa (if followed by an obstruent); > ʻúwá (if
followed by a sonorant). The expanded syllable undergoes further accent
changes defined in ‖ 22. Examples:

(TSE) + -ʻúučáwaN-qaaD > -ʻúuwáačúwan-qaa: kúuwáačúwáńa 'they
stole'

(TSE) + -ʻúuḿáacáacáaẓaN-qaaD > -ʻúwáḿáacáan-qaa:
kuwaḿáacâaẓáńa 'they made jerky'

Cf. kúučáwa 'he stole'; kúuḿáacáaça 'he made jerky'

‖ 9.3 (TSE) + ʻui > ʻuwau; the accent of the thematic syllable occurs
with the second expanded syllable:

(TSE) + -ʻúibéeẓaN-qaaD > -ʻuwáubêeẓan-qaa: kuwáubêeẓáńa 'they lied'

(TSE) + -ʻûisdâaW-aaD > -ʻuwâusdâaw-aa: suwâusdâawa 'we took a sac

Cf. kúibéeça 'he lied'; sûisdá 'I took a sack'

‖ 9.4 (TSE) + ʻi, ʻí > Qáʔa. The accent following the thematic syllabl
is usually lost. The expanded syllable undergoes further accent changes
defined in ‖ 23. Examples:

(TSE) + -ʻídyə̂əẓaN-qaaD > -Qáʔadyə̂əẓan-qaa: kaʔáatyə̂əẓáńa 'they
stretched'

(TSE) + -ʻisípaẓaN-qaaD > -Qáʔasipaẓan-qaa: ŝâasipaẓáńa 'we
blinked our eyes'

(TSE) + -ʻińáaM-qeeD > -Qáʔańáam-qee: kaʔâańáaḿe 'they looked
out'

Cf. kidyə̂əca 'he stretched'; sisípaca 'I blinked my eyes'; kińáu 'he
looked out'

‖ 9.5 (TSE) + Qau > ʻúuwáa (if the following syllable is accented);
> ʻúuwáa (if the following syllable is unaccented). Examples:

(TSE) + -QáudyáaẓaN-qaaD > -ʻúuwáadyáaẓan-qaa: kúuwáadyáaẓáńa
'they got married'

(TSE) + -QáukačaN-qaaD > -ʻúuwáakačan-qaa: súuwáakačáńa 'we
see ourselves'

Cf. kaʔáudyáaça 'he got married'; ŝáukača 'I see myself'

‖9.6 A few themes undergo irregular expansion. In the following list the theme is written without (TSE), followed by the form with the expansion. The final morphophonemic consonant is written with the forms. The first five themes are exceptions to ‖9.1 and ‖9.2; the remaining themes have thematic syllables not found in the forms treated in the preceding subrules:

- -'uʔúkaN; -'uw̥âak̇aN 'to look around'
- -'úsúmé?estaaN; -'úuw̥áasúmé?estaaN ~ -'áisumé?estaaN 'to learn'
- -'úuw̥íišaN; -'uw̥áaw̥íišaN ~ -'úuw̥íišaN 'to undress' (the second alternate irregularly shows no expansion)
- -'úuṫiM; -'áiw̥áṫiM 'to go together'
- -'úusdyúwaaN; -'áisdyúwaaN ~ -'áisdyuwaaN 'to be sweating'
- -Aû:kasdyaN; -'âiw̥akasdyaɸ 'to plan'
- -'áaṫišêeyuzaN; -'áayáiṫišêeyuzaN 'to slide'
- -'áʔudyúmiẓaN; -'úuw̥áadyúmiẓaN 'to learn'
- -'áayúudya; -'âayúudyaN ~ -'áiw̥âayúudya ~ -Qáayúudyaim 'to make a living, support oneself'
- -'ɔ́ʔəč̇âiM; Qâačai?M 'to close the eyes'
- -Qi̥isdyúB; -QáisdyúB 'to defecate'

‖9.s The plural suffix is sometimes omitted in themes that have (TSE): súw̥atâaniẓáña ~ súw̥atâani̥ça 'we worked'. The expansion alone marks such forms as plural. The plural suffix is usually found with themes that have the thematic syllables ‖'u‖, ‖'uu‖, and ‖'ui‖ (‖9.1-3), is often omitted with ‖'i‖ (‖9.4) and is usually omitted with ‖Qau‖ (‖9.5). The expansion is optional with ‖Qau‖; thus there are three possible treatments for such themes in the plural: (1) plural suffix, (2) (TSE), and (3) (TSE) and plural suffix. No themes have been recorded with all three types of treatments, but there are many recordings of themes with two of the three types: súuw̥áadyáaça ~ súuw̥áadyáaẓáña 'we got married'; śáuyéezáña ~ súuw̥áayéeca 'we made up our minds'. There seems to be no difference in meaning between the alternates.

The structural status of (TSE) is not clear. The expanded syllable is similar to the thematic syllable plus the plural prefix (cf. the synopsis of (TSE) in table 6 and of {pl} in table 5). The primary difference between the two is that coarticulation morphophonemes are found with the expanded syllables. Thus it would appear that the expansion could be treated as an allomorph, or set of allomorphs, of the plural prefix. It is not convenient, however, because a basic distinction is made between those intransitive verb themes that take the number prefixes and those that take the number suffixes (Section 410). The thematic syllable expansions, as well as the harmonic plural suffix (Section 241), make it difficult

TABLE 6

Thematic Syllable Expansion

Rule	Thematic Syllable	(TSE) Plus Thematic Syllable
9.1	ʼu, ʼú	ʼúwá
9.2	ʼúu	ʼúuwáa (before an obstruent)
	ʼúu	ʼúwá (before a sonorant)
9.3	ʼui	ʼuwau
9.4	ʼi, ʼí	Qáʔa
9.5	Qau	ʼúuwáa (before an accented syllable)
	Qau	ʼúuwáa (before an unaccented syllable)

to maintain a clear-cut distinction between these two theme types, at least in regard to the plural (the distinction is almost always clear for the dual). If the distinction were not kept, it would be more difficult to account for the allomorphy of the pronominal prefixes (Section 230).

‖ 10.0 A number of coarticulation morphophonemes have been set up to account for terminal changes of morphemes, changes that are usually conditioned by the following morpheme. There are two groups of coarticulation morphophonemes, called primary and secondary. The primary group, ‖ q, ʼ, j ‖, accounts for phonologically predictable changes and are treated in ‖ 11.

The secondary group, the subject of this rule, consists of ‖ J, J̄, Q, A ‖. They are limited to theme initial position, and account for alternations of pronominal prefixes. In effect, they are set up to account for alternations of the primary group, for example ‖ J ‖ becomes ‖ q ‖ after certain prefixes, and ‖ j ‖ after others; the effect of ‖ q ‖ and ‖ j ‖ are then described in ‖ 11.

In the following subrules reference is made to the pronominal prefixes which are listed in Section 230, table 9. The prefixes are grouped into four allomorphic sets, labeled by Roman numerals. Each of the secondary morphophonemes is found with only one set: ‖ J ‖ and ‖ J̄ ‖ with set I; ‖ Q ‖ with set II; and ‖ A ‖ with set III. There are several possible analyses of the secondary morphophonemes and of the allomorphic pronominal prefix sets. An alternate analysis of one effects the analysis of the other.

‖ 10.1 The morphophonemes ‖ J ‖ and ‖ J̄ ‖, found after set I pronominal prefixes, undergo the following changes:

(1) J, J̄ > q after ‖ j ‖, and after ‖ a ‖
(2) J > qj, and J̄ > j after ‖ u ‖

(3) J, J̄ > j after a consonant

The rule can also be stated in terms of the morphological environment instead of the morphophonemic environment:

(1) J, J̄ > q after: all the 1(-3) prefixes except the negative prefix; all obviative prefixes; all 1-2 prefixes; the expective prefix; the 3-1 negative prefix; the indefinite-obviative prefix

(2) J > qj, and J̄ > j after: all 2-1 prefixes; the 3-1 nonmodal prefix

(3) J, J̄ > j elsewhere

The first set of statements, made in terms of the morphophonemic environment, is preferred because it is more concise. In this respect the development of ‖J‖ and ‖J̄‖ differs from that of ‖Q‖ and ‖A‖ (‖10.2-3).

The nonmodal paradigms of -JîiťaaN 'to step on it, him' and -J̄ústíʔiD 'to give someone water' illustrate these changes. Three forms are given for each member of the paradigms: the morphophonemic form before the application of ‖10.1, the morphophonemic form after its application, and the phonemic form. Rules ‖11-15 in particular apply in accounting for the final phonemic form. The forms are to be glossed 'I stepped on him, you stepped on him', etc:

1-3	sj-Jîiťaa	sj-qîiťaa	śîiťa
2-3	ṣ-Jîiťaa	ṣ-jîiťaa	šîiťa
3-3	g-Jîiťaa	g-jîiťaa	zîiťa
obv.	gj-Jîiťaa	gj-qîiťaa	ćîiťa
1-2	ṣa-Jîiťaa	ṣa-qîiťaa	ṣâiťa
3-2	gəẓ-Jîiťaa	gəẓ-jîiťaa	kədîiťa
2-1	dyu-Jîiťaa	dyu-qjîiťaa	ťyûiťa
3-1	sgu-Jîiťaa	sgu-qjîiťaa	skûiťa

1-3	sj-J̄ústíʔi	sj-qústíʔi	śístí
2-3	ṣ-J̄ústíʔi	ṣ-jústíʔi	šístí
3-3	g-J̄ústíʔi	g-jústíʔi	zístí
obv.	gj-J̄ústíʔi	gj-qústíʔi	ćístí
1-2	ṣa-J̄ústíʔi	ṣa-qústíʔi	ṣástí
3-2	gəẓ-J̄ústíʔi	gəẓ-jústíʔi	kədístí
2-1	dyu-J̄ústíʔi	dyu-jústíʔi	dyústí
3-1	sgu-J̄ústíʔi	sgu-jústíʔi	sgústí

‖10.2   The morphophoneme ‖Q‖, found after set II prefixes, becomes:

(1) ‖q‖ after the 1st person nonmodal prefix, all 2nd person prefixes, and the expective prefix; and

(2) ‖ʻVʔ‖ after all 1st person prefixes except the nonmodal, all 3rd person prefixes, and the indefinite prefix (see ‖15 for the development of ‖V‖).

The nonmodal paradigm of -QáuyéezaN 'to make up one's mind' illustrates these changes. The procedure used in listing the paradigms in
‖10.1 is used here:

1st	s-Qáuyéeza	s-qáuyéeza	śáuyéeca
2nd	s̩-Qáuyéeza	s̩-qáuyéeza	śáuyéeca
3rd	g-Qáuyéeza	g-'V?áuyéeza	ka?áuyéeca
ind.	sg-Qáuyéeza	sg-'V?áuyéeza	ska?áuyéeca

‖10.3 The morphophoneme ‖A‖, found after set III prefixes, become
(1) ‖q‖ after all 1st person prefixes except the negative, all 2nd
person prefixes, and the expective prefix; and
(2) ‖a‖ after the 1st person negative prefix, all 3rd person prefixes, and the indefinite prefix.

The nonmodal paradigm of -Aúunúutii 'ankle' illustrates these changes
The procedure used in listing the paradigms in ‖10.1 is used here:

1st	s-Aúunúutii	s-qúunúutii	śúunúuti
2nd	gəz̩-Aúunúutii	gəz̩-qúunúutii	kuz̩úunúuti
3rd	g-Aúunúutii	g-áunúutii	gáunúuti
ind.	sg-Aúunúutii	sg-áunúutii	sgáunúuti

‖11.0 The coarticulation morphophonemes ‖q‖, ‖'‖, and ‖j‖ are
set up to account for three morphophonemic processes, glottalization,
aspiration, and palatalization, respectively. These processes affect the
preceding consonant, which is usually part of a pronominal prefix. The
glottalizing and aspirating morphophonemes usually condition a change in
the manner of articulation. The palatalizing morphophoneme conditions a
change in the point of articulation, and in addition the morphophoneme
sometimes becomes a vowel. The term "palatalize" is not to be confuse
with the term "palatal." The latter term refers to a class of phonemes
(Section 110).

In describing these three processes, the consonants are placed in a
morphophonemic alignment. The alignment of single obstruents and sibilant clusters is shown in Table 7. The morphophonemic alignment of the
sonorants is the same as the phonemic alignment given in Section 110. The
coarticulation morphophonemes have no effect on the manner consonants.

‖11.1 A plain (that is, unglottalized) consonant plus ‖q‖ becomes a
glottalized consonant. The glottalization takes place when a vowel or
‖j‖ intervenes. ‖q‖ has no effect on a preceding manner consonant an
is lost.

The nonmodal and dubitative paradigms of -qáusa 'to be slow' with
set I pronominal prefixes illustrates the changes. The procedure used i
listing the paradigms in ‖10.1 is used here:

Nonmodal			Dubitative		
1st	sj-qáusa	śj-áusa	śéusa	tV?j-qáusa	tV?j-áusa	te?éusa
2nd	ṣ-qáusa	ṣ́-áusa	ṣ́áusa	c-qáusa	c̣-áusa	c̣áusa
3rd	g-qáusa	ḱ-áusa	ḱáusa	dy-qáusa	č̣-áusa	č̣áusa

In the remaining examples the form is written phonemically, with pertinent morphemes written in morphophonemic forms:

    ṣ́âiťa 'I stepped on you'; prefix ṣa-, theme -JîiáaN, ‖-qîiťaa‖ 10.1

    ńîiťaagú 'he will step on it'; prefix nj-, theme ‖-qîiťaa‖ 10.1

    č̣áuk̂îini 'his friend (dubitative)'; prefix dy-, theme -qáuk̂îini

    zísúméestaańa 'they taught him'; theme -Júsúmé?estaaN, suffix

    -qaaD (see ‖1)

TABLE 7

Morphophonemic Alignment of Obstruents

Single Obstruents

	1	2	3 ←	4	5 ←	6
Occlusives:						
unaspirated	b		d	dy	z	g
aspirated	p		t	č	c	k
glottalized	ṗ		ť	č̣	c̣	ḱ
Sibilants						
plain		s	š	ṣ		
glottalized		ṡ	ś	ṣ́		
‖ẓ‖:						
unaspirated			d	ẓ		
glottalized			ť	c̣		
‖c̣‖:						
aspirated			č	c̣		
glottalized				ċ̣		

Sibilant Clusters

	3 ←	4-5 ←	6
unaspirated	sd	sdy	sg
aspirated	st	sty	sk
glottalized	sť	sťy	sḱ

Normally, dy + q > č̣. In the 3rd person dubitative prefix of set IV, however, dy- + q > č̣ ~ t́y-; and in the 2-1 person nonmodal and dubitative prefix of set I, dyu- + q > t́yu-:

    č̣áuk̂ȋiniši ~ t́yáuk̂ȋiniši 'their (plural) friend (dubitative)'

    t́yûit́a 'you stepped on me'

‖ 11.2 An unaspirated occlusive plus ‖ ʿ ‖ becomes an aspirated occlusive. ‖ ʿ ‖ has no effect in other environments, and is lost.

The nonmodal and dubitative paradigms of -ʿázəkaN 'to smoke tobacco' with set II pronominal prefixes illustrate the changes:

	Nonmodal		
1st	s-ʿázəka	s-ázəka	sác̣əka
2nd	ṣ-ʿázəka	ṣ-ázəka	ṣác̣əka
3rd	g-ʿázəka	k-ázəka	kác̣əka
	Dubitative		
1st	t-ʿázəka	t-ázəka	tác̣əka
2nd	c̣-ʿázəka	c̣-ázəka	c̣ác̣əka
3rd	dy-ʿázəka	č-ázəka	čác̣əka

Other examples:

    cíisipa 'his eyelash'; prefix g-, theme -ʿjíisipa (see ‖ 11.3)

    tíy̆u 'did he fly?'; prefix dy-, theme -ʿjíy̆u∅

    síwâaṁeestí 'I made shade for him'; stem -úwâaṁeeSD, suffix
    -ʿíʔiD (see ‖ 1.9)

‖ 11.3 Certain consonants are palatalized before ‖ j ‖. The consonants affected by this rule are listed in columns 4 and 6 of table 7, and the corresponding palatalized consonants are listed in columns 3 and 5. A sequence of two ‖ j ‖ s has the same effect as one.

The nonmodal and dubitative paradigms of -jaʔác̣iN 'to arrive' illustrate the palatalization. The pronominal prefixes (set I) are given in parenthesis:

	Nonmodal		Dubitative	
1st	seʔéc̣i	(sj-)	teʔeʔéc̣i	(tVʔj-)
2nd	šaʔác̣i	(ṣ-)	čaʔác̣i	(c̣-)
3rd	zaʔác̣i	(g-)	daʔác̣i	(dy-)

Other examples:

    zíukača 'he saw him (obviative)'; prefix gj-, theme -úukačaN

    ṡic̣âadâaya 'I am pinning it'; theme -Juc̣áadyaN, suffix ⁼jáayaN
    (see ‖ 2)

    gáizéešáat́a 'he is dreaming'; theme -áizéeṣa∅, suffix -qjáat́aN
    (see ‖ 1.13)

The palatalization takes place if ‖ q ‖ or ‖ ʿ ‖ intervenes, but not if a vowel intervenes:

číipe 'his ear', prefix g-, theme -qjíipee

sgústí 'he gave me water', prefix sgu-, theme -J̄ústí?iD,
 ‖-jústí?i‖ 10.1

The four series of palatalizable and palatalized consonants are collapsed to three for the sibilant clusters, for example, sg + j > sdyj and sdy + j > sdj. Double palatalization does not result by this rule, for example, sg + j > sdyj > sdj does not occur. Examples:

sdyáača 'someone's tooth'; prefix sg-, theme -jáača

styáamúša 'someone's beard'; theme -ʿjáamúša

stíišə 'someone's nose'; theme -qjíišəə (see ‖12)

sisíusdáaya 'I am roping him'; theme -JusíusdyaN, suffix ⁼jáayaN
 (see ‖2)

‖j‖ > ‖i‖ (1) before ‖u‖ and (2) after a consonant of a pronominal prefix that has no palatalized correspondent. The second statement applies to the following pronominal prefixes of set I: sj-, sj- 1(-3) non-modal; tV?j 1(-3) dubitative; p- 2(-3) hortative; pV?j- 3(-3) hortative; pj- obviative hortative; and nj-, nj- expective. The resulting vowel often undergoes morphophonemic changes described in ‖13. Examples:

zíukača 'he saw him (obviative)'; prefix gj-, theme -úukačaN

zíuṣá 'he approved of him'; prefix g-, theme -JúuṣâaN,
 ‖-júuṣâa‖ 10.1

séeča 'my tooth'; prefix sj-, theme -áača (see ‖13)

séemúča 'my toe'; prefix sj-, theme -ʿáamúča

The palatalizing morphophoneme ‖j‖ can co-occur with either ‖ʿ‖ or ‖q‖:

cáamúša 'his beard'; prefix g-, theme -ʿjáamúša

číišə 'his nose'; prefix g-, theme -qjíišəə

There is no priority in the order of application of ‖11.3 and ‖11.1-2. Either order yields the same results, for example, in cáamúša g > z > c, or g > k > c. If two coarticulation morphophonemes are found in a theme, ‖j‖ is written second. This convention makes necessary the statement, given above, that palatalization also takes place when ‖q‖ or ‖ʿ‖ intervenes.

‖11.4 ‖z̧‖ is not found before the aspirating morphophoneme ‖ʿ‖. It is found before the other coarticulation morphophonemes, and its development is irregular.

‖z̧‖ is not normally glottalized by ‖q‖ if it is part of a pronominal prefix:

kəz̧áukîini 'your friend'; prefix gəz̧-, theme -qáukîini

z̧áukîini 'he can be your friend'; prefix z̧-

kəz̧úunúuti 'your ankle'; theme -Aúunúutii, ‖-qúunúutii‖ 10.3

‖z̦‖, as part of a pronominal prefix, is glottalized by ‖q‖ if (1) the pronominal prefix belongs to set IV or (2) the pronominal prefix is found with a passive theme that has the passive thematic prefix {-qja?a-}:

> kǝc̦áukĩiniši 'your (plural) friend'; prefix gǝz̦-, theme -qáukĩini-ši
> sǝt́éeyu 'we (dual) went'; prefix sǝz̦-, theme -qjéeyu∅
> c̦áaskata 'drink! (plural)'; prefix z̦-, theme -qáaskaD-aaD (see ‖7.10)
> tǝc̦a?áašíica 'they borrowed it from you (dubitative)'; prefix dǝz̦-,
> theme -qja?áašíizaN

If ‖z̦‖ is not part of a pronominal prefix, it is glottalized by ‖q‖. In all our examples it is also palatalized by the application of ‖12: kudyáat́ita 'he is writing', theme -ʿudyáaz̦aN, suffix ⁼qitaaN.

‖z̦‖ is not normally palatalized by ‖j‖: kǝz̦âanú 'she gave you a bath'; prefix gǝz̦-, theme -JâanúM, ‖-jâanú‖10.1. It is palatalized by ‖j‖ only if it is part of a pronominal prefix of set IV. The auxiliary {zá} (Section 461.8) offers the only clear example of this: háak̦úusǝdá 'I am ready'; prefix sǝz̦-, theme -Já?aN. Elsewhere ‖j‖ is found with set IV pronominal prefixes in environments where the palatalization of ‖z̦‖ could be considered the result of ‖12: sǝt́éeyu 'we (dual) went'; prefix sǝz̦-, theme -qjéeyu∅.

‖12 Retroflex consonants and palatal stops are palatalized before front vowels (palatalization is defined in ‖11.3). This change is in accord with the phonemic distributional fact that retroflex consonants and palatal stops are not found before front vowels (Section 123.1).[13]

In the following examples, the forms are written phonemically and the palatalized consonant is underlined. The morphophonemic form of the consonant before the application of this rule is given in parentheses:

> kǝd̲îita 'he stepped on you' (z̦)
> sumúši̲tita 'I am digging soapweed' (z̦; see ‖29 for the change of
>   d to t̲)
> ši̲z̦áac̆úwa 'you woke up' (ș)
> sîuméekumeš̲i 'we are watching him' (ș < Ṣ; see ‖1.10)
> sugáwi̲tita 'I am threshing grain' (dy; see ‖29)
> st̲íni 'someone's body' (ty)

In the first example, the palatalization of the ‖z̦‖ in the pronominal prefix ‖g-ǝz̦‖ cannot be ascribed to the palatalizing morphophoneme (theme

---

[13]This rule reflects two historical changes that took place at different times. Proto-Keres did not have retroflex consonants before front vowels, and the historical change that this distributional feature reflects must have taken place in Pre-Keres times. Palatal and dental stops before front vowels fell together in Acoma after Proto-Keres times; most of the other Keres languages distinguish the two types of stops in this environment.

-JîíťaaN) because of forms like kəẓâanú 'she gave you a bath' (theme -JâanúM; see ‖11.4).

A palatal stop in a sibilant cluster that is from a basic ‖sg‖ is palatalized twice if it is followed by a front vowel: the first time by ‖11.3, the second time by this rule. Thus in stíni 'someone's body', the theme -'jíni, the prefix sg > sty by the application of ‖11, and > st by the application of ‖12.

When the second person dubitative ‖ç-‖ is palatalized by this rule, the resulting form is often homophonous with the third person dubitative: čiẓáačúwa 'did you wake up?; did he wake up?', prefixes ç-, dy-, theme -'iẓáačúwaM(N) (see ‖11.2).

When the ‖ẓ‖ of the empty morph ‖-əẓ-‖ (Section 230) is palatalized, a preceding ‖ẓ‖ becomes ‖dy‖ (and > ty by ‖29):

    tyədîita 'did he step on you?'; prefix ẓ-əẓ-, set I

    tyəťéeyu 'did you (dual) go?'; prefix ẓ-əẓ-, set IV

    tyədéetyu 'did you (plural) arrive?'; prefix ẓ-əẓ-, set IV

    háaḱúutyədá 'are you ready?'; prefix ẓ-əẓ-, set IV (auxiliary {zá})

‖13 Vowel contractions take place when ‖i‖, ‖a‖, or ‖u‖ is added to the thematic syllable. The ‖i‖ is from a palatalizing morphophoneme (see ‖10.1 and ‖11.3), either as part of a pronominal prefix or as a theme initial coarticulation morphophoneme. The ‖a‖ is either part of a pronominal prefix or is from a theme initial ‖A‖ (see ‖10.3). The ‖u‖ is always part of a pronominal prefix. The contractions are given in table 8. In the table, and in the formulations of rules ‖13, 14, length is written by ‖·‖ rather than by a doubling of the vowel, so as to be able to distinguish a long thematic syllable (for example, ‖u·‖) from a vowel plus a thematic syllable (for example, ‖u+u‖ or ‖uu‖).

The following examples are written phonemically. The vowel sequences, before and after the application of this rule, are given with the example:

    (i+a· > e·) śêenú 'I gave him a bath'

    (i+ai > ei) śêinazí 'I ran over it'

    (a+a > a) śázáaní 'I talked for you'

    (u+a > a) sgázáaní 'he talked for me'

    (i+i· > i·) śîiťa 'I stepped on it'

    (a+i· > ai) śâiťa 'I stepped on you'

    (u+i· > ui) skûiťa 'he stepped on me'

    (i+u > i) zístí 'he gave him a drink of water'

    (a+u > a) śástí 'I gave you a drink of water'

    (i+u· > iu) síukača 'I saw him'

    (a+u· > au) gáunúuti 'his ankle'

    (u+u· > u·) sgúukača 'he saw me'

TABLE 8

Vowel Contractions

First Vowel	Following Vowel(s)										
	a(V)	i	i·	u	u·	i+u	i+u·	ui	u:	ə(·)	ə:
i	e(V)	i	i·	i	iu	--	--	iu	iu:	i(·)	i·:
a	a(V)	--	ai	a	au	--	--	au	au:	--	--
u	a(V)	--	ui	u	u·	u	u· ~ ui	ui	u:	--	--

(u+i+u > u) skumína 'he spoke to me'

(u+i+u· > u· ~ ui) skúustyəkə ~ skúistyəkə 'he put beads on me'

(i+ui > iu) sîučaapə 'I crossed it'

(a+ui > au) gáutyu 'he is stingy'

(u+ui > ui) sgúitaaʔa 'he asked me'

(i+u: > iu:) síušanawa 'I cut his hair'

(a+u: > au:) sáušanawa 'I cut your hair'

(u+u: > u:) skušáṅawa 'he cut my hair'

(i+ə· > i·) sîigáṅi 'I am blushing'

The thematic syllable ‖ui‖ varies freely with ‖úwi·‖ if the thematic syllable is, in some of the forms of its paradigms, sometimes preceded by a vowel. The accent of the thematic syllable falls on the second syllable of the disyllabic form. This variation is not found, however, with themes that have basic ‖Jui‖ or ‖J̌ui‖. The disyllabic form is most commonly found after pronominal prefixes that have a final vowel, and the monosyllabic form most commonly after a consonant:

síwíitaaʔa 'I asked him'; prefix sj-, theme -úidaaʔaN

gúitaaʔa ~ gúwíitaaʔa 'he asked him'; prefix g-

gáwíityu ~ gáutyu 'he is stingy'; prefix g-, theme -Aúidyu

This variation is never found with a theme like -ʿúišazaM(N) 'to put on pants', a theme that takes set II pronominal prefixes and hence is never preceded by a vowel.

Some themes show alternations of the thematic syllable of the following type (prefixes si- < sj- and g-):

síusbéuca 'I whistled'   síiska 'I drank'

kusbéuca 'he whistled'   gə́ska 'he drank'

The length of the thematic syllable for other themes is constant throughout the paradigms. Therefore the variable length morphophoneme ‖:‖ has been set up to account for the variation in the length of the syllable, and

the themes given above are written -ú:sbéuzaN and -ə́:sḱaD. The morphophoneme is not lost by the application of this rule, as shown by the contractions
listed in table 8, because ‖:‖ also conditions accent changes treated in ‖20.

‖14 Certain vocalic changes are found in sequencés of two vowels separated by a glottal stop. The changes bring the sequences into conformity with
the phonemic distribution described in Section 123.4. In initial syllables:
  (1) e(·)ʔv > e(·)ʔe
  (2) $v_1 ʔ v_2 > v_1 ʔ v_1 v_2$.
The symbol v̱ stands for any vowel except ‖e‖, length, or the morphophonemic vowel ‖V‖. Rule ‖13 is reapplied to the sequence $v_1 v_2$. These
changes are expecially common with the dual prefix. Examples:
  (eʔa· > eʔe·) seʔêenú 'I gave them (dual) a bath'
  (eʔai > eʔei) seʔêinazí 'I ran over them (dual)'
  (e·ʔa > e·ʔe) sêeʔetyuša 'I covered them (dual)'
  (eʔa > eʔe) seʔéšə 'my knee'
  (iʔu· > iʔiu· > iʔiu) siʔíukača 'I see them (dual)'
  (iʔu: > iʔiu:) siʔíuṁayanikuya 'I made fun of them (dual)'
These changes do not normally occur when the possessive prefix {-qa-}
is followed by a noun root with an initial glottal stop: śaʔúyáaṁi 'my
paint brush'. There is one exception: śaʔáwáaka 'my baby'; ʔúwáaka
'baby'. The sequence ‖aʔí‖, found in three plural themes listed in ‖8,
is also unaffected. These changes also do not apply to the sequence
‖v̇ʔv‖, that is when both vowels are short, and the first vowel is accented: káuṫúkuca 'he smoothed it'; theme -ʻáʔuṫúḱazaN (see ‖23).
  The same vocalic changes are found in noninitial position with ‖ʔu‖
from ‖ʔB‖ (see ‖1.6) and with the suffix ‖≠etaaN‖, allomorph of
{≠itaaN} (see Section 441.1). The changes are regressive, however,
instead of progressive: kišâuʔu 'he urinated', theme -ʻišâaʔB; kiýêeʔeta
'he is allowing it', theme -ʻiýâaʔaW(N). No changes are found with certain irregular formations of classificatory verb themes ending with
‖kuʔíʔiD‖ (Section 453): śeṁáakuʔí 'I gave him a handful'.

‖15 The morphophoneme ‖V‖ assimilates to the vowel preceding or
following a glottal stop. In initial syllables the change is: $Vʔv_1 > v_1 ʔ v_1$.
Elsewhere the change is $v_1 ʔ V > v_1 ʔ v_1$. The direction of assimilation is
the opposite of that described in the preceding rule. Examples:
  tiʔîiṫa 'I stepped on it (dubitative)'; prefix tVʔj-
  teʔéusa 'I am slow (dubitative)'
  kaʔáuyéeca 'he made up his mind'; theme -QáuyéezaN,
    ‖-ʻVʔáuyéeza‖ 10.2

ki?íisdyú 'he defecated'; theme -QíisdyúB

cigûu?u 'she is pregnant'; theme -Jugûu?N, ‖-Jugûu?V‖1.1

śâačawai?i 'we had a stick race'; theme -QâačawaiY, suffix -?VVD
(see ‖1.7)

‖16   ?ui > ẃii

        ?iu > ẏuu

This change is optional for both sequences in medial position, mandatory
for ‖?ui‖ in initial position. ‖?iu‖ is not found in initial position (see
Section 123.4). Examples:

    ẃíičáabśni 'crossing'; prefix ?-, stem -úičaabəN (see Section 643)

    gu?úičaapə ~ guẃíičaapə 'they (dual) crossed over'

    si?íukača ~ siẏúukača 'I see them (dual)'

‖17   əCu > uCu

The change is mandatory if the empty morph ‖-əẓ-‖ is involved:
guẓúukača 'he saw you'; prefix g-əẓ-. Elsewhere the change is optional:
níupugú ~ níupəgú 'he will enter'; theme -ú:bəN.

The reverse assimilation is found with the stem -ûẓəgayaM 'to owe
money': skúc̣ukayámi 'he owes me money', theme -JûẓəgayaM-qiṢ;
gâuc̣ukaya 'he owes money', theme -AûuẓəgayaM. Cf. zícəkayámi 'he
owes him money'.

In many stems that have ‖ə‖, ‖ə ~ u‖ or ‖ə ~ a‖. In most cases
the variation is free: śépəkadá ~ śépakadá 'I used it up'. In some cases
the variation is conditioned, as -qápišəN -(´)í, -qápišuN elsewhere:
ḱapišśní 'at night'; ḱápišu 'it is night'.

‖18.0   There are three reduplicative morphemes, labeled $\{R_1\}$, $\{R_2\}$,
and $\{R_3\}$, and one length morpheme, labeled $\{L\}$. $\{R_1\}$, $\{R_3\}$, and $\{L\}$
are found with descriptive stems (Section 631), and $\{R_2\}$ with a small
class of stems treated in Section 632.1

‖18.1   A monosyllabic stem plus $\{R_1\}$ results in the total reduplication of the stem with no morphophonemic changes:

    stə́əstə́əci 'they are straight'; cf. stə́əci 'it is straight'

The second syllable of a disyllabic stem with $\{R_1\}$ is reduplicated.
The resulting form often undergoes accent changes described in ‖20, 21,
and 22. Examples:

    ćápipici 'it has lots of spots', stem ćápi-; cf. ćápici 'it has a spot'

    tákákaci 'they are square', stem táka-; cf. tákaci 'it is square'

    muŕáŕaci 'they are dented', stem muŕa-; cf. muŕáci 'it is dented'

    bérereci 'it is smooth', stem bêra- ~ befra-; cf. sénáskáibéŕeci

    'my head is smooth, I am bald' (sénáska 'my head')

‖ 18.2 {R₂} has been found only with stems of the shape Cv́v- and Cv́v-. When {R₂} is added, the syllable is totally reduplicated, and the resulting accent pattern is Cv́vCvv-. Examples:

ćaacaase 'I am breathing', stem cáa-; cf. cáase 'I took a deep breath'

híihiika 'he grinned, off and on', stem híi-; cf. híika 'he grinned'

bêepeeka 'they kept falling' (see ‖ 27), stem bée-; cf. béeka 'they fell'

‖ 18.3 {R₃} has been recorded with only two stems. The forms are totally reduplicated. One form was recorded with plus juncture between the reduplicated elements; it is probably present in both forms:

k̇údú+k̇údú 'candy', stem k̇ûdu- ~ k̇uꞎdu- 'round, spherical'

šínašína 'cookies, crackers', stem šiꞎña- 'crunch, crack'

‖ 18.4 {L} is found with stems of the shape CVCV and CV:CV. When {L} is added, CVCV > CV·CV and CV:CV > CV·:CV. The resulting forms often undergo changes described in ‖ 20. Examples:

kâayuka 'they broke', stem kaꞎyu-; cf. káyúka 'it broke'

k̇ûutuka 'several bubbles formed', stem k̇ûdu- ~ k̇uꞎdu-; k̇útuka 'it formed a bubble'

sáuk̇ûutuca 'I made them into balls'; cf. sáuk̇útuca 'I made a ball'

gûućaayuca 'he broke several of his things', stem ćaꞎyu-; cf. gûućayuca 'he broke one thing of his'

ćúuyuka 'the road is washed out in several places', stem ćuꞎyu-; cf. ćuyúka 'it is washed out'

The initial consonant of the stem ṣaꞎdi- 'tear' is glottalized when {L} is added: ṣáatici 'it has several tears'; cf. ṣádíci 'it has one tear'.

‖ 19 The morphophoneme of accent ablaut, symbolized (´), is set up to account for accent changes associated with certain suffixes. Every syllable of a word that has accent ablaut takes the high accent; any accent present in the basic form is replaced by the high accent. Accent ablaut with length, symbolized (´´), behaves like accent ablaut, and in addition the vowel before (´´) is lengthened. Under certain conditions described in ‖ 22 a short syllable may lose the high accent conditioned by (´) and (´´). Other changes are described in ‖ 23. The suffixes that contain these morphophonemes are:

-(´)í, Section 762

-(´), Section 643

-(´)wá, -(´)yá, Section 651.1

-(´)ná, Section 651.3

-(´)mí, Section 652

-(´)yá, Section 652.2

-(´)ṁa, -(´´)ṁa, Section 654.2

-(´´)ná, Section 644

-(´´)ḱáwáaka, Section 652.4

-(´´)zé, Section 653.1

-(´´)ci, Section 654.1

-(´´), Section 415

Examples:

śíiẓáačúwání 'when I woke him up', suffix -(´)í

súwáǵśní 'when I got dressed', suffix -(´)í

dyáanáwá 'four times', dyâana 'four', suffix -(´)wá

kabáaná 'pancakes', kába- 'thick', suffix -(´´)ná

šúuméəci 'graveyard', šûumə 'corpse', suffix -(´´)ci

A final syllable with an initial obstruent or glottalized sonorant is normally unaccented:

kúusťi 'when he died', suffix -(´)í

síuťáasti 'when I hung it up', suffix -(´)í

sáaṁáwáisťíṁi 'when I washed my hands', suffix -(´)í

ʔúyáasbáaṅi 'grinding stone', suffix -(´)

There are a few exceptions:

tśrśrśgá 'car', suffix -(´)

ziẃáẃáasáa 'patients', suffix -(´); see ‖ 23

‖ 20   Forms with an accented variable length morphophoneme undergo accent changes:

v:cv > v́cv́

vv:cv > v́vcv

In the formulation, v indicates any vowel and ´ indicates any accent.

In the following examples two forms are given, the first the morphophonemic form before the application of ‖ 20, the second the phonemic form. The forms often undergo further morphophonemic changes described in ‖ 22, 28, and 29.

siu:ꞗwisgəza > síuwiskəca 'I scratched it'

gu:ꞗwisgəza > gúwískəca 'he scratched it'

siu:šanawa > síušanawa 'I cut his hair'

gu:šanawa > kušáṅawa 'he cut his hair'

ća:čayuzi > ćačáýuci 'it was all shot up', theme -qja:čayuziṢ (see ‖ 5.2)

siu:čayuza > síučayuca 'I shot it'

gu:ṁayaniguya > guṁáyanikuya 'he made fun of him'

ka:yuga > káyúka 'it broke'

kaa:yuga > kâayuka 'they broke' ({ L }, ‖ 18.4)

mu:ṙazi > muṙáci 'it is dented'

If unaccented, the variable length morphophoneme is lost, and there is no accent change:

síu:sbéuza > síusbéuca 'I whistled'
gú:sbéuza > kusbéuca 'he whistled' (see ‖ 22)

‖ 21   A short unaccented syllable before an unaccented syllable with
an initial glottalized consonant is sometimes accented.[14] The change is
mandatory in forms followed by an initial vowel suffix that contains ‖ q ‖
(see ‖ 1, table 2), -tiza 'group of . . .' (Section 646), -ma(-zé) 'like'
(Section 654.3), or {R_1} (see ‖ 18.1).

Examples are listed in the same fashion as in ‖ 20:

sutâanizanədyəə > sutâanizánətyəə 'we (dual) worked', suffix -qədyəəZ
súwátâanizanaa > súwatâanizána 'we (plural) worked', suffix -qaaD
sutâanizanee > sutâanizáne 'I went to work', suffix -qeeY
ʔutâanizani > ʔutâanizáni 'to work', suffix -qiŞ
madáikutiza > madáikútiça 'Grape Men', madáiku 'grapes'
wagêeratiza > wagêerátiça 'cowboys', wagêera 'cowboy'
kasâidimazé > kasâidímazé 'it feels like summer', kasâiti 'summer'
takakazi > takákaci 'they are square' (see ‖ 22)

The change is optional in other constructions:

sêiʔicaatya ~ sêiʔícaatya 'I pinned them (plural)', see ‖ 7.2
sáudímitita ~ sáudímítita 'I am learning', suffix ⁼qitaaN

The change optionally takes place if the form is followed by the suffixes -náata (Section 442.2), -qáayaN (‖ 1; Section 441.2), or -nú (Section
412). This change takes place contrary to the restriction that the following syllable must be unaccented:

síukacanáata ~ síukacánáata 'I always see him'
sáisataaya ~ sáisátaaya 'I am spreading it out'
skucáwanú ~ skucáwánú 'I am a thief'

‖ 22.0   Under certain phonological conditions short syllables lose their
accent. The accent loss is limited to certain constructions (see ‖ 22.s).
The rule is illustrated by forms with accent ablaut. By the operation of
‖ 19 all syllables of such forms, except certain final syllables, have the
high accent.

_____

[14]This rule reflects a historical change that took place in Acoma after the break
up of Proto-Keres. Cf. Proto-Keres *húwakA, Acoma húwáka 'sky' (capitals indicate voiceless vowels). In certain morphological environments the accent is lost
on the analogy of the many forms that are not accented. Thus sêiʔícaatya 'I pinned
them' is historically correct, and sêiʔicaatya is a reformation based on the analogy
of the many forms like sêiʔipənaiʔi 'he put them in'. In those cases where the
change is mandatory the unglottalized forms are much less frequent, and the analogical shift to the unaccented forms did not take place.

‖ 22.1   A short syllable between obstruents and followed by an accented syllable loses its accent.[15] These syllables are underlined in the following examples:

śisíusdyání 'when I roped him'

ʔúubəkáakáci 'nail'

síukačání 'when I saw him'

kúistyəgśní 'when he put beads on himself'

kubśní 'at sunset'

séinúusťuzímí 'when I put the fire out'

śíiskadáwí 'when I gave him a drink'

More than one syllable can lose the accent by this rule:

kapišśní 'at night'

šapəgání 'early evening'

śipəkáawání 'when I chopped wood'

kacəkáni 'his cigarettes'

If three successive syllables of this sort occur, the second syllable does not lose the accent (cf. Section 121). The retained accent is underlined:

kəzácəkáni 'your cigarettes'

kagścədíní 'when it is in bloom'

sucítistáaní 'when I was thinking'

In one form an initial glottal stop configurates like an obstruent, in two others it does not:[16]

ʔusdyacści 'hat'

ʔícitistáani 'mind, willpower'

ʔúťidúmíci 'headband'

In noninitial position glottal stop configurates like an obstruent if either the preceding or following syllable is long (if both are short, ‖ 23 applies):

ćiuťéeʔestími 'dishwater'

ʔáiʔićáadyáni 'clothespin'

ziʔíukačańáati 'when they (plural) saw them (dual)'

There are a few irregular forms. The accent is retained in káibátyuzání 'when it banged shut' and súkaazaʔání 'when I announced'. The accent is lost from long syllables in: síuçuušání 'when I made a hole'; śéityuceeyí 'when I dragged it'; súkaazaʔání 'when I announced'. Regular variants were recorded for two of the forms: síuzúušání, śéityuzéeyí.

---

[15]This rule reflects a general historical change: Proto-Keres *ʔádàušī > Acoma ʔadáuši 'cooking pot'; *bíśśəná > pišśəná 'purple'.

[16]In the second and third form the following syllable begins with a glottalized consonant. These two forms can be accounted for by reversing the order of ‖ 21 and ‖ 22. Such a reversal cannot be used for other forms, especially forms with {R_1} (see ‖ 18, and Section 222).

‖ 22.2 A short accented syllable before or after a glottalized sonorant usually loses its accent. If both of the syllables are short, either syllable (usually the first) may lose the accent, but never both:

suẉáaméešání 'when I put up a tent'

seḿéekúyáwí 'when I gave him a handful'

gúukačánədyə́əci 'when they (dual) saw it'

ziʔíukačaṉáati 'when they (plural) saw them (dual)'

ʔúuy̨astími 'laundry'

kutáaṇiça 'worker'

șiṃíná ʔásti 'when I made stuffed tripe'

kəčaṉíši 'when he was standing'

cíčəṉíši ~ cíčə́ṉiši 'the big one' (the accent of the first syllable should be lost by ‖ 22)

suṇáćimí 'when I took a lunch'

séy̨aťáaní 'when I stomped'

The change does not always take place:

ʔúumáasgə́ṉáasti 'diapers'

sáaṃáwáistími 'when I washed my hands'

ʔúumúuŕáci 'skirt

sáasbánášúṃéní 'when I washed my hair'

șíy̨áṃa̧sti 'when I am hungry'

One would expect free variation to occur (that is, between the operation and nonoperation of this rule), but it has not been recorded.

‖ 22.s The accent losses described in ‖ 22.1-2 are limited to certain constructions:

(1) Forms with accent ablaut (see ‖ 19). All the examples illustrating the rules are such forms.

(2) Descriptives, with or without $\{R_1\}$. Rule ‖ 22.2 always applies and applies only to the syllable before the first glottalized sonorant:

muṟáci 'it is dented', stem muʃ́ra- (see ‖ 20)

muṟáraci 'they are dented' (see ‖ 18, 20)

ťaḵáḵaci 'they are square', stem ťáḵa- (see ‖ 18, 21)

(3) Themes with ‖ : ‖, the variable length morphophoneme (see ‖ 13, 20):

kusbéuca 'he whistled', prefix g-, theme -ú:sbéuzaN

kušáṇawa 'he cut his hair', theme -u:šanawaN

gumáyanikuya 'he made fun of him', theme -u:ṃayaniguyaN

ćaćáyuci 'it was all shot up', prefix g-, theme -qja:čayuziṢ

A few themes do not undergo the change: gúsú 'he knows how', theme -ú:súM.

(4) Forms with (TSE) that result in ‖úẃá‖ (see ‖9.1-2). If the following syllable is a glottalized sonorant, both syllables of the expanded form
may lose the accent:[17]

suẃáskúméńa 'we fell in the water'

súẃataȧniz̧áńa 'we worked'

kuẃam̊áacȧaz̧áńa 'they made jerky'

(5) Short syllables that result when the thematic prefixes ‖-ʽi-‖,
‖-qja-‖, and ‖-ʽ-‖ (see ‖5.2, ‖5.6) are added:

kińəəca 'he became rigid'

kikútuca 'he bunched up into a ball'

ćakútuci 'there are a whole bunch of lumps'

sum̊éyuca 'I got bruised'

This rule does not always operate, however: kísáɫa 'he is fat'.

The accent loss occurs sporadically with other forms:

ćukútiça '(both) twins', ćúku 'twin(s)', -ɫiza 'group of . . .', see
‖21 (cf. hástíɫiça 'group of old men', ‖hástì‖ 'old man')

ciyáaɫa 'he is flying', < -ʽjíyuø + -qjáaɫaN

síuskum̊áɫaaya 'I am hiding' < -ʽúiskúm̊aSD + -qáayaN (see ‖21)

hastíizá 'he is very old' < hástì + auxiliary {zá} (see ‖3.2);
hastíizéeši 'old man', suffix -zéeši (see ‖3.2)

síudimí 'I planted it for him'; séešaazimí 'I cut it for him'; themes
-JúudíM, -JáašaazíM, suffix -qíʔiD

‖23.0 The morphophonemic sequences ‖v́ʔv‖ and noninitial ‖vʔv‖ (v
stands for a short vowel) are set up in the basic forms of a number of morphemes to account for alternations that are found with accent ablaut (‖19).
These sequences do not occur phonemically. This rule describes not only
the development of these two sequences, but also the development of ‖v́ʔv́‖,
a sequence usually from ‖v́ʔv‖ or ‖vʔv́‖ plus accent ablaut.

‖23.1 The sequence ‖v́ʔv́‖ has three types of development:

(1) v́ʔv́ > vʔv́ ~ v́ʔv́ (in free variation?)

(2) v́ʔv́ > v́v

(3) v́ʔv́ > v̇v

When the glottal stop is lost and the two vowels are identical, the second

---

[17]One of the differences between (TSE) and {pl} is that both syllables that result
from the former are usually accented, and then ‖22 applies. Internal and external
evidence shows that the first syllable that resulted when {pl} was prefixed used to
be accented, and the accent was lost by the historical change reflected in this rule.
Cf. the irregular form sgúwáɫyáipa 'they (plural) looked for me' (‖8) in which the
sonorant is not glottalized and the preceding syllable is accented; and cf. Santa
Ana şáiyʔá·zúwA, Acoma şayáazúwa, < Proto-Keres *şáyáazúwA 'you paid them'.

vowel is replaced by length (there is no change in the writing, however, because of the orthographic convention of writing long vowels as double vowels).

The first type is found in stem final position and in suffixes. All of the following examples have accent ablaut:

 síwáistáni̱ʔíti 'when I dished up stew for him', suffix -ʼíʔiD

 síutáani̱ʔíti 'when I tried it for him'

 sidyaʔání 'when I held it', stem -údyáʔaD(N)

 sezáʔání 'when I talked to him', stem -záʔaN

 síubeʔéní 'when I told him', stem -béʔeN

The sequence in -qámáʔ́ágə 'daughter' (a form that does not have accent ablaut) is treated as though it were stem final: sámá̱ʔ́ákə ~ sáma̱ʔákə 'my daughter'.

The second type is found in the first of two sequences of ‖v́ʔv́‖. All of the following examples have accent ablaut:

 síustyəgə́ní̱ʔíti 'when I put beads on him', theme -J́úʔisdyəgəN-ʼíʔiD

 sezáani̱ʔíti 'when I talked for him', theme -J́azáʔaN-ʼíʔiD

 Cf. ẃiistyəgə́ńi 'beads'; sezáʔání 'when I talked to him' (both forms

  have accent ablaut)

The third type is found elsewhere. All of the following examples have accent ablaut:

 ẃíiýáasi̱usdyáńi 'hobble', stem -usí̱ʔusdyaN

 ʔúuýúuskáḿi 'pottery paint', stem -ûuýúʔuskaM̄

 síuza̱abə́ní 'when I fell in', theme -ûuza̱ʔabəN

 sədéegúiýí 'when we (plural) went', plural theme -jeʔéguY (see ‖7.10)

 sa̱ašúwíní 'when we (dual) wore shoes', dual theme -aʔášúwiM(N)

  (see ‖7.8)

There are a number of irregular forms. It is not clear whether these forms represent free variation between ‖v́ʔv‖ and ‖v́v‖ or between ‖v̇ʔv‖ and ‖v́v‖; or if allomorphs are to be set up, the choice of the allomorph being dependent on the morphological environment:

 sâumúuráca 'I have a pleated skirt' (no accent ablaut); ʔúumúuráci

  'pleated skirt' (accent ablaut); both from muːra- 'dented'

 kagə́çətáata 'it is in bloom' (no accent ablaut); suffix {-ńáataN};

  kagə́çətáatání 'when it is in bloom' (accent ablaut)

 sáuýúuskáḿí 'when I painted' (accent ablaut); ʔúuýúuskáḿi 'pottery

  paint' (accent ablaut)

‖23.2 The sequence ‖v́ʔv‖ becomes ‖v́v‖; if the two vowels are identical, the second vowel is replaced by length:

 sisi̱ustya 'I roped him', theme -Jusí̱ʔusdyaN

 síwáistaníita 'we dished up stew for him', suffix -ʼíʔiD

 sezáaní 'I talked for him', stem -záʔaN

‖ 23.3   The sequence ‖ vʔv ‖ has two developments, depénding on its
position in the word:

vʔv > v́v varying freely with vʔv in initial position

vʔv > vv in noninitial position

If the two vowels are identical, the second vowel is replaced by length:

tiʔišáaci ~ tíišáaci 'I am strong (dubitative)', prefix tVʔj-, theme
-JušáaziṢ

síucaapə 'I fell in', theme -ûuẓaʔabəN

‖ 24   Internal word juncture[18] is found before the following suffixes
and auxiliaries:

-mé́ʔe 'person of . . .', Section 647

-náaɫaN habitual suffix, Section 442.2 (see also ‖ 1)

{gú} auxiliary, Section 461.1

{zá} auxiliary, Section 461.8

{zé} auxiliary, Section 461.9

{gáa} auxiliary, Section 461.6

Internal word juncture is optionally lost. External juncture is also sometimes lost, in particular it is sometimes lost before the locative adverb
ʔée (Section 741). My recording of juncture is not accurate, and some
cases of its omission may be misrecordings. But it is clear, because of the
operation of ‖ 25 and ‖ 29, that some omissions are real and that this rule
sometimes does and sometimes does not operate. The morphophonemic
changes can be accounted for by stating that ‖+‖ is optionally lost at this
point in the sequence of morphophonemic rules. In addition, some forms
that were not recorded with /+/ are either misrecordings or else show that
this rule may be reapplied after the application of ‖ 25 and ‖ 29.

The following examples are given in pairs. The juncture has been los
at this point in the sequence of the morphophonemic rules from the first
member of the pair, but not the second:

(1) sâateeýáaɫa 'I am hauling', suffix {-náaɫaN}

(2) sâate+ýáaɫa (‖ 25 has been applied)

(1) kúudiʔée 'on the mountain', locative adverb ʔée

(2) kúutiʔée (either ‖ 24 has been applied after the application of
‖ 29, or the form is a misrecording for kúuti+ʔée)

(1) kúudíidyamé 'Cochiti Indian', suffix -mé́ʔe

(2) kúudíityamé (either ‖ 24 has been applied after the application
of ‖ 29, or the form is a misrecording of kúudíitya+mé)

---

[18]Phonemic juncture is treated in Section 140. Between words it is indicated by
space. It is not marked internally except in the exposition of this rule, where it
is marked by +.

Compare the following forms:

gúpənáaťa 'it (sun) sets', theme -ú:bəN

síuwakənáaťa 'I always wear it', theme -ú:wagəN

séečáaçanáaťa 'I always listen', theme -áačáaẓa

Either (1) this rule does not apply to short vowel plus {-náaťaN} and the forms are misrecordings for gúpə+náaťa, síuẇakə+náaťa, and séečáaça+náaťa, or (2) this rule applies to such forms after the application of ‖ 29.

‖ 25 A long unaccented vowel before juncture is always shortened:

sáyace 'I whitewashed it', theme -'áyaceeM

síyúuce 'I took it with me', theme -JúyúuzeeY

gúyəəcita 'he is hitting it', suffix ⸗itaaN

číišə 'his nose', theme -qjíišəə

sâate+yáaťa 'I am hauling', theme -QáadeeY (see ‖ 24)

A long accented vowel before juncture is usually shortened in nouns and thematic forms:

gúyá 'he butchered it', theme -ú:yáaN

súcá 'I tanned', theme -'úcáaN

síẇaisťaní 'I dished up stew for him', suffix -'íʔiD, ‖-íi‖ 23

kásí 'her breast', theme -'ásíi

But there are some exceptions:

báabáa 'grandmother'

čizáa 'they are long'

číyáa 'they are wide'

ziẇáwáasáa 'patients'

In forms other than nouns and thematic forms, long vowels with the glottal accent are retained, and long vowels with the high accent are optionally shortened:

ʔədəə 'hot'

wée 'that one'

bíyáa ~ bíyá 'tilted'

ʔáyáa ~ ʔáyá 'Oh, that!'

dáwáa ~ dáwá 'good'

zíi ~ zí 'thing'

Vowel clusters are usually retained before juncture:

síkûuyáu 'I threaded a needle', theme -JukûuyaẂ

sâačawai 'I ran a foot race', theme -QáačawaiY

zíibái 'he is sleeping', theme -jíibáiY

karaníu 'stud bull or horse'

râi 'king'

But there are some exceptions. Vowel clusters in forms of the auxiliary

{gú} are shortened before juncture: núpesí 'I will eat it', prefix sj-, theme
-ú:N. The vowel cluster is shortened in -ánásgai: sénáska 'my head' (contrast
nasgâini 'head', absolutive form). The vowel cluster in ‖házəcai‖ 'man' is
optionally shortened or assimilated to /e/: hácəcai ~ hácəca ~ hácəce.

‖26 A sequence of glottal accent followed by a glottalized sonorant
does not occur phonemically. If such a sequence occurs morphophonemically, either the glottal accent is changed to the falling accent or the
glottalized sonorant is changed to a plain sonorant:

    cíuyâaṅi ~ cíuyáani 'it was butchered', stem -úyáaN, suffix -qiṢ
      (see ‖1.1 and ‖11.1)
    síuťáane 'I visited him', theme -úuťaaN, suffix -qeeY
    saẃâiṅa 'we fought', theme -ʾaẃáiN (see ‖1.6), suffix -qaaD; cf.
      saẃáiku 'I fought'

‖27 The glottal accent apparently is optionally replaced by the falling
accent in prepenultimate syllables and in penultimate syllables that are
followed by an accent (but see Section 137):

    kaʔáaskətica ~ kaʔâaskətica 'he jerked'
    śáateeʔe ~ śâateeʔe 'we hauled it'
    síuťáaneeʔe ~ síuťâaneeʔe 'we visited him' (cf. ‖26)
    síusú ~ sîusú 'I know how'

‖28 Falling and glottal accents are replaced by high accents on short
syllables:

    gúwískəca 'he scratched it', theme -uːwisgəzaN, ‖gûwîsgəza‖ 20
    gúšiya 'he beat him', theme -úːšiyaaW
    ťúkuka 'it snapped', stem ťú̂ku-; cf. ťûukuka 'several snapped' ({L},
      see ‖18.4)
    káyúka 'it broke', stem kaːyu-; cf. kâayuka 'they broke' ({L}, see ‖18.
    gúyá 'he butchered it', theme -úːyáaN
    síẃáisťaní 'I dished up stew for him', suffix -ʾíʔiD, ‖-íi‖23, ‖-í‖2
    kásí 'her breasts', theme -ʾásíi

The falling accent remains on short vowels if the following syllable is
accented and final and begins with a plain sonorant (cf. Section 121):
gûní 'he knows him', theme -ûːníM.

‖29 Unaspirated occlusives are aspirated if there is no accent between
the occlusive and the following juncture. In most cases this amounts to
saying that they are aspirated if they are after the last accented syllable. In
the following examples the occlusives affected by this rule are underlined:

ḱúuti 'mountain'

sîukastya 'I asked him'

sîupeuca 'I called him'

gúwískəca 'he scratched it'

ḱúuti?ée 'in the mountains' (perhaps a misrecording for ḱúuti+?ée,
    see ‖ 24)

The same change also occurs if the occlusive is followed by a long
unaccented syllable:

suẘâutaa?áńa 'we asked for it'

sêi?ityaićí 'I buried them'

The change also occurs before short unaccented syllables if the following
syllable begins with a sibilant, plain occlusive, plain sonorant, or /h/:[19]

kušáńawa 'he cut his hair'

kəsḱáti 'when he drank'

kubə́ní 'at sunset'

citâańicaní 'he worked for him'

séikayáu 'I set the trap'

kəcahíišə 'your necklace'

This change does not take place before a short unaccented syllable if
the following syllable is accented and has an initial glottalized occlusive,
glottalized sonorant, or /?/:

?úubəḱáaḱáci 'nail'

sgutúpica 'it stung me'

gumáyanikuya 'he made fun of him'

sîustyəgəńáaya 'I am putting beads on him'

zi?íukačańáati 'when they (plural) saw them (dual)'

kəza?áẃáaka 'your baby'

Rule ‖ 11.2 (the treatment of the aspirating morphophoneme ‖ ' ‖) and
this rule often produce identical results. Thus the pronominal prefix g-
(3rd person nonmodal) is aspirated in both -'ubáyaN and -ú:béuzaN:

kubáýa 'he built a fire', ‖ 11.2

kubêuca 'he called him', ‖ 29

But compare the treatment of the prefix dy- (3rd person dubitative):

čubáýa 'did he build a fire?', ‖ 11.2

tyubêuca 'did he call him?', ‖ 29

The ‖ ẓ ‖ in the empty morph ‖ -əẓ- ‖ (see Section 230) may optionally

---

[19]The preceding paragraphs probably reflect historical changes of Pre-Keres:
Proto-Keres *ḱácI > Acoma ḱáci 'ten', ‖ ḱázì ‖, Pre-Keres *ḱázi. The statement in
this paragraph probably reflects recent changes in Acoma, at least those changes
that are brought about by the accent loss described in ‖ 22 (see footnote 15).

be aspirated in ambivalents (thematic prefix {-qa-}, Section 520) even when found in an environment where the change does not normally take place:

    kəza?áwáaka ~ kəça?áwáaka 'your baby'

    kəzayûuni ~ kəçayûuni 'your song'

    kəzamîná ~ kəçamîná 'your salt'

This alternation is also sometimes found in environments where only the aspirated consonants should occur: kəzaméesa ~ kəçaméesa 'your table'.

‖ 30   A plain sonorant is glottalized if it is (1) preceded by the high accent, (2) followed by a short, unaccented vowel, and (3) not followed by a syllable with another sonorant. The glottalized sonorant is underlined:

    cíya 'it is wide'   sáatúwi 'I let go of it'

    sáukáyuca 'I broke it'   síizúwa 'I paid him'

    simína 'I spoke to him'   gucáyuca 'he shot it'

If the preceding high accent is not the last accent in the word, the change is optional. No forms have been recorded that show both treatments, but there are many examples of the same theme or same construction, some showing the change, others not:

    cánamačáni 'it was sat on'; sánamačáňa 'we sat down'

    síukáyucaní 'I broke it for him'; séišáwəcaní 'I cracked nuts for him'

Contrast the following forms that only partially fulfill the requirement and show no change:

    simínaata 'we spoke to him'   bérereci 'it is smooth'

    sáatúwiise 'I keep letting go'   šašúwinu 'when I have shoes on'

    ňíizúwaasí 'I will pay him'   gumáyanikuya 'he made fun of him'

    cérereci 'it is greasy'   kadúwina 'cliff'

The sonorant is irregularly glottalized in some forms:[20] kušáňawa 'he cut his hair'; záazíi skizáacúwanu 'I didn't wake up'.

Usually ‖ 21 applies before ‖ 30: suwíidyúmítita 'I am branding it' (cf. suwíidyúmica 'I branded it'). However, the reverse order applies in one

---

[20] This morphophonemic rule reflects a historical change in which a sonorant was glottalized if preceded by a high accent and followed by a voiceless vowel: zíizúwA > zíizúwa 'he paid him' (capitals indicate voiceless vowels). Voiced and voiceless vowels were almost phonologically predictable in Proto-Keres, and a final unaccented vowel preceded by a high accent and sonorant was normally voiceless. The vowel was normally voiced if, instead of being final, it was followed by a syllable with a sonorant: *gánami > gánami 'beans'. But occasionally the vowel was voiceless and the sonorant became glottalized. Thus the morphophonemic change sometimes takes place in environments where the change is not expected: *kúsčánAwA > kušáňawa 'he cut his hair' (cf. síušanawa 'I cut his hair').

example: śéṇáťita 'I keep turning the light on' (cf. śéṇaċa 'I turned the light on', śénáẓání 'when I turned the light on', theme -JánaẓaN).

Rule ‖ 30 does not apply to a number of forms:[21]

gáwi 'his neck'   šína 'louse'
náṇa 'grandfather'   béeṛa 'pear'

220. Summary of the Morphophonemics

221. Acoma appears to have undergone a number of phonemic changes recently. The result is a simple syllabic structure, but a complicated morphophonemic system. There is a great deal of free variation in the morphophonemic system, probably as the result of analogical changes that are now taking place. The free variation creates a number of descriptive problems, and not all of them have been treated in the preceding rules. It is often difficult to delineate the limits of the free variation and to separate free and conditioned variation. In some cases forms that have been treated as free variants may actually represent different morphological forms.

A complicated morphophonemic system does have its rewards, however. By comparing the phonemic and morphophonemic distributional features it is possible to do a considerable amount of internal reconstruction.

The final morphophonemic consonants (rule ‖ 1) undoubtedly represent morpheme final consonants that used to occur in final position. They were lost in final position, but preserved when a suffix followed. But it is also clear that the particular consonant found with a morpheme does not necessarily represent the earlier consonant, because analogical changes have taken place. Judging from the amount of variation between final morphophonemic consonants, such changes are still taking place. Well over half of the morphemes end in ‖N‖. Many verb roots with ‖N‖ are probably formed, historically, with the verb forming suffix -aN (the suffix is no longer productive, however; see Section 625), and many others probably represent analogical shifts from other final consonants

---

[21]Most of the exceptions are loanwords, e.g. nana (Zuñi) and pera (Spanish). The remaining words come from Proto-Keres words ending in a long voiced vowel that were shortened in Acoma (*šínaa) or from words that ended in a short voiced vowel (*gáwi). Final short voiced vowels in this environment normally became accented (e.g. *ʔísdúwa > ʔisdûwá 'arrow'), so that words like gáwi are rare in Acoma.

to this more common final consonant. ‖M‖ is the second most common final consonant. It is found most commonly after -i, and it is the only one found after accented -í. The remaining consonants are not common.

‖M̄‖ is very uncommon and is usually followed by an unaccented vowel. ‖M‖ follows accented vowels more often than unaccented vowels. The two final consonants are distinguished by the choice of the allomorph that follow. ‖M‖ is followed by four suffixes that have the glottalizing morphophoneme ‖q‖, the same four suffixes that have ‖q‖ after ‖N‖. ‖M̄‖ is never followed by ‖q‖. It is very likely that ‖M‖ and ‖M̄‖ have the same historical source. When ‖M‖ follows an accented vowel, it is usually in an environment in which the sonorant is glottalized by the operation of ‖30. The glottalization came to be associated with particular suffixes on the analogy of forms with ‖N‖, and was applied to most forms that had a preceding unaccented vowel.

The final morphophonemic consonants ‖B, G^W, D, SD‖ are often followed by a suffix with an unaccented vowel, and the consonants are aspirated by the application of ‖29. They are also aspirated before the accented vowel of the benefactive suffix. They are rarely followed by other accented vowels, but when they are, they are usually unaspirated: śíiskadáwí 'when I gave him a drink', stem -sḱaD, suffixes -aW(N) (Section 625), -(´)í. For this reason it is stated in rule ‖1 that they become unaspirated stops, and the basic form of the benefactive suffix is set up with the aspirating morphophoneme ‖'‖. There are a few forms in whic the aspirated stop is found where the unaspirated stop is expected: kaẃáipéeti 'when they were fighting', theme -'aẃáiG^W, suffixes -eeD (plural), -(´)í. The stop probably became aspirated on the analogy of forms that have the common benefactive suffix.

Velar stops are palatalized to dental affricates before the palatalizing morphophoneme ‖j‖. It seems probable that historically the palatalization was caused by a following front vowel and that this process produce the dental affricates in Acoma. Note that a thematic syllable with a fro vowel usually has a palatalizing morphophoneme, the only exception bein the thematic syllable ‖'i‖. The palatalizing morphophoneme is also fou in thematic syllables with other vowels, for example, ‖ja‖; such a sequence could be from *ia or *ya. Additional evidence is found in the distribution of the obstruents and vowels within morphemes. Velars are rare before front vowels, and most examples are found in Spanish loanwords: géesu 'cheese' < queso; sakisdâana 'sexton' < sacristán. In addition, there are a few examples of a front vowel after a glottalized velar ʔáuḱíiníši 'friend'; gâuḱímǝni 'he has supernatural power'. The dental affricates, on the other hand are most common before front vowels. The are a number of morphemes that have /a/ after the affricate: záwini 'old'. The sequence probably is derived from *gia or *gya. Since the sequences ‖g-ju‖ and ‖g-juu‖ become /zi/ and /ziu/ (‖11.3 and ‖13), dental affricates should not occur before /u/ if the historical interpretation is correct. The sequence is found, but it is not very common: cúski 'fox, coyote'; śíizúẇa 'I paid him'; ćúku 'twins'; and a few others.

A similar interpretation cannot be made for the dental stops and /š/ (palatalized correspondents of ‖dy, č, ć, s‖), because these consonants are common before all vowels.

The phonemic alignment of the palatal stops and affricates (section 110) is recent. The older alignment, ‖dy, č, ć‖, is seen in table 7. The affricate /ž/ is found in a few Spanish loanwords and one native word (Section 123.7) and is never involved in morphophonemic alternations. The palatal stop /ty/, not found in basic forms, is either from ‖dy‖ through the operation of ‖29 or is in the cluster /sty/ and is from ‖sg‖ through the operation of ‖11.2 and ‖11.3. /t́y/ is found in the morpheme -t́yau (for example, záat́yau 'plains', see Section 654.5); elsewhere it is from ‖ẏ‖ through the operation of ‖8, from ‖dy‖ through the irregular operation of ‖11.1, or is in the cluster /st́y/ and is from ‖sg‖ through the operation of ‖11.1 and ‖11.3.

All of the Keres languages have the phonetic alignment found in Acoma, although some of them do not have a complete series of palatal stops. None of the obstruents /ž, ty, t́y/ can be reconstructed for Proto-Keres. The phonetic shift that isolated *dy from *č and *ć must have taken place in Pre-Keres times, and then the Keres languages independently filled in the gaps in the phonemic system after the split-up of Proto-Keres.

Morphophonemically, ‖c‖ is only found in some 2nd person dubitative prefixes (Section 230). Phonemically, /c/ is always from this source or from ‖z‖ through the operation of ‖29. /ć/ is always from ‖z‖ through the operation of ‖11.4, or from the pronominal prefixes with ‖c‖ through the operation of ‖11.1. *c, in the pronominal prefixes, and *z can be reconstructed in Proto-Keres, but not /ć/. Phonemically, /z̦/ is a retroflex obstruent, but it does not show the same morphophonemic patterns as do ‖c‖ and ‖s‖ (see in particular ‖11.4). It seems likely that ‖z̦‖ is historically (in Pre-Keres, not Proto-Keres) from a nonobstruent, perhaps something like *l.

The morphophonemic alignment of the sibilant clusters in table 7 represents a recent development in Acoma. Historically, the palatalized correspondents of *sg, *sk, and *sḱ are sdy, sč, and ś (Proto-Keres *sč > š: *sčísA > śísa 'six'). This alignment can be internally reconstructed. The distributive pronominal prefixes (Section 233) have two

sets of allomorphs: š-, sk- (nonmodal) and sṭ-, sč- (dubitative). If we
assume that the distributive prefixes are *s plus the 3rd person prefix
g- (nonmodal) and dy- (dubitative), the prefixes can be reconstructed as
*sgqj-, *sg'- (nonmodal) and *sdyqj-, *sdy'- (dubitative). The palataliza-
tion of *sk to š is also reflected in the allomorphs -áyaš- (before ⁼itaaN)
-áyaskaN (elsewhere) 'to sweep': sáyašita 'I am sweeping'; sáyaska 'I
swept'.

‖ṡ‖ is found in ‖ṡédyu‖ 'all day', ‖ṡečúma‖ 'daytime', and ‖ṡéeega‖
'must' (the first two are clearly historically related). Elsewhere /ṡ/ is
found as the glottalized form of the first person nonmodal prefix (‖11.1
and Section 230). The other glottalized sibilants are not common in basic
forms, but they are more common than ‖ṡ‖ (‖ṧ‖ is somewhat more common because of the development of sč to š).

Within morphemes, ‖č̇‖ is usually found before ‖a‖. There are three
exceptions: -Aúučúuziṣ 'to be willing'; č̇ə́dígá 'sparrow hawk'; č̇úu-,
č̇uu-, allomorphs of the 2nd person hortative prefix. The glottalized
affricate is found before other vowels across morpheme boundaries in
various combinations of pronominal prefix plus thematic vowel.

‖ṗ‖ is rare, and never found before ‖u‖ within morphemes. It is
found before other vowels across morpheme boundaries as a development
of the 2nd and 3rd person hortative pronominal prefixes. In ‖1.6 it was
noted that ‖Gᵂ‖ became ‖-g(u)‖ in final position and before {-u} but
‖-b-‖ before other suffixes, many of which began with a front vowel; in
one root the development was ‖-g(u)‖ and ‖-ṗ-‖. It is quite possible
that ‖Gᵂ‖ is from Pre-Keres *gᵂ, which became /g(u)/ in final position
and before /u/ and became /b/ before front vowels, or perhaps before
other vowels; and that ‖ṗ‖ is always from *k̇ᵂ.

The phonemic contrast between aspirated and unaspirated occlusives
is lost before most unaccented syllables. Cf. the following forms:
séikayáu 'I set the trap', theme -áigayaW̃; ṡáuka 'I dyed it', theme
-QáukaM̄. It is possible to determine the morphophonemic status of /k/
in these themes when they are in constructions in which either ‖19 or
‖21 apply: séigáyámí 'when I set the trap'; ṡáukámí 'when I dyed it'.
In some themes it is impossible to distinguish ‖g‖ and ‖k‖ because the
consonant is in an environment in which ‖22 and subsequently ‖29 apply
if the following syllable is accented by ‖19: síukačání 'when I saw him'
In such cases the aspirated consonant is written in the basic form. How
ever, if /ty/ or /ç/ are found in this environment, ‖dy‖ and ‖z̧‖ are
written because ‖ç‖ and ‖ty‖ are not normally found: ṡíustyəka 'I put
beads on him'; ṡíustyəgə́ní 'when I put beads on him'; theme -Júisdyəgə
The most common vowels are ‖i, a, u‖. ‖e‖ is found in the thema

syllable of a very few impersonal verb themes; $\|ə\|$ is found in a some-
what larger number of thematic syllables. In other positions $\|e\|$ and
$\|ə\|$ are not very common. In thematic syllables the phoneme /e/ is
found as a development of i + a, and it is possible that historically the
phoneme in other positions is from the same or a similar sequence.
There is some evidence that *a + i sometimes yields /e/; cf. the set
of allomorphs for the suffix ⁻itaaN (Section 441.1) and the development
of -qa- + hı́iska 'knife' ($\|5.4$). /ə/ is never the development of any
morphophonemic processes, and hence it is difficult to suggest its source.
However, its infrequency suggests that it is not original. $\|ə\|$ has simi-
lar distributional habits to $\|u\|$; it clusters with a folloiwng $\|i\|$ and
length vowel and can be followed by $\|:\|$ (the variable length morpho-
phoneme is found after no other vowels). Thus it is possible that it is
from a back vowel.

222. Most verb stems are composed of two syllables preceded by a
stem vowel and followed by a final morphophonemic consonant:
   -ázəkaN 'to smoke'
   -âačawaiY(N) 'to run a stick race'
   -usdyúwaaN 'to sweat'
Derived stems usually have an additional syllable:
   -utâani-zaN 'to work'
   -áaskayu-zaN 'to pull teeth'
Longer stems are found, but they are not frequent:
   -úwı̓istidyaaN 'to count'
   -áayáateéwi-zaN 'to step in mud'
Some verb stems are composed of one syllable, and a few are composed
of only a stem vowel plus a morphophonemic consonant:
   -áasgəN 'to fry'   -áSD 'to take a step'
   -ú:bəN 'to enter'   -áaG^W 'to bite'
Most descriptive stems are disyllabic (see Section 631). The basic
forms have been set up in the following fashion: if the medial consonant
is an obstruent, the shape is usually cv́cv-; if a glottalized sonorant, it
is usually cvı́cv-; if a plain sonorant, it is usually cv̂cv- (before {R$_1$},
cvı̂cv- (elsewhere). By setting up the disyllabic descriptives in this way,
the forms with {R$_1$} and {L} can be accounted for by the application of
$\|18, 20, 21, 28$:
   ćápi- + {R$_1$} > ćápipi-: ćápipici 'it has lots of spots'; cf. ćápici
      'it has a spot'
   táka- + {R$_1$} > $\|$tákaka-$\|18$, $\|$tákáka-$\|21$, $\|$takáka-$\|22$: takákaci
      'they are square'; cf. tákaci 'it is square'
   mu:̓ra- + {R$_1$} > $\|$mu:̓rara-$\|18$, $\|$mú:̓rára-$\|20$, $\|$murára-$\|22$:
      muráraka 'they got dented'; cf. muráka 'it got dented'

bêre- + {R$_1$} > ‖ bêrere- ‖ 18, ‖ bérere- ‖ 28: bérereci 'it is smooth'

síḱa- + {L} > síiḱa-: síiḱaka 'it got several wrinkles'; cf. síḱaka
    'it got one wrinkle'

ću꞉ýu- + {L} > ‖ ću·꞉ýu- ‖ 18, ‖ ćú·ẏu- ‖ 20: ćúuẏuka 'the road is
    washed out in several places'; cf. ćuẏúka 'the road is washed
    out in one place'

kaꞏ꞉yu- + {L} > ‖ kaꞏ·꞉yu- ‖ 18, ‖ kâ·yu- ‖ 20: kâayuka 'they broke'; cf.
    káyúka 'it broke'

There are a few forms that do not fit the canon: će꞉źə- 'broken (of
string or something long)'; sḱəꞏ꞉ di- 'round'; ḱuꞏ꞉du- varying freely with
ḱûdu- 'spherical'; sgə꞉źə- varying (freely?) with sgə́źə- 'warped'; kə꞉źə-
varying (freely?) with kə́źə- 'pink'.

Suffixes are of three phonological types: (1) initial vowel (cf. rule ‖ 1),
(2) initial replacive morphophoneme ‖ ꞊ ‖ (always followed by a vowel; cf.
‖ 2), and (3) initial consonant (cf. ‖ 4). All the suffixes of the second type
have allomorphs with a vowel, that is, without ‖ ꞊ ‖. Some suffixes of the
third type have allomorphs with an initial vowel, either by adding the
vowel (cf. -iguyaN, -guyaN, rule ‖ 1) or by subtracting the consonant (cf.
-ńáaťaN, -qáaťaN, -qjáaťaN, rule ‖ 1).

The remaining morpheme classes are not characterized by any particular canonical shape. Disyllabic morphemes are more common than monosyllabic. Most of the monosyllabic morphemes are commonly occurring
adverbs.

223. A large number of morphophonemic rules are ordered in respec
to each other. Thus in séigáyási 'when I was setting the trap' (theme
-áigayaẂ, suffixes -səø and -(ꞌ)í), rule ‖ 4 (accent loss with -səø) must
be applied before ‖ 19 (accent ablaut). Otherwise *séigáyasi would result
However, not all the rules are so ordered. Rules ‖ 1-4 pertain only to
suffixation, and ‖ 5-10 pertain only to prefixation. It would be possible
to reverse the order of these two groups of rules. The tightest ordering
of the rules is found in ‖ 18-30; some of these rules can be placed in a
different order (for example, ‖ 29 and ‖ 30 could be reversed), but the
choices are fewer than with respect to the earlier rules. Most of these
later rules reflect historical changes that have taken place since Proto-
Keres times.

Many of the earlier rules contain several subrules. If these subrules
had been treated in the same way that separate rules are treated, many
of them could be ordered in respect to each other. Thus ‖ 1.5 states
that ‖ Ẃ ‖ becomes ‖ M ‖ before certain suffixes (‖ 1.2) and becomes ‖ W ‖
before others (‖ 1.4). If these subrules were ordered, ‖ 1.5 would come
before ‖ 1.2 and ‖ 1.4.

The order between some rules is occasionally reversed. This was seen in the application of ‖21 and ‖30 (discussed under ‖30) and in the application of ‖21 and ‖22 (discussed under ‖22, footnote 16). Rule ‖21 accounts for the addition of an accent with certain short syllables, ‖22 for the loss of an accent with certain short syllables. Thus the two rules are working in opposite directions, and this is probably why there are a few exceptions in the ordering of the two. There are a large number of forms which demonstrate that the rules have been placed in the proper order. Note that ‖21 operates when (1) the following consonant is glottalized and (2) the following syllable is unaccented. One of the conditions for ‖22 is that the following syllable be accented. We may guess that historically the addition of the accent before glottalized consonants took place before both accented and unaccented syllables. The accent was then lost before an accented syllable by the later historical change reflected in ‖22. On the other hand, ‖21 optionally operates on some forms with the suffixes -ńáaťaN, -qáayaN, and -ńú, in spite of the fact that the following syllable is accented. These forms are difficult to interpret historically. It does not seem possible to treat them as analogical reformations, because most forms with these suffixes have a preceding unaccented syllable.

In ‖6, 7.2, 7.9, 9.4 accent changes are described in which the accent following the thematic syllable is either lost or shifted to the preceding syllable. The accent changes that involve ‖:‖ in ‖20 are somewhat analogous. Very likely the several rules reflect one historical change, but due to some differences in the accent changes it is not practical, in some cases not possible, to incorporate them in one rule.

230. Allomorphy of the Pronominal Prefixes

Pronominal prefixes are used with verb, ambivalent, and noun themes. There are four sets (table 9) which stand in allomorphic relationship to each other. The exact number of sets recognized is arbitrary. Fewer sets could be set up by having more complex rules for the coarticulation morphophonemes (‖10,11) and/or by listing more allomorphs within each set. More sets could be recognized by listing fewer allomorphs in each set and having less complex rules for the coarticulation morphophonemes. The crux of the problem lies in the intimate relationship between the pronominal prefix sets and the coarticulation morphophonemes.

A pronominal prefix is often a portmanteau morpheme. It indicates (1) the subject of the verb or the possessor of the noun, (2) the object

TABLE 9

Pronominal Prefixes

	Person	Nonmodal	Dubitative	Hortative
Set I	1(-3)	sj-, śj-	tV?j-	ka-
	2(-3)	ṣ-	c̣-	p-, ?-
	3(-3)	g-	dy-	pV?j-
	obv.	gj-	dyj-	pj-
	1-2	ṣa-	c̣a-	ṣa-
	3-2	g-əẓ-	ẓ-əẓ-	p-əẓ-
	2-1	dyu-	dyu-	gu-
	3-1	sgu-	d-əẓ-	n-əẓ-
Set II	1st	s-	t-, tV?-	k-
	2nd	ṣ-	c̣-	č̣-, č̣úu-, č̣uu-
	3rd	g-, s-	dy-	p-, pV?-
Set III	1st	s-	tV?-	n-
	2nd	g-əẓ-	ẓ-əẓ-	ẓ-
	3rd	g-	dy-	p-
Set IV	1st	ṣ-, s-əẓ-	d-əẓ-	n-əẓ-
	2nd	g-əẓ-	ẓ-əẓ-	ẓ-
	3rd	g-	dy-	p-

Other Pronominal Prefixes

Negative, 1-(3)	sg- (all sets)
Indefinite	sg- (all sets)
Expective	nj-, ńj- (set I)
	n- (sets II, III)
	n-əẓ- (set IV)

Set I only:

Negative, 3-1	sgj-
Indefinite-obviative	sgj-

Distributive (see Section 233):

Nonmodal	ṣ̌-, sk- (all sets?)
Dubitative	st́-, sč̣- (all sets?)

for transitive themes only, and (3) optionally, the mode for verb themes only.

All of the prefixes of Set I are used with transitive themes. The static themes use 3-1, 3-2, and obviate prefixes for the first, second, and third persons. The remaining theme classes take only those prefixes which are used for third person object with transitive themes.

There are one nonmodal and three modal series of prefixes. Two of the modes, the dubitative and the hortative, have full paradigms. The third mode, the negative, is defective.

There are also indefinite, expective, and distributive prefixes. The indefinite prefix does not distinguish mode. The expective, used with an auxiliary in periphrastic constructions (Section 471), is not properly a pronominal prefix, but it functions tactically and morphophonemically like one, and can best be treated with them. The two distributive prefixes, the nonmodal and dubitative, are treated in Section 233.

An empty morph ‖-əẓ-‖ is used after some of the pronominal prefixes. When it is found, it forms a tight unit with the pronominal prefix and behaves, tactically, as a single morpheme. It is impossible to attach any meaning to ‖-əẓ-‖ or to predict its occurrence. It is therefore listed in the combinations in which it occurs. The preceding pronominal prefix usually has identical or similar forms which lack the empty morph in other sets.

231. The occurrence of the pronominal prefix sets can be predicted in part by the initial coarticulation morphophoneme and in part by the thematic class. The thematic classes, transitive, static, intransitive-A, intransitive-B, impersonal, inalienably possessed nouns, and ambivalents are treated in Sections 410, 510, and 520. In some cases it is impossible to predict the set, and the set must be listed with the theme (when theme and stem are coterminous) or with the thematic affix (when the theme is derived from a stem).

Set I is used with: all transitive and static themes; most intransitive-A, impersonal, inalienably possessed noun themes; and a few intransitive-B themes. The few intransitive-A themes that do not take set I are also irregular in their formations with the number prefixes, and in the list given in ‖7.10 such themes are marked as to which set they take. Almost all themes with an initial palatalizing morphophoneme take set I.

Set II is used principally with intransitive-B themes. It is also used with a few impersonal and intransitive-B themes and for a part of the paradigm of one transitive theme listed in Section 234. Almost all themes with initial ‖Q‖ take set II. All intransitive B themes with initial ‖'‖ take set II.

Set III is used with themes that have initial ‖A‖ and themes formed
with the possessive thematic prefix -qa-. It is also used with the following inalienably possessed noun themes:

-qjîiḱa 'mouth, lips'
-qjîiṁúuča 'upper lip, snout'
-qjíipee 'ear'
-qjíišəə 'nose'
-Aúučíyátiṣa 'shin'
-Aûuṁa 'vagina'
-Aúumúča 'buttocks'
-Aúunúuti 'ankle'
-Aúušúkuciṣa 'elbow'
-qâanáa 'eye'
-qáiskâaṁi 'calf of leg'
-qayáatiima 'wisdom tooth'

The inalienably possessed noun themes that have initial ‖qj‖ take either
set I or III. Because of the operation of the morphophonemic rules ‖11
only the second person shows the variation:

Set I	Set III	
ṣîiṁúuča	ṣîiṁúuča	'my lip'
šîiṁúuča	kədîiṁúuča	'your lip'
čîiṁúuča	čîiṁúuča	'his lip'
sṭîiṁúuča	sṭîiṁúuča	'one's lip'

The inalienably possessed noun themes that have initial ‖A‖ may replace
the ‖A‖ with ‖a‖ and take set I. Because of the operation of the morphophonemic rules (‖10.3, 13) only the first and second persons show the
variations:

Set I, theme	Set III, theme	
-áumúča	-Aúumúča	
séumúča	ṣúumúča	'my buttocks'
ṣáumúča	kuẓúumúča	'your buttocks'
gáumúča	gáumúča	'his buttocks'
sgáumúča	sgáumúča	'one's buttocks'

When a number prefix is present, set IV is used with intransitive-A,
ambivalent, and inalienably possessed noun themes. A few intransitive-A
themes do not take set IV under these conditions. These themes are also
irregular in their formations with the number prefixes, and in the list
given in ‖7.10 such themes are marked as to which set they take. Set
IV is also used with the singular forms of: -aʔáu 'sister of a woman';
the auxiliaries {zá} and {zé} (Section 461.8-9); -jéeguyaN 'to be making',
irregular continuative form of -ʼjíizaaN 'to make'.

The pronominal prefix sets are illustrated by the nonmodal paradigms
of -úukačaN 'to see' (set I); -'úučáwaN 'to steal' (set II); -qáanáwé 'uncle'
(set III); -aʔánáwé 'uncle', dual possessor (set IV):

   síukača 'I saw him'

   s̩úukača 'you saw him'

   gúukača 'he saw him'

   zíukača 'the other one saw him'

   s̩áukača 'I saw you'

   kuz̩úukača 'he saw you'

   dyúukača 'you saw me'

   sgúukača 'he saw me'

   súučáẇa 'I stole'

   s̩úučáẇa 'you stole'

   kúučáẇa 'he stole'

   śáanáwé 'my uncle'

   kəz̩áanáwé 'your uncle'

   ḱáanáwé 'his uncle'

   s̩aʔáanáwé 'our (dual) uncle'

   kəz̩aʔáanáwé 'your (dual) uncle'

   gaʔáanáwé 'their (dual) uncle'

232. The set I prefixes śj- 1-3 person nonmodal and ńj- expective,
allomorphs of sj- and nj- respectively, are used with transitive themes
that have a number suffix. The allomorphs are illustrated with -úukačaN
'to see':

   síukača 'I saw him', prefix sj-

   síukačáńa 'we (plural) saw him', prefix śj-

   niukačagú 'he will see him', prefix nj-

   ńíukačáńəḱúuʔu 'they (dual) will see him', prefix ńj-

Stems that have initial ‖J‖ and ‖J̄‖ glottalize the prefixes sj- and nj-
by the regular application of the morphophonemic rules (‖10.1, 11.1) and
thus do not normally reflect the distinction between the two groups of
allomorphs. Compare the forms with -JućáadyaN:

   síćaatya 'I pinned it', prefix sj-

   síćáadyáńətyə 'we (dual) pinned it', prefix śj-

However, when the dual or plural prefix is used to show number of object,
the ‖J‖ or ‖J̄‖ is lost (‖7) and the alternation between the two groups
of allomorphs is seen:

   sêiʔíćaatya 'I pinned them (plural)'

   śêiʔíćaadyáńətyə 'we (dual) pinned them (plural)'

The set I second person hortative prefix has two allomorphs, p- and ʔ-. The former is used with transitive and intransitive-B themes, the latter with intransitive-A themes:

    púukača 'look at it!' (transitive)

    páinúustúzí 'put the fire out!' (intransitive-B)

    ʔíibái 'sleep!' (intransitive-A)

    ʔə́ska 'drink!' (intransitive-A)

The set II prefixes tVʔ- first person dubitative and pVʔ- third person hortative are used before ‖'i‖. Their allomorphs t- and p- are used elsewhere. Examples are with the themes -íceetaaN and -úwagəN:

    tiʔíceeta 'did you dance?'

    piʔíceeta 'let him dance!'

    túwakə 'did I get dressed?'

    púwakə 'let him get dressed!'

The second person hortative prefix of set II has three allomorphs. čuu- is used before ‖Qau‖; čúu- is used before ‖'áʔu‖ (always from the thematic prefix {-'áʔ-} plus ‖u‖ or ‖u:‖, see ‖5.3); and č- is used else-where. The vowels of čuu- and čúu- replace the thematic syllable, and the accent of čúu- replaces the accent of the thematic syllable. In this respect the prefix behaves more like a thematic prefix (‖5.1-2) than a pronominal prefix (‖13). In addition the thematic accent is sometimes replaced by the high accent after č-, and if the following syllable begins with a glottalized sonorant (through the operation of ‖5.6) it is replaced by a plain sonorant. The conditions for this change are unknown:

    čúukúya 'take them!', prefix čuu-, theme -QáukúyaW

    čúutáawaca 'boil it!', prefix čúu-, theme -'áʔutáawazaN

    čáaspanašú 'wash your hair!', prefix č-, theme -QáasbanašúM(m̊eN)

        (waN)

    čayâuʔu 'take it!', prefix č-, theme -'ayâaʔB

    čúwíica 'make it!', prefix č-, theme -'uwíizaN

    čáipéetuca 'wet your lips!', prefix č-, theme -'áʔipéetuzaN

The set II prefix s-, third person nonmodal, is used with one theme, -'jíšə: zə́əsíšə 'it is small' (prefix zə́ə-, Section 660). The first person nonmodal form is homophonous and apparently for this reason is seldom used with this theme.

Set IV has two allomorphs for the first person nonmodal prefix, s-əẓ used after ‖j‖, and ṣ-, used elsewhere:

    sətéeyu 'we (dual) went', theme -qjéeyu∅

    ṣâaʔáci 'we (dual) arrived', theme -âaʔáciN

Many more examples will be found in ‖7.10.

233. I did not record the distributive prefixes for very many paradigms, and as a result it is difficult to isolate the morphophonemic
properties of these prefixes. The allomorphs š́- (nonmodal) and st́- (dubitative) were the most common forms elicited in paradigms. They were
usually given with plural themes. Unexplained vowel changes sometimes
occur:

š́igûuʔu 'many are pregnant', theme -JugûuʔN

š́íityu, st́íityu 'they all arrived' (nonmodal, dubitative), plural
     theme -jéedyuB

š́áaẏáamáazáńa, st́áaẏáamáazáńa 'everyone helped' (nonmodal, dubi-
     tative), plural theme -áaẏáamáazaN-qaaD

š́íimə, st́íimə 'everyone left' (nonmodal, dubitative), plural theme
     -jêemə́N

š́éečâimiši, st́éečâimiši 'everyone had their eyes closed' (nonmodal,
     dubitative), plural theme -qjéečái ʔM-išiiD (?)

A few forms have been recorded with sk- (nonmodal) and sč- (dubitative). These forms have a high text frequency:

skâuʔu, sčâuʔu 'they dwelled; there was a large crowd' (nonmodal,
     dubitative), theme -Aâuʔu

skâamá, sčâamá 'they dwelled; there was a large crowd' (nonmodal,
     dubitative), theme -Aâamá

skáakuẏáaťa, sčáakuẏáaťa 'they would keep coming' (nonmodal, dubi-
     tative), plural theme -jeʔéguY plus suffix {-ńáaťaN}

234. A few themes have allomorphs that are conditioned by the pronominal prefixes.[22] Four transitive themes have two allomorphs: the
first used with the 1-3, 2-3, and 3-3 person prefixes; the second with
other prefixes (the indefinite and distributive have not been recorded):

-áaG^W, -JáaG^W 'to bite'

-âaẃistuuzaN, -JâaẃistuuzaN 'to pinch'

-û:níM, -JûníM 'to know'

-Qâaẓədeya, -JâaẓədeyaW(N) 'to run after'

The first allomorph of the last theme takes set II prefixes (the second
allomorph takes set I, as is usual for transitive themes). The nonmodal
paradigm of -áaG^W illustrates the allomorphs:

1-3	séeku 'I bit him'		1-2	ṣáaku 'I bit you'
2-3	ṣáaku 'you bit him'		3-2	kəẓáaku 'he bit you'
3-3	gáaku 'he bit him'		2-1	ťyáaku 'you bit me'
obv.	čáaku 'the other one bit him'		3-1	skáaku 'he bit me'

---

[22]Some auxiliaries have allomorphs of this type. These are treated in Section
460 rather than here.

The transitive theme 'to whip' has three allomorphs: -íišaayaN after 1-3 person prefixes, -ušáayaN after 2-3 and 3-3 person prefixes, and -JíišaayaN after other persons and the expective prefix. The first two allomorphs cannot be set up as *-u:šaayaN (for example, like -û:níM, above) because the 1-3 nonmodal form is síišaaya rather than *síušaaya.

The transitive theme 'to make, do to' also has three allomorphs: -ʼjíizaaN after 1-3, 2-3, and 3-3 person prefixes, -íizaaN after obviative prefixes, and -JíizaaN after other persons and the expective prefix.

The transitive theme 'to go after, invite' has two allomorphs: -u:deeY after ‖j‖ and ‖a‖ and the number prefixes and -u:diiY elsewhere:

    1-3   síute 'I went after him'
    3-3   kudí 'he went after him'
    1-2   sáute 'I went after you'
    3-1   skudí 'he went after me'
    {dl}   gûuʔute 'he went after them (dual)'

Three intransitive-A themes have two allomorphs:

    -JíičəB (1st and exp.), -aʔáčəB (elsewhere) 'to be enclosed, inside'
        set I
    -qâanazədeyaW(N) (3rd), -âanazədeyaW(N) (elsewhere) 'to walk,
        wander', set I
    -ázáaN (1st and exp.), -qázáaN (3rd) 'to be talkative', set III

For the last theme either allomorph could be considered as occurring after the second person, since all second person prefixes of set III end in ‖z‖ (see ‖11.4).

The intransitive-A theme zúu- 'to go' (dual -qjéeyuɸ, plural -jeʔéguY see ‖7.10) has special forms with the second person hortative prefix (ʔ- set I, z- set IV):

    ʔîimá 'go!', theme -îimá
    t́eemá 'go (dual)!', theme -qjéemá
    déegûumá 'to (plural)!', theme -jéegûumá

235. The accent is irregularly shifted to the empty morph with three themes: -û:kasdáayaN 'to invite someone', transitive theme; -û:hima 'to believe', static theme; -ázáaN, -qázáaN 'to be talkative', intransitive-A theme:

    gúc̦ukasdáaya 'he invited you'
    dúc̦ukasdáaya 'he invited me (dubitative)'
    gúc̦uhima 'you believed'

236. The pronominal prefixes nú-, zú-, and ʔé- (first, second and third persons) are found with the theme -dyu and its derivative -dyuyú (see Section 560):

nútyu 'and me?; how about me?'   nútyuyú 'my turn'

ẓútyu 'and you?'   ẓútyuyú 'your turn'

ʔétyu 'and him?'   ʔétyuyú 'his turn'

The modal, expective, and indefinite prefixes are not used with these
themes.

240. Allomorphy of the Plural Suffix

241. The plural suffix {-qeeD} has the allomorphs -qaaD, -qeeD, -eeD,
-aaD, -ʔVVD, and -iiD. The choice of the allomorph is normally dependent upon the preceding final morphophonemic consonant, as described
in rule ‖1. When the plural suffix is used as a derivational or harmonic
plural suffix, it sometimes has other allomorphs or allomorphs that are
not determined by the regular application of ‖1. The forms involved are
the passive derivations (Section 411), harmonic plurals of themes with
the possessive prefix (Section 413, 521), and the harmonic plurals of
certain intransitive-A themes. The harmonic plurals of themes derived
by the prefix {-Jaẏa-} (Section 413) always use the regular set of allomorphs.

Passive derivations take the regular set of allomorphs varying with
-qiiD (and probably -iiD before those final morphophonemic consonants
that do not take suffixes with an initial ‖q‖; see ‖1.s): ćaʔáawagə́ni ~
ćaʔáawagə́na 'his clothes were worn', stem -ú:wagəN. The speaker gave
the forms with -qiiD only in texts and always corrected them to the regular form when paradigmatic data were being elicited on the basis of the
texts.

Possessive verb and ambivalent themes have several similarities. Both
are formed by the possessive thematic prefix {-qaᵗ}, which is added to
verb stems in the case of possessive verbs or to nouns in the case of
ambivalents. Both forms take a harmonic plural suffix, which usually has
the allomorph -iiD after possessive verb themes and -šiiD after ambivalents:

ṣáastyuwaańiši 'we are sweating', verb theme -qasdyúwaaN-qiṢ
    (see ‖7.9)

ṣáwíṭuunímiši 'we are careful', verb theme -qáwíṭuunímiṢ

gáaṁáacâazáńiši 'they have jerked meat', verb theme
    -qaṁáacâazaN-qiṢ

ḱáastyuwimi 'they have suspenders on', verb theme -qáasdyuwiM

gáakabáanáši 'their cornbread', noun kabáaná

gáakawéši 'their coffee', noun kawé

A few themes take -mišiiD or other irregular endings:

gáaháišiimiši 'their tonsils', noun háišii

ṣáasíiṣumiši 'our name', noun síiṣu

gáabáaṣumiši ~ gáabáaṣuši 'their straw', noun báaṣu

gáišíimí 'they own some', verb theme -qáiši

Note that the ambivalent theme does not end with a final morphophonemic consonant, whereas the verb theme does. Most possessive verb themes have a final ‖Ṣ‖, either as part of the verb stem or as part of the completive suffix {-qiṢ} which is common with these forms. The result is that both the possessive verb and ambivalent usually have the final phonemic sequence /-ši/ in the plural.

A number of intransitive-A themes take the harmonic plural. All such themes have irregular number prefix formations and are listed, along with the harmonic plural, in ‖7.10. Sometimes the regular set of allomorphs is used:

ćéestyape 'they nursed', plural theme -qjéesdyaB, allomorph -eeD

ćêeťaatyəme 'they got up', plural theme -qjêeťaadyəM̄, allomorph -eeD

gâašiyawa 'they won', plural theme -âašiyaW, allomorph -aaD

Sometimes the allomorphs -iiD and -eeD, regular after certain final morphophonemic consonants, are used after final morphophonemic consonants that do not otherwise take these allomorphs:

səťéezáapəni 'we fell in', plural theme -qjéezáabəN, allomorph -iiD

ṣâakayani 'we are stuck', plural theme -âagayaN, allomorph -iiD

ṣâakáani ~ ṣâakáane 'we heard it', plural theme -âakáaN, allomorph -iiD, -eeD (or -qiiD, -qeeD?; see ‖26)

ṣáaćáaçaste 'we listened', plural theme -qáaćáazaSD, allomorph -eeɪ

242. The plural suffix combines with the continuative suffixes {ᵌitaaN} and {ᵌáayaN} (Section 441) to form portmanteau morphs, or more properl portmanteau allomorphs. The continuative suffixes have a number of allomorphs. All the allomorphs of {ᵌitaaN} but one include the morphophonemic sequence ‖taaN‖, and all the allomorphs of {ᵌáayaN} include the morphophonemic sequence ‖áayaN‖. The rule can be formulated as:

‖taaN‖ + {-qeeD} > ‖tiyaaD‖

‖áayaN‖ + {-qeeD} > ‖áitiyaaD‖

Any morphophonemic sequence of the continuative allomorphs that precedᵉ the sequences ‖taaN‖ and ‖áayaN‖ is retained in the portmanteau morpʰ

ća?áyəᵊcitiyaatiku 'he would be getting hit', theme -qja?áyəᵊzaN, suffixes ᵌitaaN, -qeeD (ᵌitiyaaD), -iku

kuẃáńatyumetiya 'they would get hurt', theme -‘úńadyumeN, suffixeˢ -taaN, -qeeD (-tiyaaD)

śíutaatáitiya 'we put it out to dry', theme -uːťaaSD, suffixes -qáayaN,
   -qeeD (-qáitiyaD)

A few themes show similar changes with the plural suffix (all of the
themes take (TSE), ‖ 9):

Theme	With -qeeD
-ʻucítistaaN	-ʻúwácítistitiyaaD 'to think'
-ʻubêecistaaN	-ʻúwábêecistitiyaaD 'to pray'
-ʻúuwíšáayaN	-ʻúwáwíšáitiyaaD 'to play'

These forms cannot be considered as containing a continuative suffix,
because a continuative suffix can be added: sucítistíitita 'I keep on thinking about it' (empty morph ꞊qíit- + -itaaN, see Section 441).

300. INTRODUCTION TO THE GRAMMAR

A basic division is made in this grammar between morphology (Sections 400-600) and syntax (Section 700), that is, arrangements within words and arrangements between words. The division is in part arbitrary, but none the less useful. It is not hard to maintain except in a few constructions, the most important being those that include auxiliary verbs (Sections 470, 630) and subordinating suffixes (Section 760). A few general observations can be made regarding the characteristics of the grammatical word. Plus juncture usually can occur at the grammatical word boundary, but juncture also is found within a few words (‖24). While there are certain basic rules which must be observed, a great deal of freedom is allowed in word order, and discontinuous immediate constituents are not infrequent. Morpheme order is rigid within a word; discontinuous immediate constituents occur within words, but always conforming to the strict rules of position of occurrence. Most morphophonemic alternations take place within word boundaries.

Inflection is limited entirely to verbs and nouns. Derivation is found with verbs, nouns, descriptives, and certain adverbs. The morphology is described in three sections. Section 400 describes the morphology of the verb theme, and Section 500 the noun theme. Section 600 describes the remaining morphology: verb and noun derivation that is not related to theme formation, adverbial derivation, and the use of auxiliaries and auxiliary complements.

A few definitions are in order. A verb theme is a form to which pronominal prefixes are added to form a verb. A verb stem is a form to which thematic affixes are added to form verb themes. Some verb themes do not include a thematic affix; the stem and theme are coterminous for such forms. A verb stem may be either a single morpheme, or it may be a derived form.

Possessed nouns show a similar hierarchical structure. A noun theme is a form to which pronominal prefixes are added to form a possessed noun. A noun theme may be either a single morpheme, or it may be derived from a noun.

[110]

Most of the morphology and syntax revolves around the verb. A verb includes a pronominal prefix which indicates subject and for transitive verbs also indicates object. The sentence mirrors the verbal relationships, but the reflection is not perfect: the favorite sentence type consists of a verb, which normally can take an optional noun subject, and, if the verb is transitive, an optional noun object.

The noun system, second in importance to the verb, can be characterized as a watered-down verb system. All of the inflectional affixes found with the noun are also found with the verb, but not vice versa. One subclass, ambivalent nouns (Section 520), can also function as verbs, and when so functioning can be inflected for categories otherwise restricted to verbs. A possessed noun includes a pronominal prefix which indicates possessor. A possessed noun can enter into a syntactic construction with a possessor noun, a construction that is analogous to a sentence consisting of a subject noun and a verb. Nouns can also be used to form a noun plus noun sentence. Unlike the verb, the noun need not have a pronominal prefix to be a free form.

These remarks characterize the main stream of the language system. They show that there is a parallelism between the morphology and syntax and between the verb and noun system. But there are also many eddies and some cross currents, seen for example in the infinitive (Sections 420, 720), the subordinating suffixes (Section 760), the locative adverbial phrase (Section 741), and the directionals (Section 652).

The units of morphology (morphemes) and syntax (words) can be grouped, very roughly, into three categories: (1) nuclear units, for example, verb stems, noun themes, and descriptives in morphology; verbs and nouns in syntax, (2) modifiers, for example, nonthematic verb suffixes, adverbs, and demonstratives, and (3) function units, for example, inflectional and thematic affixes, conjunctions, and certain locative adverbs. These categories have no significance for the organization of the following sections but are listed to give some idea of the character of Acoma. It would be difficult to use them as pivotal points in the grammar because many morpheme and word classes fit into more than one of these categories, their placement depending upon the given construction they are in. The nuclear units can be assigned lexical meaning; they are the basic terms in communication behavior. The modifiers limit or more carefully define the nuclear units and can less clearly be assigned lexical meaning. The function units are the glue of Acoma grammar. They define the interrelationships between the other units. The nuclear and function units figure more heavily in the morphology, the modifiers in the syntax, but all the units are common in both systems. Acoma is neither a 'syntax language' nor a 'morphology language', though morphology is given a somewhat heavier load.

There are some groups of words which are on the periphery of the grammatical system of any language and only rarely are they incorporated into it. In Acoma these are interjections and baby-talk words. Some interjections are brought into the grammatical system when they are inflected by means of auxiliary verbs (Section 632.6). Interjections include words like ʔáyáaʔá 'ouch' (man speaking), ʔáyaaʔá 'ouch' (woman speaking), ʔáiʔiši 'ouch' (child speaking), bíisti 'shut up, behave!' ('to be quiet' when inflected with an auxiliary), ʔímíi 'Oh, I'm scared', ʔáyá 'drat it' ('to dread doing it' when inflected with an auxiliary).

Baby talk is phonetically and apparently functionally similar to Comanche baby talk as described by Casagrande.[1] The Acomas used baby-talk words in speaking to their children in my presence, but this constituted only a limited experience, since I did not do any of the field work at Acoma. Unlike Comanche, the system is very much alive. It is said to be used in talking to very young children "to make it easy for them." I have collected about thirty baby-talk words, and I suspect the number is much larger. Examples are: yáayáa 'mother', dyáadyáa 'daddy', gə̂əgə́ 'rabbit', hə́əyáa 'bite', ʔáka+ʔáka 'drink', babáu 'sleep'. For every baby-talk word there is a corresponding word in adult speech.

Interjections and baby-talk words are used alone and are complete predications by themselves. The latter, especially, have a wide range in meaning when so used, for example, ʔáka+ʔáka means 'you drink!; did you drink?; I want a drink; I had a drink', etc. These words will not be further treated in the grammar.

---

[1] "Comanche Baby Language," IJAL 14.11-14 (1948).

400. VERB THEMES

The relative position of the verbal affixes is shown in table 10. Prefixes occupy positions one through three, the verb stem occupies position four, and suffixes occupy positions five through ten. Normally only one affix fills a given position at a time. Occasionally a verb has been recorded that has two affixes of the same position class. Some of these forms are possibly mistakes, ungrammatical slips of the tongue. There are some variations in the relative order, and a few affixes are not listed in the table. These are described in the course of this chapter.

The verb stem may consist of a single morpheme, or it may be derived by suffixation and/or compounding (see Sections 610, 620).

Thematic affixes fill positions three, six, and ten. The position of suffix -nú is unknown, because it has not been recorded in coöccurrence with other suffixes. It is placed in position six because it, like -'í?iD, is a thematic suffix.

Inflectional affixes fill positions one (pronominal prefixes), two (number prefixes), and seven (number suffixes). Nonthematic suffixes fill positions five, eight, and nine.

The following sections are based on the immediate constituents of the verb theme, rather than on the relative order of the affixes. Immediate constituents are often discontinuous. Illustrative examples will be given phonemically and morphemically. Forms will not be given in their morphophonemic shape except when specifically indicated. In most cases, however, the morphemic writing is identical with the morphophonemic writing.

410. Thematic Derivation

There are two general types of themes, derived and underived. Derived themes are composed of a verb stem plus thematic affix(es). Nonthematic affixes are also used in some thematic derivations. Nonderived themes make no distinction between stem and theme; the stem is the theme.

TABLE 10

Verb Affix Positions

1	2	3	4	5	6	7	8	9	10
Pron. pref.	{dl}	Thematic prefixes	Verb stem	=itaaN	-ʼʔiD	-qədyeeZ	-ńáaɬaN	-qiŞ	-sú
	{pl}			=ʼáayaN	-ńú	-qeeD	-ńáaɬaN-seɸ		
				-iguyaN			-seɸ-ńáaɬaN		
				ɸes-					
				-Gʷ					
				-qeeY					
				-izaadyaaN					
				-naiʔM					
				-duɸ(N)					

Verb themes are divided into five classes, differentiated on the basis of the kinds of combinations they enter into with inflectional affixes that mark person and number (Section 430):

(1) Transitive themes indicate subject and object for all persons. Number for subject is indicated by the number suffixes, for object by the number prefixes.

(2) Static themes indicate first, second, third, and indefinite subject by the 3-1, 3-2, obviative, and indefinite-obviative prefixes, respectively. Number is indicated by the number prefixes.

(3) Intransitive-A themes indicate subject for all persons and number by the number prefixes.

(4) Intransitive-B themes also indicate subject for all persons, but indicate number by the number suffixes instead of the number prefixes.

(5) Impersonal themes indicate third person subject and do not indicate number.

411. The transitive derivations are:

(1) {tr-1} + Stem: direct transitive
(2) {tr-2} + Stem: indirect transitive
(3) -J̄- + Stem + -'í?iD: benefactive

The morphophonemics of the prefixes is treated in ‖5.5. All the themes take set I pronominal prefixes.

The direct transitive means 'to do it to someone or something'; the indirect transitive 'to do it to something belonging to someone'; the benefactive 'to do it for someone'. Examples:

kupúḱuca 'she sprinkled it', g- {tr-1} -ûupúḱuzaN
séeskə 'I fried it', sj- {tr-1} -áasgəN
zíicitamaca 'he turned it over', g- {tr-1} -íicitamazaN
skubáya 'he burned me', sgu- {tr-1} -ubáyaN
gûupúḱuca 'she sprinkled his', g- {tr-2} -ûupúḱuzaN
séeskə 'I fried his', sj- {tr-2} -áasgəN
gúucitamaca 'he turned over hers', g- {tr-2} -íicitamazaN
sgûupaya 'he burned mine', sg- {tr-2} -ubáyaN
zíucitamacaní 'he turned it over for her', g- -J̄- -íicitamazaN
    -'í?iD
séeskəní 'I cooked it for him', sj- -J̄- -áasgəN -'í?iD
síušíicaní 'I borrowed it for him', sj- -J̄- -úušíizaN -'í?iD
síutaiskaaní 'I peeled it for him', sj- -J̄- -u꞉daiskaaM(N) -'í?iD

A number of ‖uu‖ stems that do not distinguish the direct and the indirect transitive take either {tr-1} or {tr-2}. The meaning of the resulting themes seems to be the same as that of the direct transitive:

zíuṣá 'he approved of him', g- {tr-1} -úuṣâaN

gúukača 'he saw him', g- {tr-2} -úukačaN

The morphophoneme ‖ J̄ ‖ is almost always a representation of the benefactive prefix -J̄-. Most of the exceptions are found with classificatory themes (Section 450). It is almost possible to set up {-J̄- . . . -ʼíʔiD} as a discontinuous affix. There are, however, a very few examples of the suffix with nontransitive themes that lack the prefix -J̄-: čaýáwíisṫitaaníitiku 'it would be counted for them' (passive static); gáaýáakúýapikuyaníináaṫa 'they always give away' (intransitive-A). This use of the benefactive suffix appears to be irregular. It is clearly not a thematic affix in these forms.

412. The static derivations are:

(1) -qjaʔa- + Stem (+ -qeeD): passive

(2) Stem + -du∅(N): inchoative static

(3) Stem + -ńú

The themes take set I pronominal prefixes.

The addition of the plural suffix -qeeD to the passive theme is optional. The morphophonemics of the prefix is treated in ‖5.2, the plural suffix in 241. The theme means that the subject was acted upon by an unstated agent. It is often translated by the English passive or the English active with an undefined 'they' as subject. Examples:

sᵏaʔáašíizáńa ~ sᵏaʔáašíica 'it was borrowed from me', sgu-
   -qjaʔa- -úušíizaN (-qéeD)

sᵏaʔačáwáńa 'it was stolen from me', sgu- -qjaʔa- -učáwaN -qeeD

sᵏaʔáẃagśńa 'my clothes have been worn', sgu- -qjaʔa- -ú:wagǝN
   -qeeD

The second persons of passive themes are indicated by 3-2 or 2-3 pronominal prefixes, in free variation (the 3-2 pronominal prefixes are the regular ones for static themes):

kǝċâaṁayanikuya ~ šâaṁayanikuya 'they made fun of you' (see
   ‖14, 27), prefixes g-ǝẓ-, ṣ-

çǝċâaṁayanikuya ~ čâaṁayanikuya 'did they make fun of you?',
   prefixes ẓ-ǝẓ-, ç-

The inchoative static theme is formed only with stems derived from descriptives plus the suffix -zaN (Section 621). The inchoative suffix -du∅(N), which also has a nonthematic function (Section 442.6), replaces the stem suffix -zaN. The meaning is 'something belonging to the subject got . . .'. Examples:

sgúusṫiẃíẃitu 'mine got wet', sgu- -úusṫi:ẃiẃizaN -du∅(N)

sgúusgǝ́çǝtu 'mine got twisted', sgu- -úusgǝ́ẓǝzaN -du∅(N)

sgúusṫǝǝtu 'it got straight for me', sgu- -úusṫǝǝzaN -du∅(N)

The suffix -ńú occurs with too few stems to be able to determine its morphophonemic properties. The themes often show irregular changes. The forms usually mean 'to be given to . . .-ing'. The following list is exhaustive:

-Juč́áwańú 'to be a thief', stem -uč́áwaN 'to blame, steal'

-úupanú ~ -úpanú 'to be thirsty all the time', stem -paN 'to be dry'

-J́úudyúmiẓańúuṢ 'to be smart, quick to learn', stem -úudyúmiẓaN 'to learn'

-Judyúiťú 'to have respect', stem -ûudyúiti Ṣ 'to respect'

-Jubêeťanú ~ -Jubêeťańú 'to be inquisitive', stem -JubêeťaW 'to ask for information'

The suffix -ńú is probably present in the following themes:

-J́iisťiyańú 'to be nosey' (underived static theme)

-qjúuc̀iskúmeńú 'to be absorbent' (impersonal theme; cf. c̀íci 'water', and the stem -úskúmeN 'to put in liquid')

413. The intransitive-A derivations are:

(1) -qa- + Stem (+ -qiṢ): possessive

(2) -Auu- + Stem (+ -qiṢ): external possessive

(3) -Auu- + Inchoative Static Theme: inchoative intransitive

(4) -Jaýa- + Stem

(5) Stem + -qiṢ + -ṣú

The morphophonemics of the prefixes -Auu- and -Jaýa- is treated under ‖5.2, of -qa- under ‖5.4. Themes with the prefixes -qa- and -Auu- take set III pronominal prefixes. The other themes take set I.

Most possessive themes have the completive suffix -qiṢ (Section 442.7). The plural form takes the harmonic plural suffix (Sections 241, 433). The theme indicates that the subject has something in a certain state; or that the subject himself is in a certain state, caused by an outside agent or caused by the subject himself but incidental to some other activity. Examples:

śásúḿéestaańi 'I have schooling, education', s- -qa- -úsúḿéʔestaaN -qiṢ

k̀ac̀áatya 'he has it pinned', g- -qa- -uc̀áadyaN

k̀adyáwáńi 'he has something stuck in him' (for example, a splinter), g- -qa- -udyáwaN -qiṢ

śác̀ayawáńi 'I am mad', s- -qa- -úc̀ayawaN -qiṢ

śasdyúwaańi 'I have sweat, am sweating', s- -qa- -usdyúwaaN -qiṢ

śáśáńi 'I stepped and left footprints', s- -qa- -áSD -qiṢ

Most external possessive themes have the completive suffix -qiṢ (Section 442.7). The meaning is the same as the possessive theme except that the condition refers to something belonging to the subject. Examples:

gáusúm̆eestaańi 'he has it trained', g- -Auu- -úsúmé?estaaN -qiṢ

gâusdyúwaańi 'his (for example, horse) is sweating', g- -Auu-
   -usdyúwaaN -qiṢ

śûućayawáńi 'I have (him) mad', s- -Auu- -úćayawaN -qiṢ

gâuçəkáńi 'his (for example, cigarettes) have been smoked', g-
   -Auu- -âzəkaN -qiṢ

śûućayuci 'mine has a bullet hole', s- -Auu- -u꞉ćayuzaN -qiṢ

The inchoative intransitive theme is derived from another theme rather
than from a stem. The prefix -Auu- is added to the inchoative static
(Section 412). The meaning of the two themes appears to be identical.
Examples:

gáušáẇitu 'his got fine', g- -Auu- -úušáwidu∅(N)

śúusgóçətu 'mine got twisted', s- -Auu- -úusgózədu∅(N)

Themes derived with the prefix -Jaẏa- usually mean 'to take part in
an activity'. This meaning, however, is not consistently found. The prefix is not uncommon, but the theme derivation is not productive. The
plural form takes the harmonic plural suffix (Section 433). Examples:

śeẏáćayawa 'I got into trouble', sj- -Jaẏa- -úćayawaN (stem, 'to
   get mad')

zaẏâaćawai 'he took part in a stick race', g- -Jaẏa- -âaćawaiY
   (stem, 'to run a stick race')

śeẏáamáaca 'I helped', sj- -Jaẏa- -úumáazaN (stem, 'to help')

zaẏáaḱéesi 'he is jealous', g- -Jaẏa- -úuḱéesiṢ (stem, 'to be
   jealous')

śeẏáašíica 'I borrowed (it)', sj- -Jaẏa- -úušíizaN (stem, to borrow'

Themes formed with the suffix -ṣú always have the completive suffix
-qiṢ. It would be possible, therefore, to set up the suffix as ‖-ú‖ instead of as ‖-ṣú‖ and apply ‖1.10. The meaning is 'the subject knows
how to . . .':

síẏuutaańiṣú 'I know how to sing', sj- -úyúutaaN -qiṢ -ṣú

séẏaceem̆iṣú 'I know how to whitewash', sj- -áyaceeM -qiṢ -ṣú

gáçəkáńiṣú 'he knows how to smoke', g- -ázəkaN -qiṢ -ṣú

414.   The intransitive-B derivations are:

   (1) -ʻ- + Stem: first active
   (2) -ʻá?- + Stem: second active
   (3) -ʻúu- + Stem: reflexive
   (4) -Qa- + Stem: middle voice
   (5) -ʻá?i- + Stem: 'by mouth'
   (6) -ʻi- + Stem: 'by body'
   (7) -ʻáaẏa- + Stem: collective plural

The morphophonemics of these prefixes is described in ‖5.2, 5.3, 5.6.

All the themes take set II pronominal prefixes.

The first four thematic derivations form a complex in which the thematic prefixes are in overlapping distribution. The second active prefix is found almost exclusively with long ‖uu‖ stems that are derived by the stem suffix -zaN (Section 621). The theme usually denotes action upon an object, and frequently is translated with a direct object in English. The first and second active prefixes are seldom found with the same themes, and, when they are, there appears to be no systematic difference in meaning between the two. The meaning of the first active theme is not as consistent as that of the second active theme. Sometimes the theme denotes a general intransitive activity, and sometimes it has the same meaning as the second active theme. The first active prefix is most commonly found before short stem syllables and stem syllables with an initial ‖u‖.

The reflexive prefix is only found before the stem syllables ‖uu‖, ‖u:‖, and ‖u‖. It is not entirely consistent in its meaning, but usually it denotes an intentional reflexive action.

The middle voice prefix is most frequently found before long syllables excluding ‖ui‖. If the stem is derived from a descriptive plus -zaN (stem syllable ‖uu‖; see Section 621), the theme denotes that something belonging to the subject is acted upon. Before other stems with an initial ‖u‖ the meaning is often reflexive, but the action is not intentionally initiated by the subject. Frequently the subject is the passive recipient of the action. Before stems that do not have an initial ‖u‖ (where it never contrasts with the reflexive and seldom with the first active prefix), the meaning of the middle voice prefix is less consistent. It sometimes indicates a reflexive and sometimes a general intransitive relation.

Examples of first active themes with {-ʼ-}:

    kuŕáćica 'he made a banging noise'; -ûuŕáćizaN 'to bang, slam'

    súṅatyume 'I got hurt'; -úṅadyumeN 'to hurt'

    súćayawa 'I am mad, got mad'; -úćayawaN 'to get mad'

    káçəka 'he smoked'; -ázəkaN 'to smoke'

    sáša 'I took a step'; -áSD 'to step'

    suméýuca 'I got bruised'; -ûuméýuzaN 'to scratch'

Examples of second active themes with {-ʼáʔ-}:

    káuŕáćica 'he unintentionally banged himself'; -ûuŕáćizaN 'to bang, slam'

    sáućáýuca 'I broke (it)'; -ûućayuzaN 'to break something brittle'

    sáumúŕaca 'I dented (it)'; -ûumúŕazaN 'to dent'

    káužîinuca 'she made curls, got a permanent'; -úužîinuzaN 'to make curls'

Examples of reflexive themes with {-ˈúu-}:

    kúusúméesta 'he is teaching himself'; -úsúméʔestaaN 'to teach,
      learn'

    kúurácica 'he banged himself on purpose'; -ûurácizaN 'to bang,
      slam'

    súučáyuca 'I shot myself (on purpose?)'; -uîčayuzaN 'to shoot'

    kúučáwa 'he stole (it)'; -učáwaN 'to steal'

    kúucayawa 'he got mad at himself'; -úcayawaN 'to get mad'

    súuméyuca 'I intentionally scratched myself'; -ûuméyuzaN 'to
      scratch'

    kúuṅatyume 'he is pretending that he is hurt'; -úṅadyumeN 'to
      hurt'

Examples of middle voice themes with {-Qa-}:

    śâumúraca 'something of mine got dented'; -ûumúrazaN 'to dent'

    kaʔâucayuca 'mine broke'; -ûucayuzaN 'to break something brittle'

    kaʔâurácica 'he banged himself'; -ûurácizaN 'to bang, slam'

    kaʔâuťáayuca 'he has a rash'; -ûuťáayuzaN 'to have a rash'

    śáukača 'I see myself; I have an examination'; -úukačaN 'to see'

    śáaskə 'I fried (it)'; -áasgəN 'to fry'

    śáaspanašú 'I washed my hair'; -áasbanašúM 'to wash hair'

    kaʔáašazí 'he cut himself'; -áašazíM 'to cut'

    śâačawai 'I ran a stick race'; -âačawaiY 'to run a stick race'

The 'by mouth' and 'by body' themes are not common. They are always formed from stems that have the suffix -zaN (Section 621):

    káikéçəca 'she put lipstick on', g- -ˈáʔi- -ûukéẓəzaN (stem, 'to
      make red')

    sáipêetuca 'I wet, licked my lips', s- -ˈáʔi- -úupêetuzaN (stem,
      'to lick')

    sáisťúwica 'I pointed with my lips', s- -ˈáʔi- -úusťúwizaN (stem,
      'to make sharp')

    sińəəca 'I got rigid; fainted', s- -ˈi- -úunəəzaN (stem, 'to be stiff,
      to pull')

    kikútuca 'he bunched up into a ball', g- -ˈi- -úukúduzaN (stem, 'to
      be spherical')

    kiẓéṅəca 'he shivered', g- -ˈi- -uîẓənəzaN (stem, 'to be cold')

The collective plural theme usually has a number suffix. It indicates
that the activity is done by a group of people:

    sáayáwatapətyəṅáaťa 'we would take turns', s- -ˈáaya- -úwadaW
      -qədyəəZ -ṅáaťaN

    sáayácayawitiyaṅáaťa 'we would argue', s- -ˈáaya- -úcayawaN
      =itaaN -qeeD -ṅáaťaN (see Section 242)

415. The impersonal derivations are:
      (1) -qj- + Stem + -qiṢ: perfect
      (2) -qja- + Stem + -qiṢ: dispersional
The morphophonemics of the prefixes is described in ‖ 5.2 and ‖ 5.5. Set
I pronominal prefixes are used.

The perfect theme means 'it has been . . .':
   ćʹušʹiici 'it has been borrowed', g- -qj- -úušʹiizaN -qiṢ
   ćʹucitamaci 'it has been turned over', g- -qj- -ʹiicitamazaN -qiṢ
   ćácəkáńi 'it has been smoked', g- -qj- -ázəkaN -qiṢ
   ćaasgóńi 'it has been fried', g- -qj- -áasgəN

The dispersional theme is used only with the stem syllables ‖ uu ‖,
‖ u: ‖, and ‖ u ‖. It means 'a whole bunch is . . .':
   ćaksǝ́cǝci 'there is a lot of red (as in a sunset)', g- -qja- -ûuksǝ́zǝzaN
     -qiṢ
   ćakútuci 'there are lots of lumps', g- -qja- -úuḱúduzaN -qiṢ
   ćaćáyuci 'it was all shot up', g- -qja- -u:̂ćayuzaN -qiṢ

Impersonal verb themes do not distinguish number. A stem, however,
can include a number prefix:
   ćʹutúuḱuci 'it has been smoothed', g- -qj- -úutúuḱuzaN -qiṢ
   ćiʔíutúuḱuci 'two have been smoothed, g- -qj- {dl} -úutúuḱuzaN
     -qiṢ
   ćiwáatúuḱuci 'they have been smoothed', g- -qj- {pl} -úutúuḱuzaN
     -qiṢ

The number prefixes must be considered part of the stem rather than
the theme, because the coarticulation morphophonemes of the theme are
normally lost after the number prefixes (see ‖ 7, table 5).

The suffix -(´´), accent ablaut with length (see ‖ 19), is used to form
plural stems for two impersonal verbs:
   ćʹiyáa 'they are wide', g- -qjíya -(´´)
   ćizśə 'they are long', g- -qjízə -(´´) (see ‖ 22)
Compare:
   ćʹiya 'it is wide', g- -qjíya
   ćícə 'it is long', g- -qjízə

416. The morphophonemics of the thematic prefixes is rather complex,
and a number of prefixes have the same or similar realizations before
certain stem syllables (see table 4). The prefixes often indicate subtle
voice distinctions that are not always reflected in the English glosses.
As a result, some of the prefixes, particularly those in Section 414, may
not be properly identified. In addition, there are a number of nonproductive thematic derivations which are left for dictionary listing.

417. The theme can sometimes serve as a stem. The inchoative intransitive (Section 413) is an example of this. There are a few other
examples, but they are rare: cayáamáaci 'it had been helped', g- -qj-
-Jaya- -úumáazaN -qiṢ. The impersonal theme (-qj- + Theme + -qiṢ) is
derived from the intransitive-A theme (-Jaya- + Stem).

Occasionally a third person nonmodal verb is used as a stem. The
pronominal prefix of the verb is incorporated in the resulting theme:
gáukúistiti 'his (for example, horse) is brown', g- -Auu- kúistiti. The
verb is a nonderived intransitive-A theme: kúistiti 'it is brown', g-
-qúistiti.

420. Infinitives

Infinitives are formed from verb stems by the addition of the infinitive
prefix ʔ- and the completive suffix -qiṢ. There are often unexplained
changes in the stem syllable:

ʔubáyáni 'to fire (pottery)', ʔ- -ubáyaN -qiṢ

ʔúpewi 'to eat', ʔ- -úbeW -qiṢ

ʔúudyáati 'to catch', ʔ- -údyáʔaD -qiṢ

ʔúyûupəni 'to get in', ʔ- -úːbəN -qiṢ (the /n/ is irregularly not
     glottalized)

ʔáityaani 'to gather', ʔ- -áidyaaN -qiṢ

The nonthematic verbal suffixes described in Section 440 can be used
with the infinitive:

ʔûukítaukuyáni 'to be collecting, charging money', ʔ- -ûukítaW
     -iguyaN -qiṢ

ʔɔ́tyaciši 'to always stand', ʔ- -ɔ́dyazíM -səɸ -qiṢ (expect ʔɔ́tyacis
     see ‖1.13 and ‖4)

ʔustîiyáatáni 'to habitually fetch water', ʔ- -ustîiY -náataN -qiṢ

The infinitive is presumably derived from stems rather than themes,
because thematic prefixes are never found with it. However, the benefactive suffix (Section 411) and the number prefixes for objects (Section
433) are found with the infinitive. These infinitives must be based on
transitive themes rather than on stems:

ʔaʔáwáasêeʔeníiti 'to show them (dual) how' ʔ- {dl} -J̄-
     -úwáasêeʔeN -'íʔiD -qiṢ

ʔaʔáyáidyámi 'to meet them (dual)', ʔ- {dl} -J- -úyáidyaW̄ -qiṢ

ʔúwâataiskaapi 'to keep husking them', ʔ- {pl} -uːdaiskaaM -Gʷ
     -qiṢ

So that one may account for the shape of the dual prefix, the first two

infinitives must be set up with the morphophonemes $\|\bar{J}\|$ and $\|J\|$, res-
pectively. These morphophonemes are allomorphs of the benefactive and
first transitive prefix ($\|5.5$).

430. Inflection

The verb is inflected for mode, person, and number. Person and number
apply to the subject and, in addition, to the object of transitive verbs.
Person and mode are indicated by portmanteau pronominal prefixes (Section 230).

431. Mode is the most important feature in distinguishing verbs from
possessed nouns. Only verbs and ambivalents when functioning as verbs
(Sections 520) indicate mode. Three modes are distinguished: dubitative,
hortative, and negative.

The dubitative is used (1) when there is a doubt in the speaker's mind
that the event happened or will happen, (2) when the event was not wit-
nessed by the speaker, and (3) in asking questions. It is especially common in myths. The following examples are taken from texts:

báa çəẓáwee?e 'May you have luck (the next time)!'; báa 'may';
   ẓ-əẓ- set III pronominal prefix

çáityata dyâiẏaani 'Are you gathering piñons?'; ç- set II, dyâiẏaani
   'piñons'

çəẓáwáisťiçatyai 'I guess they are your kids'; ẓ-əẓ- set II

?úutisdyáwísti ta?áukúẏawi 'I lost my saddle (and did not know it)';
   ?úutisdyáwísti 'saddle', t- set II

With second person subjects the hortative is used for commands. With
other persons it is usually translated as 'let . . .'. It is used with a
negative adverb for prohibitions. Examples:

pídyá '(you) hold it!'; p- -Júdyá?aD, pronominal prefix 2-3, set I

pu?úukača '(come out and) look at the two of them!'; p- {dl}
   -úukačaN, prefix 2-3, set I

pêe?epənai?i 'let the other one put them (dual) in!'; pj- {dl}
   -Júbənai?M, prefix obviative, set I

The negative mode is defective. It is found only with the 1(-3) and
3-1 persons. With other persons the nonmodal or (if the context is appropriate for it) the dubitative is used. The suffix -u (Section 442.9) is
often added to the verb. A sentence with a negative verb must have a
negative adverb, which is usually záazíi:

záazíi skuẃawíśáisətiyaatya 'we had nothing to play with'; sg- (TSE)
   -'úuśáiyaN -sə∅ -qeeD -u (see Section 242)

záazíi háu stíuyâaˀaníitya 'nobody gave me permission'; háu 'someone', sgj- -J̄úyâaˀaN -ˈíˀiD -u

záazíi sdyáiˀisuméestiya 'they didn't teach us anything'; sgj- {pl}
-JúsúméˀestaaN -qeeD (see Section 242)

432. The first, second, third, indefinite, and distributive persons are
distinguished for subject. The indefinite indicates 'someone, somebody'.
The distributive is not common. It indicates 'many of them', and is used
principally with plural verbs. It appears to have the same meaning as
the indefinite with plural verbs.

The object of transitive verbs distinguish the first, second, and third
persons. In addition, transitive verbs distinguish an obviative person in
which the third person subject and third person object roles ('he . . .
him') are reversed ('the other one . . . him'); the central figure of dis-
course is the object, and a secondary figure is the subject. Less commonly the obviative is used to indicate that 'the other one' is the subject
of a verb that has an inanimate object. These two usages are illustrated
by examples from a text about the War Twins, in which the War Twins
are the central figures:

daˀáyáita 'he (their father) painted them (the two War Twins)', dyj-
{dl} -JáyáitaaN

tídyá nábáasti 'she (Spider Woman, rather than the War Twins) took
hold of the spider web', dyj- -JúdyáˀaD (nábáasti 'spider web')

An indefinite-obviative pronominal prefix is found, but there is no indefinite-obviative person. The prefix is used only with static verbs to
indicate the indefinite person.

433. There are three numbers—singular, dual, and plural. Singular
number is unmarked. The dual and plural suffixes, -qədyəəZ and -qeeD
(rule ‖1), are used with nonsingular subjects of transitive and intransitive-B verbs. The dual and plural prefixes, {dl} and {pl} (‖7), are used
with nonsingular subjects of static and intransitive-A verbs and with nonsingular objects of transitive verbs. The number suffix is sometimes
omitted from transitive verbs if both the subject and object are nonsingular.

The number prefixes condition irregular stem changes for a number
of verbs (see ‖7.10). The number suffixes condition irregular stem
changes for the transitive verb theme -JáaciguyaN 'to say to someone':
-JáaciguyaN + qədyəəZ > ‖-JániyaaB-ədyəəZ‖; + qeeD > ‖-JániyaaB‖.
Examples:

śéecikuya 'I said to him'

śéniyaapətyə 'we (dual) said to him'

śéniya 'we (plural) said to him'

This theme is also irregular with the number prefixes (see ‖ 7.8).

A harmonic plural suffix is added to the plural forms of certain intransitive-A verbs: (1) possessive verbs (thematic prefix {-qa-}, Section 413), (2) verbs with the thematic prefix {-Jaýa-} (Section 413), and (3) certain irregular verbs listed in ‖ 7.10. The harmonic plural suffix is in certain respects similar to the thematic syllable expansion (‖ 9. s). The suffix is frequently irregular (see Section 241). Examples:

gáaʔáapəši 'their (plural) things are scattered', g- {pl} -qaʔáapəṢ -qeeD; cf. k̇aʔáapə 'his things are scattered'; gaʔaʔáapə 'their (dual) things are scattered' (possessive verb with {-qa-}

ṣáaýáamáazáńa 'we (plural) helped', ṣ- {pl} -JaýáamáazaN -qeeD; cf. s̆eýáamáaca 'I helped'; ṣaʔaýáamáaca 'we (dual) helped' (thematic prefix {-Jaýa-})

ṣáanáadáńa 'we (dual) bought it', ṣ- {pl} -JúnáadaN -qeeD; cf. síńáata 'I bought it'; ṣaʔáńáata 'we (dual) bought it' (irregular verb, ‖ 7.10)

The harmonic plural is the last suffix added to possessive verbs and is added without regard to suffix position classes (table 10): gáastyuwaańiši 'they are sweating', g- {pl} -qasdyúwaaN -qiṢ -qeeD ({-qiṢ}, position class nine; {-qeeD}, position class seven). The usual order is maintained when the harmonic plural suffix is added to other verbs: gáanáatitiyańáat́asə 'they would buy it', g- {pl} -JúnáadaN ꞊itaaN -qeeD -ńáat́aN -səⱷ (see Section 242 and table 10).

The plural suffix is optionally used in the thematic derivation of passive static verbs (Section 412). The suffix is sometimes irregular (Section 241).

440. Nonthematic Suffixes

The nonthematic suffixes fill positions five, eight, and nine. Two suffixes, -iku (Section 442.8) and -u (Section 442.9), have not been placed in a position class. It is not entirely certain that these are nonthematic verb suffixes.

The suffixes are not restricted in their occurrence with the five verb classes (Section 410), except that those suffixes that are used in certain thematic derivations do not again occur with these verbs. That is, they occur only once, functioning either as thematic suffixes or as nonthematic suffixes.

441. The continuative suffixes ꞊itaaN, ꞊áayaN, and -iguyaN may constitute three allomorphs or, more accurately, three sets of allomorphs

of one morpheme. (There is also the possibility that the repetitive suffixes -sə∅ and -G^W are allomorphs of the continuative suffix; see Section
442.1.) The three suffixes have the same, or at least very similar, meanings. The material does not allow us to decide, however, which analysis
is correct. I have chosen to treat them as three morphemes, because
this analysis makes it easier to state the allomorphy.

441.1. The suffix ⁼itaaN is used to express continuous action:

súẃaẏámawéetitiya 'we wedged clay (over a period of time)', s-
(TSE) -'úuẏámawéeẓaN ⁼itaaN -qeeD (see Section 242)

ća?áyə̀əcitiyaatiku 'he would be getting hit', gj- -qja?áyə̀əzaN
⁼itaaN -qeeD -iku

sgaẏáadyánâawita 'we were laughing', sg- {pl} -JíidyánâawaN
⁼itaaN

The following types of allomorphs are found:

    (1) ⁼itaaN

    (2) ⁼qitaaN ~ ⁼itaaN

    (3) -itaaN

    (4) -qitaaN

    (5) -itaaN (with empty morphs)

    (6) ⁼etaaN

    (7) ⁼é?etaaN

    (8) -taaN

    (9) -iṣaaN

The first four types are common and can be predicted by the preceding
morphophonemic sequence. The remaining types are limited to a few
themes which must be listed. The allomorphs with the morphophoneme
‖⁼‖ condition vowel loss (‖2). The suffix forms a portmanteau morpheme with the plural suffix (Section 242).

(1) ‖⁼itaaN‖ is found after most final sequences of ‖(C)aN‖ (excludin
the sequence ‖ẓaN‖; see type 2, below):

gukúsicita 'he is crippled', ‖-uîkusizaN⁼itaaN‖

śíisḱatita 'I am giving him a drink', ‖-JíisḱadaN⁼itaaN‖

śâinatita 'I am cooking meat', ‖-QâinadaN⁼itaaN‖

It is occasionally found after other sequences:

śíizúwiita 'I am paying him', ‖-JíizúwaaN⁼itaaN‖

kâusíita 'he is getting water', ‖-'á?uséeN⁼ itaaN‖

(2) ‖⁼qitaaN ~ ⁼itaaN‖ is found after most final sequences of ‖ẓaN‖
(see ‖12):

séećáatita ~ séećáatita 'I kept listening', ‖-áaćáaẓa(N?)⁼qitaaN,
⁼itaaN‖

śénátita 'I keep turning the light on', ‖-JánaẓaN⁼qitaaN‖

ka?áamitita 'he is making a nest', ‖-QáamiẓaN≠itaaN‖

(3) ‖-taaN‖ is found after ‖W, Ẃ, B, Gᵂ‖ (see rule ‖1):

séeťawita 'I have been opening his', ‖-áaťaW-itaaN‖

ka?áudyúpita 'he is finding out', ‖-QáudyúB-itaaN‖

(4) ‖-qitaaN‖ is found after ‖SD‖ (see rule ‖1.9):

súdyúťita 'I am covering myself', ‖-'údyuSD-qitaaN‖

(5) ‖-itaaN‖ is found after the empty morphs ‖≠qíiť-‖, ‖≠qiiť-‖, and ‖≠ic-‖. The empty morphs are found after certain stems and before ≠itaaN. The stems usually end with ‖sdaaN‖ or some similar sequence and are:

(with ≠qíiť-)

-umínáasdaaN 'to make stuffed tripe'

-úyámásdâaN 'to stuff in'

-áyasdaaM(N) 'to enclose; can'

-QáumúkustaaN 'to eat with big mouthfuls'

-uńúusdáaN 'to make sausage'

-udáaN 'to place in a container'

(with ≠qiiť-)

-úkudyaaN 'to gather wood'

(with ≠ic-)

-úwáisťaN 'to serve stew'

-'âicéwaN 'to wedge clay'

Examples:

síťíiťita 'I am putting them in' (theme, -JudáaN; see ‖21)

síkuťiiťita 'I am gathering wood'

kâicéẃicita 'she is wedging clay'

(6) ‖≠etaaN‖ is found after three stems that end with ‖aa?aN‖:

-ýâa?aN(W): kiýêe?eta 'he is allowing it'

-ûušaa?aN: ka?âušee?eta 'he is asking for permission'

-úidaa?aN: sûitee?eta 'I am asking for it'

(7) ‖≠é?etaaN‖ is found after six stems:

-udíišá?aN: śidíišéeta 'I am feeding him'

-úẃaakasdaaN: síẃaakasdéeta 'I am imitating him'

-áaýúuná?aN: sáaýúuńéeta 'I am moving'

-íicáaN: sícéeta 'I danced' (this stem is seldom found without the continuative suffix)

-'úcáaN: súcéeta 'I am tanning'

-úkaazá?aN: kúkaazéeta 'he is announcing'

(8) ‖-taaN‖ is found after the following stems:

-úńadyumeN: súńatyumeta 'I keep getting hurt'

-áasbanašú(M)(ḿeN)(waN): sâaspanašúḿeta 'I am washing my hair'

-ubáyaN: subáyata 'I am building the fire'

-áidyaaN: śáityata 'I am gathering'

-úyáiẓaaN: suyáiçaata 'I am weeding'

-úskúmeN: śískúmeta 'I am dipping it in water'

-ugúyaN: kugúyata 'he keeps getting on'

-âitíM: śâitita 'I measured myself'

Several of these alternate with the first type, ‖ ⁼itaaN ‖: śáitita, śáityata 'I am gathering'

(9) ‖ -iṣaaN ‖, alternating with the regular ‖ -itaaN ‖, is found with one stem that ends in ‖ B ‖: ka?áudyúpiṣa, ka?áudyúpita 'he is finding out', -úudyúB.

441.2. The continuative suffix ⁼áayaN is not as common as ⁼itaaN. It was recorded with about thirty stems. The suffix appears to have the same meaning as ⁼itaaN. The following allomorphs are found:

(1) ⁼áayaN

(2) ⁼jáayaN

(3) -qáayaN

The allomorphs with the morphophoneme ‖ ⁼ ‖ condition vowel loss (‖ 2). The suffix forms a portmanteau morpheme with the plural suffix (Section 242).

(1) ‖ ⁼áayaN ‖ is found after the following stems:

-âa?aẓaaN: śâa?aẓáaya 'I am piling wood'

-úpəẓaN: śípəẓáaya 'I am shaking it out'

-'âićéwaN: sâićéwáaya 'I am wedging clay'

-útiẓudyaN: sútiçudyáaya 'I am weighing myself'

-skədaN: śâiskədáaya 'I am scratching myself'

(2) ‖ ⁼jáayaN ‖ is found after ‖ dyaN ‖ and ‖ dyaaN ‖: śisíusdáaya 'I am roping him', ‖ -usíusdyaN⁼jáayaN ‖ śićâadáaya 'I am pinning it', ‖ -ućáadyaN⁼jáayaN ‖

(3) ‖ -qáayaN ‖ is found elsewhere: śáasgśńáaya 'I am frying it', ‖ -áasgəN-qáayaN ‖ síutaatáaya 'I am hanging it up', ‖ -uːtaaSD-qáayaN ‖ (see ‖ 1.9)

441.3. With some stems, -iguyaN expresses a continued action and appears to have the same meaning as ⁼itaaN and ⁼áayaN: síukačanikuya 'I am seeing it, am looking at it', theme -úukačaN. With other stems it expresses a repeated action and appears to have the same meaning as -səØ and -G^W (Section 442.1): sêepikuya 'I am nibbling it, I bite it several times', theme -áaG^W.

The suffix has two allomorphs, ‖ -iguyaN ‖ and ‖ -guyaN ‖. These have been treated in rule ‖ 1. In addition, there are a few irregular formations síibáakuya 'I am sleepy', ‖ -jíibáaguyaN ‖, from -jíibáiY (see ‖ 1.7)

síwádyâińawakuyańáaťa 'I find them all the time', plural theme
   -úwádyâińaW

The suffix is incorporated in a few themes:

ṣáańikuya 'we spoke', dual theme -qáańikuya (probably -qáańiguyaN);
   singular -áńaaťa (see ‖ 7.10)

síuḿayanikuya 'I was laughing at him, making fun of him', theme
   -u:ḿayaniguyaN, stem -ḿayani; cf. gaḿáyani 'he is funny'

442. The remaining nonthematic suffixes are:

442.1. -sə∅, -G^W, repetitive suffixes (see ‖ 4 and ‖ 1.6). The meaning
of these suffixes is not clear. They are sometimes translated as a continuative (cf. Section 441), sometimes as a repetitive and sometimes as
a habitual (cf. Section 442.2). There appears to be no difference in meaning between the two suffixes. They cannot be regarded as allomorphs of
a single morpheme, however, because of different positional properties
(see below). -sə∅ is the more common of the two. Any stem that can
take -G^W can also take -sə∅, but not vice versa. Most stems that take
-sə∅ do not take a continuative suffix. Examples:

   káaČasə 'it rains, keeps on raining', g- -'áaČaN -sə∅
   čîûcisťaikasi 'it is always strained', g- -qjûucisťaikaẂ -sə∅ -qiṢ
   čaʔâuťikuse 'they kept getting them', dy- -QâuťigúM -sə∅ -qeeD
   guḿəsiṣa 'where (the sun) comes up', g- -û:ḿəN -sə∅ -ṣa (see
      Section 763)
   gáitúunísi 'as they grew up', g- {dl} -'itûuníM -sə∅ -(´)í (see
      Section 762)
   sgâiʔíḿinaku 'one usually talks to them', sg- {pl} -JuḿínaaD -G^W
   dyûubíiČape 'they kept on dividing', dy- -ûubíiČaN -G^W -qeeD

-sə∅ and -G^W are normally found in position five: síukáasí, síukáapí
'I am shelling corn for him', sj- -úukáaM -sə∅ (second form -G^W)
-'íʔiD; -'íʔiD is a position six suffix. -sə∅, but not -G^W, can occur in
position eight when it occurs with -ńáaťaN. It may either precede or
follow -ńáaťaN, and it may occur in both position five and position eight
after -ńáaťaN:

   súwabáyatiyasəńáaťa 'we would build fires', s- (TSE) -'ubáyaN
      ꞊itaaN -qeeD -sə∅ -ńáaťaN
   súuwíšáayáńətyəńáaťasə 'we (dual) used to play', s- -'úuwíšáayaN
      -qədyəəZ -ńáaťaN -sə∅
   sáiwaťiseńáaťasə 'we would go together', s- (TSE) -'úuťiM -sə∅
      -qeeD -ńáaťaN -sə∅ (see ‖ 9.6)

When -sə∅ and -ńáaťaN co-occur, the habitual meaning of -ńáaťaN is
intensified.

There is one example each in which -sə∅ co-occurs with -G^W and ꞊itaaN:

zayáapatyəsəku 'he always got them out of bed', gj- {pl} -Jíipadyэ́M
-sə∅ -G^W

zîiťisitaatyanu 'when they are measuring', g- -JîitíM -sə∅ ⁼itaaN
-qeeD -u (irregularly, ⁼itaaN and -qeeD form ⁼itaadyaN instead
of the usual portmanteau morpheme; see Section 242)

When preceded by the derivative -ťuwaaN (Section 623) and followed by
another suffix, -G^W has the allomorph ‖-guyaN‖: gâamaaťuwaakuyáńa
'they are taking the leg off', g- -âamaaťuwaaN -G^W -qeeD. This allomorph cannot be considered an allomorph of -iguyaN, because ‖-iguyaN‖,
allomorph of -iguyaN, is found after ‖N‖ (see ‖1.1, and table 2). In addition, ‖-guyaN‖ was given in paradigms of forms that have -G^W:

gâamaaťuwaaku 'he is taking the leg off'
gâamaaťuwaakuyáńa 'they are taking the leg off'
gúwâaḿeeťuwaaku 'he is taking the tent down'
gúwâaḿeeťuwaakuyáńətyə 'they (dual) are taking the tent down'

442.2. -ńáaťaN, habitual suffix, normally expresses a habitual or cus-
tomary event:

kuwâańáaťa 'there would be plants', g- -'iẃá -ńáaťaN (probably
/kuẃá+ńáaťa/)
sáayáẃatapətyəńáaťa 'we (dual) would take turns', s- -'áayáẃadaW
-qədyəəZ -ńáaťaN

It sometimes expresses inevitability:

di?îuýáaťa 'it (swarm of bees) flew at them (dual)', dyj- {dl}
-ûuýu∅ -ńáaťaN

The suffix has the allomorphs ‖-ńáaťaN‖ after ‖N, W, Ẃ, Ṣ‖ and
after the plural suffix -qeeD; and ‖-qáaťaN, -qjáaťaN‖ after ‖Y, D, SD,
∅‖ (see ‖1). It does not occur after other final morphophonemic consonants, and this may account for the habitual meaning that is sometimes
found for -sə∅ (-sə∅ is especially common after ‖M‖).

The allomorph ‖-ẓáťee?eeD‖ is found after ‖-VVD‖, the allomorph of
the plural suffix -qeeD that is found after ‖Y‖ (see ‖1.7). ‖-ńáaťaN‖
optionally follows ‖-ẓáťee?eeD‖:

ća?áyúucee?eeẓáťee?e ~ ća?áyúucee?eeẓáťee?eeńáaťa 'he is always
taken', g- -qja?áyúuzeeY -qeeD -ńáaťaN
kuẃâušaaťee?eeẓáťee?eese 'they would go after meat', g- (TSE)
-'ûišaaťeeY -qeeD -ńáaťaN -sə∅

In one case -sə∅ is found between ‖-ẓáťee?eeD‖ and ‖-ńáaťaN‖:
ṡâaćawai?iiẓáťee?eesəńáaťasə 'we would have stick races'.

442.3. -qeeY, 'to go to . . ., to come . . .' (see rule ‖1). The suffix
indicates purposeful movement, usually to a definite place:

súsúḿéestaańe 'I went to school', s- -'úsúḿé?estaaN -qeeY

kuwâane 'he went hunting', g- -ʹuwáaN -qeeY (lit. 'he went to kill')
-qeeY does not occur with the continuative or repetitive suffixes because they all belong to the same position class. -náaṫaN is used instead: sináameeẏáaṫa 'I kept going to look out', s- -ʹiñáaʔW -qeeY
-náaṫaN.

-áidyaaN plus -qeeY irregularly becomes ‖-áidyaiY‖:
śaitya 'I gathered'; śaityai 'I went to gather'.

442.4. -iẓaadyaaN, inceptive suffix, 'starting to . . ., beginning to
. . .':

    gáispiẓáadyáaní 'when dawn was coming', g- -áisbîiY -iẓaadyaaN
      -(ʹ)í (see Section 762)
    tigûuṅiçaatya 'she became pregnant', dy- -JugûuʔN -iẓaadyaaN
    sîuṫuuní míçaatya 'I started to remember things', s- -ʹûiṫuuníM
      -iẓaadyaaN

There are not enough examples to determine the morphophonemic
properties of this suffix. It is probably an initial vowel suffix (see ‖1.0),
perhaps with an initial ‖q‖.

442.5. -naiʔM, 'enclosed, inside'. This suffix is not common:

    śeẏáẓáanaityə 'we (dual) made them (dolls) talk', sj- {pl} -JáaẓáʔaN
      -naiʔM -qədyəəZ (lit. 'we talked in them')
    śípənaiʔi 'I put it in', s- -JúbəN -naiʔM (-ú:bəN, 'to enter')

A few stems are always found with -naiʔM or -ńaiʔM:

    -úyaaćiciñaiʔM 'to surround'
    -úwîikúmasṫiinaiʔM 'to smother'
    -JíisdyənaiʔM 'to be constipated'

442.6. -du∅(N), inchoative:

    kaméetu 'it froze', g- -ʹaméeʔN -du∅(N); cf. kamêeʔe 'it is frozen'
    káweetu 'it snowed', g- -ʹáwée -du∅(N); cf. káwé 'it is snowy'
    ṫíipáńitu 'it (for example, river) went dry' (dubitative), dy- -qjíipáńiṢ
      -du∅; cf. ćíipáńi 'it went dry'

The suffix also functions as a thematic affix; see Section 411.

442.7. -qiṢ, the completive suffix, has several functions. It is used
(1) in certain thematic derivations (Sections 413, 415), (2) in forming the
infinitive (Section 420), (3) in certain stem derivations (Section 625), and
(4) in nonthematic constructions. As a nonthematic suffix, it emphasizes
that the action is finished:

    síwáakučáńi 'I have it hidden', sj- -JúwáakuD(čaN) -qiṢ
    cibêeṫaukuyáńańáaṫáńiši 'the questions that they had always asked',
      g- -JubêeṫaW -iguyaN -qeeD -ńáaṫaN -qiṢ -iši (see Section 761)
    súsúméestaani 'I had learned (as a child in school)', s-
      -ʹúsúméʔestaaN -qiṢ (expect /-ńi/, rather than /-ni/)

-qiṢ has two allomorphs, ‖-qiṢ‖ and ‖-iṢ‖, treated in rule‖1.

442.8. -iku has been recorded only with the nonmodal pronominal prefixes and hence may not be a verb suffix (see Section 760). It is the last
suffix in the form. The suffix means 'that's the way it's done'. It is
used primarily with the completive suffix and with the third person pronominal prefix:

    kaʔâačawaiʔizáɬeeʔeetiku 'they would race, that's the way they
        would race', g- -QâačawaiY -qeeD -ńáaɬaN -iku

    gacípətišiku 'that is what is needed', g- -acípəD -qiṢ -iku

    čídyáatiku 'that's the way he catches it', gj- -Júdyáʔad -iku

442.9. The suffix -u has three functions. It is used (1) as a subordinative suffix (Section 764), (2) with verbs in the negative mode, and (3)
with verbs that have the indefinite person. The last two functions are
considered here. Perhaps there are two homophonous suffixes, one a
subordinative suffix, the other the suffix treated here. If so, both suffixes have identical allomorphs distributed in an identical fashion (see
rule ‖1).

-u is the last suffix of the verb. Unlike other verbal suffixes, it follows the auxiliary that is used in the periphrastic expective construction
(Section 471). No meaning can be attached to the suffix, and its presence
is optional. Examples:

    sgúistyanu 'one ties it', sg- -úisdyaN -u

    ńaigámisgúńu 'one wants to catch it', n- -qaigámiṢ sg- {gú} -u
        (expective construction, Section 471)

    záazíi sdíukačanu ~ záazíi sdíukača 'I didn't see him', sgj-
        -úukačaN (-u)

450. Classificatory Verbs

The classificatory verb stems constitute a small group of stems that
undergo special thematic derivations and take special nonthematic suffixes. Some of the stems are defective, and many of the formations are
irregular. The stems are:

    -úɬ- 'to handle things in a basket'

    -úsɬ- 'to handle liquid'

    -úisd- 'to handle things in a sack or box'

    -áaḿáaku- 'to handle grainlike or sandlike objects'

    -ûišaa- 'to handle meat'

    -ûipady- 'to carry on the back'

    -âaʔB 'to handle one flexible object'

-úuku- 'to handle several flexible objects'

-úud- 'to handle one compact object'

-úuẏad- 'to handle several compact objects'

The first three stems are more regular, are found in a larger set of formations than the others, and will be considered first.

451. The thematic derivations with -úť-, -úsť-, and -úisd- follow.

(1) ‖-J̌-. . . .-í꞉iD‖, transitive, 'to give . . . to a person'. The themes are not the benefactive (see Section 454):

-J̌uťí꞉iD, śiťí 'I gave him a basket of something'

-J̌ústí꞉iD, śísťí 'I gave him a container of water'

-J̌úisdí꞉iD, śiusdí 'I gave him a sack of something'

(2) ‖-J̌- . . . -iD(čaN)‖, transitive, 'to place . . .'. The dual prefix is regular with these forms, but the plural prefix is realized as zero (see ‖7.2):

-J̌úťiD(čaN), zíťiča 'he placed a basket'

-J̌ústiD(čaN), zísťiča 'he placed a container of water'

-J̌úsdíiD(čaN), zísdíiča 'he placed a sack'

(3) ‖-J̌u- . . . . -íizaN, -áaN‖, transitive, 'to put in . . ., to fill . . .':

-J̌uťíizaN ~ -J̌uťáaN, śiťíica ~ śiťá 'I filled a basket, put it in a basket'

-J̌ustíizaN ~ -J̌ustáaN, śistíica ~ śisťá 'I poured water in'

-J̌usdáaN, śisdá 'I put it in a sack'

(4) ‖-'- . . . . -áW, -áaN, -áaW‖, intransitive-B, 'to take a . . .':

-'uťáW ~ -'uťáaN, kuťá 'he took a basket'

-'usťáaN, kusťá 'he took a container of water'

-'úisdáaW ~ -'úisdaaN, kúisdá ~ kúista 'he took a sack'

In -'uťáW the accent shifts to the preceding syllable when thematic syllable expansion is present (‖9): suẃáťawa 'we (plural) took a basket'

Additional intransitive-B derivations are:

-'uťíizaN, suťíica 'I helped myself to something from a basket'

-'áusdíizaN, sáusdíica 'I packed it (in a box, sack)'

452. The intransitive themes (type 4, above) are found with some non-thematic affixes.

(1) Suffix ‖꞊áikuY‖ 'to take . . . with oneself' (cf. -iguyaN, continuative suffix, Section 441.3)

-'uťáikuY, suťáiku 'I took a basket with me'

-'usťáikuY, susťáiku 'I took water with me'

-'úisdáikuY, súisdáiku 'I took a sack with me'

(2) Suffixes ‖꞊áikuY + -aN‖ 'to be holding, carrying . . .':

-'uťáikuiyaN, suťáikuiya 'I am carrying a basket'

-'usťáikuiyaN, susťáikuiya 'I am carrying water'

-ʼúisdáikuiyaN, súisdáikuiya 'I am carrying a sack'

(3) Extension of the thematic syllable from ‖ʼu‖ to ‖ʼuʔú‖, with loss of the following accent, 'to just now . . .':

-ʼuʔúťaW, suʔúťa 'I just now took a basket'

-ʼuʔústaN, suʔústa 'I just now took some water' (final syllable is shortened)

This formation is also found with -J̄utíʔiD (Section 451, type 1): s̄iʔitíí 'I just now gave him a basket'. The accent is not changed.

Additional forms are:

-ʼustíiY, kustíí 'he went after water (with an open container?)'

-ʼúsdíišiiY, kúsdíiši 'he took water (with a closed container?)'

-ʼúsdíišiiyaN, kúsdíišiiya 'he is carrying water (in a closed container?)'

453. The formations with the remaining classificatory stems follow.

(1) -áaḿáaku- 'to handle grainlike or sandlike objects':

-J̄aḿáakuʔíʔiD, s̄aḿáakuʔí 'I gave him a handful' (transitive)

-ʼáaḿáakúyaW, sáaḿáakúya 'I took a handful' (intransitive-B)

-ʼáaḿáakúišiiyaN, sáaḿáakúišiiya 'I am holding a handful' (intransitive-B)

(2) -ûišaa- 'to handle meat':

-ʼûišaaťeeY, sûišaaťe 'I went after meat' (intransitive-B)

-ʼûišaaseeY, sûišaase 'I went by with meat' (intransitive-B)

(3) -ûipady- 'to carry on the back'

-ʼûipatinaW̃, kûipatináu 'he put it on his back' (intransitive-B)

-J̄íipadyuiya(N?), c̄íipadyuiya 'he is carrying (several objects?) on his back' (static)

-J̄íipatiya(N?), c̄íipatiya 'he carried (several objects?) on his back' (static)

(4) -âaʔB 'to handle one flexible object'

-J̄âaʔB, s̄êuʔu 'I gave it to him' (transitive)

-ʼaŷâaʔB, saŷâuʔu 'I took it' (intransitive-B)

-QáikuY, s̄áiku 'I took it with me' (intransitive-B)

-QáikuiyaN, s̄áikuiya 'I am holding it, carrying it' (intransitive-B)

(5) -úuku- 'to handle several flexible objects'

-J̄úukuʔíʔiD, s̄íukuʔí 'I gave them to him' (transitive)

-QáukúyaW, s̄aukúya 'I took them' (intransitive-B)

(6) -úud- 'to handle one compact object'

-J̄úudíʔiD, s̄íudí 'I gave it to him' (transitive)

-JudáaN ~ JúdaW, s̄idá ~ s̄íta 'I took it' (transitive)

-JudáikuiyaN, s̄udáikuiya 'I am holding it' (transitive)

-Judîiyaa B, s̄idîiya 'I carried it (placed it?)' (transitive)

(7) -úuẏad- 'to handle several flexible objects'

  -J̌úuẏadíʔiD, síuẏadí 'I gave them to him' (transitive)

  -ʼûiẏateyaW, sûiẏateya 'I took them' (intransitive-B)

  -ʼûiẏašeeY, sîuẏaše 'I took them with me' (intransitive-B)

  -Q̇áadeeY, śáate 'I took them with me, I hauled them' (intransitive-B)

  -ʼûiẏašeeyaN, sîuẏašeeya 'I am holding them' (intransitive-B)

  -Q̇áadeeyaN, śáateeya 'I am holding them' (cf. -uːdeeY, -uːdiiY 'to fetch a person')

454. The themes listed above can serve as stems and can undergo thematic derivation of the kind described in 410. The initial coarticulation morphophoneme of the classificatory theme is dropped when it functions as a stem. A bewildering array of forms result. A few examples are given with -úisd- 'to handle things in a sack or box'.

  -(J̌)úisdíʔiD (Section 451, type 1): síusdíití 'I gave a sack to someone for him' (benefactive, Section 411); ćiisdíiti 'the sack was given' (perfect, Section 415)

  -(J̌)usdáaN (Section 451, type 3): k̇asdâani 'he has it packed in a sack or box' (possessive, Section 413)

  -(ʼ)úisdáaW (Section 451, type 4): ćîusdáawi 'the sack has been picked up' (perfect)

  -(ʼ)áusdíizaN (Section 451): ćísdíici ~ ćíusdíici 'the sack has been packed' (perfect; the vowel and accent change of the thematic syllable is irregular)

  -(ʼ)úisdáikuY (Section 452, type 2): sîusdâikuimí 'I went to give him a sack, took a sack for him' (benefactive)

In the first example the benefactive suffix is added to -(J̌)úisdíʔiD. This shows that the classificatory theme ‖-J̌- . . . -íʔiD‖ cannot be considered a benefactive theme, in spite of the similarity in shape and partial similarity in meaning. The two theme types are, however, undoubtedly from the same historical source.

460. Auxiliary Verbs

The auxiliary verbs are used to inflect the auxiliary complements (Section 630) and to form periphrastic constructions (Section 470). The auxiliary is in second position in these constructions. These verbs are few in number and often irregular. They are usually short and may be unaccented. The auxiliaries {gú}, {zá}, {gáa}, and {zé} are preceded by word juncture, but the juncture is usually lost through the operation of

‖24. The rest of the auxiliaries are joined to the preceding complement without an intervening juncture. A limited amount of thematic derivation is found with the auxiliaries.

461. Most of the auxiliaries are morphemically identified by the phonemic form of the 3(-3) person singular nonmodal. {śé} is identified by its first person singular nonmodal form because the third person form is homophonous with that of {zá}. The static auxiliaries are identified by their 3-1 person singular nonmodal form.

In the following sections the auxiliaries are exemplified by partial paradigms. The phonemic forms shown in the paradigms are those found in final position.

461.1. {gú} is found in the constructions described in Section 632.6 and in the periphrastic constructions described in Section 470. It has the following allomorphs:

	Singular	Dual	Plural
First allomorph	-ú:N	-qúuʔN	-úuS
Second allomorph	-u:máN	-u:máN	-ú:maS

Singular, dual, and plural refer to number of the subject. The auxiliary has not been recorded with nonsingular objects.[1] The first allomorphs are used with 1(-3), 2(-3), 3(-3), indefinite, and expective prefixes. The second allomorphs are used with other pronominal prefixes. The second allomorph of the dual suffix and both allomorphs of the plural take the dual and plural suffix, respectively. The first allomorph of the dual adds on the dual suffix when there is another suffix following. The first allomorphs of the dual and plural take set IV pronominal prefixes, and the remaining allomorphs take set I. The second allomorph of the plural form is unaccented if, through the operation of ‖13, the thematic syllable is long. The nonmodal paradigms of {gú} are:

	Singular	Dual	Plural
1(-3)	-sí	-ṣúuʔu	-ṣuusa
2(-3)	-ṣú	-kuc̣úuʔu	-kuz̧úusa
3(-3)	-gú	-ḱúuʔu	-gúusa
obv.	-ciumá	-ciumánətyə	-ciumasa
1-2	-ṣaumá	-ṣaumánətyə	-ṣaumasa
3-2	-kuzumá	-kuz̧umánətyə	-kuz̧úmasa

---

[1]Number prefixes have been recorded with {gú} (usually to indicate object number) in the periphrastic expective construction. This use of the number prefixes, however, does not represent the usual pattern. See Section 471.

	Singular (cont'd)	Dual (cont'd)	Plural (cont'd)
2-1	-dyumá	-dyumánətyə	-dyúmasa
3-1	-sgumá	-sgumánətyə	-sgúmasa
exp.	-níu-	-núuʔu-	-núusaa-
ind.	-sgú	-skúuʔu	-sgúusa

461.2. {sé}, an intransitive-B auxiliary verb, is used in the constructions described in Section 632.5. The forms of the auxiliary are ‖-JáʔaN‖ singular and ‖-JániyaB‖ dual and plural. The dual is distinguished from the plural by the addition of the dual suffix. Set I pronominal prefixes are used. The nonmodal paradigms of {sé} are:

	Singular	Dual	Plural
1st	-sé	-séniyapətyə	-séniya
2nd	-šá	-šániyapətyə	-šániya
3rd	-zá	-zániyapətyə	-zániya
exp.	-née-	?	?

The auxiliary {ćaaci}, a perfect impersonal thematic derivative of {sé}, has the morphophonemic shape ‖-qjáʔaziS‖. It is used in constructions described in Section 632.5.

461.3. {ci}, an intransitive-A auxiliary verb, is used as described in Sections 631 and 632.4. The forms are ‖-ji∅(S)‖ singular, ‖-qáaʔN‖ dual, and ‖-jeeY‖ plural. The plural suffix is optionally added to the plural form. Set I pronominal prefixes are used in the singular, set IV in the dual and plural. The nonmodal paradigms are:

	Singular	Dual	Plural
1st	-si	-sáaʔa	-səte, -səteeʔe
2nd	-ši	-kəćáaʔa	-kəte, -kəteeʔe
3rd	-ci	-ḱáaʔa	-ce, -ceeʔe
exp.	-ne- (?)	?	?

461.4. {ka}, an intransitive-A auxiliary verb, is used as described in Sections 631, 632.1, 632.2, and 632.5. The singular form is ‖-aN‖. The dual and plural forms are identical with those of {ci}. Set I pronominal prefixes are used in the singular, set IV in the dual and plural. The nonmodal paradigms are:

	Singular	Dual	Plural
1st	-se	-sáaʔa	-səte, -səteeʔe
2nd	-ṣa	-kəćáaʔa	-kəte, -kəteeʔe
3rd	-ka	-ḱáaʔa	-ce, -ceeʔe
exp.	-ne-	?	?

The auxiliary {gáńi}, used as described in Section 632.3, is formed from {ka} by the addition of the completive suffix -qiṢ. The plural form, ‖-jee?eṢ‖, is an irregular formation. The nonmodal paradigms are:

	Singular	Dual	Plural
1st	-séńi	-ṣáańi	-sətee?e, -sətee?eši
2nd	-ṣáńi	-kəćáańi	-kətee?e, -kətee?eši
3rd	-gáńi	-ḱáańi	-cee?e, -cee?eši
exp.	-néńi-	?	?

461.5. {ku}, an intransitive-A auxiliary verb, is found only in the singular and only with the stem zúu- 'to go' (the dual and plural themes of 'to go' are -qjéeyu∅ and -je?éguY respectively; see ‖7.10 and Section 632.7). The auxiliary has two allomorphs, ‖-aa∅‖ and ‖-ɐuu∅‖. The first allomorph is used after pronominal prefixes ending in ‖j‖, and the second allomorph is used elsewhere. The paradigm is:

	Nonmodal	Dubitative	Hortative
1st	-se	-te	-ne (prefix nj- ?)
2nd	-ṣu	-çu	... (see Section 234)
3rd	-ku	-tyu	-puṣu
exp.	-nee-		
1st neg.	-sku		

The pronominal prefixes are similar to, but not identical with, those of set I (Section 230).

The suffix ‖-qjáaťaN‖, allomorph of -ńáaťaN, is added directly to the pronominal prefixes (see ‖1.13). If the pronominal prefix ends with ‖j‖, the vowel of the suffix becomes /e/:

　　zúuśeeťa 'I kept going'
　　zúućáaťa 'he kept going'

The pronominal prefixes are palatalized before a front vowel of an initial vowel suffix:

　　zúuci 'when he went'; suffix -(´)í (Section 762)
　　?uzúuci 'to go'; suffix ‖-iṢ‖, allomorph of the completive suffix
　　　　-qiṢ

The last example is the infinitive form, in which the third person pronominal prefix is incorporated in the irregular stem formation ‖-uzúu-g-aa∅‖.

When a suffix that conditions accent ablaut is added to the auxiliary, the accent ablaut also applies to the auxiliary complement. Cf. the example zúuci, given above.

461.6. {gáa}, an intransitive-A auxiliary verb, is used in the constructions described in Section 632.8. The auxiliary has two allomorphs in the
singular, ‖-JííB‖ and ‖-á?aB‖. The first allomorph is used after the
pronominal prefixes that end in ‖j‖, and the second allomorph is used
elsewhere. The long vowel of the second allomorph is retained in final
position, in spite of ‖25. The remaining forms are ‖-âa?aB(N)‖ dual
and ‖-je?éeB(M, N)‖ plural. Set I pronominal prefixes are used in the
singular and set IV in the dual and plural. The nonmodal paradigms are:

	Singular	Dual	Plural
1st	-sí	-ṣâa?a	-səde?é
2nd	-ṣáa	-kəẓâa?a	-kəde?é
3rd	-gáa	-gâa?a	-ze?é
exp.	-níi-	-nəẓâa?a-	-nəde?ée-

461.7. {gá}, an intransitive auxiliary verb, is found only in the singular and is used as described in Section 632.9. It has the morphophonemic
shape ‖-á‖ and uses set I pronominal prefixes. The nonmodal paradigm
is:

1st	-sé
2nd	-ṣá
3rd	-gá

461.8. {zá}, an intransitive-A auxiliary verb, is used as described in
Section 632.10. It has the forms ‖-já?aN‖ singular and ‖-jaa?aB(N)‖
dual and plural. The plural is distinguished from the dual by adding the
plural suffix allomorph ‖-aaD‖ to ‖-jaa?aB‖ (the expected allomorph of
the plural suffix after ‖B‖ is ‖-eeD‖; see ‖1.6). Set IV pronominal
prefixes are used for all three numbers. The nonmodal paradigms are:

	Singular	Dual	Plural
1st	-sədá	-sətaa?a	-sətaa?apa
2nd	-kədá	-kətaa?a	-kətaa?apa
3rd	-zá	-caa?a	-caa?apa
exp.	-nədáa-	-nətaa?a-	-nətaa?apaa-

The singular form ‖-já?aN‖ plus the adverbializing suffix ‖-(´)í‖
(Section 762) results in either the morphophonemically regular form or
the irregular combination ‖-(´)ée‖. When the combination is irregular,
the long vowel is retained in final position in spite of ‖25, and the accent ablaut of the suffix operates on the auxiliary complement. In either
case the final vowel of the auxiliary complement is lengthened:
rúuníšíizée ~ rûunišiiza?ání 'when it was Monday'; cf. rûunišizá 'it was

Monday'. When the irregular combination results, ‖3.2 optionally applies after ‖19 (‖3.2 applies to forms with the morphophoneme ‖ ` ‖, and ‖19 is the operation of accent ablaut). Thus a form that contains ‖ ` ‖ has three alternate forms: mə́ədéesədée ~ mə́ədéesədée ~ mə́ədéesədaʔání 'when I was a boy'; ‖mə́ədè‖ 'boy'.

The auxiliary {sḱá}, used as described in Section 632.12, is a static derivative of {zá}. It has the forms ‖-JáʔaN‖ singular, ‖-aaʔa‖ dual, and ‖-aiʔi‖ (probably ‖-aiY‖ plus the plural suffix) plural. The plural of {sḱá} may optionally be replaced by the plural of the intransitive auxiliary {zé} (Section 461.9). The nonmodal paradigms are:

	Singular	Dual	Plural
3-1	-sḱá	-skaaʔa	-skaiʔi (or -səteeʔeši)
3-2	-kədá	?	?
obv.	-ćá	-caaʔa	-caiʔi (or -ceeʔeši
exp.	-ńée-	?	?

The auxiliary {sḱáaci}, used in constructions described in Section 632.13, is a static derivative of {zá}. It is probably derived from {sḱá} by the completive suffix -qiṢ. It has the forms ‖-JáʔaziṢ‖ singular and ‖-aaʔaziṢ‖ dual. No plural forms have been recorded; the plural of the auxiliary {zé} (Section 461.9) has been recorded instead. The nonmodal paradigms are:

	Singular	Dual	(Plural)
3-1	-sḱáaci	-skaaʔaci	(-səteeʔeši)
3-2	-kəźaaci	?	?
obv.	-ćáaci	-caaʔaci	(-ceeʔeši)

461.9. {zé}, an intransitive-A auxiliary verb, is used in constructions described in Section 632.11. It has the forms ‖-jée‖ singular and ‖-jeeʔeṢ‖ dual and plural. The plural is distinguished from the dual by the addition of the plural suffix. Set IV pronominal prefixes are used for all three numbers. The nonmodal paradigms are:

	Singular	Dual	Plural
1st	-sədé	-səteeʔe	-səteeʔeši
2nd	-kədé	-kəteeʔe	-kəteeʔeši
3rd	-zé	-ceeʔe	-ceeʔeši

461.10. {ḱá}, an intransitive-A verb, is used in constructions described in Section 632.14. It has the forms ‖-qáa‖ singular, ‖-aʔá‖ dual, and ‖-qáaši‖ plural. It takes set III pronominal prefixes in the singular and set IV in the dual and plural. The nonmodal paradigms are:

	Singular	Dual	Plural
1st	-s̯á	-ṣaʔá	-s̯áaši
2nd	-kəz̯á	-kəza̯ʔá	-kəćáaši
3rd	-ḱá	-ga̯ʔá	-ḱáaši

462. A synopsis of the auxiliary allomorphs is given in table 11.

TABLE 11

Allomorphs of the Auxiliary Verbs

Auxiliary			Singular	Dual	Plural
(461.1)	gú	1.	-ú:N	-qúuʔN	-úuS-aaD
		2.	-u:máN	-u:máN-qədyəəZ	-ú:maS-aaD
(461.2)	s̯é		-JáʔaN	-JániyaB-ədyəəZ	-JániyaB
	ćaaci		-qjáʔaziṢ		
(461.3)	ci		-ji∅(Ṣ)	-qáaʔN	-jeeY(-ʔVVD)
(461.4)	ka		-aN	-qáaʔN	-jeeY(-ʔVVD)
	gáni		-aN-qiṢ	-qáaʔN-qiṢ	-jeeʔeṢ(-iiD)
(461.5)	ku	1.	-aa∅		
		2.	-uu∅		
(461.6)	gáa	1.	-JíiB	-âaʔaB(N)	-jeʔéeB(M,N)
		2.	-áʔaB		
(461.7)	gá		-á		
(461.8)	zá		-jáʔaN	-jaaʔaB(N)	-jaaʔaB-aaD
	sḱá		-JáʔaN	-aaʔa	-aiʔi
	sḱaaci		-JáʔaziṢ	-aaʔaziṢ	
(461.9)	zé		-jée	-jeeʔeṢ	-jeeʔeṢ-iiD
(461.10)	ḱá		-qáa	-aʔá	-qáaši

470. Periphrastic Constructions

Periphrastic constructions have the following form: periphrastic prefix + theme + auxiliary {gú} (Section 461.1). The theme is either a verb theme or an ambivalent theme functioning as a verb. Noun themes are not found in this construction. The periphrastic prefix is placed in the pronominal prefix position (position class one). Person and mode are indicated by the auxiliary verb. There are three periphrastic constructions formed by one of the following prefixes:

    n- expective

    p- mandative

    ʔ- desiderative

The expective prefix has four allomorphs: nj-, ńj-, n-, and nəẓ-. Their distribution is given in Section 232. The other prefixes have no allomorphs.

    The expective is very common. The other two periphrastic constructions are rare, and the details of their formation are not known, but it can be expected that they are similar to those of the expective.

    471. The expective is used to indicate that the action is expected to, is desired to, or might take place. Thus 'I will walk', 'I was going to walk', 'I would have walked', 'I might (have) walk(ed)', and 'I want(ed) to walk' are all translated by the expective in Acoma. The following examples are taken from texts:

    nêeʔepee-kuẓuʔumá 'he might eat you up'

    ńadyáa-sgúńu 'one will keep it as a pet'

    zûunee-sgúńu 'one wants to go' (auxiliary {ku}, Section 461.5)

    ńańáci-gúńiši 'what would be used for his lunch'

    ńáudíi-sgúńiši 'what one wants to plant'

    nigûuńicaa-gúńiši 'that she would become pregnant'

The last three examples are nominalized verbs (Section 761).

    The thematic class of the expective construction is governed by the thematic class of the main verb, not by the auxiliary (see Section 410):

    gúukača 'he saw him'; ńiukačagú 'he will see him' (transitive)

    súpe 'I ate'; núpesí 'I will eat' (intransitive-A)

    kaʔáudí 'he planted'; ńáudíigú 'he will plant' (intransitive-B)

    skâanawáńi 'I am mean'; ńâanawáńisgumá 'I will be mean' (static)

    cíukúičáńi 'it has been divided'; ńíukúičáńigú 'it will be divided'
        (impersonal)

    A nonsingular subject is indicated both by the appropriate number prefix or suffix (depending on theme class, Section 433) with the main verb and by the appropriate nonsingular form of {gú}:

    ńiukačáńətyəṣúuʔu 'we (dual) will see him', transitive theme
        -úukačaN, dual suffix ‖-qədyəəZ‖, dual auxiliary

    ńiukačáńaṣúusa 'we (plural) will see him', plural suffix ‖-qaaD‖,
        plural auxiliary

    nəẓaʔáaťawikucúuʔu 'yours (dual) will be open, it will be open for
        you', intransitive-A theme -qáaťaW-qiṢ, dual prefix, dual auxiliary

    The nonsingular number of the object of a transitive verb is indicated by a number prefix with the main verb:

    niʔíuńatyumeciumá 'he might hurt them (dual)' (obviative); theme
        -ú:ńadyumeN

néyaskátaṣú 'you will give them (plural) a drink'; theme -JíiskadaN
(plural prefix irregular, ‖ 7.7)

Sometimes the number prefix (indicating either number of subject or
object, depending on theme class) is found with both the main verb and
the auxiliary:

neʔéečáaçašetiuʔúmasa 'they (dual) will be heard', static

nêeʔepeekuẓuʔumá 'he might eat you (dual) up' (transitive)

472. The mandative is used for a request or polite command. The
main verb is an intransitive verb, either type A or B, and the resulting
construction is transitive:

piẓáačúwasí 'I told him to wake up', theme -ˈiẓáačúwaM(N), intransitive-A

pâizúwaasí 'I wanted him to pay', theme -ˈáʔizúwaaN, intransitive-B
pâizúwaasgumá 'he wanted me to pay'

473. The desiderative is similar in meaning to the mandative. The
main verb is intransitive (type B only?), and the resulting construction
is also intransitive. The main verb usually, but not always, has the completive suffix and hence is usually homophonous with the infinitive (Section 420). Examples:

ʔáyaceepisí 'I asked to have it whitewashed'

ʔâizúwaañisí 'I wanted it paid'

500. NOUN THEMES

There are two classes of noun themes, inalienably possessed themes
(Section 510), and ambivalent themes (Section 520). The noun theme is
inflected for person and number (Section 530). A noun theme and pronominal prefix form a possessed noun.

510. Inalienably Possessed Nouns

The theme and root of inalienably possessed nouns are identical. This
class includes only body part terms, and almost all body part terms belong to this class. Many of the themes have an absolutive form (Section
641).

The inalienably possessed themes are given in the following list. The
theme is followed by the third person form, written phonemically, and
the gloss:

-ʼaʔášə; kaʔášə 'his knee'
-Aúučíyáatiṣa; gáučíyáatiṣa 'his shin'
-áčə́ḱaya; gáčə́ḱaya 'his armpit'
-jáača; záača 'his tooth'
-jáẓa; záca 'his horn'
-qjîiḱa; čîiḱa 'his mouth, lips'
-Aṅuṁa; gâuṁa 'her vagina'
-ʼâamaa; kâama 'his thigh'
-ʼuṁáči; kuṁáči 'his groin'
-ʼaṁáapaa; kaṁáapa 'his palm, paw'
-ʼaṁásdíi; kaṁásdí 'his hand'
-ʼáṁasdyáa; káṁasdyá 'his finger' (?)
-ʼáamúča; káamúča 'his big toe'
-ʼjâaṁúuča; câaṁúuča 'his toe'
-Aúumúča; gáuṁúuča 'his buttocks'
-qjîiṁúuča; čîiṁúuča 'his upper lip, snout'
-ʼjáamúša; cáamúša 'his beard'

[144]

-qâanáa; ḱaaná 'his eye'

-ánâaʔaẓəši; gánâaʔaçəši 'the crown of his head'

-ánâaʔaši; gánâaʔaši 'the arch of his foot'

-û:náčai; kúnáčai 'his stomach'

-ánásgái; gánáska 'his head'

-ꞌjíŋi; cíŋi 'his body'

-Aúunúutii; gáunúuti 'his ankle'

-ꞌábaa; kábá 'his testicles'

-qjíipee; cíipe 'his ear'

-aipéʇa; gaipéʇa 'his anus'

-qúupi; ḱuupi 'his forehead'

-uːsêeńiši; kusêeńiši 'his hair'

-ꞌásíi; kásí 'her breasts'

-ꞌjíisipa; cíisipa 'his eyelashes'

-jaasḱaaci; záasḱaaci 'his chin'

-qáisḱâaḿi; ḱaisḱâaḿi 'the calf of his leg'

-ꞌásdíi; kásdí 'his foot'

-aústu; gaústu 'his temple'

-qjíišəə; cíišə 'his nose'

-Aúušúkucisa; gáušúkucisa 'his elbow'

-aišupa; gaišupa 'his hip'

-aíša; gaíša 'the small of his back'

-ꞌáadáḱa; káadáḱa 'his heel'

-ꞌádáẃi; kádáẃi 'his navel'

-ꞌuẃáačə; kuẃáačə 'his tongue'

-ꞌuẃápə; kuẃápə 'his cheek'

-ꞌúẃasə; kúẃasə 'his feather, wing'

-qúwáẃi; ḱúwáẃi 'his face'

-áwi; gáwi 'his neck'

-áwíci; gáwíci 'his chest'

-jaawíiča; záawíiča 'his nail, claw'

-áwîiẓá; gáwîiẓá 'his throat'

-áwíńuska; gáwíńuska 'his heart'

-áẏa; gáẏa 'his penis'

-jáẏagəẓə; záẏakəçə 'his rib'

-qayáatiima; ḱayáatiima 'his wisdom tooth'

-ꞌjiẏúci; ciẏúci 'his upper back'

-ꞌjiẏûuḿii; ciẏûuḿi 'his arm'

-ꞌjíyusḱa; cíẏusḱą 'his tail'

-ꞌjiẏúuspii; ciẏúuspi 'his shoulder'

520. Ambivalents

Ambivalents may function as verbs or nouns. When functioning as nouns they are inflected for person and number like other noun themes (Section 530). When functioning as verbs they are additionally inflected for mode (Section 431) and may enter into the periphrastic expective construction (Section 471). Most ambivalents are translated 'to have . . .' when they function as verbs. Examples:

čadyûuni 'does she have pottery?', dubitative; theme -qadyûuni, noun dyûuni 'pottery'

ṣaʔadyûuni 'we (dual) have pottery', verb, nonmodal; 'our (dual) pottery', noun

ńadyûunigú 'she will have pottery', expective

çəẓáwiçə 'do you have a brother?', dubitative; theme -qáwiẓa

521. Derived ambivalents are composed of a free noun and the possessive prefix -qa- (‖ 5.4):

dyûuni 'pottery': -qadyûuni, for example, ḱadyûuni 'her pottery'

páńaci 'lungs': -qapáńaci, for example, śapáńaci 'my lungs'

dyaʔáu 'grandmother': -qadyaʔáu, for example, ḱadyaʔáu 'her grand mother'

ʔudyáaťitáańi 'pen': -qadyáaťitáańi, for example, śadyáaťitáańi 'my pen' (noun derived from the infinitive ʔudyáaťitaańi 'to be writing, Section 643)

522. Basic ambivalent themes are few in number and are composed of a noun root that occurs only with the possessive prefix. It is impossible to segment basic ambivalent themes into two morphophonemic parts because of the nature of the morphophonemic rule that applies to the possessive prefix (‖ 5.4). The basic ambivalent themes are:

-qaḱûiẓa 'sister of a man'

-qáwaẓə 'brother of a woman'

-qâawi 'clansman'

-qaḱúuyá 'father's clansman'

-qáaẓə 'husband'

-qâuḱui 'wife'

-qadyáa ~ -qadyáaši 'pet, domesticated animal'

-qáẃaṣu 'scar'

-qáapaa 'bag'

-qáiṣa 'field, garden'

-qáuḱïini 'friend'

The last three themes have unpossessed noun derivatives (Section 642).

Animal terms do not enter into the ambivalent construction. Instead, the theme -qadyáa(ši) 'pet' is used with animal terms: kawâayu śadyá 'my horse', díya kadyá 'his dog'.

The themes -aʔáu 'sister of a woman' and -Aâama 'house' are basic ambivalent themes in function, but not in form. The theme -aʔáu is irregular in that it takes set IV pronominal prefixes in all three numbers (see Section 231). When functioning as a verb, -Aâama has the same meaning as the intransitive-A verb -Aâuʔu 'to dwell'. The plurals of the verb and the ambivalent themes are the same: -âazəədya, for example, gâacəətya 'their (plural) house; they (plural) dwell' (see ‖7.10).

523. The kinship terms bíhí 'a woman who has married a clansman' and wáati 'a man who has married a clansman' have two ambivalent constructions. The first construction is regular, -qabíhí and -qawáati: śabíhí 'a woman who has married my clansman'; kabíhí 'a woman who has married his clansman'. The second construction, -Jubíhí and -Juwáati, is a static verb in form (Section 410), but an ambivalent in function. This construction is used to show the reciprocal relationship: śkubíhí 'my husband's clansman'. The nonmodal singular paradigms are:

śkubíhí 'my in-law'	śkuwáati 'my in-law'
kətibíhí 'your in-law'	kətiwáati 'your in-law'
cibíhí 'her in-law'	ciwáati 'his in-law'

524. A few ambivalent themes take only the third person prefixes. In this respect they are like impersonal verbs (Section 410):

kúuti 'mountain; it is a mountain'; čúuti 'is it a mountain?' (dubitative); theme -qúudì

kiwá 'plant; it is growing'; čiwá 'is it growing?' (dubitative); theme -ʼiwá

kácə 'building, house; it is a building; it is tall'; čácə 'it is a building?; is it tall?' (dubitative); theme -ʼázəəD

The theme -ʼiwá has been recorded with the nonthematic verb suffix -náataN (Section 442.2): kiwâanáata 'there would be plants'.

530. Inflection

Pronominal prefixes (Section 230) and number prefixes (‖7, especially ‖7.9) are used in the inflection of noun themes. Noun themes distinguish four persons, first, second, third, and indefinite, and three numbers, singular, dual, and plural. The singular is unmarked. A harmonic plural suffix (Section 241) is added to plural ambivalents. Person and number refer to the possessor of the noun theme. Examples:

-ʼamásdíi 'hand', inalienably possessed theme: samásdí 'my hand',
kamásdí 'his hand', skamásdí 'one's hand', ṣaʔamásdí 'our (dual)
hands', ṣayamásdí 'our (plural) hands'

-qaháazáni, ambivalent theme derived from háazáni 'hair': ṣaháazáni
'my hair', skaháazáni 'one's hair', ṣaaháazáni 'our (dual) hair',
ṣaaháazániši 'our (plural) hair'

540. Plural of Nouns

The verbalizing suffix -dyaiM (Section 624) and the nominalizing suffix
-iši (Section 761) are used with ambivalents and unpossessed nouns to
form the plural of the noun. Plurality is an optional category. Examples:

máḱatyaimiši 'dippers'; máḱa 'dipper'

ḱamáḱatyaimiši 'his dippers'; ḱamáḱa 'his dipper'

ʔúwáakatyaimiši 'babies'; ʔúwáaka 'baby'

ṣadyáatyaimiši 'my livestock'; ṣadyá 'my domesticated animal'

An ambivalent with a plural possessor (indicated by the plural prefix)
does not take the harmonic plural suffix -šiiD (Sections 241, 530) in this
formation: ṣâawityaimiši 'our (plural) relatives'. The harmonic plural
suffix is probably lost by haplology.

A few kinship terms indicate the plural with the suffix -ši: nánaši
'grandfathers'; náisdíyaši 'fathers'.

550. Vocatives

Three kinship terms have a special vocative form:

nayé 'mother!'; náaya 'mother' (cf. nayéezá 'married woman with
children')

gaʔáu 'sister!'; -aʔáu 'sister of a woman'

bíiya ~ bíiyai ~ bíhiyai 'in-law!'; bíhí 'a woman who has married
a clansman'

The vocative gaʔáu is homophonous with the third person form 'her sister'.

Other kinship terms indicate the vocative by the free noun form or,
if they are basic ambivalents, by the first person form:

dyúmə 'brother!'; dyúmə 'brother of a man'

ṣáwiçə 'brother!'; -qáwiẓə 'brother of a woman'

The first person ambivalent forms are used for the vocative of two
derived ambivalents. The free noun forms are not kinship terms:

šámə́əti 'son!'; ‖ mə́ədì ‖ 'boy'

šámáʔákə 'daughter!'; ‖ magə́ ‖ 'little girl'

These forms are also morphophonemically irregular; see ‖ 5.4.

560. Inflection of ʔédyu, ʔédyuyú

The adverb-conjunction ʔédyu and its derivative ʔédyuyú, both meaning 'and then, next', have the special thematic forms -dyu and -dyuyú. The themes are inflected for first, second, and third person by an anomalous set of pronominal prefixes (Section 236). The resulting forms appear to be nouns. Examples:

    nútyuyú 'my turn'

    ʔétyuyú 'his turn'

    nútyu 'and me?; how about me?'

600. DERIVATION

Derivational processes that apply to verb and noun themes have been described in the preceding chapters (Sections 410, 440, 520). The remaining processes are the subject of this chapter.

610. Compounds

Compounding is not a common process. Most compounds are irregular:

sémasdáistaaya 'my hand is cold', -ámasdáistaaya (intransitive-A):
-ʿamásdíi 'hand'; -áistaaya 'to be cold' (intransitive-A)

k̂aanáaši 'he has a sty', -qâanáašiM (intransitive A): -qâanáa 'eye';
-ʿáišiM 'to be swollen' (intransitive A)

húušénâani 'head or nose cold': -qjíišəə 'nose'; -qâanáa 'eye'

ka?âiciináawa 'she put on face powder', -Qâici?ináawaN (intransitive
B): -âici 'to be fair of complexion' (intransitive A); ?ináawí
'flour'

dítyabámə 'San Fidel' (place name): dídya 'north' (adverb); nabámə
'wild fruit; dry farming'

ẏáusbénáná 'sling': ẏóuni 'stone'; sbénáná 'forked stick'

The most common type of compound is composed of an inalienably possessed noun plus an intransitive verb theme, and the resulting form is an intransitive verb theme (see first two examples). The composition of other compounds is varied. The compounded elements may be verb stems or themes, nouns, descriptives, or adverbs, and the resulting compound may be a verb stem, verb theme, or noun. Adverbs are not common in compounds. Compounds composed of two verb stems or themes have not been found. If one of the elements of the compound is a verb stem or theme, the resulting form is usually a verb stem or theme.

A number of compounded verb stems are composed of a verb stem plus a preposed or postposed element of unique occurrence. Examples:

-úudâak̂adyaẂ 'to take off the lid or cover': -dâa?W 'to cover'

-úbêecistaaN 'to pray': -bé?eN 'to tell'

-ʻúticuuzaN 'to crawl: -ucúuzaN 'to move'

620. Formation of Verb Stems

621. -zaN is suffixed to descriptives (Section 631) to form verb stems.
The stem syllable ‖úu ~ ûu‖ is used with these forms:

gáutákaci, gâutákaci 'his got square', stem -úutákazaN, -ûutákazaN;
    táka- 'square'

sáusíkica 'I folded it', stem -úusíkizaN; síki- 'wrinkled'

cíuspátaci 'it has been dampened', stem -úuspátazaN; spáta- 'damp'

A descriptive that has the shape ‖cvːcv-‖ and a medial glottalized
sonorant (see Section 222) becomes ‖cv́cv-‖ in this formation:

sîumúraca 'I dented his', stem -úumúrazaN, -ûumúrazaN; muːra-
    'dented', for example, muráci 'it is dented'

sîušínaca 'I crushed it', stem -ûušínazaN; šiːna- 'crushed', for
    example, šinánaka 'it got crushed' (reduplicated, ‖18.1)

Other unpatterned accent changes often occur:

-uːsgəzəzaN 'to bend'; sgə́zə-, sgəːzə- 'bent, warped'

-ûucáyuzaN, -úucáyuzaN 'to break'; caʔyu-, cáyu- 'broken'

-úušauzaN 'to pop out'; šáu- 'popped out'

The initial consonant of nə́ə- 'rigid, stretched' is deglottalized in the
verb stem: cíunəəci 'it has been stretched'.

In addition to the descriptives, members of other auxiliary complement
classes (Section 632) sometimes form verb stems with -zaN. In this case,
however, the formations are unproductive and irregular:

-íišupəzaN; šúpə- (Section 632.1): síišupəca 'I spit on him'; šúpəse
    'I spit'

-ucúuzaN; cúu- (Section 632.1): cicúuca 'he moved it'; cúuka 'he
    moved'

-ûuwakazaN; wáka- (Section 632.5): kaʔâuwakaca 'it all spilled from
    him'; wákazá 'he spilled it'

A large number of verb stems are always found with -zaN. The majority of these forms have the stem syllable ‖uu‖:

-úušíizaN 'to borrow', gúušíica 'he borrowed it from him'

-ûupayazaN 'to laugh', sgûupayuca 'I laughed'

-ûupátizaN 'to scatter', cîupátici 'it has been scattered'

-áaskayuzaN 'to pull teeth', sgáaskayuca 'he pulled my tooth'

-íicitamazaN 'to turn over', síicitamaca 'I turned it over'

622. -zaN 'to make . . ., to get . . . ready' is suffixed to nouns to
form verb stems. The resulting forms usually have the unaccented stem

syllable ‖u‖. An initial plain sonorant is glottalized. The noun suffix
-ni (Section 642) is often lost in this formation:

    súmúšiça 'I gathered soap weed', stem -úmúšiẓaN; múši 'soap weed'

    súmazíça 'I made blue corn paper bread', stem -úmazíẓaN; mazíni
        'blue corn paper bread'

    súuwabáça 'I put feathers together', stem -úuwabáẓaN; wabáni
        'feathers'

    súumáacáaça 'I made jerky', stem -úumáacáaẓaN; máacáani 'jerky'

    síukiiniça 'I made friends with him', stem -úukiiniẓaN; -qáukiini
        'friend' (basic ambivalent, Section 522)

    kázámǝniça 'he made prayer sticks', stem -ázámǝniẓaN; házámǝni
        'prayer stick'

The allomorph ‖-iẓaN‖ is sometimes used: siméesiçaní 'I made a
table for him', méesa 'table'. .

A number of stems are always found with -ẓaN:

    -ûpǝẓaN 'to shake', sípǝça 'I shook it out'

    -úwákuiẓaN 'to get married', skúwákuiça 'I got married' (cf.
        -qâukui 'wife')

    -udyáaẓaN 'to write', sudyáaça 'I wrote'

    -usbéẓaN 'to string', susbéça 'I strung it'

    623. -ƚuwaaN 'to take . . . off' is added to inalienably possessed
noun themes (Section 510) to form verb stems. There are sometimes
changes of the final syllable and the initial vowel:

    zâawíiƚuwaaní 'she cut his nails', stem -âawíiƚuwaaN; -jáawíiča
        'nail, claw'

    síuyúuspiiƚuwa 'I took the shoulder off', stem -ú:yúuspiiƚuwaaN;
        -jiyúuspii 'shoulder'

    gâamaaƚuwa 'he took the leg off', stem -âamaaƚuwaaN; -'âamaa
        'thigh'

    gúnásgáiƚuwa 'he took the head off', stem -ú:násgáiƚuwaaN; -ánásga
        'head'

The suffix is found with one verb stem: síwâameeƚuwa 'I took the ten
down', stem -úwâameesD-ƚuwaaN; -úwâameeSD 'to make shade, put up a
tent'.

    624. -dyaiM 'to have several . . .' is added to ambivalents (Section
520). The resulting forms are verb themes (intransitive A) rather than
verb stems:

    čámǝǝtityai 'she had sons' (dubitative): -qámǝǝdì 'son'

    kámúšityai 'he has lots of soap weed': -qámúši 'soap weed'

    náwáasƚiçatyaigú 'he will have offsprings' (expective): -qáwáasƚiẓa
        'young one'

ƙadyúm̓ətyai 'he has brothers': -qadyúm̓ə 'brother'

The final syllable of -qám̓ə́ədì is sometimes dropped before the suffix: ƙám̓ə́ətyai, ƙám̓ə́ətityai 'he has sons'.

625. The suffix -aN is added to some verb stems. The resulting form
may be a verb stem or a verb theme. The suffix has a number of morphophonemic shapes; ‖-aN‖, ‖-áaN‖, and ‖-áawaN‖ are typical. The
suffix is not productive. Examples:

-âinaD 'to cook meat'; -âinadaN 'to cook meat' (stem)

-sƙaD 'to drink'; -JíisƙadaW(N) 'to give someone a drink' (transitive theme)

-qabáa 'to have a fire going'; -ubáyaN 'to build a fire, to burn'
(stem)

-učáwaN 'to blame, steal'; -Jučáwidáawa 'to blame someone' (transitive theme)

-pəkadá?aN 'to use up'; -ûupakadáawaN (see ‖17) 'to use up' (stem)

A few stems that appear to contain the suffix -aN are paired with
forms that have the completive suffix -qiṢ. The forms with -qiṢ are
usually impersonal themes rather than stems:

-áyáitaaN 'to paint'; -qjáyáitiṢ 'to be painted' (impersonal theme)
-úuyúuskaM̄ 'to paint, decorate'; -ûuyúušiṢ 'to be painted' (impersonal theme; cf. Section 221)

-áayátaW(M̄, N) 'to get smeared'; -ayátiṢ 'to be smeared' (stem)

-úgúta 'to make a bridge'; -ʻjúgútiṢ 'to be a bridge' (impersonal
theme)

-áyasdaaN 'to enclose'; -áyasdiiM, -ʻjúyasdiiM 'to be enclosed'
(stem)

Instead of occurring in position nine (see table 10), the completive suffix
is added directly to the stem in these forms: cíyastináata 'they graze',
lit. 'they keep being enclosed'; -náataN, position eight suffix. Contrast
cíwâaneeyáataɲi 'there used to be hunting', in which the normal relative
order of -náataN and -qiṢ is maintained.

630. Auxiliary Complements

Auxiliary complements are inflected by a following auxiliary verb (Section
460). The complements fall into a number of classes that are defined by
their occurrence with particular auxiliaries. Only one class, the descriptives (Section 631), is of much importance. The remaining classes (Section 632) tend to be small and do not enter into as many constructions
as the descriptives.

631. The descriptives are inflected by the auxiliaries {ci} (Section 461.3) and {ka} (Section 461.4). There are two formations with {ci}, one intransitive and the other impersonal. {ka} is used impersonally. The intransitive forms use the full paradigm of the auxiliary and mean 'to be . . .'. The impersonal forms use only the third person auxiliaries and with {ci} mean 'it is . . .', with {ka} 'it got . . .'. The impersonal constructions with {ci}, unlike other impersonal constructions (Section 410), distinguish number. The plural, in this case meaning more than one is indicated by using the plural forms of {ci}. The dual forms are not used. Examples are given with skúu- 'wet':

    Intransitive forms with {ci}
        skúusi 'I am wet'
        skúuci 'he is wet'
        skúukáaʔa 'they (dual) are wet'
        skúusəteeʔe 'we (plural) are wet'
    Impersonal forms with {ci}
        skúuci 'it is wet'
        skúuceeʔe 'they (two or more) are wet'
    Impersonal forms with {ka}
        skúuka 'it got wet'

$\{R_1\}$ or {L} (reduplicative and length morphemes, see ‖ 18) is added to the descriptive to form the distributive, meaning 'to be . . . all over, everywhere'. A given descriptive can occur with one or the other morpheme, never both (except under special circumstances described below). Examples:

    cápipici 'it has lots of spots'; cápici 'it has a spot'
    muráraci 'they are dented'; muráci 'it is dented'
    mátyutyuka 'it got steamed up everywhere'; mátyuka 'it got steame up'
    kâayuka 'they broke'; káyúka 'it broke'
    kûutuka 'several bubbles formed'; kútuka 'a bubble formed'

A number of descriptives always occur with $\{R_1\}$ in auxiliary constru tions. The reduplication in this case does not indicate the distributive:

    cérereci 'it is greasy, has one grease spot'
    bérereci 'it is smooth'
    šináŋaka 'it got cracked, crushed'

{L} is used with the unreduplicated form of these descriptives to form the distributive: céereci 'it has lots of grease spots'.

$\{R_1\}$ is not ordinarily found with the descriptive in the verb stem formations with -zaN (Section 621). Those descriptives that are always reduplicated in auxiliary constructions are unreduplicated in this formation: saušíṅaca 'I crushed it'. {L}, however, is used with descriptives in this formation:

    saušíiṅaca 'I crushed them (as in chewing popcorn)'

    saukûutuca 'I made them into balls'; saukútuca 'I made a ball'

    kaʔâukaayuca 'his things broke'; kaʔâukayuca 'something of his broke'

{R_3} is used with two descriptives to form nouns:

    kúdú+kúdú 'candy'; kûdu-, kuîdu- 'round, spherical'

    šíṅašíṅa 'cookies, crackers'; šiîṅa- 'crunched, cracked'

A list of the descriptives follows. Forms that are always reduplicated in auxiliary formations are written with -R_1. Forms with a medial plain sonorant have two allomorphs, cv̂cv- with {R_1}, cv̂cv- elsewhere (see Section 222). Only the second allomorph is written. Other descriptives that have allomorphs (presumably in free variation, see Section 222) are listed with both forms:

    ćápi- 'spotted'

    ćaîyu- 'broken' (something brittle)

    ćeîẓə- 'broken' (something long)

    ćéka- 'grease stained'

    ćeîre-R_1- 'greasy, grease spotted'

    ćíyúu- 'wet'

    ćuîyu- 'washed out, gullied' (of a road)

    čə́ə- 'cracked'

    kába- 'thick'

    kaîyu- 'broken' (something not brittle)

    kə́ẓə-, kə:ẓə- 'pink, purple'

    kûdu-, kuîdu- 'round, spherical'

    mádyu- 'steamed up'

    mísdyə- 'black'

    muîra- 'dented'

    ṅə́ə- 'stiff, stretched'

    beîre-R_1- 'smooth'

    peʈá- (accent?) 'split'

    bə́ə- 'bloated, blown up'

    píša- 'flat'

    bûubu- 'cool'

    sə́ə- 'rough, ugly'

    síki- 'wrinkled'

    sgáci- 'hard, stiff'

    sgə́ẓə-, sgə:ẓə- 'warped; in bloom'

    skúu- 'wet'

skûdu- 'dome-shaped'

skə꞉di- 'round, circular'

spáta- 'damp'

sdyə꞉ri-R_1- 'dangling, jingling'

sdúku- 'wrinkled'

stə́ə- 'straight'

stúku- 'pointed, conical'

stu꞉wi- 'sharp'

ste꞉re- 'dirty'

sti꞉wi-R_1- 'damp'

ša꞉wi- 'fine' (for example, sand)

šáci- 'have a hole, burst'

ša꞉mə- 'white'

šápa- 'light' (in weight)

šáu- 'popped open'

ša꞉wə- 'tender, fresh'

ši꞉na-R_1- 'crushed, cracked'

sa꞉di- 'torn'

ṣu꞉wi- 'crooked'

táka- 'square'

táawa- 'boiling'

túku- 'neat; smooth (of wood)'

632. The remaining classes of auxiliary complements follow.

632.1. The complements that are inflected by {ka} (Section 461.4) to form intransitive constructions are:

ʔésu- 'to sneeze'

cáa- 'to take a deep breath'

cúu- 'to move'

čúu- 'to burp, belch'

háu- 'to yawn'

híi- 'to grin'

káča- 'to be afraid, apprehensive'

múci- 'to squirt water from the mouth'

búuṣu- 'to smell (have an odor), stink'

šúpə- 'to spit'

šúu- 'to swallow'

šúṣu- 'to cough'

yáṣa- 'to be out of breath, to pant'

Monosyllabic complements form a continuative with {R_2} (see ‖18.2):

háuhause 'I was yawning'; háuse 'I yawned'

cáacaaka 'he is breathing'; cáaka 'he took a deep breath'

632.2. The third person forms of {ka} form impersonal constructions with the following:

šápə- 'to be early evening'

câamu- 'to be dawn or early evening'

guŕáŕa- 'to be smoky, dusty'

búu- 'to fall' (one object)

bêe- 'to fall' (several objects)

kə́ə- 'to glow' (a fire)

sáwawa- 'to throw up small piles of sand' (of a raindrop)

tə́rərə- 'to roar' (machinery)

guŕáŕa- also occurs in the thematic formation -quŕáŕagaN with the same meaning: kuŕáŕaka 'it is smoky'; čuŕáŕaka 'is it smoky?' (dubitative).

Two forms occur with {R₂} to express the continuative:

kə́əkəəka 'it glowed'; kə́əka 'it glowed once'

bêepeeka 'they kept falling'; bêeka 'they fell'

bêe- can be used intransitively in the plural: bêesətee?e 'we fell'.

632.3. {gáŋi} (Section 461.4) is used with the following:

dyə́ə- 'to be slow'

híi- 'to smile'

kə́ə- 'to be red'

Two of the forms have different meanings when they are inflected by {ka} (Sections 632.1, 632.2):

kə́əka 'it glowed'; kə́əgáŋi 'it is red'

híise 'I grinned'; híiséŋi 'I smiled'

dyə́ə- and híi- are inflected intransitively with the full paradigm of the auxiliary, and kə́ə- is inflected impersonally with the third person forms of the auxiliary. The intransitive verb theme -'ə́əgáŋi 'to be red' is used with the full set of pronominal prefixes:

síigáŋi 'I am red, am blushing'

ṣə́əgáŋi 'you are red'

kə́əgáŋi 'he, it is red'

The anomalous third person dubitative form čə́ədyáŋi 'is it red?' is marked twice for person and has the same meaning as čə́əgáŋi (dy- + the theme -'ə́əgáŋiṢ) and as kə́ədyáŋi (kə́ə- + dy- + the auxiliary theme -áŋiṢ).

632.4. The following complements are inflected by {ci} (Section 461.3):

nə́wəwə- 'to be strong, healthy'

bási- 'to be bushy haired'

wínunu- 'to be quick'

báska- 'to be fine, well woven' (basket)

šúku- 'to be a lump'

wáaṣuu- 'to be dusty'

The first three complements are inflected intransitively; the last three are inflected impersonally.

632.5. The following complements are found in three auxiliary constructions:

wáka- 'to spill, empty (any object?)'

wáa- 'to spill water'

míi- 'to spill, throw away large granular objects (for example, wheat)'

wíi- 'to spill, throw away small granular objects (for example, sugar)'

Intransitive constructions are formed with {ṣé} (Section 461.2), impersonal constructions with {ka} (Section 461.4), and perfect impersonal constructions with {ćáaci} (Sections 461.2, 415):

wákazá 'he spilled it, threw it away'

wákaka 'it spilled'

wákaćáaci 'it has been thrown away'

632.6. Complements inflected by {gú} (Section 461.1) are:

ʔámúu- 'to love' (transitive)

ʔañée- 'to like (of a man)'

ʔañíuḿée- 'to like (of a woman)'

ʔáníu- 'to like (food)'

ʔáyáa- 'to dread doing it'

ʔáyáamaa- 'to regret it'

ʔé- 'to consent, allow it'

ʔeʔé- 'to remember'

máagù- 'to be quiet (noiseless)'

bíisti- 'to be quiet (still)'

tenée- 'to value it'

One of the complements forms a transitive construction, and is so marked in the list (ʔámúusguḿá 'he loves me'). Some complements seem to be intransitive (for example, máakusí 'I am quiet'). Other complements, because of their semantic content, may be transitive (for example, ʔeʔésí 'I remember [him?])', but the diagnostic forms have not been recorded.

Many of the complements also occur as free forms, sometimes with a different shape. Two complements appear to be nouns. The rest are interjections:

ʔámu 'love' (noun?); ʔámúusí 'I love him'

ʔañée 'nice' (man speaking); ʔañéegú 'he likes it, him'

ʔaníumé 'nice' (woman speaking); ʔaníuméegú 'she likes it, him'

ʔáníu 'goody!'; ʔáníusí 'I like it (food)'

ʔáyá (interjection showing disgust); ʔáyáasí 'I dread doing it'

máaku 'quiet (quietness?)'; máakugú 'he is quiet, noiseless'

bíisti 'keep still, behave!'; bíistigú 'he is quiet, still'

632.7. {ku} is used with zúu- 'to go': zúuse 'I went'; zúuku 'he went' (see Section 461.5).

632.8. {gáa} (Section 461.6) is used with adverbs to form intransitive constructions. Examples:

dyə́gáa 'he is riding horseback'; dyə́ 'up'

ʔáiyâaníśí 'I was in front'; ʔái 'there', ɣâaní 'in front'

ʔáiṣâaʔa 'we (dual) stayed there'; ʔái 'there'

siśí 'I am sitting down'; si 'back, again'

núwánášuśí 'I am the only one surviving'; cf. núwáná 'separate, different'

632.9. The auxiliary {gá} (Section 461.7) has been recorded with only two forms:

ʔáinəsé 'I was lying there (dead drunk)'; ʔái 'there', nə 'down'

šínašinágá 'they are crackers'; šínašína 'crackers' (see Section 631; note accent change)

632.10. The auxiliary {zá} (Section 461.8) is used primarily with nouns:

náwâaʔaisədá 'I am middle-aged'; náwâaʔai 'adult'

hûuruzá 'he is stubborn'; hûuru 'donkey'

ḱúudíizá 'it is mountainous'; ḱúuti 'mountain'

It is also used with noun qualifiers, adverbs, and third person non-modal verbs:

čameʔéezá 'there are three'; čameʔé 'three'

téeʔezá 'it is far'; téeʔe 'far' (adverb)

ḱúistitizá 'it is brown'; ḱúistiti (verb, same meaning)

səəcizá 'it is ugly'; səəci (auxiliary construction with {ci}, same meaning)

632.11. {zé} (Section 461.9) is added to a small group of complements to form intransitive or impersonal constructions. Some of the complements are derivatives formed by the suffix -ma (Section 654.3). Some of the other complements have the final sequence -ma, but no underlying forms can be identified:

ʔée- 'to have initiative' (intransitive)

ʔadéema- 'to be untidy' (intransitive)

ʔədə́əmáa- 'to be sunny'; ʔədə́ə 'hot'

kaṣádíima- 'to be chartreuse'

náawíikáma- 'to be oval'; náawíika 'egg'

kúi- 'to be spoiled; strange'

máa- 'to look like'

kaṣâidíma- 'to feel like summer'; kaṣâiti 'summer'

kúugúma- 'to feel like winter'; kúuku 'winter'

t́iizáma- 'to feel like spring'; t́iiça 'spring'

háyáacíma- 'to feel like fall'; háyáaci 'fall'

632.12. The static auxiliary {ská} (Section 461.8) is used with:

šónáa- 'to have a nose cold'

záa- 'to tingle (limbs, from being asleep)'

púuna- 'to have hunger pangs'

632.13. The static auxiliary {skáaci} (Section 461.8) is used with one complement, wíidi- 'to be sullen'.

632.14. The intransitive auxiliary {ká} (Section 461.10) is added to nouns and noun qualifiers:

šáaku-šá 'I have a pipe'; šáaku 'pipe'

ʔúusíusdyáni-šá 'I have a rope'; ʔúusíusdyáni 'rope'

hée-ká 'that is his'; hée 'that one'

The auxiliary is similar in form and meaning to the possessive prefix -qa- that is used to form ambivalents (‖5.4, Section 520). Cf. šašáaku 'I have a pipe; my pipe'. In contrast to the ambivalent construction, the auxiliary construction is always a verb construction, never a noun construction, and the auxiliary is always accented.

640. Nominal Derivation

641. Most inalienably possessed noun themes (Section 510) have an absolutive form, that is, a free noun form that is not inflected. The absolutive is formed by the following means:

(1) Affix h- . . . -ni:

háçani 'horn', theme -jáza

háawíičani 'nail, claw', theme -jáawíica

háačani 'tooth', theme -jáača

háaskáacini 'chin', theme -jáaskáaci

hiisipani 'eyelash', theme -ʿjíisipa

háamúšani 'beard', theme -ʿjáamúša

háamúučani 'toe', theme -ʿjâamúuča

hádáwini 'navel', theme -ʿádáwi

hamásdíini 'hand', theme -ʿamásdíi

háamaani 'thigh', theme -ʿáamaa

háadákani 'heel', theme -'áadáka

háamúčani 'big toe', theme -'áamúča

háiskâamini 'calf', theme -qáiskâami

húwáwini 'face', theme -qúwáwi

hûumani 'vagina', theme -Aûuma (/n/, irregularly glottalized)

húumúčani 'buttocks', theme -Aúumúča

(2) Affix h- ... -ni, with the thematic syllable changed:

húwanáani 'eye', theme -qâanáa

húyani 'penis', theme -áya

háabáani 'testicles', theme -'ábáa

háasíini 'breasts', theme -'ásíi

háamasdyáani 'finger' (?), theme -'ámasdyáa

háasdíini 'foot', theme -'ásdíi

(3) Affix w- . . . . -ni (perhaps ?u- . . . . -ni, see ‖ 16):

wîikani 'mouth, lips', theme -qĵiika

wîimúučani 'upper lip, snout', theme -qĵimúuča

wíipeeni 'ear', theme -qĵíipee

wíišəəni 'nose', theme -qĵíišəə

(4) Loss of the thematic syllable:

nâa?açəši 'crown of the head', theme -ánâa?azəši

wínuska 'heart', theme -áwínuska

(5) Suffix -ni and loss of the thematic syllable:

núutiini 'ankle', theme -Aúunúutii

wícini 'chest', theme -áwíci

yúuspiini 'shoulder', theme -'jiyúuspii

yûumiini 'arm', theme -'jiyûumii

(6) Suffix -ni, loss of the thematic syllable, and accent changes:

yagéçəni 'rib', theme -jáyagəzə

yuskáni 'tail', theme -'jíyuska (see ‖ 30)

wasə́ni 'feather, wing', theme -'úwasə (see ‖ 30)

wáačə́ni 'tongue', theme -'uwáačə (see ‖ 30)

máapâani 'palm, paw', theme -'amáapaa

nasgâini 'head', theme -ánásgai

The preceding list of absolutives is exhaustive.

Ambivalents may be derived from absolutives, and a contrast between alienable and inalienable possession results:

káháçani 'his horn' (for example, a horn belonging to a person), ambivalent theme -qaházani

záça 'his horn' (for example, a deer's horn), inalienably possessed theme -jáza

642. Nouns are derived from verb stems, descriptives, other nouns, and adverbs by several techniques: (1) suffixes -ni and -ši; (2) prefixes ʔ- and h-; (3) loss of the stem syllable; (4) accent changes; and (5) irregular stem changes. Two or more of these techniques are often used. Many of the derived nouns resemble the absolutive forms of the inalienably possessed nouns (Section 641). These processes are not productive, in spite of the fact that such noun derivatives are common. Examples:

   pâani 'bag'; -qáapaa 'bag' (basic ambivalent, Section 522)

   ʔáukíiníši 'friend'; -qáukíini 'friend' (basic ambivalent)

   ʔičə́ni 'building'; -JíičəB, -aʔáčəB 'to be enclosed' (see ‖ 30)

   ʔagə́çəci 'flower'; -ˈagə́zə-du∅ 'to bloom'

   ʔíiwáçəni 'snot'; -qáiwázəkaya 'to have a runny nose'

   húutyašini, húutyašani 'fast'; -Aúudyaši 'to fast (abstain)'

   húuwáipi 'whip'; -awáiGᵂ 'to fight'

   hâamé 'ice'; -ˈamêeʔM 'to freeze'

   hâawé 'snow'; -ˈáwée 'to snow, to be snowy'

   ýûuni 'song'; -úyúutaaN 'to sing'

   čáyáani 'medicine man'; -ûučayáazíM 'to finish penance, to renew'

   cayá 'oldest sibling'; cáyá 'first' (adverb)

   wáisťâani 'dish'; -úwáisťaN 'to serve stew, soup'

   pišánani 'peelings'; píša- 'flat' (descriptive)

   ýâuni 'stone', ýáuši 'flat cooking stone'; cf. ýáu-sbə́náná 'sling'

   kašéeši 'white corn; navy beans'; cf. kašéená 'albino, blond' (cf.
      Section 644)

   naháayaši 'day after tomorrow'; nahâaya 'day before yesterday'

   dúwímiši 'socks'; -udúwíM(N) 'to have, wear socks'

   súgúčáci 'crucifix'; -û:čáčizaN 'to make the sign of the cross'

   gáwici 'seeds, pits'; -ugáwidyaaD(N) 'to thresh grain'

The underlying stems of a number of nouns with -ni are only found in the noun formation:

   máacáani 'jerky'

   házámǝni 'prayer stick'

   zêeni 'language, word'

   ýûubíini 'soot'

The suffix -ni is sometimes lost when the noun is denominalized by the suffix -ẓaN: súumáacáaça 'I made jerky' (see Section 622).

A number of noun derivatives appear to include the third person non-modal prefix g-:

   záiṣa 'garden'; -qáiṣa 'garden' (basic ambivalent, Section 522)

   gáibéeši 'The Liar' (a constellation); -úibéeẓaN 'to lie'

   cibáaši 'fire'; -qabáa 'to have a fire going'

kúuskə́ədíci 'wheel'; sk̓ə:di- 'round' (descriptive)

káačáníši 'rain water'; -ʿáačaN 'to rain'

kúmásdána 'patches, quilt'; -ûumaasdánaaSD 'to make a patch'

k̓ásti 'stirrup'; -ʿásdíi 'foot' (inalienably possessed noun)

búuṣuka 'odor, stench'; búuṣu- 'to smell' (auxiliary complement,
    Section 632.2; cf. the homophonous form búuṣuka 'he smells')

cáaci 'breath, air'; cáa- 'to take a deep breath' (auxiliary comple-
    ment, Section 632.2)

    643. The suffix of accent ablaut, -(´) (see ‖ 19), is added to infinitives
and third person nonmodal verbs to form nouns. Nouns with an infinitive
or impersonal verb base indicate the instrument of action, those with an
intransitive or transitive base indicate the agent of the action, and those
with a static base indicate the recipient of the action:

ʔáasbánášuméni 'shampoo'; ʔáaspanašuméni 'to wash hair'

ʔúyáasbáani 'grinding stone'; ʔúyáaspaani 'to grind'

ʔúuyə́ʔə́ci 'hammer'; ʔûuyə́əci 'to hit'

cíumáaci 'donation'; cíumáaci 'there was help' (impersonal)

tə́rə́rə́gá 'car'; tə́rərəka 'it (machinery) is roaring' (impersonal
    auxiliary construction)

káizúwíita 'taxpayer'; káizúwiita 'he is paying' (intransitive)

ziw̓áw̓áasáa 'patients'; ziw̓áwaasá 'they are sick' (static)

The singular, dual, or plural subject form of the verb is used in the
derivation to indicate the appropriate number for the noun:

gáubíičáni 'Divider' (a Kachina dancer); guʔúubíičáni 'Dividers'
    (dual); guw̓áabíičáníši 'Dividers' (plural)

kiceʔéta 'dancer'; kaʔáaceedíya 'dancers' (plural)

kutáaniça 'worker'; kúw̓ataaniça 'workers' (plural)

kusumeʔésta 'student'; káisumeʔésta 'students' (plural)

    644. -(´´)ná is added to descriptives to form nouns:

kabáaná 'cornbread; pancake'; kába- 'thick'

sdyə́ríiná 'bells worn by dancers'; sdə:ri- 'dangling, jingling'

sgacíiná 'bread crumbs'; sgáci- 'hard, stiff'

The suffix was recorded with a verb form in a text from an older
speaker: díinazáaná 'whoever wants to shoot'; dîinaça 'he shoots' (dubitative). This suffix does not seem to be used by younger speakers with
verbs.

  -(´´)ná is probably also contained in:

kašéená 'albino, blond'; cf. kašéeši 'white corn'

sk̓əzə́əná 'crumbs'

pišə́əná 'purple'

ýáapadíiná 'pebble'

ʔúuk̇udúuná 'kidney'; cf. k̇uːḋu- 'round, spherical'

ʔúunádáaná 'measles'

645. The prefix ẏáa- is used to form nouns which usually mean 'lots of little . . .'. This formation is not productive, and the examples are exhaustive:

ẏáač̇íni 'shelled corn, corn seed'; -qúuč̇íniṢ 'to be yellow'

ẏáašáwí 'temper of ground pottery'; šaːˀwi- 'fine (like sand)'

ẏâapéetukani 'Ice Caves' (place name); cf. háapéetukani 'icicle'

ẏáasbá 'dough', ẏáasbátawé 'mud, adobe'; cf. -úyáaspaawaẂ 'to knead'; -úyáasbaaN 'to grind'

ẏáaspáiṣuma 'alter'; cf. cáaspáiṣuma (same meaning)

ẏáasti 'early morning' (probably an adverb); -qáastitya 'to be early morning'

646. -tiẓa 'group of . . .' is added to nouns:

wagêeráṭiça 'cowboys'; wagêera 'cowboy'

náwâaˀaiṭiça 'adults'; náwâaˀai 'adult'

ċuk̇úṭiça '(both) twins'; ċúk̇u 'twin(s)'

The allomorph ‖-ẓa‖ is used after -méˀe 'people of . . .' (Section 647):

sêenimⷴéeça 'Zuñi tribesmen'; sêenimⷴé 'Zuñi Indian'

múucimⷴéeça 'Hopi tribesmen'

The allomorphs ‖-ẓa‖, ‖-siẓa‖, and ‖-ẇaẓa‖ occur in:

wáastiça 'young ones'; wáasti 'young one'

máasiça 'group of unmarried girls'; magó 'little girl' (cf. also -qámáˀágⷴ 'daughter')

k̇úyâaẇaça 'group of girls'; cf. k̇úuyá 'Navajo lady'

hánuça ~ háṅuça 'clan'; háṅu 'people'

Rule ‖30 optionally does not apply to the last form.

647. -méˀe 'people of . . .' is added to locative adverbs to form nouns:

báasúumⷴé 'Mexicans'; báasu 'Mexico'

sêⷴⷴnimⷴé 'Zuñi Indian'; sêⷴⷴni 'Zuñi Pueblo'

ʔáak̇úumⷴé 'Acoma Indian'; ʔáak̇u 'Acoma Pueblo'

bⷴnísdíimⷴé 'Orientals'; bⷴnísti 'across to the west'

This suffix probably also occurs in hínumⷴé, šínumⷴé 'I' and híṣumⷴé 'you'. The underlying forms do not otherwise occur.

648. -ẓáṅi 'imitation, not real' is added to a few nouns. Irregular stem changes sometimes occur:

ʔúwánáaẓáṅi 'eye glasses'; húwanáani 'eyes' (absolute form, Section 641)

ċíyáuẓáṅi 'adobe bricks'; ẏâuni 'stoneˌ' (suffix -ni, see Section 642)

k̇ánâayaẓáṅi 'his foster mother'; k̇ánâaya 'his mother'

ḱámə́ətiẓáṅi 'his foster son'; ḱámə́əti 'his son'

649. -ẓá is found with three nouns that refer to women:

ḱúuyáuẓá 'Old Woman' (a Kachina dancer); ḱúuyáu-zá 'she is an
   old woman' (auxiliary {zá}, Section 642.10)

nayéeẓá 'married woman with children'; náyée-zá 'she is a mother'

máagə́əẓá 'young lady'; magə́ 'small girl', -qámá?ágə 'daughter'

650. Adverbial Derivation

Adverbial derivation is treated in the following sections, along with some
nonadverbial derivation that it is convenient to treat at this point.

651. The numerals, a separate syntactic class (Section 733), occur
with a special set of adverbializing suffixes. The numerals, written morphophonemically, are:

?ísga, ?ísḱé 'one, other'	šísà 'six'
dyûu, dyûuwée 'two'	máidyaana 'seven'
čámi, čame?ée 'three'	kuḱúmišu 'eight'
dyâana 'four'	máyúḱù 'nine'
tâama 'five'	ḱázì 'ten'

The first three numerals have two forms. The first form is an indefinite
('one, another'), the second a definite ('the one, the other'). The indefinite
forms are used in the adverbial derivations.

651.1. -(´)wá 'times' has two allomorphs. ‖-(´)yá‖ is used with two
and three, and ‖-(´)wá‖ is used with higher numerals. The suffix is not
used with the numeral one (the adverb háiḱámíizé 'the first time, once'
is used instead). The allomorph ‖dyú-‖ 'two' is used in this construction:

dyúyá 'twice'	šisáwá 'six times'
čámíyá 'three times'	ḱazíwá 'ten times'

These forms are followed by 'ten' to indicate units of ten: dyáanáwáḱáci
'forty' (lit. 'four times ten'), ḱazíwáḱáci 'one hundred' (lit. 'ten times
ten'). Units of one in the higher numbers are indicated by adding the
appropriate number and the verb zíẓá 'it is more, extra': dyúyáḱáci
?íska zíẓá 'twenty one' (lit. 'two times ten, one is extra'). The numbers
eleven through nineteen are indicated in the same fashion, using ḱázì as
the base: ḱáci ?íska zíẓá 'eleven' (lit. 'ten, one is extra').

651.2. -ḱaa '. . . places, the . . . -th place'. In this formation the
allomorphs for one and two are ‖ísḱa-‖ and ‖dyúwi-‖, respectively. The
suffix has the allomorphs ‖-ḱuu‖ when used with one and ‖-ḱaa‖ when
used with higher numerals. Rule ‖21 operates on these forms:

ʔískáku 'one place, the first place'

dyúwíka 'two places'

dyâanáka 'four places'

máityaanáka 'seven places'

This suffix is also used with háasí 'somewhere': háadíka 'either place'.

651.3. -(ˊ)ná 'by . . . -s' has two allomorphs. ‖-(ˊ)ná‖ is added to the numbers two through five, and the independent word ‖gáaná‖ is added to the forms with -(ˊ)wá (Section 651.1) for the numbers six through ten. The allomorph ‖dyúwi-‖ 'two' is used in this formation. The suffix is not used with the number one:

dyúwíná 'by twos'

táamáná 'by fives'

máidyáanáwá gáaná 'by sevens'

kazíwá gáaná 'by tens'

651.4. -sáʔi '. . . days', -bíšu '. . . nights':

dyûusái 'two days'

dyâanasái 'four days'

ʔískasái 'one day'

dyâanabíšu 'four nights'

The suffix -bíšu is related to the impersonal verb theme -qápišuN, -qápišəN 'to be night'. The suffixes are also added to adverbs:

hácəsái 'how many days?'; hácə̀ 'how many?'

héeméesái 'so many days'; héemée 'enough; within a certain area or period of time'

héeméebíšu 'so many nights'

The suffix -sáʔi behaves morphophonemically as a separate word in that accent ablaut (‖19) applies only to the suffix, not the preceding word: cámisaʔíizé 'on the third day', suffix -(ˊˊ)zé, Section 653.1.

651.5. The numeral one, ʔísga, occurs in the following nonproductive derivations:

ʔisgâawa 'together'

ʔísgáya, ʔísgáyâa-si 'on the other side' (si, 'back, again')

Perhaps ʔíské, the definite form of 'one', occurs in:

skáiná, skáinâaka, skáiwá 'both'

skáinâaya 'both sides'

652. The directionals are a subclass of locative adverbs (Section 741). The serial arrangement starts with north, like English, but proceeds in a counterclockwise direction: north, west, south, east. This order is ceremonially significant. Written morphophonemically, the directionals are:

    dídya 'north'

    bə́ 'west'

    kúwa, ku- 'south' (see Section 741)

    hâa 'east'

    A number of derivational suffixes are added to the directionals. Some of these suffixes are also added to the locative adverbs dyə́ 'up' and n̓ə 'down'.

    Nouns are formed by the suffix -(´)mí (allomorphs ‖-(´)mí‖ and ‖-(´)námí‖):

    tidyámí 'the north'

    bə́námí 'the west'

    kúwámí 'the south'

    háanámí 'the east'

    dyə́námí 'the zenith'

There is apparently no corresponding term for 'the nadir'.

    In the remaining derivations (with one exception, Section 652.2) the resulting forms are directionals, that is, they belong to the same syntactic subclass of locative adverbs as the stem. The stems dyə́ and n̓ə belong to a different subclsss of locative adverbs. The derivatives of these two stems, however, are directionals.

    All of the directional derivatives are based on a form with the suffix -ní. Portmanteau and irregular allomorphs are common, both when the suffix -ní is used and when suffixes are added to forms with -ní. The resulting forms are grouped into four sets (table 12), and the derivations in the following sections are described in terms of these sets. The abbreviation Dir is used for the directional stem.

    652.1. Set I forms consist of Dir plus -ní and are used in the derivations:

    (1) Dir -ní '. . . -ern part, in the . . .'

    (2) Dir -ní -saa (see ‖3.1) '. . . side' (unattested with díní and n̓ə́zí)

    (3) Dir -ní -saa -wá 'from the . . . side' (unattested with díní and n̓ə́zí)

Examples:

    dídí 'northern part, in the north', < {dídya -ní}

    díní 'above, on top', < {dyə́ -ní}

    dídiisa 'the north side', < {dídya -ní -saa}

    dídiisaawá 'from the north side, < {dídya -ní -saa -wá}

    652.2. Set II forms consist of Dir plus -ní and -(´)yá. The two set II forms for south are in free variation. The derivations are:

TABLE 12

Directionals

Set	North	West	South	East	Up	Down
I	dídí	bə̂ní	kuní	hâaní	díní	nə́zí
II	díyá	bə́níyá	kúyá, kúiyá	háaníyá	díníyá	nəzîyá
III	tíišuu	bə́iníišuu	kúiníišuu	háaníišuu	. . .	. . .
IV	díi-	bə̂ní-	kúi-	háaní-	díní-	. . .

(1) Dir -ní -(´)yá (used as first member in compound directions)

(2) Dir -ní -(´)yá -ʔV (see ‖ 15) 'the one further to the . . .'

    (unattested with díníyá and nəzîyá)

The compound directions are used to indicate the intermediate points of the compass. Acoma has all eight possible combinations of two member compounds. The order 'north-east' indicates somewhat north of northeast, and 'east-north', somewhat east of northeast. When díníyá 'up' and nəzîyá 'down' are used as first members of compounds, the following form indicates the direction of motion. Examples:

    díyáhá 'north-east', < {dídya -ní -(´)yá hâa}

    háaníyádítya 'east-north', < {hâa -ní -(´)ya dídya}

    díníyákúẃa 'across the top, going south'

    nəzíyákúẃa 'down below, going south'

The vowel preceding the suffix -ʔV is lengthened, and the high accent is replaced by the falling accent. The derivatives are nouns and are used to compare the spacial relationship of two persons or things. The shape of the suffix is similar to the dual prefix (‖ 7). Examples:

    díyâaʔa 'the one further to the north', < {dídya -ní -(´)yá -ʔV}

    kúyâaʔa 'the one further to the south'

In compound directions, -ʔV is suffixed to the first direction: díyâaʔasabə́ 'the one back again further to the northeast', < {dídya -ní -(´)yá -ʔV si bə́}. All the recordings of -ʔV in compound directions include ‖ sa- ‖ or ‖ s- ‖, allomorphs of {si} 'back, again' (locative adverb of a different subclass, Section 741). It is probably not necessary part of the construction.

    Set II forms are used in place of set I forms when ṣu 'in both or all directions' or ʔée 'on, at' follow:

    háaníyáṣa 'in the eastern part in all directions'

    díníyáṣa 'above and back and forth'

    háaníyá ʔé 'at the eastern part'

652.3. Set III forms are used in a derivation consisting of Dir plus -ní and -šuu, meaning 'by the . . . edge, side':

tíišu 'by the north side', < {dídya -ní -šuu}

kúiníišu 'by the south side'

This derivation can be followed by another directional. The first directional indicates the location, and the second the direction of motion: tíišuusabé 'along the north side, going back west', < {dídya -ní -šuu si bə} (‖ sa- ‖, allomorph of {si} 'back, again').

652.4. Set IV forms consist of Dir plus -ní and are used in the derivations:

(1) Dir -ní -sdì 'across to the . . .'

(2) Dir -ní -(´´)káwáaka 'on, at the . . . end'

Examples:

díisti 'across to the north', < {dídya -ní -sdì}

háanísti 'across to the east', < {hâa -ní -sdì}

díikáwáaka 'on the north end', < {dídya -ní -(´´)káwáaka}

háaníikáwáaka 'on the east end', < {hâa -ní -(´´)káwáaka}

653. The suffixes -(´´)zé, -zéeši, and -zéeṣa are similar in shape and meaning to forms of the auxiliary {zé} (Sections 461.9, 632.11) and are undoubtedly historically related to it. The suffixes are productive and are found with a large variety of preceding forms, whereas the auxiliary is restricted to a small number of preceding complements.

653.1. -(´´)zé 'at the time of . . .' is added to adverbs. The resulting forms are adverbs (Section 740; cf. Section 762). Examples:

šisáwáazé 'the sixth time'; šisáwá 'six times' (Section 651.1)

kaṣáidíizé 'summertime'; kaṣâiti 'summer, year'

ʔíska kaṣáidíizé 'the first year'; ʔíska 'one'

héyáwáašúuzé 'the last time'; héyáwáašu 'again'

rúuníšíizé 'on Monday'; rûuniši 'Monday'

gáayúuzé 'in the morning'; gâayu 'this morning'

dyâanasaʔíizé 'on the fourth day'; dyâanasái 'four days' (Section 651.4)

653.2. -zéeši 'the one that is . . ., the part that is . . .' is added to nouns and adverbs to form nouns (cf. the suffix -iši, Section 761). Examples:

dáwáazéeši 'the good part'; dáwáa 'good'

piẓâamizéeši 'the beams, the part of a building composed of logs'; piẓâami 'log'

máadáašúkúuzéeši 'the part that is like a ball'; máadáašúku 'ball'

náyáazéeši 'the underneath part'; náyáa 'under'

sənáazéeši 'the middle sibling'; sóna 'middle'

háamáašuzéeši 'the next person'; háamáašu 'next'

This suffix conditions an accent change when it follows the morpho-phoneme ‖ ˋ ‖: yúuẉíizéeši 'the side part', yúuẉi 'along, beside', ‖yúuẉì‖. This change is described in ‖3.2. There are, in addition, some accent changes that cannot be accounted for by this rule: ḱuuyáuzéeši 'old lady, "grandmother"', cf. ḱuuyáuẓá 'old woman'; čáizéeši 'Last Little Chief', čâi 'last'.

653.3. -zéeṣa 'the place where . . ., the part where . . .' is added to nouns and descriptives to form locative adverbs (cf. Section 763). The suffix sometimes conditions accent and length changes of the pre-ceding syllable, but there are not enough examples to determine its morphophonemic properties. Examples:

ṣuẉíizéeṣa 'at the curve'; ṣu꞉ẉi- 'crooked' (descriptive)

pâaniizéeṣa 'cave, hollow'; pâani 'bag'

háacizéeṣa 'on earth'; háaci 'land'

čónáazéeṣa 'where there is a river'; čóná 'river'

654. Additional suffixes that form adverbs:

654.1. -(´´)ci 'place belonging to . . ., pertaining to . . .' is added to nouns to form locative adverbs:

sóəníici 'Zuñi Pueblo'; sóəni 'Zuñi Indian'

šúumóəci 'graveyard'; šûumə 'corpse'

šəzóníici (name of a kiva); šóçəni 'seeds'

wóəróróəci 'cliff trail at Acoma' (place name); cf. wərórə-ci 'it
    is zigzagged'

héemíšíici 'Jemez Pueblo'; hêemiši 'Jemez Indian'

ḱaunamáaci 'heaven'; cf. ḱaunamée 'beautiful'

wašandúníici 'Washington, D.C.' (no underlying form)

wéenímáaci 'Wenimatsi, home of the Kachinas' (no underlying form)

654.2. -(´´)ma 'each . . ., every . . .' is added to adverbs and in-flected verbs to form adverbs. The suffix has two allomorphs: ‖-(´´)ma‖ after adverbs and ‖-(´)ma‖ after verbs:

gáayúuma 'every morning'; gâayu 'this morning'

rúuníšíima 'each Monday'; rûuniši 'Monday'

sónáama 'half'; sóna 'middle'

ka꞉áidyáanúma 'as she gathered (them), one by one'; ka꞉áityaanu
    'as she gathered'

ḱapišúma 'every night'; ḱápišu 'it is night'

šapəgáma 'every evening'; šápəka 'it is evening'

A related suffix (perhaps allomorph?), -(´´)čáama, is found with a few forms. It seems to have the same meaning:

gâayúučáama 'every morning' (= gáayúuma?)

kaṣáidíičáama 'every year'; kaṣâiti 'year'

rúuníšíícáama 'each Monday' (= rúuníšííma?)

A related suffix, -(´´)šáama 'from . . . to . . .', has been recorded with three forms:

kúudíišáama 'from mountain to mountain'; kúuti 'mountain'

hánušáama 'from person to person'; hánu 'people'

háagúušáama 'one after another' (no underlying form)

654.3. -ma is added to a few nouns and adverbs to form auxiliary complements of {zé} (Section 632.11). The forms have been recorded only in the auxiliary construction, but very likely they are adverbs meaning 'like . . .':

kasâidímazé 'it feels like winter'; kasâiti 'winter'

nâawíikámazé 'it is oval'; nâawíika 'egg'

654.4. -mée 'like . . ., as if . . .' is added to nouns and adverbs to form adverbs:

putistántimée 'like a Protestant'; putistánti 'a Protestant'

hánumée 'like people'; hánu 'people'

ʔáakumée 'like an Acoma Indian'; ʔáaku 'Acoma Pueblo'

The suffix is common with verbs that have been nominalized by -iši (Section 761):

kaʔâušaaʔanišimée 'as if he had permission'; kaʔâušaaʔa 'he has permission'

záipasaišimée 'as though he were chasing them'; záipasa 'he was chasing them'

654.5. The suffixes -tyau and -dyai are added to the stems záa-, čáa-, and zə́zə- to form locative adverbs. The stems and suffixes are found only in these derivations. The suffix -dyai has two allomorphs, ‖-dyai‖ and ‖-dya‖:

záatyau 'plains, flat area'

čáatyau 'side'

zə́cətyau 'edge'

záatya 'plains, flat area'

čáatya 'outside; side'

zə́cətyai 'edge'

The two suffixes probably differ in meaning, but the difference has not been determined.

654.6. -pədá 'just any . . .' is added to adverbs and noun qualifiers:

háadíipədá 'just any place'; háadí 'somewhere'

háupədá 'just anyone'; háu 'someone'

guwáapədá 'anyway'; guwáa 'how'

hámapədá 'any time in the past'; háma 'formerly'

660. The Prefix z̢ə́ə-

661. The diminutive opposite prefix z̢ə́ə- is prefixed to the inflected
forms of three verbs:

    -ʼíčə, -ʼíšə 'to be large' (irregular; see ‖ 7.10)

    -qjízə 'to be long'

    -qáci 'to be deep (of water)'

Examples:

    z̢ə́əsíšə 'it is small' (s-, third person nonmodal prefix, see Sec-
tion 232); z̢ə́əgáašá 'they (plural) are small'

    z̢ə́əcícə 'it is short'; z̢ə́əticə 'is it short?' (dubitative)

    z̢ə́əkáci 'it is shallow'

Compare:

    gáašá 'they (plural) are large'

    cícə 'it is long'

    káci 'it is deep'

662. A few forms are always found with the prefix:

    z̢ə́ə- . . . -qašəka 'to be narrow (for example, a room)', z̢ə́əkašəka

    z̢ə́ə- . . . -qasəka 'to be narrow (of cloth)', z̢ə́əkasəka 'it is narrow'

    z̢ə́ə-čánana- 'to be thin (of cloth)', inflected by the auxiliary {ci},
z̢ə́əčánanaci 'it is thin' (cf. čánanaci 'cloth, yardage')

    z̢ə́ə-máa- 'to be short (in stature)', inflected by the auxiliary {zá},
z̢ə́əmáasədá 'I am short'

    z̢ə́əma 'short time' (adverb?)

    z̢ə́əpišíšə 'a small piece' (noun), derived from -ʼíčə, -ʼíšə 'to be
large'?

    z̢ə́əgáašáaši 'little ones' (noun), derived from the plural of -ʼíčə,
-ʼíšə? (see ‖ 7.10)

700. SYNTAX

Most of the syntactic analysis is based on the text material and only slightly on material given by the speaker in response to questions. Since I was not able to gather an extensive body of texts, only a sketch of the syntax can be given.

Seven major word or syntactic classes have been set up: verbs, infinitives, nouns, numerals, demonstratives, adverbs, and conjunctions. A verb on the syntactic level is defined as a simple inflected verb theme (Section 430), a periphrastic construction (Section 470), or an auxiliary verb construction (Section 630). Three of the classes can be expanded to form phrases. The noun, infinitive, and adverb phrases are endocentric constructions consisting of one or more words in which the head is a noun (or noun substitute), infinitive, or adverb, respectively.

The major word classes and phrases may serve in one or more of the following syntactic functions: predicates, subjects, objects, secondary objects, noun modifiers, noun possessors, noun qualifiers, noun substitutes, adverbials, interrogatives, and connectives.

710. Predication

There are three kinds of predicates: finite verbs (Section 711), infinitives (Section 712), and nouns (Section 713). These three are used to form corresponding predication or sentence types: verbal, infinitival, and nominal sentences. The verbal sentence is by far the most common of the three.

711. A minimum verbal sentence is composed of a finite verb. Persons indicated by the pronominal prefix of the verb can optionally be indicated by a noun phrase:

máagǝǝzéeši kánâaya dyúubé 'The girl told her mother'.
   (máagǝǝzéeši 'girl', subject; kánâaya 'her mother', object; dyúubé 'she told her')
šadya?áu sgúwáasêe?eníináaťasǝ 'My grandmother gave me directions.' (šadya?áu 'my grandmother', subject; sgúwáasêe?eníináaťasǝ she showed me how')

[173]

ṣuwée ḱapišə́ní ḱáṁaskuḱúuyá dya?âiçaaču̇wa ṁaaséėwi ?ée ?úyûuyai
'In the night Spider Woman woke up Masewi and Uyuyai'.
(ḱáṁaskuḱúuyá 'Spider Woman', subject; dya?âiçaaču̇wa 'she woke
them (dual) up'; ṁaaséėwi ?ée ?úyûuyai 'Masewi and Uyuyai',
object)

ṣuwée ḱadyúṁə dáacikuya 'Then he said to his brother.' (ḱadyúṁə
'his brother', object; dáacikuya 'he said to him')

háṁa siñâaya ṣ́áawȧaya ẏáačíñi 'My mother and I used to grind
corn.' (siñâaya 'my mother', subject; ṣ́áawȧaya 'we (dual) ground'

A first or second singular person of a verb is never indicated syntactically. If it is nonsingular, however, it can be indicated syntactically
(see the last example, above). The forms šínuṁé, hínuṁé 'I' or 'me',
and híṣuṁé 'you' are never used as the subject or object of a verb.
They are used, instead, as answers to questions such as 'Who is it?',
'Who did it?'.

Many impersonal verbs (Section 410) can take a syntactic subject:
cáyá ẏáuši gacípətiku 'First, a flat stone is needed.' (ẏáuši 'flat stone',
gacípətiku 'it is needed'). Some impersonal verbs have never been recorded with a syntactic subject, and because of semantic considerations
it seems unlikely that they can occur with syntactic subjects, for example, ḱáača 'it is raining', kucáṁaca 'it is evening'.

Some verbs can take a secondary noun object, an object that has no
referent in the pronominal prefix. If the Acoma verb is transitive, the
secondary object is translated in English as an indirect object, preposi-
tional phrase, or (if the verb is a benefactive transitive, Section 411)
direct object. If the verb is intransitive, the secondary object is translated as a direct object:

ḡaabáabáa da?áwîiçaaní husdyâaka 'Their grandmother made bows
for them.' (da?áwîiçaaní 'she made (it) for them (dual)', transitive; husdyâaka 'bow', secondary object)

dîunáṁa dyáiẏaani 'She thanked him for the piñons.' (dîunáṁa 'she
thanked him for (it)', transitive; dyáiẏaani 'piñons', secondary
object)

?ée wá náanú núuwée ča?áityata dyáiẏaani 'The next day she was
gathering piñons.' (ča?áityata 'she was gathering (it)', intransitive; dyáiẏaani 'piñons', secondary object)

?ai ṣáacəətya čáatya ṣúyáná ṁaadáašúḱu suwáwîititiyañáaṫa 'We
used to make snowballs by the side of our house.' (ṁaadáašúḱu
'(snow)ball', secondary object; suwáwîititiyañáaṫa 'we used to
make (it)', intransitive)

The order of the syntactic elements in the verbal sentences is: subject + object + secondary object; and subject + verb. The verb may be
in any position in relation to the two objects. The order subject + object
is reversed when an obviative pronominal prefix is used with a transitive
verb. The obviative is used to indicate that the third person subject and
third person object roles ('he . . . him') are reversed ('the other one
. . . him') (see Section 432):

    dúwa máagózéeši kánâaya záazíi háu mâamé ʔanéetiumáńu 'Nobody
    liked this girl's mother.' (dúwa máagózéeši kánâaya 'this girl
    her-mother', object; záazíi háu 'not anybody', subject;
    ʔanéetiumáńu 'the other one likes her')

Some verbs can take an infinitive phrase (Section 720). The structural
position of the infinitive phrase in the sentence is not known, but, judging
from the English translations, it appears to be roughly similar to the
English infinitive phrase:

    ṣáadáabûupuši skaʔâiʔiząána ʔûukítaukuyáńi 'Our Governor asked me
    to collect.' (skaʔâiʔiząána 'he asked me'; ʔûukítaukuyáńi 'to col-
    lect', infinitive)

    máamé ṣaʔáu gúsú karêeta ʔúwîiçaańi 'My sister really knew how
    to make wagons' (gúsú 'she knew how'; karêeta ʔúwîiçaańi 'to
    make wagons', infinitive phrase)

712. The infinitive is used as the predicate in sentences that give
directions:

    ṣuwée ʔainə cíci ńíya ʔúyaaspaawámi 'And then you knead it with
    water.' (ʔúyaaspaawámi 'to knead')

    kúistiti kaʔáiząaní yúuku síńə ʔúukúyawi 'When they get brown,
    you take them off (the fire).' (ʔúukúyawi 'to take')

    ṣuwée ʔáyadíišáańi 'Then you feed them.' (ʔáyadíišáańi 'to feed
    them')

The structure of the infinitival sentence is the same as that of the infinitive phrase (Section 720).

713. The nominal sentence consists of two main noun phrases and is
used to indicate a copulative relationship (the auxiliary {zá}, Section
632.10, indicates the same relationship and is more common):

    wá ṣuwée wée cáyaazéeši máaséewi ʔée háamáašu múudêezéeši
    ʔúyûuyai 'The first one was Masewi, and the next boy was
    Uyuyai.' (wée cáyaazéeši 'that first-one'; máaséewi 'Masewi';
    háamáašu múudêezéeši 'next boy'; ʔúyûuyai 'Uyuyai')

    wá ʔétyu dúwa cáacawaiyáatáńiši 'Now this is about stick racing.'
    (dúwa 'this'; cáacawaiyáatáńiši 'stick racing', nominalized verb,
    Section 761)

720. Infinitive Phrases

The infinitve phrase may be used as a component of a verbal sentence
(Section 711) or as a predication (Section 712). In either case the structure of the phrase is the same.

The infinitive is morphologically similar to the finite verb (Section
420). The primary difference between the two is that the infinitive does
not indicate person and does not indicate number for subject, whereas
the verb does. These differences are reflected in the structure of the
infinitive phrase. The infinitive phrase may not include a syntactic subject, but it may, like the verbal predication, include a syntactic object
(if the infinitive is transitive) and a secondary object:

   ʔétyuyú ṣuw̓ée ʔíṣáti ʔâayaasti 'Next you mix in the lard.' (ʔíṣáti
      'lard', object; ʔâayaasti 'to mix', transitive)

   ḱám̓askuḱúuyá ía̓ʔáyanikuyán̓a ʔa̓ʔáyáidyámi w̓ée ṣúyati 'Spider
      Woman was asked to meet the boys.' (ʔa̓ʔáyáidyámi 'to meet
      them (dual)', transitive; w̓ée ṣúyati 'those boy(s)', object)

   ṣáum̓áacaní dyáiy̓aani ʔáityaan̓i 'Let me help you gather piñons.'
      (dyáiy̓aani 'piñons', secondary object; ʔáityaan̓i 'to gather',
      intransitive)

The suffix of accent ablaut, -(´), is added to the infinitive to form
nouns (Section 643). There are, however, many text examples of such
forms in which the translation would seem to indicate that the form is
an infinitive. Very likely there are two ambiguous constructions. Compare the following sentences, both of which contain ʔúyáasbáan̓i. In the
first sentence it appears to be an infinitive ('to grind'). In the second
sentence it is clearly a noun ('grinding stone'):

   gáiḱa ṣaʔáu níuši̓icasí ḱa(osterizer) kí zíi w̓ée héey̓a ʔúyáasbáan̓i
      'I was going to borrow my sister's osterizer to grind it with.'
   záa háu sgúuyâaʔaníitya y̓âuni ʔúyáasbáan̓i dyə́ suy̓áaspa 'Since
      nobody let me use it, I ground it on a grinding stone.'

730. Noun Phrases

731. A noun may be modified by certain verbs, certain adverbs, or by
another noun. The verb, when functioning as a noun modifier, takes the
third person nonmodal pronominal prefix and may either precede or
follow the noun:

   cíčə ḱúuti 'the big mountain' (cíčə 'big; it is big')

ḱúuti cíčə 'the big mountain'

šámə́ci háńu 'white man' (šámə́ci 'white; it is white')

kawâayu ḱúučíńi 'palomino horse' (ḱúučíńi 'yellow; it is yellow')

yáwasti stə́əci 'a straight stick' (stə́əci 'straight; it is straight')

Some of the adverbs that are commonly used as noun modifiers are:

núu, núuyú 'alone, only, own'

háaḿaašu 'following, next'

ńańámí 'different'

ńâuya, ńáuná 'lots, many'

máamé, mâamé 'very, many'

dáwáa 'well, good'

When functioning as a noun modifier, the adverb precedes the noun.
Examples:

núuyú sḱúwáastiçatyaimiši 'one's own children'

háaḿaašu múudêezéeši 'the next boy'

ńańámí husdyâaḱa 'different bow(s)'

ńâuya dyáiyaani 'lots of piñons'

A modifying noun precedes the modified noun:

wáakaši ʔésgá 'cow hide'

wáakaši ʔíisa 'cow manure'

kanêeru yáakaṣúuni 'sheep tripe'

dyûuni ʔáyáyáitáańi 'pottery paints'

háatyani múši 'yucca soap'

732. A third person possessed noun (Section 500) can be preceded by
a syntactic possessor:

ṣúyati ćíipe 'the boy's ear' (ćíipe 'his ear')

ṣúyati gaʔáńaisdíya 'the boys' father' (gaʔáńaisdíya 'their (dual)
      father')

sadyúḿə gâaḿa 'my brother's house' (gâaḿa 'his house')

máagə́zéeši ḱánâaya 'the girl's mother' (ḱánâaya 'her mother')

wabûuri ḱahíyâani 'railroad tracks' (wabûuri 'train'; ḱahíyâani 'its
      road')

The possessor can be a modified noun (Section 731):

šámə́ci háńu ḱasuḿéestáańi 'the white man's school' (ḱasuḿéestáańi
      'his school')

This construction probably has the same restrictions that apply to the
subject and object of a verb (Section 711), that is, any possessed noun
except a first or second person singular possessor can take a syntactic
possessor. The diagnostic forms, however, have not been recorded.

733. Numerals and demonstratives may be used as noun qualifiers.
A qualifier may be used with a single noun, a noun and its modifier

(Section 731), or a possessed noun and its possessor (Section 732).

The numerals are composed of the numbers one through ten (Section 651) and the indefinite numeral háċə 'some (amount); how much? how many?' The numeral may either precede or follow the noun or noun phrase:

> dyûuwée ṣúẏati 'two boys' (ṣúẏati 'boy')
>
> husdyâaḳa kukúmišu 'eight bows (husdyâaḳa 'bow')
>
> háċə mîiya 'a few miles, several miles' (mîiya 'mile')
>
> hâaçəni háċə 'a little bit of onion, an indefinite amount of onion'
>   (hâaçəni 'onion')

The most common demonstratives are:

> wée 'that (further)'
>
> hée 'that (nearer)'
>
> dúẇa 'this'
>
> míika 'others' (plural reference)
>
> zíi 'some (thing); what (thing)?'
>
> háu 'some (person); who?'
>
> háidí 'a few, one of the; which?'

The demonstrative wée 'that' is often used to indicate a definite thing or person, and in this usage is best translated 'the'.

Demonstratives always precede the noun or noun phrase:

> wée ?úẇaaka 'that baby, the baby' (?úẇaaka 'baby')
>
> wée kuháẏa ḱáwaasṭi 'the bear's cubs' (kuháẏa ḱáwaasṭi 'bear her-cubs')
>
> dúẇa máagézéeši ḱánâaya 'this girl's mother' (máagézéeši ḱánâaya 'girl her-mother')
>
> míika háńu 'other people' (háńu 'person')
>
> zíi čə̣eri 'things such as chili'

Numerals and demonstratives may co-occur. In this case the position of the numeral is fixed, and the order is demonstrative + numeral + noun: wée dyûuwée dyáiẏaani 'those two piñons'.

734. Numerals and demonstratives (Section 733) can function as noun substitutes:

> dúẇa núpeṣú 'eat these'
>
> sḱâawi ku ?íska 'one's relatives, or others' (?íska 'one, other')
>
> wée sə̣ə̣ci nîiçaadyú 'those will be destroyed' (lit. 'that will be made ugly')
>
> háu ṣuwée ?ai ṭíyáidyáu 'someone, then, met her there'

A noun substitute can take a noun qualiifer:

> dúẇa dyâana 'these four'
>
> wée míika 'the others'

There are probably some restrictions in the possible sequences.

735. Two noun phrases may stand in apposition to each other. There appears to be no internal difference between this construction and the nominal predication (Section 713):

sanisdêewa wée yûusi 'St. Stephen, the saint'

čapiyú kadyáaši wée kawáayu 'Chapiyu's horse' (lit. 'Chapiyu his-pet, the horse')

wée cíyáidyámiši, ?ușâaçə páyadyámə 'the one that met her, Sun Youth' (cíyáidyámiši 'the one that met her', nominalized verb, Section 761)

gâačáaši wée dyáni 'the large deer' (lit. 'large-one, the deer')

The second noun phrase usually has the demonstrative wée 'that, the'. It is probably used to distinguish the construction from the noun modifier plus modified noun construction (Section 731).

740. Adverbs

The adverbs are divided into a number of classes, but only one class, the locative adverbs (Section 741), has been clearly identified. The adverb or adverbial phrase is usually placed just before the verb. It can occur in other positions, however, and usually does if there is more than one adverb or adverbial phrase in the sentence. There appear to be certain positional limitations that are governed in part by the adverb class.

741. The locative adverbs are divided into the following subclasses:

1 ?ái 'there, at (that place), to (that place)'

2 háu 'to, towards'
   wée 'from'
   kée 'through, along, to'
   yúuku 'away, off'
   wâa 'on out, over there (closer)'
   wâi 'on out, over there (further)'

4 (open class)

5 directionals (see Section 652)

6 adverbs formed with the suffixes -tyau, -dyai (see Section 654.5)

7 ?ée 'on, at'
   si 'back, again'
   șa 'in both directions, in all directions'
   nə 'down'
   dyś 'up'

The locative adverb phrase consists of one or more of these adverbs and under certain conditions may include a noun. The class numbers correspond to the position of the adverb in the phrase. Only one member of a class can occur in the phrase, with the exception of class 7. If more than one adverb of class 7 is found in a phrase, the adverbs are in the order given in the list.[1] Classes 1 and 2 and 5 through 7 are small classes, and the list given above is complete. Class 4 is a large and open class which includes place names and adverbs such as ṣuní 'together, from all sides', náyáa 'underneath', sə́nà 'middle', y̓âaní 'in front', and many others.

In the following examples of adverb phrases the class number is placed after the adverb. The adverbs are written as single phonological words, and without the morphophonemic changes that sometimes apply (see below):

> kámasku wâasťiça ʔái (1) čáaťyau (6) ṣa (7) dyə́ (7) čáaʔâaťa 'The young spiders sat all around up on the side (of the wall).'
> kée (2) ʔáaku (4) ʔée (7) si (7) zûuneegú 'It will go back to Acoma.'
> ʔái (1) kúiníišuu (5) si (7) ńə (7) ʔusuméestáaníizá 'Back down at the south side there is a school.'

Position 3 is filled by a noun, rather than an adverb, and is filled only if position 1, 6, or 7 is filled:

> ʔái (1) čə́ná (3) 'at the river'
> ʔái (1) čə́ná (3) yúuẃi (4) 'beside the river' (yúuẃi 'beside')
> čə́ná (3) zə́çəťyau (6) 'the edge of the river, the river bank'
> čə́ná (3) zə́çəťyau (6) ʔée (7) 'on, along the river bank'
> háaċi (3) si (7) dyə́ (7) 'back up from the ground'

The adverb ʔée has little concrete meaning when it is used alone with a noun: čə́ná ʔée 'at the river' (less specific than ʔái čə́ná).

The words in the locative phrase usually have no intervening juncture. If the phrase is long, however, it can be broken into two or three phonological words.

Three of the class 7 adverbs are unaccented: si 'back, again', ṣa 'in both or all directions', and ńə 'down'. These words are phonologically affixed to a preceding or following word, usually to another adverb of

---

[1] Locative adverbs have been recorded that do not conform to these rules. In every case juncture occurred between the adverbs (see below). It is assumed that the sequences represent two or more locative phrases, since sentences with more than one locative phrase are common. Many sentences consist of long strings of locative phrases followed by a finite verb (sometimes the verb is forgotten, probably because the speaker loses track of where he is).

the same phrase. Since ńə has an initial glottalized consonant, it can condition the accent change described in ‖21. Therefore, when it follows either si or ṣa, a phonological word results: síńə 'back down'; ṣáńə 'down and in all directions'.

The directional ku 'south' has two allomorphs, ‖kúwa‖ before juncture and ‖ku-‖ elsewhere:

    kúẇa 'south'   kúńə 'south and down'
    kudyə́ 'south and up'   kuzə́çətyai 'south edge'

When si 'back, again' (class 7) occurs with a directional (class 5), the normal order is usually reversed. In addition, the following allomorphs of si are used before a directional and dyə́ 'up' (class 7): ‖s-‖ before dídya 'north', hâa 'east' (the ‖u‖ is dropped), and dyə́ 'up'; and ‖sa-‖ before ku 'south' and bə́ 'west'. These allomorphs are also used with the directional derivations (Section 652). The allomorph ‖si‖ is used elsewhere. Examples:

    sdítya 'back from the north'
    sabə́ 'back from the west'
    sakúẇa 'back from the south'
    sá 'back from the east'
    sdyə́ 'back up'

742. The remaining adverb classes probably include at least manner, temporal, and modal adverbs.

Manner adverbs include:

    ńíẏa 'by means of'
    díḱa 'pertaining to'
    guẇáa 'about, how, as to'
    héeẏa 'with'

These adverbs may be used with a noun or noun phrase to form an adverbial phrase:

    kaṣâiti ʔái ṣáaránčuši ʔée dyə́ sədeʔéku karêeta ńíẏa 'We went up
        to our ranch in the summer by wagon.' (karêeta 'wagon')
    sińaisdíẏa wáakaši díḱa ʔée sḱúyúuceẏáaťa 'My father used to take
        me on roundups.' (wáakaši 'cattle')
    máamé zíi guẇáa háçəcai daʔáiça 'They (dual) became very manly.'
        (háçəcai 'man')
    ʔée wėe kuháẏa ḱáwáasťi héeẏa čúuwíš̌áayáńətyə 'And they played
        with the bear's cubs'. (wėe kuháẏa ḱáwáasťi 'the bear's cubs')

Manner adverbs may also be used without a noun:

    záazíiná ṣuẇée háu guẇáa dyáńaaťa 'Nobody, then, said anything
        about it.' (záazíiná háu 'not anybody'; dyáńaaťa 'he said')
    mûuḱaiça diʔíupêetucita, héeẏa čuẇawíš̌áitiya 'The lions licked them
        (dual), and played with (them).'

Temporal adverbs include certain derivations (Sections 651.1, 651.4, 653.1, 654.2, and 762) and adverbs such as:

háḱamiṣu 'first time'	kaṣâidi 'year'
háma 'once, formerly'	kúugu 'winter'
gâayu 'this morning'	rûuniši 'Monday'

Some locative adverbs may be used in temporal phrases: siyúuḱu 'from that time on; in the future' (si 'back, again'; yúuḱu 'away, off'). The same adverbs are used in the locative phrase, but in the order prescribed for the locative phrase (Section 741): yúuḱusi 'back off, apart again'.

Modal adverbs are semantically related to the modes distinguished by the verb (Section 431) and sometimes govern the mode. Some of the modal adverbs are:

ʔáku indicates a question (governs the dubitative mode?)

ʔe- 'if' (indicates a conditional statement)

záazíi, záa 'not' (governs the negative mode when the verb is used with those pronominal prefixes that distinguish this mode)

báa 'may, might' (governs the dubitative mode)

Examples:

zíi dyáiyáani ʔekaʔáica hawée ṣáityatiyanáaḱa 'If there were any piñons, we would gather them.' (zíi dyáiyáani 'some piñons'; kaʔáiça 'it becomes, there is')

ʔézé ṣuwée ʔái zíkaná báa çəẓáweeʔe 'May you again be fortunate.' (çəẓáweeʔe 'you are fortunate, you have luck', dubitative)

Certain verbs can be used as adverbs, probably the same verbs that can be used to modify nouns (Section 731). When functioning as an adverb, the verb takes the third person nonmodal pronominal prefix:

ʔée wá gaʔâaná ṣúyáná daʔáyáita kəəgáni 'And he painted red around their eyes.' (daʔáyáita 'he painted them (dual)'; kəəgáni 'red; it is red')

wée səəci nîiçaadyú 'It will be destroyed.' (lit. 'It will become ugly.'; səəci 'ugly; it is ugly')

750. Conjunctions

Conjunctions are used to connect words and phrases of the same syntactic class. The most common conjunctions are:

ʔée 'and' (nontemporal)

ṣuwée 'and, and then' (temporal)

ʔédyu, ʔédyuyú 'and, but' (contrastive; also used as an adverb meaning 'then, next')

ʔédyu . . . ʔédyu 'but if . . . then'

Zero (probably marked by a juncture) 'and'

ku 'or' (probably inclusive)

zíi 'or' (probably exclusive)

zíi . . . zíi 'either . . . or'

The conjunction ku is unaccented and is often phonologically attached to
the preceding or following word.

Examples:

 tâama ʔée šísa dikáne 'in the fifth and sixth grades' (díka 'pertaining to', Section 742; ne 'down', here meaning 'in')

 zíi ʔubéwí ʔée zíi wágéni 'things like food and clothing' (zíi demonstrative 'some, things such as')

 máamé gái gáçaasti, ʔétyu gái ʔanéezá 'it is very hard, but it is
  fun'

 wáakaši ku kanêeru ẏáakaşúuni 'cow or sheep tripe'

 zíi tâama zíi šísa kaşâiti 'either five or six years (old)' (kaşâiti
  'year')

760. Subordination

Dependent clauses are formed from verbal sentences (Section 711) by
adding a subordinating suffix to the verb. The verb must be a nonmodal
form (Section 431). Since a finite verb can be a complete verbal sentence, the dependent clause is frequently simply a subordinated verb.

 761. -iši, nominalizing suffix (see rule ‖ 1 for allomorphy):

 şúyati tẏâanikuya ḱée gaʔánaisdíẏa níuťáaneetyekúunetyeciši 'The
  boys said that they would go to visit their father.' (ḱée
  gaʔánaisdíẏa níuťáaneetyekúuʔu 'they will go to visit their father';
  see Section 461 for the treatment of the auxiliary)

 şuwée ʔai čaʔáutyu ʔémí wée cigûuniçaatiši 'She found out that she
  was getting pregnant' (cigûuniçaatya 'she is getting pregnant')

 záazíi zíi dínâiźánişa dúwa dyáiẏaani díkasi nigûuniçaagúniši 'She
  did not think that she would become pregnant from these piñons.'
  (dúwa dyáiẏaani díkasi nigûuniçaatyagú 'she will become pregnant
  because of these piñons')

 The suffix can also be used to form nouns. The nominalized verb has
all the synthctic properties of other nouns:

 wée cíẏáidyámiši, ʔuşâaçe páẏadyámə, şuwée ťaacikuya "çáityata
  dyáiẏaani?" 'The one that met her, Sun Youth, then said to her
  "Are you gathering piñons?"' (wée cíẏáidyámiši 'the one that

met her' subject, in apposition to ʔuṣâacə páyadyámə 'Sun Youth';
cíyáidyáu 'he met her', obviative)

místyəciši k̓úudiʔée cíuyateyapikuyáni 'The black ones are gathered
in the mountains.' (místyəciši subject; místyəci 'it is black')

The allomorph ‖-i‖ (see ‖1.10) is used after the completive suffix
-qiṢ (allomorphs ‖-qiṢ‖ and ‖-iṢ‖, the combinations yielding ‖-qiši‖
and ‖-iši‖). In the first case, the glottalization of the final morphophonemic consonant is the only overt sign of the completive suffix:
cibáyániši 'one that has been fired' (theme ‖-qjubáyaN-qiṢ‖ + ‖-i‖);
cíutigúmiši 'that which has been taken out' (theme ‖-qjû:t̓igúM-qiṢ‖ +
‖-i‖). In the second combination, ‖-iši‖, there is no overt sign of the
completive suffix, but it can often be inferred from the morphology:
cíutikusiši 'that which was being taken out' (‖-qjû:t̓igúM-sə∅-iṢ‖ + ‖-i‖;
a perfect theme which must have the completive suffix, Section 415).

762. -(´)í forms temporal adverbial clauses:

déetya gúukačánədyə́əci dîinazáñə 'When they saw a rabbit, they
shot.' (déetya gúukačáñətyə 'they (dual) saw a rabbit')

wée háu zaʔáacədéyáwí neʔéekuzíumáni ṣuwée dîutyəgə́ñətyə 'When
she charged them, when she was about to bite them, then they
put it in her mouth.' (wée háu zaʔâacəteya 'she charged them';
neʔéekuciumá 'she will bite them')

cíci súwast̓iʔi háu sədéedyúpi 'We went after water when we
arrived.' (háu sədéetyu 'we arrived')

The usual morphophonemic shape of the suffix is ‖-(´)í‖ (see rules
‖1 and ‖19 for morphophonemics). The allomorph ‖-(´)ú‖ has been recorded with a few forms: skubə́nú 'when one enters'; zaʔácínú 'when he
arrived'. This allomorph alternates freely with the regular form:
zaʔácíní 'when he arrived'.

The singular theme ‖-âanazədeyaW‖ 'to be walking, wandering' plus
-(´)í irregularly yields ‖-áaní‖: sêenacəteya 'I was walking', séení
'when I was walking'. The dual and plural themes, -qjéeyáaN and
-jéʔegúyaN (see ‖7.10), are regular with this suffix.

763. -ṣa forms locative adverbial clauses:

gáabáabáa dâaʔapuucitañáat̓a záa máamé téeʔe ʔuzúucáat̓ani hawée
wée mûuk̓aiça ʔée kuháya zeʔêema 'Their grandmother warned
them not to go very far to places where there were mountain
lions and bears.' (wée mûuk̓aiça ʔée kuháya zeʔé 'there are
mountain lions and bears')

The suffix has a large number of allomorphs: -ṣa, -iṣa, -ma, -ima,
-ṣuma, -dya, and -ća. There are not enough examples to determine the
distribution of the allomorphs. The distribution does not seem to be

governed by the final morphophonemic consonant of the preceding morpheme. Examples:

s̓kabáaṣa 'at one's fire'; s̓kabá 'one has a fire going'

gúistyaniṣa 'where he made a knot'; gúistya 'he made a knot'

gun̓áaṭáayuma 'where there is a cave'; gun̓áaṭáayu 'there is a cave'

zítyapiima 'forest'; zítyapi 'it is thickly wooded'

gáaspeeṣuma 'where it is warmed by the sun'; gáaspeeʔe 'there
      are sunrays'

káçəətya 'building'; káçə 'it is tall; there is a building'

gúwâaneeća 'where there is a hunt'; gúwâane 'there is a hunt'

764. -u 'when, if, since, as a result' forms conditional clauses (see
rule ‖ 1 for allomorphy):

héem̓ée sáuseen̓aatya ʔái ránču ʔéesi sədeʔéku 'When we got
      enough water, we went back to the ranch.' (háam̓ée sáuseen̓a
      'we got enough water')

ʔétyu sái kaʔaućán̓aatya ʔétyu ṣuw̓éewá sái háubá w̓ee nəćáašiidyúusa
      'But if they divide it all up, it will belong to everyone.' (sái
      kaʔaućán̓a 'they divided it all up')

This suffix, or a homophonous suffix, is also used as a nonthematic
suffix (see Section 442.9).

770. Indefinite-Interrogatives

Many of the word classes have one or more indefinite members. The
most common indefinites are:

háćə 'some (amount); how many?' (numeral, Section 733)

zíi 'something; what (thing)?' (demonstrative, Section 733)

háu 'someone; who?' (demonstrative, Section 733)

háidi 'one of the; which?' (demonstrative, Section 733)

háadí 'somewhere; where?' (locative adverb, Section 741)

héku, hékudáa, hékuma 'some direction; which direction?' (direc-
      tional adverb, Section 741)

These words function in a manner that is appropriate for their class:

ṣuw̓ée wá ćéeyáaní háu dâaʔámina 'As they were on their way,
      someone spoke to them.' (háu 'someone', indefinite demonstra-
      tive, here functioning as a noun substitute)

In addition, the indefinites are used to form interrogative sentences and
to introduce dependent clauses. The appropriate response to an interrogative sentence is a word or phrase belonging to the same syntactic class
as the indefinite. A nonmodal form of the verb is used both in interroga-

tive sentences and in dependent clauses introduced by an indefinite:

  háu təẓâaʔámina? 'Who spoke to us?'

  kéꞣudáa zúuṣu? 'Which way are you going?'

  héꞣudáa ćéeyu zíkaná wá haẃée nəẓaʔáuyâaʔanaťyúuʔu 'They will
   be permitted wherever they go again.' (héꞣudáa ćéeyu zíkaná
   wá 'they went some direction again'; the main verb
   nəẓaʔáuyâaʔanaťyúuʔu is dubitative, but the dependent verb
   ćéeyu is nonmodal)

TEXTS

INTRODUCTION TO THE TEXTS

The texts were recorded on tape by a number of different speakers and were transcribed and translated with the help of Mrs. Hansen (see Introduction). The translations follow the Acoma as closely as grammatical English will allow. Parenthetic material in the translation represents English words and phrases that have been added to make the translation more understandable. Parenthetic material in the Acoma represents English words that were used with English phonology. The first text is provided with a grammatical analysis; it is hoped that the reader can provide his own analysis for the remaining texts by using the grammar in conjunction with a forthcoming dictionary.

The manner in which the texts are punctuated is described in Section 142 of the grammar. Space is used to separate words that are potentially delineated by juncture. There are a number of short adverbs, many of obscure meaning, that are characterized by the Acoma speakers as "little words." Sequences of three or four "little words" normally occur run together with no intervening plus junctures. In sequences of nine or ten, not uncommon in some texts, they are grouped together into three or four phonological words. The position of junctures in these longer sequences appears to be arbitrary. I have, however, written space between all the "little words."

The texts of Mr. Garcia (texts 32 through 37) require special comment. Mr. Garcia was in his fifties when the texts were collected, and he belonged to an older generation than Mrs. Hansen. He occasionally used words and phrases that Mrs. Hansen did not know or was not familiar with, and sometimes his style was obscure. In most cases Mrs. Hansen understood what was meant, probably because of contextual cues, and was able to offer a translation. But she was not always able to identify with certainty the individual compenents of the sentence. As a result Mr. Garcia's texts have been translated quite freely, and it is possible that the translation is wrong in some cases.

"The Birth of the War Twins" (text 38) is a translation by Mr. Lewis of the tale published by Stirling (1942, pp. 92-98). It is not translated sentence by sentence, however, but rather paragraph by paragraph. The story was well known to Mr. Lewis, but apparently not well enough for him to tell the story without any props.

1. Baptizing
(By Mary Histia)

1. kí   (Solomon)[2]   ćíci[3]   ćíizáaní[4]   wâasu[5]
(Adv.)   Solomon   water   when he did   starting now
                           it to him

šísa[6]   kaṣâiti[7]   ka?aiċa.[8]   2. (Santa Ana)[9]   sǝde?éku[10]
six   year   it became.   Santa Ana   we went

ṣa?ánâaya[11]   ?ée[12]   ṣa?ánaisdíya[13]   ?ée[12]   (Margaret).
Our mother   and   our father   and   Margaret.

3. háu[14]   sǝdéedyúpi[15]   ṣuwée[16]   (Tommy)[17]   gâama[18]
Towards   when we   then   Tommy   his house
               arrived

sǝde?éku.[19]   4. háu[14]   sǝdéedyúpi,[15]   kabáabáa[20]   síupéeńa.[21]
we went.   Towards   when we   his grand-   we told her.
                    arrived   mother

5. ṣuwée[16]   skadíiná[22]   šemáaku?íitya.[23]   6. ?amaháa[24]
Then   cornmeal   we gave it to her.   (Interjection)

séniyaapǝtya[25]   (Tommy)[26]   záa[27]   ?ée[28]   ńúućuucidyú[29]   ćíci
we said to her   Tommy   not   in   he will be   water
                                willing

ńiiċaaciumá[30]   wâa[31]   ṣa?ámǝǝti.[32]   7. ṣuwée[16]   gáńaaťa[33]   "wa[34]
he will do   now   our son.   Then   she said   now
it to him

dáwá?ee,[35]   wá[34]   sguwâanáma[36]   ṣuwée[16]   ?áci[37]   ńíyuucee?e[38]
thank you   now   we are   then   later   let us take him
                   grateful

míisa   kâiya."[39]   8. ṣuwée[16]   kúuyáuzéeši[40]   gáńaaťa[33]   "ńakée[41]
Mass   room.   Then   Grandmother   she said   go!

báa[42]   sakisdâana[43]   pudí."[44]   9. ṣuwée[16]   ćáadîi?i.[45]
might   sexton   you go get him.   Then   they sent for
                                         him.

[191]

10. wée[46]   zúuci[47]   ṣuwée[16]   ċaʔamáakuʔíita[48]   skadíiná,[49]
    From   when he   then   he was given a   cornmeal
             went   handful

ṣuwée[16]   ʔai[50]   gái[51]   rusá   cíiċa.[52]   11. rusá   sái[53]
then   there   (adv.)   prayer   he did it.   Prayer   all

gaṅáaṫaṅí[54]   ṣuwée[16]   míisa   ḱâiẏa[39]   ʔéesi[55]   zúuku[56]   ʔai[50]
when he said   then   Mass   room   back in   he went   there

tudáaci[57]   dyúubé.[58]
priest   he told him.

12. ṣuwée[16]   míisa   ḱâiẏa[39]   háu[14]   sədéetyu,[59]   ḱée[60]
    Then   Mass   room   towards   we arrived   through

sədeʔéku.[19]   13. ṣuwée[16]   gái[51]   ʔai[50]   zíi[61]   míiṣu[62]
we went.   Then   (adv.)   there   things   already

háaku[63]   zíi[61]   míiṣu[62]   tíiċa.[64]   14. ṣuwée[16]   míiṣu[65]
prepared   things   already   he did it.   Then   already

séṅa[66]   héeṁée[67]   zíi[68]   gáya[69]   ʔamaháa[24]
middle   at the end   things   (adv.)   (interj.)

nuẓuwáunáutaṣúuṣáati[70]   ṣuwée[16]   ċáacikuya[71]   ʔamaháa[24]
when we would be finished   then   he said to her   (interj.)

(Florinda)[72]   "hiṅá[73]   gánáska[74]   dəi[75]   wáistâaṅi[76]   díḱa[77]
Florinda   (adv.)   his head   here   bowl   with

háu[14]   pídyá."[78]   15. méeṣu[79]   ʔétyu[80]   sái[81]   háuṅə[82]
towards   you hold him.   Instead   but   all   downward

ṅípənaiʔiciuṁá.[83]   16. ʔai[50]   háubá[84]   sáaẏasúkucitiya,[85]
she was going to   There   everyone   we were pushing each
put him inside.   other with our elbows

sgaẏáadyáṅâawita.[86]   17. ṣuwée[16]   sái[81]   ṣuwáunáudáṅí[87]   ṣuwée[16]
we were giggling.   Then   all   when we were   then
                                                   finished

tudáaci[88]   skaiʔicikuya[89]   wá[34]   gáiḱa[90]   ʔéźéźíi[91]   sái[81]
priest   he said to us   now   (adv.)   (adv.)   all

hǎunə[82]	nípənaiṁeetuzúusa, [92]	putistántiṁée. [93]	18. ṣuwée[16]
downward	we should have put him inside	like a Protestant.	Then

gái[51]	ṣuwée[16]	sguwâanáṁa. [36]
(adv.)	then	we are grateful.

19. ṣuwée[16]   ḱéesi[94]   sədeʔéku[19]   gáacəətya[95]   ʔái[50]
Then   on back   we went   their house   there

sâuẏatawa, [96]	ʔée[12]	sóṅa cidíyá[97]	siyúuku[98]	ṣuwée[16]
we ate dinner	and	noon	in the future	then

ka ʔ áacéetiya. [99]   20. ṣuwée[16]   mâaméṣu[100]   šapəgání[101]
they danced.   Then   starting right at   early evening

wée[46]	kawâayu[102]	gûuṁə. [103]	21. ṣuwée[16]	saʔánáisdíya[13]
from	horse	they left.	Then	our father

(Solomon)	ʔái[50]	zídyá[104]	kawâayu. [105]
Solomon	there	he touched him	horse.

Analysis of "Baptizing"

In the following notes single morphemes are written morphophonemically. For this reason some monomorphemic words will not be written the same in the text and the notes, for example, item 7 appears in the text with a 't', but in the notes with a 'd'.

[1]kí, adverb. Indicates that the event took place in the past or is completed.

[2]Solomon, object of ćíiẓáaní.

[3]ćízi̇̀ 'water', secondary object of ćíiẓáaní (Section 711).

[4]ćíiẓáaní; the combination with ćíci means 'when he baptized him (obviative)'. -'jiiẓaaN ~ -JiiẓaaN (Section 234) 'to make it, to do it to', transitive theme of the verb stem -iiẓaaN 'to make, become' plus the first transitive prefix ($\|$5.5, Section 411). gj-, obviative nonmodal prefix ($\|$10.1, Section 230, 432); -(′)í, adverbializing suffix ($\|$1, $\|$19, Section 762).

[5]wâaṣu 'starting now, at this time', adverbial phrase (Section 742). wâa 'now'; ṣu 'starting'.

[6]šíṡà 'six', numeral (Section 733).

[7]kaṣâidi 'year, summer', adverb.

[8]kaʔâiċa 'it became', impersonal verb. -QáiẓaaN, impersonal theme derived from the verb stem -iiẓaaN 'to make, become'. g-, 3rd person nonmodal prefix ($\|$10.2).

[9]Santa Ana, locative adverb.

[10]ṣədėʔéku 'we (plural) went', intransitive-A verb. -jeʔéguY, plural theme of zúu- ($\|$7.10); s-əẓ-, 1st person nonmodal prefix (Section 230). The syntactic subject of the verb (Section 711) is ṣaʔánâaya ʔée ṣaʔánái̇sdíya ʔée Margaret; the English translation 'I' results from the fact that the verb has a 1st person prefix.

[11]ṣaʔánâaya 'our (dual) mother', derived ambivalent (Section 521). ṣ-, 1st person nonmodal prefix; dual prefix ($\|$7.9, Section 530); -qa-, possessive prefix ($\|$5.4); ńâaya 'mother'. The dual was used because Mrs. Histia was telling one of her sisters, who was not present at het baptizing, about the event.

[12]ʔée 'and', conjunction (Section 750).

[13]ṣaʔánái̇sdíya 'our (dual) father', derived from ńái̇sdíya 'father'. Analysis identical to ṣaʔánâaya (note 11).

[14]háu 'to, towards', locative adverb.

[15]ṣədéedyúpi 'when we (plural) arrived'. -jéedyuB, plural of the intransitive-A verb theme -jaʔáċiN ($\|$7.10); s-əẓ-, 1st person nonmodal prefix (Section 230); -(′)í, adverbializing suffix (Section 762).

[16]suẃée 'them, and then, next', conjunction (Section 750) and adverb (Section 742).

[17]Tommy, possessor of gâama 'his house' (Section 732).

[18]gâama 'his house', basic ambivalent (Section 522). -Aâama, theme; g-, 3rd person prefix.

[19]ṣədeʔéku (see note 10).

[194]

²⁰k̇abáabáa 'his grandmother', derived ambivalent (Section 521). g-, 3rd person nonmodal prefix; -qa-, possessive prefix (∥5.4); báabáa 'grandparent, grandchild of the opposite sex'. Object of the verb síupéeňa.

²¹síupéeňa 'we (plural) told her', transitive verb. -úubé?eN 'to tell someone', transitive theme derived from the verb stem -bé?eN 'to tell'. sj-, 1st-3rd person nonmodal prefix; ∥-qaaD∥, allomorph of the plural suffix -qeeD (∥1.1). For the glottalization of ∥s∥ see Section 232; for the glottalization of ∥b∥ see ∥1.1.

²²skad́iiná 'ceremonial cornmeal', secondary object of the verb śeḿáaku?iityə (Section 711).

²³śeḿáaku?iityə 'we (dual) gave her a handful', transitive verb. -Jaḿáaku?í?iD, transitive theme of the classificatory verb stem -áaḿáaku- 'to handle grainlike or sandlike objects' (Section 453). sj-, 1st-3rd person nonmodal prefix; ∥-dyəəZ∥, allomorph of the dual suffix -qədyəəZ (∥1.8).

²⁴?amaháa, interjection. Indicates a hesitation, much like English 'er'.

²⁵śeniyaapətyə 'we (dual) said to her', transitive verb; here, meaning 'to ask'. -JániyaaB, suppletive theme for dual and plural subject for -JáacikuyaN (Section 433). sj-, 1st-3rd person nonmodal prefix; ∥-ədyəəZ∥, allomorph of the dual suffix -qədyəəZ (∥1.6).

²⁶Tommy, subject of the verb núuč́uucidyú.

²⁷záa 'not', a negative adverb.

²⁸?ée 'in, at, on', locative adverb. Here it means 'in this affair, concerning this'.

²⁹núuč́uucidyú 'he will be willing', intransitive-A verb. -Aúuč́uuci, theme. n-, expective prefix (Section 230 and Section 471); /-dyú/, 3rd person singular dubitative form of the auxiliary gú (Section 461.1). The expective is used because the event was to take place in the future, the dubitative because the request had been made but not yet accepted.

³⁰ćíci ň́iiçaaciuḿá 'he will baptize him' (see notes 3 and 4 for syntactic construction and theme). nj-, expective prefix; /-ciuḿá/, obviative singular nonmodal form of gú (see note 29).

³¹wâa 'now', adverb.

³²sa?áḿə́əti 'our (dual) son', derived ambivalent (∥5.4, Section 521). mə́ədì 'boy'; see note 11 for construction.

³³gánaaťa 'she said', intransitive-A verb. -ánaaťaN, theme; g-, 3rd person nonmodal prefix.

³⁴wá 'now', morphophonemic variant of wâa, note 31 (∥25).

³⁵dáwá?ée 'thank you', lit. '(there is) good in (it)'. dáwáa 'good'; ?ée 'in, on, at'.

³⁶sguẘâanáḿa 'we (plural) are grateful, thankful', static verb. -ûunáḿa, theme. sgu-, 3rd-1st person nonmodal prefix (Section 230); plural prefix (∥7.6).

³⁷?áci 'later, in a little while', adverb.

³⁸ň́iyúucee?e 'let us take him', transitive verb. -Júyúuzee Y, theme. nj-, 1st-3rd person hortative prefix (Sections 230, 431); ∥-?VVD∥, allomorph of the plural suffix -qeeD (∥1.7).

³⁹ḿiisa k̇âiẙa 'church'. ḿiisa 'Mass' modifies k̇âiẙa 'room, inside' (Section 731).

[40]kúuyáuzéeši, respectful term for an old lady. -zéeši 'the one that is . . . ., the part that is . . .' (Section 653.2).

[41]ńakée 'go!', modal adverb.

[42]báa 'might, may', modal adverb.

[43]sakisdâana 'sexton', object of the verb pudí.

[44]pudí 'you go get him', transitive verb. -uːdeeY ~ -uːdiiY (Section 234) 'to go after, invite'. p-, 2nd-3rd person hortative prefix (Section 230).

[45]cáadîiʔi 'they sent for him', static verb. -qjaʔaːdîi-ʔVVD 'to be sent for', static theme of the verb stem -uːdiiY plus the passive prefix -qjaʔa- (‖5.2, Section 412); and ‖-ʔVVD‖, allomorph of the plural suffix -qeeD (‖1.7, Section 412). See ‖23.3 for the initial glottal accent. gj-, obviative nonmodal pronominal prefix.

[46]wée 'from', locative adverb (Section 741).

[47]zúuci 'when he went'; the combination with wée means 'when he came'. zúu- 'to go', singular intransitive verb theme inflected with an auxiliary (‖7.10, Section 632.7). /-ku/, 3rd person singular nonmodal auxiliary (Section 461.5); -(ˊ)í, adverbalizing suffix (Section 762).

[48]caʔamáakuʔiita 'he was given a handful', static verb. -qjaʔamáakuʔíʔiD-aaD, static theme from the classificatory verb stem -áamáaku- 'to handle grainlike or sandlike objects' (Section 453) plus the passive prefix -qjaʔa- (‖5.2, Section 412); and ‖-aaD‖, allomorph of the plural suffix -qeeD (‖1.8, Section 412). gj-, obviative nonmodal prefix.

[49]skadíiná 'ceremonial cornmeal', secondary object of the verb caʔamáakuʔiita (cf. note 22).

[50]ʔái 'there', locative adverb (Section 741).

[51]gái, adverb of unknown meaning.

[52]ciica, transitive verb (see note 4); the combination with rusá 'prayer' means 'he said a prayer'. g-, 3rd-3rd person nonmodal prefix.

[53]sái 'all, everything, whole', adverb. Here it indicates the completion of the action.

[54]gańáaťání 'when he said'. gáńaaťa 'he said' (note 33) plus -(ˊ)í, adverbializing suffix (Section 762).

[55]ʔéesi 'back in, in again', locative adverbial phrase (Section 741). ʔée 'in, at, on'; si 'back (to starting point)'.

[56]zúuku 'he went', intransitive verb (see note 47).

[57]tudáaci 'priest', object of the verb dyúubé.

[58]dyúubé 'he told him', transitive verb (see note 21). dy-, 3rd-3rd person dubitative prefix (Section 230). The dubitative is used because the speaker was not present when the sexton told the priest (Section 431).

[59]sədéetyu 'we (plural) arrived' (see note 15).

[60]kée 'through, along', locative adverb.

[61]zíi 'thing(s), something(s)', indefinite demonstrative (Section 733) functioning as a noun substitute (Section 734) and object of the verb tiica.

[62]míisu 'already, completed', adverb. The repetition of the words zíi míisu appeared to represent a hesitation and backtracking on the part of the speaker.

[63]háaku 'prepared', adverb.

[64]tiica 'he did it, made it', transitive verb (see note 4). dy-, 3rd-3rd person dubitative prefix (Sections 230, 431).

[65]míisu (see note 62).

[66]sə́nà 'middle', adverb.

[67]héemée 'at the end of, at the completion of', adverb.

[68]zíi (see note 61).

[69]gáya, adverb of unknown meaning.

[70]nuẓuẃáunáutaṣúusáati 'when we (plural) would be finished'. -Aûinaudan 'to finish', intransitive-A verb theme. n-əẓ-, expective prefix (Sections 230, 471); plural prefix (‖7.4); ṣ-, 1st person nonmodal prefix (Section 230); -úuS-aaD, an allomorph of the auxiliary gú and the plural suffix (Section 461.1); -(´)í, adverbializing suffix (Section 762).

[71]cáacikuya 'he said to her', transitive verb. -JáacikuyaN, theme. gj-, obviative nonmodal prefix.

[72]Florinda, object of the verb cáacikuya.

[73]hiná, modal adverb indicating a command (Section 742).

[74]gánáska 'his head'. -ánásgai 'head', inalienably possessed noun theme (Section 510); g-, 3rd person prefix.

[75]dəi 'here', adverb.

[76]ẃáisťâani 'bowl', noun. Derived from the verb stem -úẃáisťaN 'to dish up liquid' (Section 642).

[77]díka 'with, pertaining to', adverb. Forms and adverbial phrase with ẃáisťâani, the combination meaning 'pertaining to the bowl' (Section 742).

[78]pídyá 'you hold him', transitive verb. -Júdyá?aD 'to hold, catch, touch', transitive theme from the verb stem -údyá?aD plus the first transitive prefix (‖5.5, Section 411). p-, 2nd-3rd person hortative pronominal prefix (Section 230).

[79]méeṣu 'instead', conjunction (Section 750).

[80]?édyu 'but', conjunction (Section 750).

[81]sái 'all', adverb.

[82]háunə 'downward', locative adverbial phrase (Section 741). háu 'towards'; nə 'down'.

[83]nípənai?iciumá 'she was going to put him inside', transitive verb. -JúbəN, theme from the verb stem -ú:bəN 'to enter'. nj-, expective prefix (Sections 230, 471); -nai?M 'enclosed, inside' (Section 442.5); /-ciumá/, obviative singular nonmodal form of the auxiliary gú (Section 461.1).

[84]háubá 'everyone'. Derived from háu 'someone; who' plus -bá, an element that occurs only in this word.

[85]sáaẏasúkucitiya 'we were pushing each other with our elbows', intransitive-B verb. -'áaẏasúku-zaN, theme from the verb stem -û:súku-zaN 'to elbow, jostle' plus the collective plural prefix -'áaẏa- (‖5.2, Section 414); -zaN, stem formative (Section 621). s-, 1st person nonmodal prefix; =itaaN, continuative suffix (Section 441.1); the continuative suffix and the plural suffix -qeeD yield the portmanteau form ‖=itiyaaD‖ (Section 242).

[86]sgaẏáadyánâawita 'we (plural) were giggling', static verb. -Jíidyánâawa, theme. sg-, 3rd-1st person nonmodal prefix; plural prefix (‖7.7); =itaaN, continuative suffix (Section 441.1).

[87]suẃáunáudání 'when we (plural) were finished'. -AûinaudaN 'to finish', intransitive-A verb theme. ṣ-, 1st person nonmodal prefix; plural prefix (‖ 7.4); -(´)í, adverbializing suffix (Section 762).

[88]tudáaci 'priest', subject of the verb skaiʔicikuya.

[89]skaiʔicikuya 'he said to us (plural)', transitive verb. -JáaciguyaN, theme. sg-, 3rd-1st person nonmodal prefix; plural prefix (‖ 7.8). This is one of the words that, contrary to the general rule, may have no accent (see Section 121, ‖ 7.8).

[90]gáiḱa, adverb of unknown meaning.

[91]ʔézézíi, adverb of unknown meaning.

[92]nípənaiḿeetuzúusa 'we (plural) should have put him inside', transitive verb. -qeeD, plural suffix (‖ 1.2); /-tuzúusa/, 1st person plural dubitative form of the auxiliary gú (Section 461.1). See note 83 for the rest of the construction.

[93]putistántiḿee 'like a Protestant', adverb. putistánti 'Protestant'; - ḿee 'like . . ., as if . . .', adverbializing suffix (Section 654.4).

[94]ḱéesi 'on back', locative adverbial phrase (Section 741). ḱée 'through, along'; si 'back'.

[95]gáacəətya 'their (plural) house', ambivalent. -áazəədya, plural theme of -Aâḿa, basic ambivalent (Section 522).

[96]ṣâuẏatawa 'we (plural) ate dinner', intransitive-B verb. -QâuẏataW 'to eat several things', for example, 'to eat a meal (of people), to graze (of animals)', theme. s-, 1st person nonmodal prefix; ‖ -aaD‖, allomorph of the plural suffix -qeeD (‖ 1.4).

[97]The verb theme -júdyu is only used with the adverb sə́nà 'middle': sə́na zítyu 'it is noon'. The form with the adverbializing suffix -(´)í (Section 762) is irregular: sə́na cidíẏá 'when it is noon', (or simply) 'noon'.

[98]siyúuḱu 'in the future, from that time on', adverbial phrase (Section 742). si 'back, again'; yúuḱu 'away, off'.

[99]kaʔáaceetiya 'they (plural) danced', intransitive-B verb. - ʻícáaN, theme from the verb stem -iicáaN 'to dance' plus the first active prefix - ʻ- (‖ 5.6, Section 414). g-, 3rd person nonmodal prefix; thematic syllable expansion (ʻí > Qáʔa, ‖ 9.4); ‖ ᵊéʔetaaN‖, allomorph of the continuative suffix ᵊitaaN (Section 441.1); the continuative suffix and the plural suffix -qeeD yield the portmanteau form ‖ ᵊéʔetiyaaD‖ (Section 242). This stem is seldom found without the continuative suffix.

[100]mâaméṣu 'starting right at, exactly at', adverbial phrase (Section 742). mâamé ~ ḿáamé 'very, exactly'; ṣu 'starting'.

[101]šapəgání 'when it is early evening'. šápə- 'early evening (before sunset)' is inflected with the auxiliary ku (Sections 461.4, 632.2). The adverbializing suffix -(´)í (Section 762) has been added. The adverbial phrase mâaméṣu indicates that it was the beginning of the time period covered by šápə-, namely the middle of the afternoon.

[102]kawâayu 'horse(s)', subject of the verb gûuḿə.

[103]gûuḿə 'they (dual) left', intransitive-A verb. -ûuḿə, dual theme of -û·ḿə (‖ 7.10). g-, 3rd person nonmodal prefix. The locative adverb ẃée indicates movement from a location (in this case, unspecified) to the area of interest; hence, in this sentence the verb means 'they came'.

[104]zídyá 'he touched (that is, patted) him', transitive verb.   -JúdyáʔaD 'to hold, catch, touch', theme from the verb stem -údyáʔaD plus the first transitive prefix (‖ 5.5, Section 411).   g-, 1st-3rd person nonmodal prefix.

Note that the singular is used for both the subject and object. There are two syntactic subjects (ṣaʔánáisdíýa Solomon), and the object (kawâayu) probably refers to two horses since the preceding sentence made it clear that there were two horses involved. The category of number is optional for transitive verbs (Section 433), and this is one of the rare instances in which it is not indicated.

[105]kawâayu 'horse', object of the verb zídyá (see note 104).

Free Translation of "Baptizing"

1. Solomon was baptized six years ago.   2. Our mother and father and Margaret and I went to Santa Ana.   3. When we arrived, we went to Tommy's house.   4. We told his grandmother when we got there. 5. Then we gave her corn meal.   6. We asked her if Tommy would not be willing to baptize (that is, sponsor) our son now.   7. She said "Thank you, we are grateful; in a little while let's take him to the church."   8. Then the Grandmother said, "Go and get the sexton." 9. They sent for him.   10. When he came, he was given some corn-meal, and he said a prayer.   11. When he finished the prayer, he went back to the church and told the priest.

12. We arrived at the church and went in.   13. He (the priest) already had things prepared there.   14. When we were halfway through, he said to Florinda, "Put his head towards (over) the bowl."   15. But instead she started to put him all the way inside.   16. We were pushing each other with our elbows and giggling.   17. When we were finished the priest told us that we should have put him all the way in, like a Protestant.   18. We were grateful.

19. Then we went back to their house and ate dinner there, and from noon on they danced.   20. In the middle of the afternoon two horses came.   21. Our dad and Solomon patted the horses.

2. All Souls' Day
(By Anne Hansen)

1. dúwa wá ńíibéesí šûumə dâawáaçaṣu[1] náwâaʔaiṭiça sizéedyúpi.[2]
2. cáyáṣu hástíṭiça kuwâušaaṭeeʔeezáṭeeʔeesə, ʔétyu kúyâawaça báhá
kuwáwîititiyańáaṭa.   3. ṣuwéeṣu wá ʔémé ʔée ʔískɛ́ háuńə kubóńí
šapəgání wéeméé háçə ʔai sgâama ʔamaháa háusi nədéetyugúusaatya,
ṭée ʔémé ʔée núuyú skáwáasṭiçatyaimiši nêiʔitiišáasgúńišiméé ʔémé
ʔée ʔée káuzáańi.[3]   4. cáyáṣu ʔubéwí zíi sái ʔai háaku stîiçanu, ʔée
wée ṣáamíi zíi sgayánamaṭíitya[4] ṣuwée ʔíṣáti ńíya ʔánázáńi sdyánaçanu
ṣuwée rusá stîiça ṣuwée káimináʔáatišiku.[5]   5. zíi yúuṣusgúńu zíi sái
kaʔâuyatawaatya ṣuwée ʔáasa díka dyə́ ʔuṭâańi ʔubéwí ʔée ṣuwée skadíiná,
wíispi ʔée círi háaku stîiça ṣuwée záiṣa ʔée kuwaṭaikuiʔizáṭeeʔe.   6. ʔai
háu sdyaʔacínú ṭúu ʔémé ʔée zíkaná sgâiʔíminaku ʔée ṣuwée ʔaińə
ʔúuwíišáńi héeméé ṣuwée kaʔáizáaní ʔíyaça zíi wée zéegúya gái ciyúu
dyaiʔipewíitańáaṭa.

7. ʔée wá ṣuwée kapišóńí ʔétyu wéeméé kuc̓ámázáńí hawéé kasdyə́rá
zéegúiyáaṭasə rusá gáawâatitiyaníitańáaṭa.   8. wéeméé zíi háu
sdíwaaceeku rusá sdyâawáaçaniitya séegáazé zíi gayáaʔáapi[6] zíi ʔubéwí
zíi ʔézé zíisgúńu.   9. ʔétyu ṣuwée wá gáayúuzé ṭúu meyûuna héeméé
háçə nêiʔitiišáasgúńi ṭúu ʔémé ʔée zíkaná ʔétyu ṣuwée wéeméé ʔáasa
díka dyə́ ʔuṭâańi, ʔétyu ʔai míisa káiya ʔai čáatya háusi zíkaná
ʔuwánáciiyi.[7]   10. ṭúu dyəəçəṣa ʔai skâuʔuńáaṭa.   11. háikámíná míisa
ciiça.   12. ʔai káiya ʔée cáyá kée ʔuṭáikúiyíizá.

---

[1] šûumə dâawáaça 'November, month of the dead', lit. 'corpse month', so called
because All Souls' Day occurs in this month.

[2] náwâaʔaiṭiça sizéedyúpi 'All Souls' Day', lit. 'when the old people come back'.

[3] The main verb is káuzáańi, and in combination with the adverb ʔée 'thus, so'
it means 'it is done, prepared this way'; ambivalent (Section 521) derived from a
nominalized infinitive (Sections 420, 643), theme -úuzaaN 'to make for somebody'.
kubóńí 'when it (the first date) arrives', theme -ú:bəN 'to enter'. šapəgání, see
note 101, text 1. nədéetyugúusaatya 'when they will return', see note 15, text 1,
and Grammar, Section 764. nêiʔitiišáasgúńišiméé 'as if one (indef.) will feed
them', theme -JudiišáʔaN; see ‖7.2, Section 761, and Section 654.4.

[4] sgayánamaṭíitya 'when one sets a chair for them', theme -JánamaD(čaN)-ʔíʔiD.

[5] káimináʔáatišiku, theme -JumínaaD 'to speak to', ambivalent derived from
nominalized infinitive (see Sections 521, 643, 442.8).

[6] gayáaʔáapi, theme -JâaʔB 'to give (light object) to someone' (see ‖1.6, ‖7.8).
This is a subordinate verb in form (Section 762), but it appears to translate as
the main verb.

[7] The cemetary is beside the church.

2. All Souls' Day
(By Anne Hansen)

1. I'm going to tell about All Souls' Day in November.   2. First the
men go after meat, and the ladies make bread.   3. Then on the first
evening, you prepare for however many will return to your house, just
like you would prepare food for your own children.   4. First you get
the food all ready, and when you have the table properly set for them
then you light a candle and pray and talk to them.   5. When you think
that perhaps they have eaten everything you put the food in a pan, and
then you prepare corn meal, cigarettes, and water, and you take them
to the garden.   6. When you get there you talk to them again and then
put them down, and when this is done, if there are children wandering
about, they will probably eat them (the several items in the pan).

7. Then in the evening when it is dark, Mexicans come and pray for
them.   8. If they come to someone's (place) to say prayers for them,
he must give them things such as food or whatever he has.   9. And in
the morning, in the same way, you will feed them enough again, and
you put it in a pan, and you take it to feed them outside the church.
10. There is always a crowd there.   11. Sometimes there is a Mass.
12. First (before Mass) you take it inside the building.

3. The Parish Priest
(By Anne Hansen)

1. ʔée dúẃa zíka túu kánáa ʔeʔésí, ýuu zíi ḱauku (1933) háti kaṣâiti
ḱaaní.   2. kí ṣáanáisdíẏaši tudáaci⁸ zúuku (New York) ḱaukume zíi (1935)
háti záazíi mâamé ʔeʔésgúńu.   3. kí ʔémé ṣáanâayatyaimiši zaẏáyanikuya
háu ṣuní ʔai míisa ḱaiẏa ʔutáikuiyi ʔubéẃí ʔémí yúunáa há ńanáćigúńiši.
4. ʔégú gái háubá zíi dáẃaa diẃauça ṣuẃee zíi ʔézé zíi ʔesdîuçaanu háu
ʔémí zíi háu ʔée cíiçaańa.   5. šée ʔamaháa ńiibéedyú guẃáa ʔai
ḱaháńutyaimiši guẃáa ḱâaẏúutyaniši.

4. St. Stephen's Day
(By Margaret Lim)

1. ʔáaku sanisdêewa (September) háuńə dyûuẃee kubéní⁹ sái háu ṣuníisi
skáakuẏáata ʔáaḱuumé.   2. ʔée merigâanu zíi kasdyéŕá ʔée míika zíi
háu ṣuní zéedyúpisə dîiẃá ʔée ḱaẃaigamé sêəni ʔée zíi tené.   3. wâa
dyûuẃee háuńə kubéní gáayúuzé staẃáaẃadyámeeʔeezátee'e tudáaci míisa
cîiça.   4. ṣuẃee wá héemée ʔai míisa kaʔaiça, sántu ćaʔátikuse.   5.
ṣuẃee sái ʔai ʔáaku haẃée záastiyaagúmeetya ṣuẃée wá sái míisa kaʔaiça
ḱée ćaʔaastiyaagúmeetya ṣuẃee ḱaakaati ʔai kúwâameeća ćaʔápənaime
ćaʔáẏuuceeʔeezátee'e.   6. ṣuẃee gái ḱúyâaẃaça zíẃáẏaidyáasə zíi báhá,
merûuni, ʔée ʔišâani.   7. ṣuẃée ʔée ʔai báasku kaʔaacêetiyańáata.
8. ʔée ʔama gáiḱa háma čapiyú zaʔáćisəńáata ʔáaku ʔée santiyâaku.¹⁰
9. ṣuẃée záazíná ciẃá gái háu ʔémé ʔée zíẏúukaiyu.   10. gái ʔétyu
háma wá čapiyú síukačáńí ʔamaháa kaẃâayu ńíẏa ẃée zúuku ẃée dyé
gaʔápi.   11. sái místyəci kúẃakə ʔée ʔémí ʔée cíçə ḱauspíici.   12. ʔée
ʔétyu santiyâaku zíka ʔémí zéəsíšə kaẃâayu ńíẏa dyé gáa.

---

⁸ṣáanáisdíẏaši tudáaci, lit. 'our (plural) father, the priest' (See Section 735).

⁹háuńə dyûuẃee kubéní, lit. 'towards-down two when-it-arrives'; this combination is used to specify dates (cf. note 3, text 2). St. Stephen is the patron saint
of Acoma.

¹⁰According to Mrs. Hansen, Santiago is the horse and man combined, and
Chapiyu is a man who accompanies Santiago, riding his own horse. This account
differs from that given by White (1943, p. 313).

3. The Parish Priest
(By Anne Hansen)

1. And this also I remember a little, happening perhaps about the year 1933.   2. Our Holy Father went to New York, perhaps about 1935, I don't remember very well.   3. He asked our mothers to help to gather food together at the church for his provisions going east.   4. Everyone's things turned out well (that is, they had good crops that year), and if one had things (crops), they prepared them.   5. Thus he would be able to tell how his people there made their living.

4. St. Stephen's Day
(By Margaret Lim)

1. On St. Stephen's day, the second of September, all the Acomas come together at Acoma.   2. And Anglos and Spanish Americans and others gather together, Isletas, Lagunas, Zuñis, and those such as Navajos. 3. On the morning of the second, everyone goes (to church) and the priest says Mass.   4. Then the Mass is over, and the Santo is taken out.   5. When everyone at Acoma goes in the procession, then the Mass is over, and when he (the Santo) is taken in the procession he is put into the shrine in the plaza, and he is taken (there).   6. The ladies toss out things such as bread, melons, and meat.   7. Then they have a dance.

8. Formerly Chapiyu used to come to Acoma with Santiago.   9. No one observes (the tradition) now.   10. One time when I saw Chapiyu he came by horse riding on top (that is, was riding the horse).   11. He was dressed all in black and (had) a lone whip.   12. And Santiago (came) the same way, mounted on a small horse.

5. Chicken Pull on San Juan's Day
(By Andrew Lewis)

1. wá ṣuwéeṣu záatyau húučani ka?áukúyáwáati ýáapi, ṣuwée wá tîiça háu za?ácíní, wá ṣuwéeṣu sawá dâawáaça háu za?ácíní, ṣuwéeṣu wá húučani zíiýáadyúwi[11] neyáyanikuyagú ṣúyati da?áa wá sawá zíucáasti dyúyá káci dyâana zízá háuṅ̇ə kubéní héemáaku ṣuwéeṣu guwáaku ṅ̇əṅ̇idáwáaguusatiši. 2. ṣuwée wá táa ṣúyati gái gáyáwáasêe?ení guwáa néṅ̇aatasgúṅ̇u, guwáa nubêecistaasgúṅ̇u kawâayu santiyâaku,[12] čapiyú kadyáaši wée kawâayu. 3. gái dəi sukúuná yúuná dítya, bə́, kúwa, sá héemée dəi dyə́ gáisbîiyu kawâayu ze?êemiši sái héemée ?ai dyə́ zitíyáaniciši ?émí ?ézé zíi ?íyâaní níçaagú nubêecistaagú wée ?aiṅ̇ə ṅ̇ítagúṅ̇iši.[13]
    4. ṣuwée wá háu za?ácíní héemáaku zíucáasti ?ai ṣuwéeṣu wá gái háaku níçaaṅ̇aguusa wéemée háṅ̇u háubá kúyâawaça, máasiça, háçəcai, ṣúyati, sái.   5. ?ée wá ṣuwée ?ai háu cətée ka?áizáaní, ṣuwée ciwá ?ai káakaati ?ai há húučani núkaazáagú.   6. ṣuwéeṣu wá cətée zíuzáaní ?ai héemáaku ṣuwée ?ai zíuzáaní ṣuwée wá ?aiṅ̇ə šúku ?éeṅ̇əkə nədə?ékuguusa ṣúyati kawâayu níya dyə́ sgáagúnú.[14]   7. ṣuwée wá gái kée ?amaháa kée cišáaci nədéeguiyáatáguusa ?ai yâunizíwáanáyuu wée sakuṅ̇í ?ée kée tíišuusabə́ ?ée wée bə́iṅ̇íišuusakúwa dyáanáwá kée ṣúyáná zéeguiyí.[15]
    8. wée ṅ̇əṅ̇ítagúṅ̇iši ?ai yâaṅ̇í zíiýáatyuwiṅ̇áata ?ée háamáašu níuwataciumáṅ̇iši.   9. ṣuwée wá ?ai sdídyáṅ̇ə bəṅ̇ícíyâama[16] ?ée dídyáṅ̇ə ?ée yúuku dídyáṅ̇ə kée díyásabə́ kée háma santiyâaku zúuciṣa ?ée yúuku bə́ zístikáca[17] wée sâaní ?ai zístikáca kée háaníyásakúwa ?ée yúuku sakúwa ?ai hámastíyani[17] sdíyásá ?ée yəkée sâa dyə́ bəṅ̇ísti háu sabəṅ̇í dyə́ yâunizíwáanáyuu stíišuusá dyə́, ?ai háu sâa dyə́ za?ácínú ?ai ṣuwée ?ai níuwataciu má ?ai háamáašu háuzéeši.   10. ?ai zíuwata[18] ṣuwée ?ai sabəṅ̇ə zíkaná níyúuceegú zíkaná ?émí yəkée hakée zúuciṣa bəṅ̇ícíyâama ?ée sdídyáṅ̇ə ?ée yəkée díyásabə́ ?ai zístikáca wée hâaní ?ée kée sakudyə́ ?ée zíkaná hakée ?ée sâa dyə́ ?ai háu sâa dyə́ za?ácínú ṣuwée háiti háuyée

---

[11]húučani zíiýáadyúwi 'First Chief', or War Chief. Unmodified, húučani 'chief' would also designate the War Chief.

[12]Santiago is the patron saint or protector of horses.

[13]ṅ̇ítagúṅ̇iši 'the one that will take it (down, -ṅ̇ə)' (theme -JúdaW 'to take', see Sections 471, 761) is the subject, and nubêecistaagú 'he will pray' is the verb. The meaning of zitíyáaniciši is unknown, but it is probably a derivative of - ĵíýáaN 'to be born, to be alive'.

[14]The Acoma mesa is the starting point.

[15]The group circles Lonesome Rock four times in a counterclockwise direction. It is not clear if the chicken is taken down before or after circling. The chicken

5. Chicken Pull on San Juan's Day
(By Andrew Lewis)

1. When the Country Chiefs accept the staff of office, when spring arrives, when the month of San Juan (June) arrives, the First Chief will ask some boys for San Juan's feast day, the twenty-fourth (of June), to take down the chicken. 2. Then he instructs the boys in what to say, how to pray to the horse, Santiago, and to Chapiyu's horse. 3. The one that will take it down will pray from this point far towards the north, west, south, back to the east, places on this earth where horses dwell, all places, so that it will give zitíyáanicisi and life.

4. When it is almost time for the feast day the people will get things ready, everyone, ladies, girls, men, boys, everyone. 5. When it is ready the War Chief will announce it in the plaza at the east (side). 6. When it is ready, when it is time, the boys will go down below riding horses. 7. They keep going fast to Lonesome Rock, (approaching) from the south and on along the north side (going) back west and along the west side (going) back south, going around four times. 8. The one who is going to take it down is in the lead, and following (is) the one who will relieve him. 9. Then north and down (hill) again to West Gate, and north and down, off north and down along to the northeast where Santiago once went and off west to Zishtikatsa, by the eastern side of Zishtikatsa, on back southeast, off south to Hamashtiyani, back northeast and that way back east and up, across the western part, back and up from the western part by the north side of Lonesome Rock and up, and when he arrives back in the east (at the base of Acoma) the following (person) will relieve him. 10. He relieves him there, and then he will take it back to the west and down again, the place where he went (before) to West Gate and back north and down, that way north and back west, to the east of Zishtikatsa, and off again south and up, again that way back east and up, to the east and up,

---

is strung between two poles to the south of Lonesome Rock, and the riders pass beneath the chicken.

In this and the following sentences the cardinal points are used in places where English would use "left" and "right". This text illustrates the tendency of Acoma to indicate rather exact geographic locations by using a well-developed set of directions (Section 652) and complex locative phrases (Section 741).

[16]Compound (Section 610) of bəní 'in the west' + cíyâama 'door'. The name of a passage between two rocks to the west of Acoma.

[17]The name of a rock, unanalysable.

[18]zíuwata 'the other one relieves him', obviative. The obviative is used to indicate that the following boy relieves the one who had been in the lead.

ʔémí ṣúẏati háu sâa dyə̀ zaʔaćínú zíudíitya.[19]   11. ṣuẃée ʔai sabə́nə
nədeʔékugúusa ʔée ćíyâama ʔée sdídyáńə ʔée yúuku díyásabə́.[20]

12. ṣuẃée wá ʔai gái héeẏa zíi ʔamaháa nitûunisəsgúńiši ńíẏa wée wá
máaséewi[21] ḱámáawítâańi héeẏa zíi ńitûunisəsgúńu ʔai ṣuẃée ʔai dyáanáwá
ćaʔáaspíizáńa.   13. ʔai ṣuẃée yúuku ńítagú ʔée wá ṣuẃée ʔai sá dyə́ ḱée
sá dyə́ ʔée ṣuẃée ʔai núwáẏáanəəcadyúusa wée wá dyâana šuḱúuná haẃée
wée ʔíyatiku háḿa haẃée ćaʔáwiṣaçataniṣa.   14. ʔémí haẃée wée dyáanáwa
yúuku núwáẏáanəəcadyúusa guẃáaku.   15. ṣuẃée háuyée ʔémí zíi zíšiya
ʔémí wée ṣuẃée sái gáwaaʔaiti zíi ʔićáatyani wée ṣuẃée sái ńaadyú
guẃáaku zítaku.   16. ʔétyu sái kaʔâućáńaatya ʔétyu ṣuẃée wá sái háubá
wée nəćáašiidyúusa.   17. daʔáa ʔémí dúẃa wá ʔáaku zíyúukaiʔi.

6. Around Acoma
(By Anne Hansen)

1. ʔai ṣâaḿa dídyí zə́çətyai ʔai sdyə́ máamé cíčə ḱúuti káwéestiima
ʔéegá.   2. ʔée ṣuẃée ṣáaçəətya wée kúyásabə́ máakina híyâanizá.
3. ʔée ʔai ʔée kúńə wée sabə́ dyə́ wabûuri ḱahíyâani.   4. ʔée ṣuẃée ʔai
kúińíišu síńə ʔusuḿéestáańíizá.   5. wée ʔée háańíyásakudyə́ híyâanizá
ʔáaku háu sdyə́.   6. ʔai díićíyâaḿa[22] díńíyákudyə́ ʔai sdyə́ ḱúuti cíčə gâa
ʔétyu wée ṣâakayá ʔéegá.   7. ʔai nəzîyá sdídyáńə ʔamaháa zítyapi, haẃée
ʔamaháa háçəcai kúẃábîiʔizát'eeʔeńáat'a.   8. ṣuẃée ʔai sâańə dííčə́ná[23]
ʔai ʔée háańíyá t'íišu sdyə́ zíka ḱúuti zə́əsišəgâa ʔétyu wée ʔagə́çəci
ḱúutíizá.   9. ʔée ṣuẃée ʔai sâańə yúu háçə mîiya zúusti yəḱée sdyə́
híyâanizá ʔai ʔáaku ʔémí háu sdyə́ zíka.   10. ʔáaku nəzíyáhâańə ʔai
sdyə́ zə́əsíšə ḱúutigâa ʔétyu kazîima ćaʔáńiya.   11. ʔée ṣuẃée wá ʔáaku
ńəzíyáṣáńə, ḱée díibə́çə há kubéwiwá, haḱée ḱúuku wáakaši cíyastińáat'a.
12. ʔée haẃée hâaní bə́çəkúẃa zíka ʔémí haẃée zeʔéńáat'a.   13. ʔée
haẃéeńə záiṣazá ʔétyu yúuku kučə́nâaẏa zíka haẃée wáakaši
gûuẃawaaʔańáat'a háyáaći.   14. ʔée ṣuẃée yəḱée kúyábə́ dyə́ haẃée zíi
kanêeru dyûuẃawaaʔańáat'a.   15. ʔée kaṣâiti yəḱée sdyə́ wáakaši
gút'ikuseeńáat'a.   16. ʔétyu yúuku bə́ dyə́ čə́nâaẏa zíka haẃée pesdúuracizá
ʔée haẃée bə́ńíyádídyáńə yəḱée zíka záiṣazá.   17. ṣuẃée ʔai dítya čáat'yau
gúḿi ʔai sdyə́ guḿə́sə ʔée haẃée ńauẏa gái haẃée ẏúu cíci dyuḿə́sə.

---

[19]He gives the chicken to the first boy to arrive.

[20]Apparently the group travels the same course four times, each time with a
different boy in the lead carrying the chicken.

[21]máaséewi, one of the war twins (see text 38).

and when he arrives, when one of the boys arrives, he gives it to him.
11. Then they will go back to the west and down and to West Gate and further
back to the northeast.

12. In order that one will grow up with Masewi's atonement, if one wants
to grow up with this, he is then whipped four times (with the chicken).   13.
Then he will take it back up to the east there, along to the east and up, and
the group will pull it to the four corners which Iyatiku named long ago.   14.
They will pull the chicken four times.   15. Whoever wins it will have all the
fruits of life and fortune, if he takes the (whole) chicken.   16. But if they di-
vide it all up, then it (the fruits of life) will belong to everybody.   17. This
is the way they observe the tradition at Acoma.

6. Around Acoma
(By Anne Hansen)

1. From my house (running) along in the north there is a very big mountain
called Mt. Taylor. 2. To the southwest of our house there is an automobile
road. 3. And (further on) to the south, on down, and back up to the west
there is a railroad track. 4. And there down by the south side there is a
school. 5. From (that point) up to the southeast there is a road on up to
Acoma. 6. Above McCarties, south and up, there is a big mountain, and it
is called Rustling of the Trees. 7. Below there, back down to the north,
there is a forest where men usually gather wood. 8. East and down to
Acomita and (still further) east again there is a small mountain off to the
north, and that one is Flower Mountain. 9. Then to the east and down, going
a few miles, there is a road up to Acoma that way, another way (to get) up
to (Acoma). 10. Below Acoma to the east and down there is a small mountain (going) up, and it is called Enchanted Mesa. 11. Spreading out to the
north and east below Acoma is grassland, where the cattle are kept in the
winter. 12. They (cattle) are also along to the east and on south. 13. There
are fields down there (in the south), and still further on is South Canyon
where they keep cattle in the fall. 14. And on up to the southwest they keep
sheep. 15. And they take cattle up that way in the summer. 16. And still
further west and up in a canyon there is a sheep camp, and down to the north-
west there are fields. 17. And there on the north side is Gumi Spring, and
there are many other springs there.

---

[22]díićíyâama 'McCarties' (lit. 'north door'), the location of Mrs. Hansen's house.
[23]díićśná 'Acomita', lit. 'north river'.

7. What We Used to Do as Kids
(By Mary Valley)

1. wá dúẃa dɘisi ʔée názáasí guẃáa zíi háma ʔíyáz̜áasədáaʔabáati
suẃawíš̜áitiyaatiši. 2. ʔai s̜úyáná súẃáýáabéecitiyańáaťasə. 3. zíi ýúu
ḱáuku ťúuná zíi tâama zíi š̜ísa kas̜âitisədeʔéemí ʔée s̜áwaçətyaimiši ʔai
s̜úyáná súẃáýáabéecitiyańáaťa ḱée s̜úyáná míi ʔémí héeméeş̜a cáatyuma
ʔai s̜áaçəətya. 4. ʔée zíi zíka ʔamaháa ŝâac̜awaiʔiizáťeeʔeesəńáaťasə
ʔai s̜úyána héemée ḱáš̜əka ʔai ʔamaháa s̜áaçəətya ʔai kuc̜ónâaya ʔée ẃée
háaníbóçə sdítya ʔée ẃée ʔée sâaní. 5. ʔée ʔézí háiti zíi ýúu záazíi zíi
háma mâamé gái zíi skuẃawíš̜áisətiyaatya. 6. ʔézé ťúu ʔai háaťi zíi
haẃée zíi c̜óná ʔée zíi haẃée c̜áaťyau ʔée s̜âaʔaz̜áitiyańáaťasə.

7. gái ẃai máamé zíi ńańámí zíi kaʔáatuuńími ʔíyaça. 8. zíi
gáanáatitiya ʔétyu yuẃée háma zíi ťúu ʔézé zíi zíi háiti zíi háarú ńiyáka
zíi yâuni haẃée s̜úyáná héeya ŝâaʔaz̜áitiyasə, zíi ẃée súẃabáýatiyasəńáaťa
haẃée c̜áaťyau ʔée zíi zíi skúuc̜áwáńí ʔézé zíi ʔišâani cîipáńiši zíi.
9. ʔée zíi haẃée ḱáńi zíi s̜áasgəńaitiya ťúu zíi háiti zíi suẃámasawáaťaitiya
ťúumá zíi.[24] 10. suẃáwîititiyaasə zíi sguẃáýáidyáasə zíi háarú zíi ḱéeńə
s̜áiyadíťuwityaimiši.[25] 11. haẃée zíi ʔée zíi dénta sədéegúiyáaťasə zíi
ʔézé háiti zíi haẃée c̜áaťyau ʔée zíi síẃáťyâipaatikuyáńańáaťasə.

8. What We Used to Do as Kids[26]
(By Anne Hansen and Margaret Lim)

Margaret: 1. ʔée ʔáaku ʔée z̜ózə́ťyau ʔée sədéeyasəńáaťa. 2. ʔée ḱáac̜áńí
ʔamaháa súẃastíizáťeeʔe haẃée ḱáẃáyáńis̜a ʔée. 3. záama kuz̜óçədyaʔée[27]
çustíí?

Anne: 4. hímá, míi máiḱúiná ẃée sêenaçəteyańáaťa, ŷaapéetukani ẃée
dídyáńə s̜áamáaš̜úẃaacitiyańáaťa.

---

[24]That is, they would do pretend-cooking with pieces of cedar and the like if
they had no real food at hand.

[25]They were pretending to toss out food to spectators, as is done at some of
the dances (for example, see text 4).

[26]This is the only sample of conversation that I was able to collect. The situation was rigged and is reflected in the stiffness of the style.

[27]kuz̜óçətyai, lit. 'South Edge', the name of a water hole.

7. What We Used to Do as Kids
(By Mary Valley)

1. I'm going to talk about our playing when we were children. 2. We used to race around. 3. When we were probably about five or six years old my brothers and I would race around, on to as far as the fence by our house. 4. And we would also have foot races around in larger areas, from our house to South Canyon, and (then going) to the east, and back north, then (coming) back from the east. 5. We never had anything very special to play with. 6. We would build (play) houses just any place as at the river or on the hillside.

7. Today they raise kids very differently. 8. They buy things, but in those days we would build (play) houses with anything such as tin cans or stones (which were) around, or we would build a fire on the hillside when someone had sneaked away things such as dried meat or the like. 9. And we fried cedar there or just anything (we could find) and we boiled things just for fun. 10. We would make things and toss them, and what we threw out (were) things like tin cans. 11. When we went to the store or anyplace we would look for things at the side (of the road).

8. What We Used to Do as Kids
(By Anne Hansen and Margaret Lim)

Margaret: 1. We used to climb along the edge (of the cliff) at Acoma. When it rained we went for water at the waterholes. 3. Did you ever get water at kuẓóçətyai?

Anne: 4. Yes, we used to go around there lots of times, and we used to slide down from the north side of the ice caves.

Margaret: 5. díićíyâama wée saʔáwiša ʔáyáni, ʔai hâaćáatya.
6. saʔâama ʔai hâaćáadyaʔée, hawée guńáaťaayuma ʔée hawée zíi ḱáni kiẃáća yúuwi ʔée súwabáyatiyańáaťa. 7. ʔée yáaćíni sáasgəńaitiyańáaťa.
8. ʔée hawée zíi záisa ʔée hawée zíi sədéepəsəńáaťa, wíćəńíisətaaʔańáaťa.
9. hawée zíi kínáti yúuku siẃáutitiyańáaťa, sâayawitiyańáaťa ʔée zí merûuni záanáa gánáti zíi saaʔapeeńáaťa súuẃaćáwáitiyańáaťa. 10. ʔée zíi yaʔáaná sáutyatiyańáaťa, yuʔústu zíi yáaspusu súwasbóťitiyańáaťa.
11. suwée ćóná ʔéenə suẃawáišáwazáńeeʔeẓáťeeʔe ʔée suẃáyáapəsəńáaťa.
12. ʔée míi zí saẃaipeeńáaťa, sáayáćayawitiyańáaťa ʔée wée zíi sədéegúiyání zíi sáayáwaaníitańáaťa.

Anne: 13. ťúuná ʔíyáẓáasədée zóəsíśə sâaʔaʔáu, sáayáwatapətyəńáaťa ʔúutitiyani. 14. ʔée háiḱámíná suʔúwíibáaťáaťasə, ʔétyu sińaaya ʔáisi zíyûuḳami sgâaʔayuuḳamińáaťa hámaaća wéesi ńíyúuceṣúuńətyəciši.
15. ʔétyu wée suẃawíšáitiyaatya ʔétyu ʔai dyúuni ćuwîititańáaťa.

Margaret: 16. ʔái ćóná yúuwi háarú ńíya zíi suẃawíšáitiyańáaťa.
17. máamé saʔáu gúsú karêeta ʔúwîiçaani, wée sḱáašu héeya cáyastiimiši—kusbóťitańáaťa. 18. suwée zíi tené hyêesta zéegûiyišiḿée ḱáwiša ʔáyáni. 19. ḱáwáika báasku sḱáakuuyańáaťa ʔémé ʔée ḱáwiša ʔáyáni.
20. hâawíski ḱáwíititáani. 21. šápəka ʔái saʔâama bó ẓóçətyai súuwíšáayáńətyəńáaťasə. 22. mánta ńíya súdyúťâayáńə suwée saʔáwáaka ʔamaháa séyáẓáanaityə suẃáaguťâayáńətyə zíi wée ćíšé záipaṣaišiḿée suẃáaguťâayáńətyə.

Anne: 23. seiyáńiyaapətyəńáaťa "ńâa ʔai ʔímíi abâaći zeʔéku."

9. Growing Up

(By Anne Hansen)

1. wá dəisi ńíibéesí guẃáa háḿa sitûuniši. 2. cáyáṣu ʔéeséeši, sáyúusitya ʔéesé. 3. kí ʔémé təçaʔáiṣaẓáńa sáastíyáagúḿi. 4. ʔée suwée sḱúmáawání təçaʔáiṣaẓáńa zîusdyawí. 5. máyúḱúusətaaʔa saʔáutyaimiši ʔée sáwaçətyaimiši dyûuwée sáẃaçətyai ʔétyu ḿáityaana ḿáasiçasətaaʔa. 6. yúu zíi ḱáuku šísa kaṣâiti šíipi siyúuḱu wá ʔémí ńíibéesí. 7. sińaaya dyəəçəsa dyúuni kuwîitita, ʔétyu suwée saʔáutyaimiši sáwaaníińáaťa. 8. wéeḿée ćóná ʔéenə seiẓúuceyáaťasə, hawée zíi suẃáyâapəsəńáaťa.

9. suwée wéeḿée kaṣâiti yúuḱu kućání, suwéeṣu ʔusuḿéestáani ḱáaʔáaťáwí háiḱamiṣu súsúḿéesta (McCartys). 10. záazíi mâamé ʔeʔésgúńu zíi gúitódéekuya. 11. gái yúu zíi wá dyâana diḱáńə

Margaret: 5. We used to play at McCarties on the east side. 6. Along the east side of our house, where there are caves and along the side where there are cedar trees we used to build fires. 7. We would parch corn. 8. We would go into the fields and snitch things. 9. We would pick fresh corn, and roast it, and we would eat melons before they were ripe, we would snitch them. 10. And we would pick skunk brush berries, and we would string cedar berries and cottonwood berries. 11. And we would go swimming and wading down at the river. 12. And we would fight and wrangle, and while we went about (doing these things) we would look after (smaller) children.

Anne: 13. When I was still young, we had a tiny sister, and we took turns carrying her on our backs. 14. Sometimes she would go to sleep for us, and my mother would wait, she would wait a while for us to bring her back. 15. Then we would play while she made pottery.

Margaret: 16. We would play with tin cans beside the river. 17. My sister really knew how to make wagons with the ones that fish are in (that is, with sardine cans)—she would string them. 18. Then she would play as if they were Navajos going to a fiesta. 19. She would play as if they were going to a Laguna dance. 20. She made little rag dolls. 21. In the evening we used to play by the west side of our house. 22. We covered ourselves with large sheets, and we made our dolls talk, and we would hide them as though the Apaches were chasing them (so) we would hide them.

Anne: 23. We would say to them, "Oh, the Apaches are coming!"

9. Growing Up
(By Anne Hansen)

1. I'm going to tell about my growing up. 2. First my name, ṣáyúusitya, is my name. 3. They named me at my naming ceremony. 4. When they initiated me they named me Storm Clouds. 5. There were nine of us, my sisters and my brothers, my two brothers and seven of us girls. 6. I'm going to tell from about the time I was six years old and beyond. 7. My mother was always making pottery, and I would take care of my sisters. 8. I would take them down to the river, and we would wade there.

9. When summer was over, and when school was open I went to school for the first time at McCarties. 10. I don't remember very well what I used to do. 11. When I was in about the fourth grade, I finally started

śíičúpi[28] ṣuẃéeṣu gáitiṣu ṣáamíi súitunímiçaatya.   12. háyáaci (picnics)
sədéegúiyáatasə, zíi dyáiyaani ʔekaʔaiça hawée śáityatiyańáata.   13. ʔée
ṣuẃée tâaṁa, ʔée śísa dikáńə sədéečúpi zíi wágəńi suẃáwîititiya.   14.
ʔée zí kusinêeru ʔûutitaani sgâiʔisúṁéestiya.

15. ʔée wá ṣuẃée ṁáityaana, kukúṁišu ʔée máyúku dikáńə śíičúpi
ʔarawagêeki súsúṁéestaańe.   16. máamé ńâuya ʔáakúuṁéeça ʔaisədeʔé.
17. ṣaʔáu ʔisgâawa ʔáiṣâaʔa, túu dyəəçəṣa háaṁáašu háu sêenaçəteya.
18. ʔée ṣuẃée wá máyúku súináudání ʔétyuyú šáməci háńu kasùṁéestáańi
ʔée ʔétyu háu síupə.   19. kúimí zí káusa wée zíi héeya ʔusuṁéestáańi.
20. wéeṁée šápəka (bus) ńíya háu síńə seʔecí sińâaya zíka
śíumáacitaaníńáata.   21. háyáaci zíi śéyastíititaańətyəńáata zíi čəəri
ʔée ʔišâani.   22. ʔée háikámíná dyáiyaani śáityaiʔizátéeʔeńáata zíi
ʔekaʔâiçaanu.

23. ʔée wá ṣuẃée héeṁée ʔai súináudání ṣuẃée duẃée sîuṁə.

10. When I Was a Guide at Acoma
(By Anne Hansen)

1. tâaṁa kaṣâiti kaʔâiça sińâisdíya húučani káuyáaʔańíši.   2. ṣáadáabûupuši
skaʔâiʔizáńa ʔûukítaukuyáńi, hawée dyə́ háńu zéegúiyí ʔai ʔáaku
gúukačáńaatya.   3. dyə́ zêeṁənu kúuẃáadyâatita.   4. šáməci háńu
káayáazúwiitiya ʔétyu skáukîini ʔíntyu túumá wée zéegúiyáata.   5. cíčə
húučani[29] stitâańiçańiitya záazíi káayáazúwiitiyaatya.   6. wee ʔáaku
cîukítaukuyańiši ʔai zístíititiya hékudáa kaʔáizáaní[30] héeyasi háaci
nəẓáanáadáńagúusa ʔée mísa kâiya cîukítaukuyańiši ʔétyu héeya sdyə́
ńâaʔaçaańagúusa, ʔée hawéesi zíi dáẃáa ńeyátitiyagúusa.

7. zíi šáməci háńu máamé zíi káupeetawiši, sái zíi cibêetaukuyáńa
háadí cíci sáusíitiyaatiši ʔée guẃáa ʔáakúuṁéeça kâayúutyaniši.   8. ṣuẃée
siẃáapeeta cidyâayawiši ńíya kâayúutyaniši ʔée záiṣa sdyə́ ńíya
çayâaʔaukuyáńiši ńíya ʔéṁé ʔée ʔáakúuṁé ʔaigáa.   9. ʔée háadí ʔíyaça
káisuṁéestaaniši ʔée zíi cíčə húučani sgayáazúwiitaaniši ʔéṁí sái zíi
cibêetaukuyáńi.   10. zíi šáməci háńu cibêetaukuyáńańáatáńiši ʔáaku
nəẓíyáṣáńə.   11. ·ʔáaku ʔai nəẓíyáhâanə kazîima ʔai sdyə́ gáa, háṁa ʔai

---

[28]díka 'pertaining to' (Section 742; see ‖ 21, ‖ 22 for accent changes); nə 'down'
(Section 741); śíičúpi 'when I was inside, enclosed' (theme -aʔáčəB, see Sections
234, 762). The whole combination means 'when I was in the . . . grade' (cf. sentence 13, 15, following).

remembering things well. 12. We used to go on picnics in the fall, and if there were any piñons we would gather them. 13. When we were in the fifth and sixth grades we made clothes. 14. And they taught us to cook.

15. When I was in the seventh, eighth, and ninth grades, I went to school in Albuquerque. 16. We Acomas were very numerous there. 17. My sister and I were there together, and I always followed (her) around. 18. When I finished the ninth grade I went to the white man's school. 19. The studies were kind of hard. 20. It was evening when I got back (home) by bus, and I also helped my mother. 21. In the fall we used to can things like chili and meat. 22. Sometimes we went to gather piñons if there were any.

23. After I finished (school) I came to this place (San Francisco).

10. When I Was a Guide at Acoma
(By Anne Hansen)

1. It was five years ago that my father served as War Chief. 2. Our Governor asked me to collect (the fees) when the people came up to see Acoma. 3. When they arrived they signed their name (registered). 4. White people pay, but friends of the Indians just come in (free). 5. Those working for the U. S. government don't pay. 6. They put away that which is collected for Acoma for future use, and they will buy back land with it, and they will rebuild and repair (the church) with that which is collected for the church.

7. The white people are very inquisitive; they keep asking everything, about where we get our water and how the Acomas make a living. 8. I tell them they make a living with livestock and with what they raise in the fields; this is how the Acoma people are (that is, how they live). 9. And where the children go to school, and if the government pays us, they ask all these (questions). 10. The white people always ask about what is around below Acoma (in the valley). 11. Down to the east of Acoma is Enchanted Mesa (sticking) up, and people once lived up there.

---

[29] cíčə húučani 'the U.S. government' (Section 731). cíčə 'big, it is big'; húučani 'chief', or, in contexts such as this, 'government'.

[30] hékudáa ka?áiẓáaní 'when it gets to be some time'. Theme -QáiẓaaN 'to become', impersonal.

sdyə́ sčâuʔu.   12. ʔémí ʔaisi yúuku sčáaku ʔai ʔáaku ṣuwée ʔémí ʔai
dyə́ t́igúyáñi.   13. ṣuwée šámə́ci háñu w̓ée kubə́ní, ʔusumə́eestáañi
káaʔáat́áwí ʔaisi yúuku sčáaku.[31]   14. díičíyâama hawéenə čáaʔâat́a ʔée
díičə́ná, hawée čízíizéeši ñíy̓a.   15. héemée sái ʔai ʔáaku gúukačáñaatya
ṣuwéeṣu t́ée síñə zéegúiyí gáanáatitiyañáat́a dyúuni.

11. Selling Pottery
(By Margaret Lim)

1. dyúuni śiy̓âat́itiyañáat́asə (highway) ʔée.   2. merigâanu ʔémí
gáanáatitiyañáat́asə dyúuni wáast́iça.   3. ʔáñíumə́eezáañáat́asə skáy̓aneeyu.
4. zíi sáiwat́iseñáat́asə sgaʔáu zíi skâawi.   5. máamé gái merigâana
ziwâaw̓aniucañáat́a dyúuni.   6. ʔée gáanáatitiyañáat́a zíi skáuk̂íini
gáaw̓âanaatitiyañíitañáat́a.   7. háit́áa ʔémí zíi sčáakuy̓áat́asə, máamé gái
ṣúwánámaaṣa zéegúyañáat́a máakina ñíy̓a.   8. ʔée máamé gái zíi
zâiʔipeet́añú háadí ṣáaçəətiši ʔémí mâamé káupéet́áwiši, ʔée guw̓áa
ʔéeṣay̓áaši, ʔée háadí skúsúmə́eestaaniši, ʔée míika gái mâamé t́úumá zíi
cibêet́aukuy̓áña.   9. ʔée míika gái záazíi zíi gáaw̓adyúitišiitya, t́úumá zíi
ʔíntyu ñíy̓a kúw̓amát́itiyañáat́asə.   10. ʔée gái míika máamé ʔáñíumə́eecaaʔa.
11. háik̓ámíná zíi gáay̓âačaapeñáat́asə zíi ʔubéwí ʔée zíi wágə́ñi
gáay̓aakúy̓apikuyañíiñáat́a.

12. A Trip to Mt. Taylor
(By Anne Hansen)

1. k̓í háma kaṣâiti ʔai ṣáaráncuši ʔée dyə́ sədeʔéku karêeta ñíy̓a.
2. gáayúuzé dyâwá sət́éepatyəni ʔai kučáatyai gumə́siṣa k̓ée dyə́
siñáisdíy̓a sgáizúuce.   3. číci súw̓ast́îiʔi háu sədéedyúpi.   4. ʔai číci
ñíy̓a suw̓awíšáitiya héey̓a wâawaasayáñiya.   5. héemée sáusêeñaatya
ʔai ránču ʔéesi sədeʔéku.

---

[31]Acoma is still considered home, and all of the important dances and cere-
monies are conducted there. But most of the people now reside in McCarties or
Acomita so as to be nearer to the fields.

They moved away from there, and Acoma was settled.   13.. When the whites came, when the schools were opeend, they moved away from there (from Acoma).   14. They settled at McCarties and Acomita where there is water.   15. After they have seen everything at Acoma, they buy pottery when they go down.

11. Selling Pottery
(By Margaret Lim)

1. We used to sell pottery by the highway.   2. White people would buy small pieces of pottery.   3. It is nice when you sell.   4. We would go together with a sister or a clan relative.   5. The white people would admire the pottery very much.   6. And they would buy some (for themselves), or they would buy some for their friends.   7. We wondered where they came from; they would come by car from many different places.   8. And they were very inquisitive about where we lived—that was their main question—and about our names, and where one went to school, and others just asked (foolish) questions.   9. And others didn't have any respect; they just made fun of the Indians.   10. And others were very nice.   11. Sometimes they would give away things; they would give away things like food and clothing.

12. A Trip to Mt. Taylor
(By Anne Hansen)

1. One summer we went up to our ranch by wagon.   2. Early in the morning when we got up, my father took us up to a spring on the south side (of Mt. Taylor).   3. We got water when we arrived.   4. We played there with water and threw it (had a water fight).   5. After we got the water, we went back to the ranch.

13. Prairie Dogs
(By Margaret Lim)

1. háma sə́əníici sədeʔéku karêeta níya sináaya ʔée sináisdíya.   2. ṣuwée
yuwéesi sədéeguíyí ʔái háadí yúu ʔai saṣáanáati, sináisdíya séecikuyasə
díya wáasti ʔúudyáati, kaṣumé ʔémí nə́ti wée dyə́ kaʔáanáase.
   3. ʔée ṣuwée ʔamaháa dyáiyaani kiwáca náyáa yúu taṣâaṅa, ṣuwée ʔémí
sináaya ḱée dyə́ ḱáyâuṫuwiitya, níwâayəəcagú dyáiyaani.   4. ʔée wéemée
čə́ṫi gúwâayəəca wéenə dyáiyaani béepeeka.

14. Snow
(By Anne Hansen)

1. wéemée kúuku káwéetu.   2. čə́ná ʔéenə suwastîiʔizáteeʔenáaṫa.   3. ʔée
hawée kamêeca sáayáiṫišêeyucitiya.   4. ʔée ṣuwée ʔai ṣáaçəətya čáatya
ṣúyáná máadáašúku suwáwîititiyaṅáaṫa.   5. kí zíi wée[32] (snowman)
suwáwîititiyaṅáaṫa.   6. ʔée héeya máadáašúku níya sáamašáacitiyaṅáaṫa.

15. Gathering Salt
(By Anne Hansen)

1. kí háma sináisdíya sgáizúuce kamínáace ḱamáakina níya.   2. máamé
tée ʔ ezá, ḱapišə́ní ʔai sáaʔâaṫa.   3. háu sədéedyúpi záazíi zíi háu
ʔaigáagúnú, náanú gáayúuzé dyâwá səṫeepatyəniitya ḱée ʔai mîná ḱée
gaʔáčupiṣa háunə ṣuwáyáapə, dyə́ síuṫâaʔakasə ʔáyáa skásdí nəzîyá
ḱáwaasá.   4. ṫúu sái sḱáwagə́ni zíi sgaćícici kaʔâitita.   5. záazíi
ʔeʔésgúṅu háćə suwáustaaṅaatiši.   6. gái ʔétyu háma máikúiná
déegúiyáaṫa karêeta níya yúumíi zíi ʔíska tamîiku gáaná déegúiyáaṫa.
7. záazíi sgúutuníma guwáa ḱáyúugáiyíšiitya, túumée gái sîuní šâawitya
hánuça ʔée dâani hánuça ḱáiwáṫiseetya.

---

   [32]kí zíi wée 'what you call, that which is'. The meaning cannot be determined
by an analysis of its parts: kí (adverb) indicates completed action; zíi '(some)-
thing', indefinite demonstrative; wée 'that one', demonstrative.

13. Prairie Dogs
(By Margaret Lim)

1. Once my mother and father and I went to Zuñi by wagon. 2. When we were coming back, when we had stopped someplace, I asked my father to catch a puppy; but they were just prairie dogs looking out (of their holes).

3. I think we stopped under a piñon tree, and my mother was throwing (cones) up (into the tree) in order to hit the piñons. 4. And when she hit them directly, the piñons fell down.

14. Snow
(By Anne Hansen)

1. During the winter it snows. 2. We would get water down at the river. 3. And we would slide where it was icy. 4. And we used to make (snow-balls around by the side of our house. 5. We used to make what you call snowmen. 6. And we would fight with (snow)balls.

15. Gathering Salt
(By Anne Hansen)

1. My father took us once to the salt lake in his car. 2. It was very far, and we spent the night there. 3. When we arrived nobody was there, and when we got up early the next morning we waded into where the salt was, and drained it up (that is, scooped it out), and oh! it hurt under your feet. 4. All your clothes just get stiff. 5. I don't remember how much we gathered. 6. But formerly (in the old days) they used to travel by wagon for a long time, perhaps they would travel for a week. 7. I don't know how the traditions were carried on, I only know that the parrot and pumpkin clan went together.

16. Picking Prickly Pears
(By Anne Hansen)

1. wéeméeṣu háyáaċi ʔáníuṁée kaʔaiçaanu dyaiẏaani sâiteeʔeẓáteeʔe, ʔai ṣaaçəətya díníyákúwa.   2. wéemée ḱáni díḱa náyáa ʔée hawée dyó hawée náyáa dyó ʔiitya kiwáṅáata.   3. ʔée ṣuwée ʔai yúuḱu siwâutitiyaṅáata ċáasdyúṁiṣa níẏa, ʔée ẏáabísi wéemée sâateeʔeetya héeẏa siwáabáaḱacitiya 4. ʔée ṣuwée šûumə dâawâaça ʔai ṣaaçəətya díiċáatyau bó dyó wéemée ʔíẏaça ṅauẏa sədéegúiẏáatasə.   5. zíi ʔáasa níẏa ʔamaháa súwatíicitiya ʔiitya.   6. hawée zíka ʔémí sáẏastiipeeṅáata.   7. ʔétyu záagú gái háṁa ča ʔâipaaṅaawitiyaṅáata ʔée ʔamaháa ča ʔâatiwâitiya ṣuwée ḱí zíi wée díḱa ʔée dyáyâatâitiya hâati.   8. wéemée zíi ʔáaḱu guwáa kaʔâititaanu héeẏa yúu dyuwâuċiiçaiʔiẓáteeʔeṅáata.   9. ʔée zíka diwáadyâawá héeẏa zíi ʔúukasi habúuša héeẏa ʔúukami níẏa.

17. Making Soap
(By Anne Hansen)

1. dúwa wá ṅíibéesí guwáa hâatyani múši ʔáasbánášuṁéni ċiutikusiši. 2. wéemée ḱúuti ʔée dyó skubîiyu, cáyáṣu ʔai hâatyani skâuċəəçəca ṣuwée wáawáiçəni ċiwáušaipi.³³   3. ṣuwée ṣáamí sguwáabáaḱaca ʔai sgâaṁa háusi sdyaʔáċínú ʔamaháa skáusáapaca ṣuwée ḱí zíi wée díḱa dyó skûitainata hâaḱaani díḱa, ṣuwée ʔədóəṁazéeṣa dyó ċâipaaṅaawáṅitaaṅi 4. ṣuwée níudyâawáastiuṁáṅu cáyáṣu wîitaaʔazíṁi, ṣuwée sái ċíyúugáni ṣuwéeṣu sái čətée kaʔâititaaṅáata.

18. Indian Medicine
(By Anne Hansen)

1. nahâaya háṁa kaṣâiti ʔíẏaça gúwáaši ʔémé ʔée ʔədóəṁáazeʔéši, máaṛ sái ḱánani díníẏá zíwáača.   2. ṣuwée sḱaʔániya "záa ḱáni ṣayáyáaspaaní, néẏaskátaṣú?"   3. ṣuwée gáiḱa ṣaʔáu níušíicasí ḱa-(osterizer) ḱí zíi wée héeẏa ʔúyáasbáaṅi.   4. ṣuwée záazíi háu stíuyâaʔaniitya, skáʔániya "sái

---

³³Soapweed is normally obtained on wood-gathering trips.

16. Picking Prickly Pears
(By Anne Hansen)

1. During the fall, when they were nice (that is, got ripe), we would go to gather piñons above and south of our house. 2. Under the cedar trees prickly pears would be growing up. 3. We would take them off with a forked stick, and we would take y̓áabísi (a stiff grass) and brush them (to take the stickers off). 4. And in November many of us children would go up to the west of the hillside north of our house. 5. We would gather prickly pears in pans. 6. We would also sift them. 7. Long ago they used to dry and grind them and mix them into a meal. 8. When some (event, ceremony) took place at Acoma they would go to pray with it (that is, use it as an offering). 9. Also they used to dye things with it, such as to dye wool with it.

17. Making Soap
(By Anne Hansen)

1. I'm going to tell how soapweed shampoo is taken out (of the ground). 2. When one goes for wood in the mountains, first one cuts down the soapweed, then the roots are dug up. 3. Then you shake them well (to remove loose dirt), and when you get gack home you pound them; then you cook them on charcoal; then you dry them where it is sunny. 4. Then when you are going to use them, first soak them, and when they are thoroughly soaked they are all ready to use.

18. Indian Medicine
(By Anne Hansen)

1. The year before last the children had diarrhea because it was hot, and they were overcome by the heat. 2. Then they said to me, "Why don't you grind cedar for them and give it to them to drink?" 3. I was going to borrow my sister's osterizer to grind it with. 4. Nobody would let me use it; they told me, "It will get the odor all (through it)." 5. Since

ńiucaaʔaciumá." 5. ṣuẃée záa háu sgúuyâaʔańiitya ẏâuni ʔúyáasbáańi dyə́ suẏáaspa. 6. ṣuẃée ʔíẏaça séẏaskáta, túu ṣuẃée ʔéeṣusi dáẃáa ziẃáuça. 7. wéeḿée ʔíẏaça gúwáašiinu ʔíntyu ḱáwawáašiku ẓə́əpəšíśə ḱáńi.

19. School
(By Margaret Lim)

1. túuná háḿa ʔarawagéki susuḿéestáaní ʔamaháa ʔíẏaça duẃée wá míiná yúuku zaiʔisuḿéestiya záa ʔéḿí zíi ʔusuḿéestáańi túuná šíipi ʔéḿí zíi súsúḿéestaani. 2. túuná wá ʔai šíipi túuḿée ʔéḿí zíi ʔíntyu wẽe guwáa ʔáaẏúudyáńi zaiʔisuḿéestiya dyúuni ʔúwîiçaańi ʔée zíi kanâasta ʔúwîititaańi ʔée zíi wagêeta ńíẏa, ʔée zíi ʔamaháa báani ʔúwîititaańi zíi ʔúuťisdyáńi pisâari. 3. ʔée hawée zíi ʔutâańizáńi ʔúuẏastíḿi díka ʔée, zíi máakina ńíẏa ʔée zíi ʔaẏáaťidyə́əci, ʔée ʔai ʔúuẏadáẃi ʔai. 4. ʔée zíi guwáa ʔubéwizáńi, wágə́ńi ʔúwîititaańi, zíi ʔáẏašitaańi. 5. záazíi gái ʔéḿí duẃéewá wá zíi ʔéḿí gái sdyaiʔisuḿéestiya.

20. Cowboy Life as a Kid
(By Andrew Lewis)

1. kí háḿa túuná ʔíẏáẓáasədée sińaisdíẏa wáakaši díka ʔée sḱúyúuceẏáaťa 2. wẽe háiti kawâayu ḱúučíńi šadẏá máaḿé ṣúukúiťuuní. 3. ʔée wá ṣuẃée gáayú sədéegúiyúunú šíwádyâinaukuyáńańáaťa wáakaši. 4. máaḿé záawáatyušu. 5. ʔée ṣuẃéeṣu háaḿáašu haḱée šáupašáaťasəńáaťa. 6. ʔée máaḿé háadíiku zíi šapəgáńí séiʔidyáatikuyáńańáaťa. 7. ʔée záazíi háḿa zíi sə́ńa cidíẏá háadí zíi túuṣu dyâwá zíi háḿa sgâaʔapeetya zíi wẽe skáaskataatya. 8. máaḿé gái gáçaasti, ʔétyu gái ʔańéezá. 9. háḿa ṣuẃée ʔai ḱáḿasku ḱáwáiṣa ʔai hâačáaťyau gáaspeeṣuma díníẏáhá háḿa ʔai ʔúuťisdyúwísti taʔaukúẏawi. 10. záazí skaʔautyuku kí míi ḿéńaṣu ʔai ḱáḿasku ḱáwáiṣa nəšúku háusi sədéedyúpi šapəgáńí ḿéńaṣu ʔai šáuty 11. núu wẽe ʔai háusi seʔéci gámpu. 12. ḱée ʔéesi gáika síwáťyápaate. 13. ṣuẃée háaḿáašu gái sińaisdíẏa ṣuẃée gái dyúwádyâińa ʔée kasdyə́rá wẽe zéegúẏa. 14. túuḿée skáaḿáyanikuyáńańáaťa. 15. ʔée wá ṣuẃée sitúunisi ṣuẃée gái ṣuẃée sáudyúḿíťita ʔúusiusdyáń 16. máaḿé gái ʔańéezá sgúsúḿa. 17. ʔée wá ṣuẃée zíi kaʔaiẓáaní gái

nobody let me use it I ground it on a grinding stone. 6. I gave the children a drink, and they just got well (right away). 7. When the children have diarrhea a little bit of cedar is medicine for Indians.

19. School
(By Margaret Lim)

1. (Compared to) when I was in school in Albuquerque, they teach the children more these days, things I didn't learn when I was in school.
2. When I was there they just taught them to do everyday Indian things, to make pottery, to make baskets, to make things with leather, to make kilts, belts, blankets. 3. And how to work in the laundry, with machines, how to iron, and how (to work) in the dining room. 4. And how to cook, make clothes, keep house. 5. They don't teach this (that is, Indian crafts) these days.

20. Cowboy Life as a Kid
(By Andrew Lewis)

1. When I was still a child, my father used to take me to the roundups.
2. I had a very well-trained palomino horse. 3. When we left in the morning we would go out to find cattle. 4. They were very skittish.
5. And I chased them like (others did). 6. And sometimes we would (finish) gathering them up when it was very late in the evening. 7. And sometimes we would not eat or drink early at noon. 8. It was very hard, but it was fun. 9. One time on the east side of Spider Springs, where it was sunny (that is, on the north side of a ravine), above and going east, I lost my saddle without realizing it. 10. I didn't know it until we got back below to Spider Springs in the evening, and it was then that I found out. 11. I arrived back at camp alone. 12. I went back to look for it. 13. My father (arrived) next, and he had found it, and they (other men) and a Mexican were coming. 14. They just kept teasing me.

15. And as I was growing up I learned how to rope. 16. It is very nice when you know how. 17. As time went on, I used to ride at those

ṣuw̓ée wâa dúw̓a haw̓ée dyə́ káaˀáat̓itan̓áat̓a (rodeo) gái ˀémí zíi w̓ée dyə́ sugúy̓atan̓áat̓a. 18. máamé t̓úum̓ée sgúsúm̓iši n̓iy̓áazá. 19. ˀée m̓íika haw̓ée wagêerát̓iça kuw̓án̓atyumetiya. 20. ˀée wá ṣuw̓ée kaˀáiẓáaní záazíiná hám̓a gái w̓ée mâamé sk̓âanu. 21. gái zíkaná k̓éesi zûuneesí hám̓apədá.

21. Getting a Drum at Cochiti
(By Andrew Lewis)

1. hám̓a wá kúusdyúuci súuw̓áy̓a ˀúw̓îiçaan̓i w̓ái k̓úudíityam̓é s̓áuk̓îini s̓íyanikuya. 2. wáakaši ˀésgá k̓ée dyə́ s̓êeteemí. 3. ṣuw̓ée gái tədíw̓íiçaaní. 4. háam̓áašúuzé k̓ée dyə́ zúusi haw̓ée sgûuyuuceemí. 5. ˀái s̓adyúm̓ə gâam̓a háusi zíyúuce.[34] 6. máamé ˀan̓ée k̓áazá. 7. ˀézé híiẓâaˀai n̓íy̓a čuw̓íiça. 8. ṣuw̓ée wá gái ˀái sk̓aˀáaš̓íicitiyan̓áat̓a, ˀée wá míi (San Francisco) w̓ée k̓âanaçəteya. 9. ˀée zíka ˀái sái c̓aˀáyúuceeˀeeẓát̓eeˀe. 10. sái haw̓ée k̓âanaçəteya. 11. wá zíkaná k̓ée ˀáak̓u ˀéesi zûuneegú t̓úu mâamé háaw̓éná.

22. Irrigation Ditches
(By Andrew Lewis)

1. dúw̓a ˀétyu wá kúupáastyuwíc̓a. 2. kúupáastyuwíc̓a tâan̓izá gái máamé dúw̓a ˀémí gáitiṣu tâan̓izáan̓áat̓a. 3. wâaṣu mayarûuma gúuyéeca háidík̓aaku díic̓íy̓âam̓a ku díičə́n̓á.[35] 4. gái ṣuw̓ ée ˀái cáyá k̓áiw̓adyám̓eetiku. 5. háubázá gái háçəcai, ṣúy̓ati. 6. wâaṣu háidík̓aasi cáyá nuw̓ádúucagúusa, w̓ée sâaní ku w̓ée sabə̂ní. 7. gái cáyá c̓íci čə́ná dík̓a háu sín̓ə cigúyán̓aatiku. 8. ṣuw̓ée dúw̓a kúuku gái héem̓ée kaˀáiẓáaní báagú gái záam̓a c̓íci k̓ée k̓âanu. 9. wá ṣuw̓ée gái guy̓áist̓ikuseetiku k̓ée čə́nâay̓a ˀée zíi haw̓ée gə́n̓aci zít̓akase zíi ˀíska zíi haw̓ée háun̓ə zéepəsə. 10. ṣuw̓ée wá guw̓áunáudání ˀétyuyú yuw̓ée kúistisá ku díistisabə́. 11. háidík̓a zíi háidík̓a zíi cáyá kúw̓atâan̓iça. 12. məəwá zíi ˀái háaníyâaˀán̓ə díičə́ná dik̓án̓ə guw̓âunauta ṣuw̓ée ˀétyuyú ˀái bə́níyâaˀán̓ə díic̓íy̓âam̓a zíkaná t̓úu ˀémí ˀée. 13. hak̓ée ˀéesi gái ˀémí kúsgáy̓u tâan̓izá.

---

[34] Mr. Lewis' brother lives at Cochiti.

[35] The ditch runs from McCarties in the west to Acomita in the east.

places where they had rodeos.   18. You really have to know how in order to do it.   19. And some of the cowboys would get hurt at the places (where they had rodeos).   20. As time went on I didn't go very much.   21. I will go again sometime.

21. Getting a Drum at Cochiti
(By Andrew Lewis)

1. Once I asked my Cochiti friend to make a drum for me.   2. I took some cow hides up there for him.   3. Then he made it for me.   4. The next time I went up there he took it to me.   5. He took it to my brother's house.   6. It was nice and loud.   7. He made it from cottonwood.   8. It is always being borrowed from me, and it even goes (as far as) San Francisco.   9. It is always being taken (borrowed) by everyone there (in San Francisco).   10. It goes everywhere.   11. It will go back to Acoma again very soon.

22. Irrigation Ditches
(By Andrew Lewis)

1. Now this is about ditches.   2. A ditch is work; it is really (hard) work.   3. The ditch boss plans (to start) at either McCarties or Acomita.   4. First they assemble.   5. It is for everyone, men and boys. 6. They will start at either end, (coming) from the east or from the west.   7. First they let the water wander (that is, flow) through the river (that is, ditch).   8. When the winter is over, the water does not flow through.   9. They take the sand out along the ditch and burn the weeds or anything else that gets in.   10. When they finish, they go across to the south side and (come) back east or to the north side and back west.   11. They work from either place first.   12. For instance, they finish the part in the east at Acomita, and then (it is) just the same again in the west at McCarties.   13. The work is the same on back (going the other direction).

14. ṣuwée wá zíkaná kaṣâiti zíi hakée čə́nâaya ʔée kȧwina kaʔáiẓaaní
gȧi hawée kudâaʔaseetiku.   15. dyə́ kȧwina kútikuseetiku zíi gə́nəci ṣunínə
kuwȧyâiçatiyaatiku.   16. zíkaná gȧi ʔémí ʔée skȧinâaka tâanizȧanȧata
díičə́ná ʔée ʔai bə́níyâaʔánə, zíkaná gȧi ʔémí héemȧaku háubá gȧi
kȧyȧamȧaci.   17. ʔétyu záa ʔaisgȧagúnú gȧi kȧizúwȧani.   18. ʔée ṣúyati
háiti zíi záa kȧnȧisdíya ʔáigȧagúnú gȧi ṣuwée kée zȧagúyȧnatiku hakée
číci kustȧikuiyȧataniku zȧyaskȧtitaaniši.   19. gȧi gamȧyanišiku zíi hawée
skúwatâaniça háubá.

23. Planting
(By Andrew Lewis)

1. wá tîiça kaʔáiẓaaní ʔúutisi čətée kaʔáiẓáaní hawéenəkə gȧi báagú
šaʔautunímasa háiti zíi nȧudíisgúniši.   2. wâamə́ yȧaka gȧi skȧiná
stiwíwici ku túuwé ćipȧni gȧi skȧiná túuwé dúwa kȧudímišiku.   3. wá
gȧi zíi míiná cȧyȧ gȧi wâaṣu kâumišuméewȧnišiku hawée záiṣa ʔée.
4. gȧi ʔískasȧi zíi sə́náama kaʔáiẓáaní ćipȧniti dínívȧaku kȧudímišiku.
    5. ʔétyu wá gánami.   6. gánami ʔúudími čətée kaʔâiçaaniku wâaṣu
ʔiibȧni kagə́çətȧataní.   7. gȧi ʔémí dúwa héemȧaku čətée kaʔâiçaaniku.
8. ʔée wá dâani.   9. dâani gȧi zíka ʔémí héemȧaku háti zíi čətée
kaʔâititanȧata.   10. ʔée wá ʔaṣáni ku čə́əri zíi ʔíska zíi ʔaisi gȧi máamé
túu dyə́əçəṣa kȧušȧkȧanišiku, ʔémí máamé ʔúyâiçaani túu dyə́əçəṣa
ʔusdyúwisti.   11. ʔétyu dúwa nabámúuzéeši báagú túu ʔémí háu dínínə
kȧačasə níya báagú dúwa ʔémí túuméе skȧunáizȧniši gȧi kȧuyúukȧmiši.
12. guwȧa ʔétyuṣu zíi gȧi kȧača gȧi báagú dȧwȧa kaʔâititaaniku.

24. Harvest
(By Andrew Lewis)

1. wâaṣu háyȧaci kaʔáiẓáaní ʔúwâityaani čətée kaʔáiẓáaní gȧi túu
kȧwȧatišȧnišiku túu yúuku.   2. ʔée wá ṣuwée gȧi kȧyȧašə́əcišiku
ʔúwâataiskaapi yȧaka.   3. kúyâawaça gȧi mâamé ʔéezêeʔeši báagú ʔémí
díiskámá ʔémí díka háu ʔúdíici mágúcuyúuná ʔúwíizȧani.   4. ʔée wá
ṣuwée wȧaka gȧi kȧusdȧanišiku gȧi kúuku, ʔée wá ṣuwée kúuku kawâayu

14. And again in the summer when it gets mossy along the ditch bank, they take it out. 15. They take the moss out and rake the weeds together. 16. Again they work both at Acomita and in the west, and again at this time everyone helps. 17. If you are not there you pay a fine. 18. If some boy's father is not there, they send him (the boy) and he carries water in order to provide them with drinking water. 19. It is fun when everyone works (together).

23. Planting
(By Andrew Lewis)

1. When it is spring, when it is the right time to plant, everyone usually knows what they want to plant. 2. For example, corn is planted both wet or dry; both ways (are practiced). 3. For the first way you must moisten (that is, irrigate) the field. 4. After the first day when the upper half becomes dry, you plant.

5. Now for beans. 6. It is the right time to plant beans when the cholla cactus are in bloom. 7. This is the right time. 8. And now squash. 9. It is the right time for squash also. 10. And one must always take good care of wheat or chili or anything else, especially (being sure) to hoe and to always irrigate. 11. Then for dry farming, it must rain, (making it) necessary for you to depend and wait for this (rain). 12. If it turns out well (or not) depends on (how much) it rains.

24. Harvest
(By Andrew Lewis)

1. When fall comes, when it is time to harvest, you just peel them (corn ears) off. 2. And you invite people to husk the corn. 3. The women are very eager to grab the corn husks in order to make tamales. 4. And the corn stalks are stored for the winter, (to be used) to feed the horses in

ʔáiẃáašániʔíti. 5. sanisdêewa dâaẃáaca[36] gái wá dyûuẃée háunə kubə́ní
ʔémí héemáaku ʔáaku zíucáastitya. 6. sanisdêewa ẃée yûusi ʔéegú gái
báasku kaʔâitita. 7. ʔée wá ṣuẃée káwáika zíka káci máyúku zízá háunə
kubə́ní sahusé[37] ʔétyu zíucáastitya. 8. túu ʔémí ẃée sái kúsgáyu ʔémí
ẃée háyáaci báasku ʔai kaʔâititanáaťa.

25. Grinding Corn
(By Margaret Lim)

1. ʔáaku háma kúyâawaca ťyâawâitiyanáaťasə cáastiima ʔéenə. 2. gái
háma ʔamaháa sinâaya ṣáawáaya ýáačíni.

26. Cornmeal Mush
(By Ruth Valley)

1. wá dəisi níibéesí guẃá ʔamaháa háyani ʔúẃíizáaníizéeši. 2. cáyáṣu
ʔamaháa ʔináawí ʔainə stíťáaní ẃáisťâani díka. 3. ṣuẃée ʔamaháa zíi
háiti ʔíské (cup milk) skáuťáawazání ʔama(one quart) wá hímá ʔée ṣuẃée
ʔamaháa dyə́ ťáawaneegú dyúyá háti čámíyá. 4. ʔée ṣuẃée háunəkə
húwîini níiséeṣú ʔai ʔináawí ciťîima ʔée ṣuẃée níẃácəšaṣú záa ʔamaháa
húrúẃáašu zíi háiti náicaagúniši. 5. ʔée ṣuẃée túuná gáẃáičáaci ʔúpewi.

27. Tortillas
(By Mary Valley)

1. wá dúwa ʔaisi níibéesí guẃáa háráméuṣa ʔúẃíizáaníizéeši. 2. cáyáṣu
ʔináawí skuťáaní ʔée ṣuẃée kíi zíi ẃée mîná ʔée wá kaṣáti ʔáayáasti
ťúumá héemée ʔée háčənu ẃíicaasgúniši. 3. ṣuẃée ʔamaháa ʔainə cíci

---

[36]sanisdêewa dâaẃáaca 'September', lit. 'St. Stephen's month'. St. Stephen is
Acoma's patron saint, and his feast day is September 2.

[37]sahusé 'St. Joseph'. St. Joseph is Laguna's patron saint, and his feast day is
September 19.

the winter. 5. On the second of September they have a feast at Acoma. 6. There is a dance for St. Stephen, the saint. 7. They also have a feast at Laguna on the nineteenth of September. 8. It is all the same; there is a dance in the fall (at Laguna, also).

25. Grinding Corn
(By Margaret Lim)

1. Formerly at Acoma the ladies used to grind corn in metates. 2. Once my mother and I ground corn.

26. Cornmeal Mush
(By Ruth Valley)

1. Now I'm going to tell how to make cornmeal mush. 2. First you put flour in a dish. 3. Then you boil one cup of milk, I mean one quart, for sure, then it will boil up two or three times. 4. Then you will put the milk in where the flour is, and you will stir it so that bubbles won't form. 5. Then while it is still warm you eat it.

27. Tortillas
(By Mary Valley)

1. Now I'm going to tell how to make tortillas. 2. First you get flour, and then you mix in salt and baking powder, (the amount depending on) how much you want to make. 3. Then you knead it with water, and when

níya ʔúyáaspaawámi ṣuwée sái dyə́ skuyáaspáawání ʔétyuyú ṣuwée ʔíṣáti
ʔáayaasti. 4. ṣuwée sái dyə́ ṣáamíi sgáyáasti ṣuwée ʔétyuyú ʔúukûutuci
wée dyə́ héemée gáaša túumá ńuwíizáasgúni. 5. gái háadíiku záazáma
skə́dítici kaʔâiçaanu hárámeuṣa. 6. ṣuwée wîitainaidáni ʔai dyə́ (stove)
díka díníyáńədyə́. 7. ṣuwée kúistiti kaʔáizáaní túumée ʔézéṣu skáinâaya
ṣuní báa túu záa mâamé zíi guwá záama háu mâamé káusgáaćicanu.[38]
8. túumá héemáaku ṣuwéeṣu skáinâaya kúistiti kaʔáizáaní yúuku síńə
ʔúukúyawi. 9. ṣuwée ʔáyadíišáańi.

A Warning
(By Ruth Valley)

10. bâaṣu gái háma ńauya čubáya zíimáa ʔée čubáya hárámeuṣa
skuwíizáaní šée čítačəčəəka, místyəci kaʔâitita.

28. Stuffed Tripe
(By Mary Valley)

1. guwáa wá dúwa yáakuṣúuni ʔumíńaasdáańiizéeši ʔée názáasí. 2. túu
gái háiti zíi wáakaši ku kanêeru yáakuṣúuni ʔúwízáańiizá. 3. kí zíi wée
ʔišâani skaʔáuyáawízání ʔée wá hâaçəni háćə ʔée káńi túu mâamé háćə
ʔíntyu káwawáašiku, ʔée wá ṣuwée kí zíi wée mîná sái sgáyáasti, ṣuwée
kée náyá ʔûupənaimi,[39] túumá háćə háuńə (water) ʔustâani záa héeya
ńéyačəgúniši.

29. Pottery
(By Mary Valley)

1. wá daʔáa ʔáakúuméeça dyûuni suwáwîititiya. 2. cáyáṣu míici
síutaatáitiya, ʔée ṣuwée wá táaskáná sáusáapacitiya ʔée ṣáatiwâitiyańáata.
3. ṣuwée sái ṣáatíwáańáati ʔée wá ṣuwée kí zíi wée míici sítâaʔatáitiya.

---

[38] That is, if they brown quickly they can be taken off the stove before they get
hard.

[39] Underneath the stove, that is, the oven.

you have kneaded it thoroughly then you mix in lard.   4. When you have it all well mixed you will make them into balls that are large enough. 5. Sometimes the tortillas don't get round.   6. Then you cook them on the top of the stove.   7. When they become brown on both sides you don't have to make them so hard.   8. As soon as they get brown on both sides you take them off (the stove).   9. Then you serve them.

A Warning
(By Ruth Valley)

10. Don't ever make the fire too big or make too much fire when you make tortillas, or else they (will) burn and get black.

28. Stuffed Tripe
(By Mary Valley)

1. Now I'm going to tell how to season tripe.   2. It is made from either cow or sheep tripe.   3. After you slice the meat and some onion and just a very (little) bit of cedar for an Indian treat, and then after you mix it all with salt, then you put it in underneath and pour in some water so that it will not burn.

29. Pottery
(By Mary Valley)

1. Now this is how we Acomas make pottery.   2. First we put the clay out to dry, and then we pound and grind up potsherds.   3. Then when we finish grinding, we soak the clay.   4. Then we wedge it, and when

4. ṣuẃée súẃay̓ámawéetĩtiya ʔée ṣuẃée sái súẃay̓ámawéeẓání zíi ʔískaṣái
háti ʔáisi gaʔápi suẃáwîititiyańáaťasə ṣuẃée.

5. záazíi gái mâamé sái zíi sgúsúṃa, wá ťuu ʔéẓé daʔáa ṣadyaʔáu
sgúẃáasêeʔeníińáaťasə.   6. ʔée ṣuẃée gái ḱáusa dyûuni ʔúwîiçaańi ṣuẃée
míi wá háćəṣái kaʔâititaasə ṣuẃée skuẃíiẓ̓áaní míi ʔúuyáakáici ʔée wá
ʔuẃáaẃáaçəci míi ʔémí ṣáubîiticitiyańáaťa ḱí zíi wée ʔípiša sgay̓áyáitáaní.
7. ʔée ṣuẃée zíkaná sái gay̓áyáitáaní ṣuẃéeyú ʔúuyúuskami.   8. sái
skaʔáuyúuskámí ʔétyuyú ṣuẃée ʔubáyáńi.   9. zíi ʔéẓé wáakaši ʔíisa
sḱáišiinu, ʔée ṣuẃée wá ʔubáyáńi, ṣuẃée sgudáukáṃa ʔéẓé zíi héḱuma
ʔâateeyi ʔáyaneeyi.   10. gái záazáṃa háiḱámíná dáwáa gâinatya ṣuẃée
zíizáa dáwáa sḱâinatya ḱée ʔéesi ʔuwîiçaańi.   11. wá y̓úu héeṃé.

30. Pottery Paints

(By Anne Hansen)

1. ńíibéesí guẃáa ʔúuyúuskámi ćîuy̓ateyaukuyáńiši.   2. místyəciši ḱúudiʔée
ćîuy̓ateyapikuyáńi, máamé wée sgaćíciciši.   3. ʔétyu ʔípiša míi ʔái háti
ćîustíititáaní, ʔée wá ḱúučíńiši zíka ʔéṃé ʔée.

4. sái ťuu ʔémí háaći sdy̓ə guṃ́əsəši ʔémí héey̓a ḱí zíi wée místyəciši
ćîuk̓ayaukuyáńi ʔái ʔúuyúuskámi ʔúuḱáyámi dy̓ə, ćíci dikáńə stidáaʔazími.
5. ʔée wá ḱúučíńiši sditáaʔazími ʔée míi ṣuẃée ćîucisťaikase, ʔée ʔémí
ʔée zíka ʔípiša wée dyûuni ʔay̓áyáitáańi zíka ťuu ʔéṃé ʔée sditáaʔazími
ʔée skaʔáućisťáiskámí.   6. ṣuẃée ʔétyu ćíubîiticitáaní ṣuẃée ʔémí
bérereci kaʔâitita sḱáubíitizání.   7. ṣuẃée ćibáyáńiši gái ṣuẃée mâamé
ḱí zíi wée ḱúuẃáadâaťaukuyáńa wée místyəciši, ʔée ḱúučíńiši, ʔée šáṃóci.

31. Hunting

(By Andrew Lewis)

1. wá dúẃa dyáńi ḱúyáiti ʔúwáaneeyí[40] ńíy̓a ʔétyuyú nemáṣasí.   2. wâaṣu
háay̓áaći kaʔáiẓáaní gái ḱúyáiti ʔúwâaneeyi ḱáaʔáaťáwí,[41] zíi ṣúy̓ati

---

[40]dyáńi ḱúyáiti ʔúwáaneeyí, lit. 'deer game hunting'.

[41]ḱúyáiti ʔúwâaneeyi ḱáaʔáaťáwí 'when it opens to hunt game': ʔúwâaneeyi 'to go
hunting' (theme -úwáaN-qeeY, Sections 420, 422.3); ḱáaʔáaťáwí 'when it opens'
(theme -ʼáaʔáaťaW).

we finish wedging it and when we set it (out to dry) at least one day, we make it then.

5. I'm not very skillful (at making pottery), but this is how my grandmother instructed me. 6. It's hard to make pottery, and it takes several days when you begin to mold and scrape it, (and taking still) more (time) we polish it after painting on the white slip. 7. When you have finished painting (the slip), you paint the design. 8. When you are finished painting the design you fire it. 9. When you have cow manure, you fire it, and when you take them out (of the oven) you take them some place to sell. 10. Sometimes they don't fire well, and if you don't have them well fired you make them again. 11. Guess that's all now.

30. Pottery Paints
(By Anne Hansen)

1. I'm going to tell how paint is gathered. 2. The black is gathered in the mountains, they (are) the hardest. 3. The white paint is gathered from a distance, and again the yellow (is also gathered from a distance).

4. They all come out of the ground, and the black ones are ground in the paint mortar, after you have soaked them in water. 5. After you soak the yellow ones they are strained, and the same way with the white pottery paint, when you soak them and strain them. 6. Then (after the (pieces of) pottery have been painted) they are polished, and they get smooth when you polish them. 7. Then (the colors) that have been fired stand out very much, the blacks, the yellows, and the whites.

31. Hunting
(By Andrew Lewis)

1. Next I'm going to talk about deer hunting. 2. When it is fall, when hunting season opens, the boys plan for the (hunting) trip. 3. First you

skâiẃastya gáiḱa zúucišiku.   3. ʔézé cáyá gái ʔái zíi skúuẃabázánú zíi
skázámǝca skáastíyáagúmi šáyâika dúẃa gái wášu ḱazúuci.   4. ʔái háadí
zíi háiti ḱúuti háu sgûukuyáṅaatya gái ʔái zíi skaʔâastiyaagúmeetya zíi
šáyâika[42] ṣuṅí zíi sgúwâapeuca báagú ʔémé dúẃa héeẏa ʔémí dúẃa zíi
ṅíudyaʔátigúṅi ḱúyáiti.   5. ṣuẃée wá gáayúuzé sdêemǝnu gái ṣuẃée ʔái
héḱuma núu ṣuẃée héḱuma zíi zûuneesgúṅu ḱazúucišiku.   6. ṣuẃée wá
stídyáaku gái ṣuẃée ʔái ḱacǝḱáṅišiku—ʔée ḱúyáiti ḱacǝḱáṅišiku gái ʔái.
7. ʔée wá ṣuẃée gái sgúyâawaaťigúma ʔái náyáazéeši gái ṣuẃée ʔái yúuku
sgûuťigúma ʔái gái míiná zíkaná háusi zíbêecisti ṅíẏa ʔémí ḱáumínaʔáatišiku.
   8. ṣuẃée wá sái sgâiʔidyâataatya hácǝstyaaʔatya ṣúyati, ṣuẃée gái
sgáacǝǝtya sgâama ʔéesi gái ṣuẃée haḱéewási báagú ʔémí ḱazúucišiku gái
ṣuẃée.[43]   9. ṣuẃée ʔái háṅu báagú gái zíyûukamišiṅáaťa, gûunámazáṅaatiku.
10. ṣuẃée wá háu sdéetyuku gái ḱáušáaʔáṅi: "ḱâiẏa nǝdéepǝṣúusa ḱúyáiti,
tíimí ʔicáatyani sgáuyáaní záa gái dǝi číyûuḱamiši."   11. "háaʔa" gái
ṣuẃée yuẃéemée cibêeẏudyáṅaatiku, ṣuẃée wá ẃée sdípǝṅaima ʔaiṅǝ
sdíizíma zíkaná gái ṣuẃée ʔái cârŷiršáaṅaatiku skadíiná, háaťawé zíi ʔíska
háiti zíi tíimí skáaṣa gái ʔái dyǝ́ ḱátitiku ẃiistyǝgóṅi.   12. ṣuẃée wá
gái ʔáisi náanú kuwámasawáatiitya kuẃáẃaateeʔeetiku skâawi ku ʔíska,
gái háupǝdá ḱáwáadéeyíšiku.   13. "ʔézé ṣuẃée ʔái zíkaná báa cǝzáweeʔe"
zíi daʔáa ʔái ṣúyati zíi háuyée ʔémí zídyâatiši daʔáa caʔáyanikuyáṅaatiku.

32. Traps and Snares
(By George Garcia)

1. dúẃa wá zíi háma yuẃée ʔíyázásǝdée zíi ʔáigámíšíizéeku.   2. zíi
bíisbíiná zíi ṅídyáasgúṅu ku zíi śeikayaseṅáaťa.   3. ṣuẃée ʔétyu guẃáa
ʔémé ʔée ʔáigáyámíizéeši ʔétyu gái ʔétyu wá daʔáa ʔétyu.   4. cáyá
ẏáuši gacípǝtiku ṣuẃée zíi ʔái háadí zíi skáucécǝcanu zíi cáasdyúmiši
ʔée ṣuẃée ʔíska zíi ẏáwasti stǝǝci ṣuẃée ʔái síṅǝ cíuḱúmi ḱée
sdíupastyaniitya ʔée ʔái zócǝtyai ṣuẃée ḱáigáyámišiku.   5. néigáyáusgúṅi
ʔái náyáaṅǝ zíi ʔézé háiti zíi zíi ḱáuẃíišáṅišiku.   6. ṣuẃée báagú ṣuẃée
zíi háti zíi ḱáná, zíi ḱúistidíiši zíi ḱúizé zíi bíisbíiná zíi háiti ẃée
kugúyanu.   7. ṣuẃée ḱéeṅǝ náyáa kubóṅí ʔái náyáa skáaṣa ẃée ḱée náyáa
cáatyuma ʔái dyǝ́ kašáṅí ʔémí ṣuẃée háu síṅǝ ẏáuši ḱáibátyuzáṅí ṣuẃée

---

[42]The Shayaika are both the hunting charms (animal fetishes carved from stone)
and the beings responsible for successful hunting.

[43]That is, when each boy catches (kills) one.

make prayer sticks when you put feathers together—things you pray with, hunting charms—(then with) these you are ready to go. 4. You head for some place in the mountains, you pray, and you call together the Shayaika, so that you will, perhaps, catch game this way. 5. When everyone leaves in the morning, you will (each) go your own way. 6. When you catch one you smoke—you smoke to the game there (as an offering and prayer). 7. When you take the inside part (entrails) out, and when you take it apart (butcher it), then you pray some more by speaking (to it).

8. When you all catch some, for however many boys there are, then you go back to your homes. 9. The people there are probably waiting, looking forward (to your return). 10. When you arrive you ask for permission (to enter): "(You) inside, we are going to enter with game, and the wealth, good fortune, and fruits of life that you are probably waiting for." 11. "Yes, (enter)," they would answer, and you would bring it in and lay it down, and again it would be fed corn meal and pollen, and any valuables that you own would be put on it, (things such as) beads. 12. On the following days you cook (the game) and invite your relatives or others, just anyone who you happen to invite. 13. "May you again be fortunate," the boy who caught it is advised.

32. Traps and Snares
(By George Garcia)

1. This is about setting traps, back when I was a child. 2. When you wanted to catch things such as birds or (other) things we would set traps. 3. The following is about how the traps were set. 4. First a flat rock is needed, then you cut a forke'd stick somewhere, and another one, a straight stick, then you tie a string to the end (going) back down and through, and then you set the trap. 5. When you set the trap you put some things (bait) down underneath. 6. What ever kind of bird it might be, ḱáná, ḱúistidíiši, or whatever, it sits on it (the trap). 7. When he goes down underneath where you have a line extending across, when he

cídyáatiku. 8. daʔáa háma ʔémí zíi câiʔidyáatikuyáni bíisbíiná. 9. ʔétyu
zíi cíyáanîśi zíi nídyáasgúnu bíisbíiná, zíi nadyáasgúnu ku zíi náutasgúnu,
ʔétyu ʔái náyáanəkə gáušakácišiku ṣuwée ʔémé ʔée túu ṣuwée zíka
bíisbíiná kée kubéní ʔái náyáa yáuši díka ṣuwée záama ʔémé kúustu, báagú
ʔáinə gáušákaciṣa ʔái háunə ʔáinə ṣuwée kubéniku. 10. ṣuwée kée náyáa
skamásdí níya yúuku káugúmišiku ṣuwée cíyáanîśi káudyaʔátišiku ʔémí.
11. daʔáa ʔétyu háma ʔémí zíi śeiʔidyáatikuyána zíi bíisbíiná zíi
kúistidíiśi, káná zíi naigámisgúnu.

    12. ʔétyu zíi sîiya, kúuku ṣuwéeṣu ʔétyu gái zíi sîiya zíi
káigáyámitáanišiku zíka ʔétyu zíi wéemée káwéetunu ʔái háadí yúuku
skáyaskanu ʔái čáatya háti zíi wéemée ṣuwée kí zíi wee yáwasti zíka
cíçə sgayâaʔaakunu ʔée ṣuwée háazáni, kawâayu háazáni zíi skušánawanu.
13. ṣuwée ʔémé ʔée túu wée dyə́ sgúistyanu. 14. ʔée ṣuwée ʔái háadí
wéemée zíka ʔáiṣa yúuku skáyaskanu ṣuwée ʔáiṣa kí zíi wee ʔémí wá
dúwa wáasa, ʔémé ʔéegáašiku wáasa. 15. héeyaka câiʔidyáatikuyániśi,
ṣuwée wée dyə́ skaʔáunásbúuṣání ṣuwée ʔémí dúwa ṣuwée ṣuwéeṣu ʔégú
zíi sîiya, ku zíi háiti zíi bíisbíiná háu ṣuní káaʔáatáati ṣuwée hée wáasa
wée dyə́ kûunaspətiśi ʔémí gayánaska ʔée ku gayamásdí[44] zâiʔidyâatikuya
záiʔidyaʔáti ʔama sdyə́ gáayúní ṣuwée ʔémí záama sdyə́ gáayúní
zâiʔidyáatikuya.

    16. ʔée ʔémí ʔée zíka sdúuṣu zíka ʔémé ʔée ʔáiʔidyaʔátigúyániizéeku
ʔémí wáasa niyáka. 17. ʔétyu ʔáinə stičání ṣuwéeṣu dyúwíná yâuni ṣuwée
wée dyə́ káuyáatáanišiku ṣuwée báagú ʔémí záama wáasa sdyə́
kayâaʔawaatyanu. 18. daʔáa ʔétyu ʔémí kí zíi sdúuṣu zíi ku zíi sîiya
ʔémí câiʔidyâatikuyániśi háma. 19. dúwa wá daʔáa ʔétyu gái ʔézé dúume
zíi ʔégú ṣawâabé. 20. daʔáa wá háma ʔémí zíi śeiʔidyáatikuyána zíi
sîiya zíi sdúuṣu zíi skuwâanu zíi.

33. Building Houses
(By George Garcia)

1. báagú gái ʔétyu dúwa ʔáaku dyəə́na zíi stíimóní haʔáastiiça kaʔáazáaní
ku ʔémé ʔée ku záagú tâaʔaçaaní díikáwáaka hâaní, ʔée wée sóna hâaní,
ʔée wée kúikáwáaka hâaní.[45]   2. háma záagú sáyúuzé gái tayáamáaci

---

[44]gayamásdí, lit. 'their hands'.

[45]Old Acoma is made up of three rows of buildings, running east and west (see
map in Stirling 1942, facing p. 18). In some places the buildings are three stories
high.

steps on (the line), and when the flat rock snaps back down, he is caught. 8. This is how birds used to be caught. 9. If you want to catch the bird while he is alive, if you want to keep it (as a pet) or (later) kill it, then you hollow it out underneath, and then when the bird goes underneath again he is not killed by the flat rock, because he goes down where it is hollow. 10. You take it out from underneath with your hand, and (thus) you catch it alive. 11. This is how we used to catch birds, such as ḱúistidíìši and ḱáná, when one wanted to catch them.

12. As for larks, you set the traps in winter the same way, and when there is snow you clear away a spot and you get a long stick and a hair, (that is) you cut a horse hair. 13. Then you just tie it (the hair) on (to the stick). 14. And you clear away (some snow) again, and this (which is placed) across is a snare—it is called a snare. 15. With it they are caught, and when you have the tension adjusted, and when those such as larks or any birds sit together in a bunch, then the snare that is strung (set) catches them by their heads or feet when it catches them; when they (try to) fly back up, it catches them before they fly up.

16. And also the way to catch bluebirds is with a snare. 17. When you set it down you set two stones on it so that they cannot pick up the snare. 18. This is how bluebirds or larks used to be caught. 19. I have told you all (I know) about it. 20. This is how we used to catch larks and bluebirds when one went hunting.

33. Building Houses
(By George Garcia)

1. When they came to the top of Acoma, when (Acoma) became a village, (a row) was built on the north side running east, and (a row) in the middle running east, and (a row) on the south side running east. 2. Every-

kazóətíišu.   3. dúwa daʔáa ṣuwéeṣu kumezáagú ʔičóni taʸâacáni.⁴⁶

4. ʔétyu ʔémé ʔée ṣuwéeṣu wâi nózí sdyôena tiʸáišiʸáatáni zíi ʔézé skûipatinámá yaʔái šáwíciši ʔée héeʸa nîuyauskamigúmiši zíi.

5. ṣuwée ʔégú zíi číyáuzáni ʔémí dúwa gái zíi tíwîiçaani.   6. zíi wáašíini, ʸáwasti, míišai gáyáaci kúuméyawéeçanu.   7. ṣuwéeṣu daʔáa ʔémí kúwaʸámawéezánaatya zíyáuzáni ʔémí číyáuzáni čuwáwîititiya.

8. ṣuwéeṣu číyáuzáni čîipánitunu ṣuwéeṣu záagú kée ʔémí ṣuwéeṣu ṣúyáná cáyá taaʔaçaani méṣu.

9. ʔée ṣuwéeṣu záagú gái méṣu ṣuwée dyûubíičape sóna ʔéesi, méṣu dyôena ṣuwéeṣu ʔée díyúucee ʔe.   10. ʔée kumezáagú gái ʔémé ʔée ṣuwée ṣuwéeṣu háma zíi ʔégú hâani kúudyuʔée zíi yúukuṣa gáika zíi ʔézé ʔaazóəsdyáwísti skaʔautyaanu hâani, háapani, ʔée ʔémé ʔée ṣuwéeṣu gái zíi ʔézé ʔazóəsdyáwísti dúwa zíi dyuwáadyâawá.

11. méyûuna gái wái zíi ʔémí sîukačána wée zí záwini ʔái dyôena zíi túuná káçəətiši.   12. ʔée ṣuwéeṣu kumezáagú zíi ʔégú wéesi zíi kaʔâatee ʔeetyanu ʔémé ʔée ṣuwéeṣu yúuná kúutyu zíi ʔégú wéesi zíi háma čaʔâatee ʔezáteeʔe zíi ʔégú zíi hûuru dyuwáadyâawá.   13. ku túuná zíi wêeyəsə⁴⁷ háma dyuwáadyâawá ʔáaku sdyôena zíi ʔégú čaʔautikuse zíi pizâami názóəsdyáwíisgúniši.   14. ʔée ṣuwéeṣu ʔémé ʔée zíi zíka méyú ʔái dyó ʔúuwíišáni zíi zukâwá gái zíi ʔémí dúwa daʔáa zíi káni ziwáawazóci zíi dyuwáadyâawá ʔái dyó.   15. daʔáa dúwa kumezáagú gái háma zíi taaʔaçaani.

16. ṣuwée túu wée ʔégú díikáwáaka hâaní yúuná ṣuwéeṣu taaʔaçaani túu ʔíské dyôena tîukuyáni ʔičóni, ʔée ṣuwée díyásabó zíka ʔémé ʔée. 17. ṣuwéeṣu ʔée sóna ʔée tîubíicáni kumezáa ʔégú túu méṣu dyôena daʔáa tîuyuuceeʸáatáni.   18. wá zíi gái wái ʔémé ʔée zíi hácə káaši zíi dyónámí dyó cámíyá dyó zíi dúwa daʔáa káçə.   19. ʔée ʔémé ʔée kumezáa ʔétyu ṣuwéeṣu zíi gái ʔézé wée sónaʔeezéeši ʔétyu zíi zíi ṣuní náaçasgúniši ʔétyu kumezáa ʔégú dyuwáadyâawá háma hâaskáani.   20. dúwa daʔáa gái ʔétyu ʔémí dyuwáadyâawá kumezáa ʔégú wée ṣuní zíi zíi néešasgúnu ʔézé wéenə dêeʔemi nədáagúniši.   21. daʔáa ʔétyu ʔémí gáika zíi háma dyuwáadyâawá záanáa háadí zíi mendâana zíi zaʔání ʔétyu ʔémí háaskáani gái zíi dyuwáadyâawá ṣuní náaʔaʔasgúniši.   22. ʔée ʔémé ʔée zíi háadíiku gái zíi wái méyûuna daʔáa zíi gái zíi ʔúukačániizá.

23. ṣuwéeṣu dúwa daʔáa zíi ʔégú háma kumeʔétyu kumezáagú gái sái sáyúuzé hánu ʔái dyó haʔâastiiça zíi ʔégú hánu zíi čáaʸáamáacitiya ʔíské

---

⁴⁶taʸâacáni 'they were divided'. Perfect theme, -qjaʸâacaN-qiṢ; stem, plural prefix plus -JûučaN (Section 415).

⁴⁷wêeyəsə was not known to Mrs. Hansen, but the context suggests 'oxen', from Spanish buey, a common Spanish loanword throughout the Pueblo area.

body helped with each building.   3. This is how, I believe, the buildings were made.   4. The building materials were carried up from down below, things like fine sand being carried on the back to be used for plaster.

5. This is how adobe bricks were made.   6. Bark, sticks, and ashes were mixed together.   7. Then they mixed the adobe with this, and the bricks were made.   8. When the bricks dried, they built around (laying the foundation), and they kept on (going up).

9. And continuing on, they divided (into rooms) the middle part (that is, the second floor), and they continued on up this way.   10. And I believe they used to haul pine and oak from Pine Mountain for beams, and they used them (also) for the crossbeams.

11. Today we still see the old buildings up there.   12. When they brought things back from the mountains, they used to use donkeys to bring them back.   13. Or they used oxen, and they brought up to Acoma the logs that they were going to use for beams.   14. And then for the things placed on top, willow and scraped cedar were used on top (of the main beams for crossbeams).   15. This, I believe, is how they were built.

16. In the northern section (and proceeding) from the east the building was built and was put up as a single unit, and likewise (for the middle section and proceeding) from the west.   17. It was divided up into halves (that is, rooms), and this was continued on up (for the higher stories).   18. Today the building is three stories high in several places. 19. And for the middle part (that is, the second floor) they used mica for that which was going to be made on the sides (that is, windows). 20. This is what they used on the sides for light.   21. This is what they used to use; before there were windows they used mica for that which was going to be built on the sides.   22. And today it can still be seen in some places.

23. And formerly, I believe, all the people up at the village helped, and it was built as a single unit.   24. And each building, I believe, was

sái dúẇa daˀáa ṣuẇéeṣu zíi ṫâaˀaçaańi.   24. ˀée ṣuẇéeṣu kaẓə́əṫiišu
kumezáagú daˀáa ṣuẇéeṣu čáaẏáaẏadíita, ˀeṫé ṫaẏâaçaańi guẇáa yúuná
ˀémé ˀée zíi ˀégú ńíičəsgúńiši.   25. ẇái há ḱáwáaka sabə́ ˀée yúuná
bə́ sái cínáudáńí, sə́ńa sá zíkaná, yuẇée kúiḱáwáaka sabə́ bəẓáatya háu
sabə́ daˀáa ˀégú tínáuta.[48]   26. dúẇa daˀáa ṣuẇée háḿa kumezáagú ˀégú
ˀáaḳu dyˆəna zíi ˀégú ṫâaˀaçaańi zíi ča̧ˀai̧ça.

27. ˀée ṣuẇée gái zíi ˀégú ẇaˀii̧zéeši ˀétyuyú yúuná dúẇa daˀáa
yúuná ˀétyu gái zíi ẇái zíi daˀáa ˀégú zíi ẇéeńə zíi ĉâaˀaçaańi sái
ṣúyáná zíi yúuḳu kúẇa zíi háadí síńə sgúńu.   28. daˀáa zíi ẇái ˀétyuyú
ˀée háadii̧ku síńə daˀáa zíi ĉiukuuṫawi zíi záwini ḱáçəətiši.   29. wá ẇái
dúẇa daˀáa gái zíi ˀáaḳu dyˆəna zíi ˀétyuyú sîukaĉáńa.

30. daˀáa ˀétyu kumezáagú háḿa gáiḳa zíi ˀégú ˀáaḳu dyˆəna zíi
gáiḳa zíi ˀémé ˀée zíi čáçə, zíi ṫâaˀaçaańi sáyúuzé zíi ċaẏáamáaci.
31. ṣuẇée ˀée zíi pizâaḿizéeši zíi gái zí ˀ ańéezí gáiḳa zíi gáatyaẓáńiši
zíi daˀáa dúẇa.   32. dúẇa daˀáa kumezáagú háḿa zíi ˀégú míiṣu ˀáaḳu
dyˆəna zíi ˀémé ˀée zíi ˀégú ˀičə́ńi zíi ča̧ˀai̧ça.   33. daˀáa dúẇa wá
ˀégú háḿa zíi ṫâaˀaçaańi.

34. Shinny
(By George Garcia)

1. dúẇa wá guẇáa ĉiuḿaataaašúḳucitaańiši háḿa zíi yuẇée ˀíyáẓáasədée.
2. yuẇée zíi ṣ́auḿaataaašúḳucitiya ˀai ˀáaḳu dyˆəna.   3. ṣuhaẇéˀéná zíi
naĉuwêenu ˀáaḳu háu sdyə́ ŝîiḿənu.   4. ˀai ḱáakaaṫi ṣ́auḿaataaašúḳucitiya,
ẇée ṣuńí zíi ṣúẏati ku háçəca ku háu zíi ˀ ańéegúńu zíi ˀûuḿaataaašúḳucitaańi.
5. ṣuẇée ˀégú sái zíi ḱáaẏâaĉíikumíitaatya, sáńáḿí dyə́, ˀée yəḱée bə́náḿí
ṣúwánáḿaaṣa čə́nâaẏa.[49]   6. yəḱée ṣúyánáṣa ṣuẇée ˀéḿí zíẏúuceeˀeetiku
ṣúyáná.   7. ṣuẇée háu cáyá ḱáakaaṫi háusi zíẇacínâiḿa ḿáadáaašúḳu ṣuẇée
ˀéḿí gáašiyawaatiku.   8. ṣuẇée ˀétyu ḿáadáaašúḱúuzéeši ˀétyu ˀémé ˀée
ẇéeḿée zíi ĉíwîititaańiši zíi wáakaši ˀésgá ku zíi píici zíi ĉíuyámasdâańiṣa.
9. ṣuẇée ˀaińə́kə ṣuẇée stidyâiĉíḿeetya ṣuẇée ˀûuḿáadáaašúḳuci.   10. ṣuẇée
ˀétyu gái zíi háadí gúuci skaˀáutyaanu ku zíi háapani skaˀáutyaanu ˀée

---

[48]The direction of construction for the three rows of buildings was the shape of
an 'S', starting with the northern row in the east and finishing with the southern
row in the west.

bəẓáatya 'West Floor', name of the first dancing station (see White 1932, p. 66).

[49]čə́nâaẏa 'canyon', here referring to the alleyway between the rows of buildings
at Acoma.

distributed (divided up among the families), and they were (each) entitled to be in it. 25. When the (northern) part was finished, (building) from the east back to the west, and the middle part, (building) back to the east again, then the southern part, (building) back to the west, was finished at the first dance station. 26. This is how, I believe, Acoma was built on top (of the mesa) and how it came to be.

27. But nowadays they build around (just anywhere), all around in the south (part of the mesa) whereever they choose. 28. In some places the old buildings are torn down. 29. This is what we see up at Acoma to-day.

30. This is how, I believe, the buildings used to be up at Acoma; they were built with everybody's help. 31. And the beams used to be beauti-fully carved. 32. This, I believe, is how the buildings came to be up on top at Acoma. 33. This is how they were built.

34. Shinny
(By George Garcia)

1. This is how shinny was played when I was a boy. 2. We played shinny up at Acoma back in those days. 3. Near Christmas time everyone came up to Acoma. 4. We played shinny in the plaza, together with the boys or men or anyone who liked to play. 5. Everyone paired off up in the east and to the west along the separate corridors. 6. They would take it (the ball) around (the building). 7. Whichever (side) got the ball back to the plaza first would win. 8. The ball was made from cowhide or buckskin, which was stuffed. 9. They would bury it to play shinny. 10. They gathered wood some place, or they gathered oak (sticks) that

ʔémé ʔée ṣuẇée ʔai zǫ́cǝtyai ṣuwícisa, héeẏaka ʔúuṁáadáašúkucitáani.
11. ṣuẇéeṣu ńáuṁáadáašúkucisgúńi ṣuẇée ʔaińǝkǝ stidyâicíṁeetiku ʔaińǝ
skáusdúuca.   12. ṣuẇée ʔégú sáanámí dyǝǝzéeši haẇée dídí nǝ́tyazíigú,
ʔétyu sabǝ́námíizéeši ṣuẇée ẇée kuńí nǝ́tyazíigú.   13. ṣuẇée ʔai háu
ṣuńí ṣuẇée ḱée gúwískǝzáńaatiku.   14. ṣuẇée ʔétyu sái yǝḱée bǝ́námí
čǝ́nâaẏa sabǝ́námíńǝǝzéeši ḱée kaṣâańaatiku, ʔétyu hánámízéeši yǝḱée há
čǝ́nâaẏa ṣuẇée kaṣâańaatiku.   15. ṣuẇée ʔégú kuwîistityaańǝtyǝǝciku háu
ṣuńí ṣuẇée méṣu ćêeyiku, ʔée ṣuẇée ʔai ńǝzáatya ʔémí ṣuẇéeṣu ʔaińǝ
ṁáadáašúku cidyâiciima.   16. ṣuẇéeṣu dyǝ́ gúubáicitaańa, ʔée méṣu dyǝ́
gúubáicitaańa.   17. ṣuẇéeṣu dyǝ́ gúmǝ́ní ṁáadáašúku zíi ẇée dídíisaawá
gǝ́čáńiṣa cáyá gúubáicanu ṣuẇée ʔégú háanámí yǝḱée wá nupǝ́náucagú.
18. ṣuẇée yuẇée ʔai sá dyǝ́ ṣuẇéeṣu sabǝ́námí čǝ́nâaẏacaaʔaatiši ṣuẇéeṣu
háu nuẇáduucagúusa ʔée ʔémé ʔée ṣuẇéeṣu sabǝ́námíńǝ níẏuucee ʔeegúusa.
19. ʔée méṣu ṣuẇée yǝḱée ṣuẏáná káaẏazúucee ʔeetiku, túu ʔaiṣa ʔémé
ʔée ṣuẇéeṣu čǝ́nâaẏa ṣuẇéeṣu kaʔâuṁaataašúkucitiyaasǝ.   20. ʔée ṣuẇée
gái háuyée ʔémí gái ṣuẇéeṣu zíi ʔégú tée ʔe ṣuẏáná zíẏuuceenu, yǝḱée
ṣuẏáná háusi zíẇacínâiṁa ʔai ḱaakaati ṣuẇéeṣu ʔémí dǝ́i díḱa ṣuẇée ʔémí
dúẇa gáašiyaawaatiku háiti ʔai díḱa.   21. ṣuẇéeṣu sái ʔískǝ́ zíkaná
cîicaańaatiku.   22. dúẇa daʔáa ʔétyu ʔémí cîuṁaataašúkucitaańi háṁa.

35. Target Practice
(By George Garcia)

1. ʔétyu wá dúẇa zíi yuẇée zíka ʔíyázáasǝdée zíi ẇeeṁée zíi
zíińátitiyaatiku.   2. ṣuẇée ʔégú husdyâaka ʔée ʔisdûwá gacípǝtišiku.
3. ṣuẇée ẇeeṁée zíi ʔai háti zíi háćǝ skáaʔâacaanu ṣúyati.   4. ẇeeṁée
zíi skáistuwáaṣa skáhusdyâakaṣa ẇeeṁée ṣuẇéeṣu ḱée kaṣâańaatiku.
5. ṣuẇée ʔétyu kí zíi ẇée ʔémí ziẇáadyâawâaniku múkuzíši.   6. ʔémí
ṣuẇée dúẇa ʔétyu zíi múkuzíši kanêeru ʔésgá ku zíi ćíuyámásdâańi zíi
ẇeeṁée.   7. ṣuẇéeṣu ʔai háadí ẇeeṁée zíi zíitisitaatyanu, ṣuẇéeṣu ʔémí
zíińátitiyaatiku ṣuẇéeṣu mâamé ʔémí ṣuẇéeṣu ʔekúẇáyâacaańaatiku háu
ṣuẇéeṣu haćǝ́wá díińazáaná dúẇa kí zíi ẇée múkuzíši séniyaatiši.   8.
ʔémí ẇeeṁée háṁa zíi ẇîińátitaańi zíi káisuṁéestaaniku ẏúu ṣuẇée
ṣuẇéeṣu.   9. ʔée ṣuẇéeṣu ʔémé ʔée skáudyúmicanu ṣuẇéeṣu ʔémí zíi
ʔégú haẇéenǝ zíi kaʔaiça gúwâaneeça, zíi yúuná zíi ṣuẇéeṣu ʔémí zíi
zíi déetya, zíi síitya, zíi káẏaṣu zíi ʔáẏańátitáańíizéeku zíi skuwâaneeyu.
10. zíi ćǝ́na háṁa ćíwâaneeyáatáńi.   11. daʔáa dúẇa háṁa ʔétyu zíi
zíińátitiyaatiku.   12. daʔáa wá dúẇa ʔétyu ṣuẇéeṣu háṁa ʔétyu zíi

had a curve at the end to play shinny with. 11. The ones that were going to play ball dug a hole and buried (the ball). 12. Then the eastern team would stand in the north, and the western team would stand in the south. 13. Then they (each) scratched (a line) that (came) together (in the middle). 14. Then everyone on the western team would get in position in the west corridor, and the eastern team would get in position in the east corridor. 15. Then they would count and keep coming together to the place in the ground where the ball was buried. 16. Then they hit it up and kept hitting it up. 17. When the ball came up, if the one standing on the north side hit it first, it would roll to the east. 18. Then the ones who were in the west corridor would jump in, and they would try to take it to the west. 19. They would keep taking it around (the building), and they would play shinny back and forth along the corridor. 20. Whichever (team) took it around the furthest and arrived back around in the plaza, they would win in this way. 21. Then they would all make it one again (that is, start over). 22. This is how shinny was played.

35. Target Practice
(By George Garcia)

1. They used to shoot this way back when I was a child. 2. Bows and arrows were needed. 3. You would gather together a number of boys. 4. When you had arrows and a bow you would stand (take your position). 5. They would use a target. 6. The target was (made of) sheepskin or something stuffed. 7. When they measured off a certain distance they would shoot and compete very (intensely to see) who could shoot the most at that which we called the target. 8. In former times they learned to shoot this way. 9. When you had learned, there was a hunt, and you hunted rabbits, squirrels, and chipmunks by shooting them. 10. Pack rats used to be hunted (too). 11. This is how they used to shoot.

gúudyâawá zíi súwawíŝâitiyaatya ku ʔémé ʔée dúwa ćíwiṅáťitaaní zíi ʔégú
ʔisdûwá ṅiẏáka ʔée husdyâaka zíi ʔémí sguẃáadyâawá.   13. wá dúẃa
daʔáa ʔétyu ʔémí.

36. Stick Racing
(By George Garcia)

1. wá ʔétyu dúẃa ćâaćawaiẏáaťáṅiši.   2. háḿa zíi gáiḱa
kaʔâaćawiʔizáťeeʔeetiku.   3. háçəcai, ṣúẏati ku ʔíẏaça zíka gái ʔémé
ʔée zíi kaʔâaćawaiʔizáťeeʔeetiku.   4. ṣuẃéeṣu wéeḿée ʔétyu zíi ciĕəṅíši
ṅâaćawaigúṅu wéeḿée ṣuẃéeṣu háu zíi ćaʔáiṣaẕáṅaatyanu, ṣuẃéeṣu ʔémé
ʔée zíi kâadyúmenu, ṣuẃéeṣu ṅíuťâanikuyáṅagúusa háçəcai háćə zíi
káaʔâaçaanu.   5. háiḱáмíṅá gái dyáanáwá guẃâaćíikumeṅáaťa.   6. ṣuẃéeṣu
wéeḿée ṅêećawaiyigúṅu, ṅeẏâaćawaiyisgúṅu wéeḿéeṣu ẃéeṣu
gúuťâanikuyáṅaatya gái zíi ʔégú zíi ḱáistyuwaapeetiku.   7. ʔée wéeḿée
ḱápišu ṣuẃéeṣu kaʔáašawaitiyaatiku.

8. ʔétyu ʔémé ʔée ṣuẃéeṣu dúẃa háḿa zíi kaʔâaćawaiʔizáťeeʔe ʔáaku.
9. háu sdyə́ zíi stíiḿənu ku ʔémé ʔée dúẃa daʔáa dâawâaça zíi ʔégú
ĕəťee ʔémí ṣuẃéeṣu dúẃa zíi dâawâaça ḱáaní zíi kuréesima záanáasi
kućáyâazíḿi ʔétyu ʔémí ṣuẃéeṣu zíi ka ʔâaćawaiʔizáťeeʔeetiku háḿa.
10. ʔée ṣuẃéeṣu gái zíi ḱáiséeťaaniši háçəcai zíi háiti zíi ṅîuséeťasgúṅu.
11. ṣuẃéeṣu dúẃa daʔáa gái ṣuẃéeṣu kaʔâaćawaiʔizáťeeʔe.

12. ṣuẃéeṣu ʔégú háuyée ʔémí zíi ṣuẃéeṣu ṅeẏâaćawaigúṅu ʔétyu báa
ṣuẃéeṣu dúẃa ṣuẃéeṣu ʔémí núuwâaćíikugúusa.   13. ṣuẃéeṣu ʔai háadíṅə
zîiťíḿeetyanu, ṅeẏâaćawaisgúṅu, ṣuẃéeṣu ṅâa ṣuṅí ʔégú skâakuniku háu
ṣuṅí zíi háiti héḱuma, héḱuma nədáasgúṅu.   14. ṣuẃéeṣu ḱáiséeťaniku.
15. ʔai dyə́ zíi ćíišiimiku, ʔaiṅə záadyáṅə zíi pisâari kaʔáišataatya, zíi
háitisgúṅu zíi ṅîuséeťasgúṅu ṣuẃée ʔémí ʔai dyə́ zíišiitiyaatiku.   16.
ṣuẃéeṣu ĕəťee kaʔáazáaní, ṣuẃéeṣu ḱée gûuĕáṅaatiku ṣuẃée ʔáaćáwáiyí
dúẃa ʔáaćáwáiyízéeši ṣuẃéeṣu ʔaiṅə ziẏâaťaaṅətyəəciku.   17. ṣuẃéeṣu
ḱée ḱáťyazíḿətyəəciku, ʔée yəḱée ẏâaṅí ṣuẃéeṣu kaṣâaṅaatya guẃâaćíikumiši.
18. ṣuẃéeṣu ʔáisi ćaẏáwíisťitaaníitiku, ṣuẃéeṣu dyáanáwá kuẃíisťidyáaní,
ṣuẃéeci kaʔáatikuyaniku ʔée ṣuẃéeṣu yəḱée ẏâaṅí háu méṣu ťúu káaẏâaťawi.
19. ṣuẃée yúuná ṣuẃéeṣu háidíḱa zíi ṅeẏáḱumegúusaatyanu, ṣuẃéeṣu yəḱée
ṣúyáná záyáḱumeeʔeetiku.   20. ʔée ṣuẃéeṣu gái haḱée zíi ʔégú zíi ʔémé
ʔée zíi háçəcaiḿéesgúṅu zíi stíiyâiṣanu ʔée ṣuẃéeṣu gái zíi ḱée
ḱazúucišiku.

12. This is how it was useful when we played, how the bow and arrow was shot, and what we used.   13. This is how it was.

36. Stick Racing
(By George Garcia)

1. This is about stick racing.   2. Formerly they used to have stick races.
3. Men, boys, or kids had stick races.   4. When there was going to be a big stick race someone was named (to be in charge), and if he was willing, then a number of men gathered together and started practicing (that is, training).   5. They usually formed groups of four.   6. If there was going to be a stick race and if a person was going to take part in the stick race, they would practice and would go to take sweat baths.
7. They would race (to get in shape) in the evenings.

8. This is how they had stick races at Acoma.   9. When the people came back up (to Acoma), on the right month, during the month of Lent (February), before Easter, they would have stick races.   10. The men would place bets on whoever they wanted to bet on.   11. This is the way it was with stick racing.

12. Those who were going to take part in the stick races paired up.
13. When the date was set, and if you were going to take part in the stick races, then you went (on that date) with whichever (side) you were going to be on.   14. And they placed bets.   15. There would be valuables there, and they would put them (the valuables) on a blanket that they would spread on the ground so that you could bet whatever you wished.
16. When it was ready, they would mark the course, and they would put down the racing sticks for the stick race.   17. (Each team) would stand (in position), and the teams would line up in front.   18. Someone would count for them, and when he counted four times, then they would go forward.   19. The crowd would go with (the racers), and they would go all the way around (the mesa).   20. If you were man enough, if you were a fast racer, then you went along (and kept up with the rest).

21. ʔétyu túu dyǝǝçǝṣa ṣuwéeṣu háu gâuyuukainu ṣuwée zíyúukaiʔiitiku
ʔáačáwáiyí, záa ʔai háadí zíi náyawagúñiši díˀka.   22. ʔée ṣuwéeṣu yúuná
ʔémé ʔée ṣuwéeṣu zíyúuceeʔe.   23. yuwéesíizé ṣuwéeṣu máamé gái
ṣuwéeṣu kúwáyâaçaatiku, háu cáyá háusi neʔéčigúñiši ʔaisi dyútigúˀmeeṣa
ʔáačáwáiyí.   24. ʔéeṣu wée háusi gái ṣuwéeṣu háu cáyá háusi
zíwačínâiˀmanu ṣuwéeṣu háiti zíi ʔáačáwáiyí zíi mâamé hawéʔéná
káayapaẓáyawaatyanu, háiti ṣuwéeṣu ʔáačáwáiyí cáyáñǝ gûidyáčinu, ʔai
gûučáñiiṣa ṣuwéeṣu háusi zíwačínâiˀma cáyá ṣuwéeṣu ñǝgûidyáči, ṣuwéeṣu
ʔémí ṣuwéeṣu dǝi díˀka ṣuwéeṣu zíšiyawiku ṣuwéeṣu dúwa káawášiyawaatiku.
25. dúwa daʔáa ʔétyu háˀma zíi ʔégú ʔétyu dúwa zíi čâaččawaiyiyáaťáñi
daʔáa wá dúwa daʔáa ʔétyu háˀma zíi kaʔâaččawaiʔizáťeeʔeetiku.   26. ʔétyu
waʔíizéeši báagú záaná háadí ʔémé ʔée zíi gái zíi háu zíi háˀma
kaʔâaččawaiyu.   27. dúwa ʔétyu zíi daʔáa čaʔâaččawaiʔizáťeeʔe.

37. Growing Up in the Old Days
(By George Garcia)

1. zíi háˀma ʔíyáẓáasǝdée, gái wáiṣa zíi ʔégú máamé ṡaatuuní.   2. ʔétyu
yuwée gái zíi skánâaya, skánáisdíya, zíi skabáabáa, skanána zíi háˀma zíi
dyâwá zíi zayáapatyǝsǝku.   3. wéeˀmée háˀma zíi gái míiṣu zíi ʔégú dyâwá
zíi dyǝ ṡtaʔáipadyǝ́ˀmeetyanu mâamé túuná dyǝ ʔáaˀku skáaˀmi.   4. hawée
ṣuwéeṣu dyǝ ṡtaʔáipadyǝ́ˀmeetyanu, pisâari ʔézé zíi ṡtyaʔátyušaatyanu, ʔai
čáatya ṡtyáagúyáñaatyanu ṣuwéeṣu sdíyúukamišaatya háˀmaaˀča
néisbíˀçaatyagúñiši.   5. dúwa daʔáa háˀma ʔétyu yuwée záagú zíi gáiˀka zíi
dáwáa zíi ʔémé ʔée zíi tîuyuuceeyáaťáñi.   6. gái ʔémé ʔée zíi gáiˀka
dyuwáasgíici hástíˀtiça háˀma.   7. báagú míiṣu ʔégú dúwa ʔémé ʔée zíi
gáiˀka zíi ʔégú dáwáazéeši zíi dyúukušana guwáa ʔémé ʔée zíi ʔégú zíi
dáwáa zíi nitúuníisgúñiši zíi héeya zíi ñâayúutyasgúñiši.   8. ku yuwée
háˀma ʔégú kumezáa ʔégú zíi ʔégú čúwasti.   9. wéeˀmée zíˀka ʔémí ṣuwéeṣu
zíi ʔégú míiṣu gái zíi ʔégú dyúutuuníˀmasa zíi ʔégú zíi ñiuwaizáˀmasgúñiši
dǝi yâañí, gái ʔémí duná gáiṣu zíi ʔémí zíi ṡíukačáña.[50]   10. ʔétyu yuwée
záagú míiṣu gái zíˀka ʔémé ʔée zíi ʔégú ṡtawâaawaizáˀmasa ʔáaˀku dyǝǝna.
11. ñâa ṣuñí zíi ʔégú tené, číšé zíi háˀma čúuwáaččáwaitiya.   12. ʔémí
héeyaka kuˀmezáa ʔégú gáiˀka zíi dyúunáˀmacitiya záa yúuwi zíi
ʔúuskatikuyáñi, ku zíi skuwâaneyu pâñí záa ñêečaayustiuˀmáñiši ñiyáˀka
ʔémé héeya gái zíi záaˀma zíi mâamé zíi ñâuya ʔúpewi, ku ñâuya zíi

---
[50] Referring to the Second World War and the Korean War.

21. Somebody would always watch, and they would keep track of the sticks so that they would not get lost. 22. They would take (the sticks) way out. 23. Coming back, they would compete in earnest in trying to be first one back from where they started with the sticks. 24. The one who got back first with the racing stick while the others were closing in, the one whose stick landed first when he arrived at the (finish) line—he would win; this is how they won. 25. This is how there used to be stick races and how they used to race. 26. But nowadays nobody does stick racing any more. 27. This is how they would have stick races.

37. Growing Up in the Old Days
(By George Garcia)

1. Long ago I was a child, but today we have all grown up. 2. At that time (when I was a child) your mother, father, grandmother, and grandfather made you get up early. 3. And long ago when they made you get up early they still lived at Acoma. 4. They got you up, wrapped you in a blanket, and put you outside, and you waited until the sun rose. 5. This custom was practiced in the old days. 6. The older people were stronger in those days. 7. They knew beforehand the good things of life and how they would grow up and make a living. 8. And in the old days it was dangerous. 9. They already knew that in the future they would have to go to war, and now we have seen this. 10. In the old days they went to war from up at Acoma. 11. Nearby Navajos and Apaches used to steal things. 12. They used to advise (you) not to drink (too much), or else when you went hunting you would get mixed up in your directions because of thirst, and (they advised you) not to

háawéná zíi yúuẇi ʔuuskati ćíci. 13. dúẇa daʔáa kumezáa ʔégú gái háma
zíi dyuẇáasgíici ku zíi dyâwá wíipatyəsi dúẇa daʔáa kumezáa ʔégú gáiḱa
zíi ʔégú ʔañée zíi háu zíi nénatuçu, dáwáa zíi nitûuníiçú zíi.   14. daʔáa
ʔémí háma kumezáa gáiḱa zíi ʔégú čáiwâaẏuutya ẇai ḱáatya míişu.   15.
ʔée şuẇéeşu ʔémé ʔée zíi yúuná zíi ʔégú gûuwaiẓámanu, ku zíi skuẇâane
záazíi zíi ʔégú zíi háiti zíi zíi pâní zíi yámasti zíi şúwamə díníyá
ṅeẇáčadyúṅu.   16. ʔémí héeẏa gái zíi gúunámacitiya ku múudéesdyáanu
zíi gái zíi nánaši zíi sdyáṅatiši zíi záa mâamé zíi ʔúkuyautâayáni,
guwâakaaşuma şúyáná zíi ʔátyaciši.   17. ʔée ʔémé ʔée zíi ḱúẇizáanu
zíḱa ʔémé ʔée gái zíḱa záa máaméti zíi ʔúkuyautâayáni zíi ẇéesi skubúnú.
18. ʔémí gái dúẇa zíi daʔáa zíi hástítiça háma zíi duẇáasgíici zíi
máiḱúiná zíi deʔé.   19. ẇeemée zíi ʔégú háçəcai zíi múudéesdyáanu zíḱa
meẏú záanáa héema hau dyə́ stíiẓáaní zíi záa ʔáçəkasi, míi ménaşu zíi
cúski kusgáicanu.   20. dúẇa daʔáa ʔétyu kumezáa ʔégú gái zíi díyúukaiʔi
şuẇéeşu ménaşu zíi ʔégú héemáaku gái ʔégú zíi náçəkasgúṅu.   21. şuẇée
ʔétyu zíi ḱúẇizéeši ʔétyu ʔémé ʔée zíḱa meẏú zíi háma şuẇée
daẏáapatyəku dyâwá.   22. zíi tyâawaitiyaatiku gáayúuzé dyâwá, ʔée ʔémé
ʔée zíi ʔustíiẏáatáṅi zíi ʔégú.   23. dúẇa daʔáa ʔétyu zíi ʔégú ḱúẇizáa
báagú gáiḱa zíi tyáaši zíi ʔégú.   24. ʔée ʔémé ʔée zíḱa meẏú záa mâaméti
zíi yúuná zíi ʔúyûuməsi zíi ḱápišu kaʔáiça máasiça gáiḱa zíi daʔáa
bâaşúudá.   25. ku ʔémé ʔée zíi háçəcaizéeši zíḱa meẏú ṅâaya, ṅáisdíẏa
gáiḱa zíi dyúunámacitiya záa háaẇéná zíi ʔúudyâatitaaní.   26. ʔétyu ʔézé
zíi skánâaya, skáṅáisdíẏa ʔézé zíi mâiḱui ṅíumáazáníisgúṅi cáacêema
ʔéeṅə́kə.   27. dúẇa daʔáa sdiẏáḱa záagúu ʔémé héeẏa gái zíi ʔégú záazíi
gáiḱa háaẇéná ʔúudyâaẓáṅi.   28. ku ḱúẇizéeši zíḱa meẏú ʔémé ʔée zíi
ʔégú dúẇa daʔáa záa túu ẇée zíi yúuná nêenaçəteyagúṅiši.

29. daʔáa háma zíi kumezáagú gái zíi ʔégú gáiḱa zíi čáiwâaẏuutya.
30. ẇaʔíizéeši gái ʔétyu ṅaṅámíizá dúẇa daʔáa záazíi zíiná
sguẇáasgíicişanu, ku ʔíẏaça záazíiná háaẇéná kitûunisə.   31. ʔétyu háma
yuẇée zíi báagú zíi ʔégú zíi ẏáaka kíṅatiši ku zíi ʔíska hâací sdyə́
çaẏáaʔáẇiši dúẇa zíi ʔégú ʔémé ʔée gâaʔapeetiši ṅiẏáka dáwáa zíi
gáṅatiši dáwáa zíi kíṅatunu ʔémí héeẏaka zíi dyuẇáasgíici háma.   32.
daʔáa dúẇa kumezáa ʔégú gáiḱa zíi ʔégú ʔémé ʔée háma zíi táiwâaẏuutya.
33. wá dúẇa gái zíi ʔézé dêeʔemi sgûuçanu daʔáa gái zíi ʔégú zíi héeme
sîutuuní daʔáa.

eat too much and not to drink too much water. 13. They were strong in those days, and they got up early; you would mature in a nice way, and you would grow up properly. 14. This is how they lived in earlier days. 15. And when one went to fight or to hunt he would not be overcome by thirst or hunger or misery. 16. Grandfathers advised boys who were hardy not to warm themselves by standing around the fire place. 17. And girls were (told) not to warm themselves when they came in (the house). 18. That is why people were stronger in the old days and lived longer. 19. Men and boys were (told) not to smoke before they grew up, not until the fox howled. 20. This is the way they believed in regard to when a person should smoke. 21. And as for girls, they got them up early, too, in the old days. 22. They would grind (corn) early in the morning, and (do) such things as fetch water. 23. This is how things used to be done in regard to girls. 24. Also girls had to be careful not to go out too long after it was dark. 25. Mothers and fathers used to advise boys not to get married right away. 26. The mothers and fathers expected them to help the family for a while. 27. This is the reason they didn't get married right away. 28. And as for girls, they didn't run around.

29. This is how they used to live in the old days. 30. Nowadays it is different, and this is why we are not strong any more, and children don't grow up quickly. 31. But in the old days the things they ate were fresh corn or other things grown from the land, good things such as fresh fruit, good things such as fresh corn, and because of this they were strong in the old days. 32. This is how we used to live. 33. This is what is clear to me; this is all I know.

38. The Birth of the War Twins
(By Andrew Lewis)

1. ṣuháṁa wá dítya kašiskáçəətya wá ʔai ḱúwíizá ʔai dyâuʔu, čámáʔákə.
2. dúwa máagə́zéeši ḱánâaya záazíi háu mâamé ʔaṅéetiuṁáṅu.   3. núuyú
gái ṣuwée dyúwiikaašáaṅətyəṅáaṫa gaʔaiṣa zíi ʔézé wéeṁé guwáaa
zaʔámiẓáṅətyəəka.   4. záazáṁa háu zíi dâaʔáṁinaatikuya, ku zíi háu
diʔíušə́əca wée wá ṁíika háṅu gåaçəətya.   5. ʔétyu ḱáazíná gái
diwâanáṁaṅáaṫa dyə́əçəṣa gái håusi ʔámúuṁaateeʔekuyaṅáaṫa.

6. ṣuwée wá háṅu, gái háṅu ḱée dêeməsəṅáaṫa, dyaiẏaani
čaʔaityaiʔiẓáťeeʔe, ʔée ʔíitya.   7. ṣuwée ʔaiṅə háṁa čəťée kaʔáizáaní,
máamé ṅâuẏa dyaiẏaani gaťáwáníši náẏeezá zíi skámáʔákəṣa dyúubé ḱée
dyaiẏaani ṅâityaigúṅiši.   8. ḱánâaya ťáacikuya "wá záazíi háu ḱée
ṅiućaayukuẓuṁáṅu."   9. ṣuwée ʔée máagə́zéeši ťêeçəəci, núuwée ʔée ḱée
zúuneedyú.   10. ṣuwée wá gái čuṅáći, ḱée háaṁáašu čaʔáupaṣa háṅu.

11. ṣuwée wá gái håu déetyu ʔai čâaʔaaṫa.   12. záazíi háu díušə́əca
ʔai, núuwée ṣuwée ʔai čugúya, ṣuwée núuwée ʔai kapišóní ťíẏaaska, ʔée
wá náanú núuwée čaʔaityata dyaiẏaani.   13. só̄na cidíẏá háu ṣuwée ʔai
ťíẏáidyáu.   14. wée ćíẏáidyáṁiši, ʔuṣâaçə páẏadyáṁə, ṣuwée ťáacikuya
"ćaityata dyaiẏaani?"   15. "háaʔa; ťúu wá ťyubúuca."   16. "ṣáumáacaní
dyaiẏaani ʔaityaaní.   17. wá wée ṣâuẏašeemí dyûuwée dyaiẏaani.   18.
dúwa núpeṣú."   19. ṣuwée dyúupeeťa háuzéeši.   20. "wée múudéezéeši
wá ʔuṣâaçəsədá."   21. "ṣuwée ʔétyuyú háadí kuzâuʔu?"   22. "hâagáwáikuçu."
23. gái ṣuwée dîunáṁa dyaiẏaani dúwa ćîuẏadíitiši.

24. ṣuwée wá dúwa gái dyaiẏaani čúpe zíi háti zúuci.   25. ṣuwée wá
ʔaisi háṁa ẏúu kaʔáizáaní ṣuwée tigûuṅiçaatya.   26. gái ťáacikuya
ṅíumáacaṅíiciuṁáṅiši dyaiẏaani ʔaityaaní.   27. wéeṁée kaʔáidyáanúṁa
dyaiẏaani kaʔâityanu ʔée máamé ṅáuná dîutita gúyásťi dikáṅə.   28. máamé
ṅâuẏa guwákača ʔée guwáaa ṅáuná dîutita.   29. ṣuwée ḱéesi zúutyu gâaṁa
ʔéesi, čûipatináu, záazíi gái dyáẏúutaaya.

30. håusi zaʔáćíní ḱánâaya dîunáṁa.   31. "máamé wá ṅâuẏa çaitya
dyaiẏaani."   32. ṣuwée ṁíika háṅu dyuwákačáṅə čaʔáipaaṅaawitiya
dyaiẏaani hawée ʔičóṅi díní ʔée dyə́, ʔée tîiçaaṅə.   33. ṣuwée ṅə́kə
wákazáṅíẏáapədyə́əci máamé ṅâuẏa čaʔaiça zíkaná.   34. ṣuwée
máagə́əzéeši ḱánâaya dyúubé guwáaa wée ʔuṣâaçə háçəcai ćíuṁáacaṅíitiši.
35. ʔée dyúubé wée dyûuwée dyaiẏaani ćîuẏadíitiši.   36. ṣuwée ʔai
čaʔáutyu ʔémí wée cigûuṅiçaatiši.   37. záazíi zíi dínâiẓáṅiṣa dúwa
dyaiẏaani díkasi nigûuṅiçaagúṅiši.

38. ṣuwée wá kaʔáizáaní cigûuṅiši dêeʔemi dîutita.   39. ḱánâaya zíka
čaʔáutyu ṣuwée dîupeeťa cigûuṅiši.   40. "záa" dyáṅaaṫa, ʔégú záṁa háu

38. The Birth of the War Twins
(By Andrew Lewis)

1. Long ago in the north at White House there lived a woman, and she had a daughter.   2. Nobody liked the girl's mother very much.   3. They took care of their garden by themselves, doing their job (as best they could).   4. Nobody ever spoke to them, nor did the other people ever invite them to their house.   5. But the Kachinas were grateful (to them) because they always prayed to them.

6. As for the people, the people usually went out and gathered piñon nuts and cactus fruit.   7. Then one time when they were ready (that is, ripe), when there were lots of piñons, the daughter asked the woman if she could gather piñons.   8. Her mother said to her, "Nobody will look after you."   9. But the girl insisted; she wanted to go alone.   10. She took some food and went after the people.

11. They arrived and camped there.   12. Nobody invited her there, so she camped alone, spent the night alone, and the next day she gathered piñons alone.   13. At noon somebody met her.   14. The one who met her, Sun Youth, said to her, "Are you gathering piñons?"   15. "Yes; how you scared me."   16. "Let me help you gather piñons.   17. I brought two piñons for you.   18. You will eat them."   19. She asked him who he was.   20. "I am the Youth of the Sun."   21. "And where do you live?"   22. "At the Sunrise."   23. She thanked him for the piñons that he had given her.

24. She ate the piñons soon after he left.   25. Some time after that she became pregnant.   26. He told her that he would help her gather piñons.   27. As she gathered piñons her gatherings became many (that is, multiplied) in her basket.   28. The more she saw them, the more they multiplied.   29. Then she went back home, she put them on her back, and they were not heavy.

30. When she arrived back (home) her mother praised her.   31. "You certainly have gathered lots of piñons."   32. They saw other people drying piñons on top of the buildings, (so) they did it (too).   33. When they poured them out they multiplied again.   34. The girl told her mother how the Sun Man had helped her.   35. And she told her about the two piñons that he had given her.   36. Then she found out that she was pregnant.   37. She did not think that she would become pregnant from these piñons.

38. As time passed her pregnancy became noticable.   39. Her mother also found out and asked if she was pregnant.   40. "No," she said, because

háadí hác̜əcai zíɣaidyámiši. 41. ʔée míika háńu čúuẃaatyu zíka ʔémí
cigûuńiši. 42. s̜uẃée wá gái tíẃáɣa dyûuẃée s̜úɣati. 43. wá s̜uẃée wée
cáɣaazéeši máaséewi ʔée háamáašu múudêezéeši ʔúɣûuyai. 44. s̜uẃée
čucítista guẃáa ʔémí wée cigûuńiši, s̜uẃée ʔeʔédyú wée dyûuẃée
dyáiɣaani kúbéwiši wée ʔus̜âac̜e páɣadyámə c̑îuɣadíitiši.

45. wée ʔúẃaaka z̜ə́ədyáišá, záazíi mâamé dyuʔúmə́ədáẃaanu, ʔétyu
mâamé háaẃéná dyáitûunisə. 46. túu mâamé háaẃéná čúticuucitaanə,
záanàa kaʔáizáaní míi s̜uẃéesu téeyá kəčańíši, mâamé dyâwá dyaʔamás̜a.
47. ʔée s̜uẃéesu têeɣáata záazíi zíi daʔautyušus̜a ḱée ʔúɣûumə́ni. 48.
gáabáabáa gái diʔíunámacitańáata záa mâamé téeʔe ʔai zaʔáastiic̜a yúuḱu
ʔuz̜úucáatasi, s̜uẃée wá ʔétyu zíi cidyâayawiši báamée niɣúuńatyumeciumá
ʔai háti. 49. záazíi háma ʔémí zíi dyaʔáačâac̜a.

50. máamé s̜uẃéesu ʔúẃaani bíisbíiná ʔée déetyu čaʔâuẃaniuzáńə.
51. hàusi gâaʔác̜inu ʔémí s̜uẃéesu dyáazáańáata zíi guẃákačáńətyəəka
haẃée. 52. déetyu guẃákačáńətyəəka s̜uẃée ʔémí dyaɣác̜atińáata démis̜utyu.
53. s̜uẃée gáabáabáa dyúupeeta zíi háidíicaaʔa. 54. "wá wée déetyaacaaʔa."

55. s̜uẃée gáabáabáa daʔáwíic̜aaní husdyâaka héeɣa nuẃâanətyəḱúuńətyəə-
ciši. 56. kí zíi wée gúɣásti ḱée z̜ə́z̜ə́tyau ʔée ḱée gaʔáčupiši sə́ńa ʔéesi
čáukáɣuca s̜uẃée ʔáis̜a dáatya dâatautya. 57. s̜uẃée dúẃa ʔémí husdyâaka
ʔémé ʔée dyáɣas̜ác̜a. 58. s̜uẃée daʔáwíic̜aaní zíka ʔisdûwá s̜uẃée
daʔáẃaasêeʔení s̜uẃée guẃáa ʔúudyáaẃáńíizéeši.

59. dyə́əc̜əs̜a gaʔánáisdíɣa ʔus̜âac̜ə diʔîuméekumeńáata ʔée
daʔáumáacańíińáata túu guẃáa náɣáa ʔée. 60. ʔée zíka ʔémí núu
ʔus̜âac̜əzéeši ʔémí ʔémí núu ʔus̜âac̜əzéeši ʔémí núu šaz̜ə́ə daʔâiʔituuní,
dyaʔâinámaca. 61. s̜uẃée déetya gúukačáńədyə́əci dîińazáńə, túumée
ʔisdûwá háu zíi zíubáakazáńí ʔée háuńə čúuẃíišitańáata. 62. núu ʔémí
dúẃa ʔus̜âac̜ə ʔémí ʔée ʔée daʔâutitaaní wée díníńə, gáabáabáa ʔée
gaʔánâaya máamé diʔîunáma.

63. haẃée háadíiku čuẃawíšáitiyańáata ʔíɣac̜a míika díka haẃée
čúudâataayáńətyəńáata. 64. máamé dyáišáaci ʔée dyâiʔipeetawáńətyəńáata
ʔée núuẃée têeɣáata ḱée ḱúuti ʔée. 65. s̜uẃée mâamé gáačáaši zíi
čuẃác̜ətaańətyəńáata dyáńi ʔée kə́əci. 66. ʔus̜âac̜ə ʔémí núu háu
daʔâuɣateyapikuyańáata.

67. gáačáaši wée dyáńi kuẃâańətyəəka záazáma dyâiʔitiyaapətyəəka,
s̜uẃée gáabáabáa núu ḱéesi čaʔâateɣáatasə daʔáẃaasêeʔení s̜uẃée guẃáa
ʔuẃáɣáańíizéeši. 68. ʔée túuyú gáabáabáa dâaʔapuucitaańáata záa máamé
téeʔe ʔuz̜úucáatani haẃée wée mûuḱaic̜a ʔée kuháɣa zeʔêema, ʔémí
záazáma zíi čúubúuzáńətyəəka. 69. s̜uẃée tâaʔacikuya "báamée háma
kuháɣa nêeʔepeekuzuʔumá." 70. s̜uẃée ḱée čuẃâaneetyə.

71. háma zíkaná s̜uẃée gái ʔai dyûukačáńətyə kuháɣa. 72. s̜uẃée
ɣáwasti čaɣâaʔapətyə s̜uẃée wée háu zaʔáac̜ədéɣáwí neʔéekuzíumáńi s̜uẃée

she had not met any men anywhere. 41. And the other people found out
about her pregnancy, too. 42. She gave birth to two boys. 43. The first
one was Masewi and the next boy was Uyuyay. 44. She gave thought to
how she became pregnant, and then she remembered that she ate the two
piñons which Sun Youth had given her.

45. The babies were small and not very handsome, but they grew up
rapidly. 46. Very soon they were crawling, and it was not very long
before they were walking standing up, and they talked very early. 47.
They would leave (the house) and they were not afraid to leave. 48.
Their grandmother would warn them not to go too far away from the
pueblo, because wild animals might hurt them some place. 49. But they
never listened.

50. They grew fond of hunting birds and rabbits. 51. When they
came back they would talk about what they had seen. 52. When they
saw rabbits it seemed that they had horns. 53. They asked their grandmother what they were. 54. "Those were rabbits."

55. Their grandmother made bows for them so that they could hunt
with them. 56. She cut a basket rim in two and put a line across and
connected (the two ends). 57. She named this husdyâaḱa (bow). 58.
Then she made arrows for them and showed them how they were used.

59. Their father the sun always looked after them and helped them
down below. 60. And it was only because of the sun, just because of
the sun that they grew rapidly, and matured. 61. When they saw a
rabbit they shot; when they shot an arrow they (the rabbits) would just
fall. 62. The sun alone, from above, did this for them, and their grandmother and mother were very glad.

63. Children would be playing some places, and they would join in
with the others. 64. They (the twins) were very strong and they would
make them (the children) cry, and (so) they would go into the mountains
alone. 65. They would kill the largest deer and antelope. 66. The sun
alone gave them these.

67. When they killed large deer they were not able to carry them, so
their grandmother carried them back alone and showed them how to
butcher them. 68. Their grandmother warned them not to go too far
where mountain lions and bears would be, but they were never afraid.
69. She said, "Sometime a bear might eat you up." 70. Then they went
out to hunt.

71. Again at another time they saw a bear. 72. They took a stick
and when she charged and was ready to bite them they put it in her

dîutyəgə́nə́tyə.   73. ʔée wée kuháya káwáasti héeya čúuwíšaayánə́tyə t́uumá
ʔée dyayâatitaanə́tyə, ṣuwée wée kuháya wáasti gáanâayaši hawée wée zúuci
ʔémí ṣuwée wée ýáwasti dîutəgə́nə́tyə ṣuwée máaséewizéeši.   74. ṣuwée
ʔaiṣasi kuháya wáasti gáanâayaši ʔaiṣa t́uuyú dyúnášíya ʔée ýáwasti
tîudíkaya, méeṣu t́uuṁée daʔáidyanâawita.

    75. ṣuwée wá gáitúunísi dyə́əci ṣúyati dyáazáanáata háu gaʔánaisdíyaši.
76. t́uuyú tibêetaukuyánə́tyə "zéegúmá záa ṣaʔánaisdíya wá hawéeṁée
ʔíyaça gáanaisdíyaši?"   77. ṣuwée gaʔánâaya diʔiubé záa gaʔánaisdíyaši
də́i gâaṁiši, tibêetapə́tyə háadí gâaṁiši.   78. ṣuwée gaʔánâaya diʔiubé
"míi ʔai hâagúwáikəçə ʔémí ʔai gâuʔu."   79. tibêetapə́tyə hacə́mazéeši.
80. gáabáabáa taaʔacikuya "hawée dyə́ ʔuṣâaçə gumə́sisa ʔémí ʔai gâuʔu."
81. ṣuwée ṣúyati týâanikuya kée gaʔánaisdíya níutáaneetyəkúunə́tyəəciši.
82. gaʔánâaya taaʔacikuya máamé téeʔezéeši záa ʔai háu
nəẓâaʔácikúunə́tyəəciši.   83. záazíi dínâizániṣa háu nəẓâaʔácikúunə́tyəəciši
ʔai.

    84. dyâwá gáayúuzé káipatyunu ʔézézée háu sá kaʔáastiyaagúmə́tyə wái
sá téeyu.   85. dyúutáaneetyə gaʔánaisdíya.   86. ṣuwée wá ʔuṣâaçə dyə́
gumə́ní wá t́uu mâamé ʔai ʔuṣâaçə gumə́sisa ʔai wá kúuti hâaníšúku ʔémí
ʔai.

    87. ṣuwée wá céeyáaní háu dâaʔáṁina, dúwa wá káṁaskukúuyá.
88. ṣuwée taaʔacikuya "šabáabáatyaimiši, çúutáaneetyə kəẓaʔánaisdíya?"
89. ṣuwée týâanikuya "háu təẓâaʔáṁina?   90. háu híṣuṁé?"   91. dyánaata
káṁaskukúuyá.   92. "háadí?"   93. "wá də́i."   94. ʔaiṣa čuʔúkasətyə záazíi
háu háadí dyâagúnú.   95. ṣuwée týâanikuya "ʔáku ʔémí káṁaskukúuyá?"
96. "háaʔa."   97. ṣúyati týáanikuya gaʔánaisdíya gúutáaneetyəəciši.   98.
ṣuwée káṁaskukúuyá taaʔacikuya záaná ʔuzúuci míi háti nâačámá.   99.
ʔuṣâaçə míiṣu ʔétyu dyúutuuní hawéenə nətêeyukúunə́tyəəciši.   100. ṣuwée
káṁaskukúuyá táʔáyanikuyána ʔaʔáyáidyáṁi wée ṣúyati ʔaʔáwáasêeʔeníiti
guwáa háu ʔuwácíni.

    101. ṣuwée káṁaskukúuyá gái kée dâaʔayuuca ʔai gâaṁa.   102. "də́i
ṣâuʔu, hawée nə́kə ẓâaʔadyá."   103. ṣuwée ʔai kéenə dyáapə gúçuutiṣa ʔai
háaci díka.   104. "ʔégú wá mâamé zə́əkášəka kéenə gúçuutí."   105. "t́uu
ʔai dyə́ nášaṣu, gái ṣuwée káčəka nâiçaagú ṣuwée."   106. wée máaséewi
cáyá ṣuwée gái ʔai dyə́ čáša, ṣuwée ʔai dyə́ kašání káčəka čaʔaiça, ṣuwée
ʔai číṁa kéenə dyúpə.   107. ṣuwée kadyúṁə dáacikuya "háamáašu wéenə
ʔúpə.   108. gái káčəka wá."   109. ṣuwée ʔai číṁa hâunə gáapə gái máamé
ʔai kâiýaadá.

    110. káṁasku wáastiça ʔai čáatyauṣa dyə́ hawée sái kúdútuci hawée
čáaʔâata.   111. dâiʔipuuca ṣúyati wéenə gáabə́ní.   112. ṣuwée
káṁaskukúuyá dâaʔatiišá.   113. ṣuwée káṁaskukúuyá čáṁə́əti ʔíské, ṣuwée
dáacikuya kí zíi wée nábáasti kée ʔaityaaní ʔée ṣuwée ʔúukútuci kúdúci,

mouth.   73. They just played with the bear's cubs and teased them, and when the bear cubs' mother came towards them they put the stick in her mouth; it was Masewi (that did it).   74. The bear cubs' mother, (going) back and forth, was just frantic and the stick was in her mouth, but they were just laughing.

75. As the boys grew up, they kept wondering who their father was. 76. They kept asking, "Why don't we have a father like (other) children have fathers?"   77. Their mother told them that their father didn't live here, and they asked where he lived.   78. Their mother told them, "He lives at the Sunrise."   79. They asked how far it was.   80. Their grandmother said to them, "He lives where the sun comes up."   81. The boys said that they would go to visit their father.   82. Their mother told them it was too far and that they would not get there.   83. She did not think that they would get there.

84. When they got up early in the morning they prayed to the east and they went to the east.   85. They went to visit their father.   86. When the sun had come up a little from where the sun comes up, it was in the mountains in the eastern area.

87. When they were walking someone spoke to them, and it was Spider Woman.   88. She said to them, "My grandsons, are you going to visit your father?"   89. They said "Who spoke to us?   90. Who are you?"   91. The Spider Woman spoke.   92. (They said) "Where (are you)?" 93. "Over here."   94. They looked around and nobody was there. 95. Then they said, "Is it you Spider Woman?"   96. "Yes."   97. The boys said that they were going to visit their father.   98. Then Spider Woman told them not to go until tomorrow.   99. The Sun already knew that they would be going.   100. Spider Woman had been asked to meet the boys and show them how to get there.

101. Then Spider Woman took them to her home.   102. "This is my home, step down here."   103. They went to where there was a hole in the ground.   104. "But the hole is too small (to go) down in."   105. "Just step there, and it will become big then."   106. Masewi stepped in it first, and when he stepped in it it became big, and he went down below.   107. Then he said to his brother, "Come on down next.   108. It is large (enough)."   109. They went down below and there were lots of rooms.

110. Young spiders, all around on the wall like balls, sat there. 111. The boys scared them when they came in.   112. Then Spider Woman fed the two of them.   113. Spider Woman had one son, and she told him to get a spider web and roll it into a ball, because they would get to

ʔémí héeẏa wée ʔuṣâaçə gâama ʔémí héeẏa háu nəẓâaʔáćiṫyúuʔu.
114. ṣuwée wá gái ʔai ṣúẏati čugúyánətyə daʔáa kapišóní. 115. dyâwá
ṣuwée nəṫêeyuṫyúuʔu gáayúuzé ẏúu nûwé kapišóní. 116. máamé téeʔedá
dyâwá čaʔâizímətyə.

117. ṣuwée kapišóní kámaskukúuyá dyaʔâiçaačuwa máaséewi ʔée
ʔúyûuyai ʔée kámaskukúuyá kámóəti dáacikuya kí zíi wée kanâasta díkánə
ʔúyûupəni, ʔémí héeẏa ʔée nêeʔeyuuceetiumá wái ʔémí ʔuṣâaçə gâama.
118. ṣuwée wée kámaskukúuyá tídyá ʔai ʔísgáẏâasi nábáasti. 119. ṣuwée
wée kámaskuméəti ṣuwée kéenə tidúutya ʔée wá ṣuwée kée dyûisbóṫaukuya
zéegûiẏáaṫání. 120. ṣuwée wée ṣúẏati čáyawaanətyə záazíi háiti
dyûutuuníma hékudá ćêeyiši. 121. záazíi zíi ʔétyu ṣuwée ṫúumá wéemée
ṫéeyu ʔétyuṣu stíẏa. 122. ṣuwée wá háu zéedyúpi kámaskuméəti dáacikuya
máaséewi ʔai ćíipe ʔai káatyasi ʔûukuyáni, ʔémí ṣuwée ʔaisi
ńimínaatikuyatiumá zíi wéemée ʔai háiti zíi guwáa ʔée ńiiçaagúniši.

123. ṣuwée wá gái ʔai háu zéedyúpi ʔai ʔičóni díka kée dyó ṣuwée
guwâaṫíima kée dyó déeya. 124. ṣuwée háu kúwíizá diʔîukača "wá
dyûuwée ṣúẏati kée dyó gáaya, máamé wá ṫúuzúšu steréreci. 125. ẏúu
wá wée ṣáawaçəši čámóətyai, záazíi wá ṣáawaçəši démetyu ʔémí
ńáwáastiçatyaigúnu." 126. ṣuwée ṣúẏati háu gáaʔaćíní ṫúu ṣuwée ʔéeṣu
kée dyáapə kaṣárîimée záa háiti zíi kaʔâuṣaaʔanišimée. 127. ṣuwée
ʔuṣâaçəméəti ṫaʔáapéena "wá dyûuwée ṣúẏati dəi gâaʔáći, ẏúukáuku ʔémí
çəzáwáastiçatyai, məəwée dyó puʔúukača." 128. ṣuwée gaʔánáisdíẏa
tibêeṫapətyə.

129. ṣuwéeṣu gái ʔuṣâaçəméəti wée zúuci "wée tyəṫéeyu ṣámóətityaimiši?"
130. ṣuwée ʔai dyó dâaʔakuya ʔée kée kâaʔaçə ʔéenə dâaʔapənaiʔi. 131.
ʔuṣâaçəméəti čadyúmətyai ʔai kâaʔaçə, ṣuwée tyaiʔicikuya "wá
ṣámóətityaimiši hawée ćéeyu," ṫúumée méeṣu ṣúẏati diʔíumayanikuyáńa.
132. "káu ʔémí hée wéemézé çuzáwáastiçatyai ṣúẏati!" 133. ṣuwée háiti
dyáńaaṫa "hée kəzáwáastiçatyaimi ʔémícaaʔa wái dídíisa ʔai mûukaiça
cíẏastiima ʔai pêeʔepənaiʔi zíi ʔée ʔémícaaʔa dêeʔemi kée ẏâańisi
nuẑûuməkúuʔu."

134. ṣuwéeci ṣúẏati záa háiti zíi zaʔáutyušuuṣa, ṫúumé ʔai záaʔabóńáimi
mûukaiça diʔíupêetucita, héeẏa čuwawíšáitiya. 135. ṣuwée háiti háçəcai
dyó dyəṫáatyə ʔémí kée dyúukačáńe zíi zâaʔapeeńiši, méeṣu záazíi ʔée.
136. ṫúumé héeẏa mûukaiça níẏa čúuwíšáayáńətyə. 137. "ṣuwée ʔétyuyú
ʔai bóńiisa kâiẏa ʔétyuyú ʔai kákana cíẏastiima ʔai pâaʔapənaiʔi."
138. zíkaná ṣuwée wéesi káiẏáaní sdyó, ṣuwée ʔétyuyú ʔai kuńíisa ʔai
ṣúuhúuná[51] cíẏastiima zíkaná meẏûuna wéesi dyûumə. 139. ʔée ʔétyuyú
ʔai hâańiisa kâiẏa ʔai ćíisdíini cíẏastiima sái wée diʔîuẏáaṫa. 140. ṣuwée

---

[51]It is not clear whether ṣúuhúuná means lynx or jaguar. See Stirling (1942,
p. 23, footnote 57).

the Sun's house with it.   114. The boys stayed there for the night.
115. They would leave early in the morning, probably at midnight.
116. It was very far, (so) they went to bed early.

117. In the night Spider Woman woke up Masewi and Uyuyay, and
Spider Woman told her son to get into a basket, because by means of
(the basket) she would take them to the Sun's house.   118. Then Spider
Woman took hold of the other side of the web.   119. Spider Boy hung
down and kept unwinding it as they went.   120. The boys got lost, and
neither one knew where they went.   121. They did not simply go (for
fun), but for a reason.   122. When they arrived, Spider Youth told
Masewi to (let him) sit behind his ear, so that he could talk to him
whenever he was going to do something.

123. When they arrived there at the house they climbed up a ladder.
124. A woman saw them (and said) "Two boys are climbing up, and
they are just filthy.   125. They are probably our brother's sons, (but)
our brother wouldn't be apt to have (such) children."   126. When the
boys arrived they just went right in like clowns as if they had permission.   127. Then Sun Youth was told, "Two boys have arrived; maybe
they are your children; come up and see."   128. They (the boys) asked
for their father.

129. When Sun Youth came (he said), "Did you come, my sons?"
130. He installed them and put them down in the kiva.   131. Sun Youth
had brothers in the kiva, and he said to them "My sons have come here,"
but they just laughed at the boys.   132. "Is this the kind of kids you
have!"   133. Then one of them said, "If these are your children put
them in the lion den in the north, and if they are as they seem they
will come out in front (that is, as victors)."

134. The boys were not afraid, and when he put them in the lions
just licked them and played with them.   135. One of the men stood up
and went to see if they were eaten up, but they were not.   136. They
were just playing with the lions.   137. "Then put them in the wolf den
in the cave in the west."   138. When they came out alive again, then
the lynx den was next, and they still came out again.   139. Next was
the beehive in the cave in the east, and they all flew (in a swarm) at
them.   140. One (bee) sat on one of the boy's ears and went into his

háiti ṣúẏati ćîipeesi dîukuya ćîipe ʔéenə díuyúupə 141. ṣuẃée kadyúmə
ťaʔacikuya "dúẇa ʔaɴéezá—kuwêeʔe."⁵²   142. ṣuẃée mîika sái dyâaʔape,
sái ćîisdíini dyâaʔape.   143. ṣuẃée mîika háçəcai ẃée ziʔíukačaɴáati
záazíiná ṣuẃée háu guẃáa dyáɴaaťa.   144. sái ćîisdíini čuẇâaɴətyə.

145. ṣuẃée ʔétyuyú ʔai hâakaani díka dyé ʔai cibáaṣa háu dyə́
dâaʔakuyáɴa, méeṣu ʔétyu háu dyə́ zaʔáyákání háu dyə́ gaʔáyání máamé
zíi guẃáa háçəcai daʔaiça, ʔétyu méeṣu guʔuméədâwá daʔaiça
gaʔáɴaisdíẏamée.   146. ṣuẃée gáitiṣu mîika díwâahima ʔémí ẃée
ʔuṣâaçə páẏadyámə káwáastíçatyaimiši.

147. ṣuẃée gái náanú kée gaʔâaṁa ʔéesi pêeyutiuʔumá.   148. ṣuẃée
gaʔáɴaisdíẏa mâaméti guʔuméədâwá neʔêiçaatiuʔumá.   149. ṣuẃée ɴaɴámí
husdyâaka daʔáwîiçaɴíita, ɴaɴámí ʔisdûwá díka ẃée zə́çətyai húuseni, ʔée
hîisťíyani ẃée zə́çətyai ʔée ʔée daʔâuçaaní.   150. ʔée ʔisdûwá pədîina
ʔisdûwá ʔúipədíẏámi daʔáwîiçaani ʔémí haẃéenə ʔisdûwá dyaʔáistiiɴáaťa.

151. ṣuẃéeṣu wá ʔuṣâaçə páẏadyámə dyaʔáyanikuya káwáastíçatyaimiši
ṣúẏati mâamé nuẓuʔûukímənikúuɴətyəəciši.   152. ʔée wá gái daʔáwîiçaaní
záipičáaná ʔée diʔíunáṁaca záa ʔúudyâawáaɴi mâamé ťúu háṁapədá.
153. máamé zíi guẃáa haẃée ẃée səəci ɴîiçaadyú héeẏaka.   154. zíi gái
máamé ẃéeka niʔíudyâawáaciuṁá gái ṣuẃée ʔétyuṣu niʔíudyâawáatiuṁá.
155. ʔétyu háiti zíi ẃéeṁée kaʔáutapətyəəka záa ʔémé ʔée zíi ziʔíuṣâanu
ťúu ẃée ẏáapi ku kí zíi ẃée hîisťíyani ʔai héeẏa ʔai dyə́ zíčáɴətyəəka
ṣuẃée gái zíi kaʔáutyuku héeẏasi níẏáadyú.   156. gaʔáɴaisdíẏa taʔáwîiçaaní
husdyâaka kukúmišu, dyâana núwáná dyaʔáiši.   157. dúẇa dyâana ṣuẃée
gái piʔíudyâawáatiuʔumá haẃée ʔai máamé ṣuẃéeṣu zíi ʔai háadí mâamé
čabáazúṁa háu zíi ʔai ziʔíuyéeca, gái ẃée mîika ṣuẃée gái mîika héeẏa
ʔúwáanéeẏí ʔémí héeẏa niʔíudyâawáatiuʔumá.   158. ṣuẃée gái wá
taaʔacikuya hékudá ćêeyu zíkaná wá haẃée nəẓaʔáuyâaʔanaťyúuʔu tidyámí,
bə́námí, kúwámí, háanámí, haẃée mâamé cidyúmiṣa ʔée haẃée
neʔéečáaçašetiuʔúmasa guẃáa káaɴətyəəka.

159. ṣuẃée gaʔáɴaisdíẏa taaʔacikuya "gái zíkaná ẃéesi kəťêeyu də́i
ṣâaṁa, də́i ćíyâaṁa gái nəẓaʔáaťawikuçúuʔu.   160. ʔée wá
kəẓaʔáunádíisti neʔéukuʔíiṣauʔumá mâamé dúwáya nuẓuʔúméədáwáakuçúuʔu."
161. háaṣúwími daʔâuẏadí ʔée búkuyawi, ʔée gaʔaṁásdíbə́çə ʔée mušâiça
ʔésgá daʔâiṁáçayawisiustya.   162. dúwáẏa ʔémí héeẏa nəẓaʔáwáiɴiťúuʔu,
záazíi háṁa dúẇa ẏúuku ɴîiçaaɴəťyúuɴətyəəka haẃéenə dyaʔáwínuskaati
haẃéenə dyaʔáisti.   163. ʔée ẇíistyəgə́ɴi daʔáukuʔí šúwimi—šúwimi
ẇíistyəgə́ɴi.   164. "dúwáẏa ʔémí máamé nuẓuʔúméədáwáakuçúuʔu."
165. ʔée wá gaʔâaná ṣúẏáná daʔáyáita kəəgáɴi, dúẇa ʔétyu mâamé
ʔúusgíici ʔémí wá dúẇa daʔáyáita.

---

⁵²Probably 'mouth' rather than 'ear' is meant, as in Stirling (1942, p. 96).

ear.   141. He said to his brother, "This tastes good—it's sweet."
142. They ate all the others, and they ate all the honey.   143. When
the other men saw them, nobody said anything.   144. They had killed
all the bees.

145. Then they put the two (boys) on the hot coals in the fire, but
when they were burned and when they climbed out they had become
very manly, and he made them handsome like their father.   146. Then
the others finally believed that they were Sun Youth's children.

147. He asked them to return to their home the next day.   148. Their
father was going to make them still more handsome.   149. He made different (that is, new) bows for them, and he made different arrows for
them with feathers on (one) end and arrowheads on (the other) end.
150. He made arrow quivers for them to carry arrows in.

151. Sun Youth asked his boys to be very powerful.   152. He made
a rabbit stick for them and advised them not to use it just any time.
153. Everything would be made ugly (that is, destroyed) by it.   154. But
if they had to use it, then it would be all right to use it.   155. If they
killed something and were not satisfied, they could place the staff of
office or the flint on it, and it would know and come to life again.
156. Their father made eight bows for them, and each one had four.
157. He wanted them to use four arrows if they were suddenly attacked
somewhere, and the others, they would use the others to hunt with.
158. He said to them that wherever they went again they would be
allowed, in the north, west, south, and east, where there are very
sacred places, and what they said would be listened to.

159. Their father said to them, "If you should come back to my
house here, the door will be open for you.   160. And now I will give
you clothing, and you will become very handsome with it."   161. He
gave them moccasins and a sash, and he placed a bow guard of buffalo
hide on their wrists.   162. These would be their weapons, and they
should never take them off (because) they had their soul in them.
163. And he gave them beads and turquoise—turquoise beads.   164. "You
will be very handsome with these."   165. He painted red around their
eyes; he painted this way for bravery.

166. ʔée wá dyəəçəṣa ḱámaskuméəti taaʔacikuya záa hawée zíi ʔúbúuci.
167. ṣuwée wá gaʔánaisdíya daʔáwîiçaaní ʔusdyaćści háiti zíi ʔémí ʔai
gaʔánáska ḱáatyasi hawéenə dyaʔáapaçutya.   168.   ʔée kí zíi wée skadíiná
wíisdáani daʔáwîiçaaní, ʔémí dúwa dyəəçəṣa ʔée puʔúuçaanitiuʔumá.
169. hawéenə ʔémí dyaʔaisti šáyâika dúwa ʔémí túu dyəəçəṣa zíka ʔée
puʔúuçaanitiuʔumá.   170. ṣuwée wá ćíyáuṣa "wá hímá dúwáýáka ʔée
ńâiçaagú wâaṣu sái dúwa ʔémí ʔúusgíici zíi mâamé ʔušáaci dúwa ʔémí
ṣaʔáwîiçaaní."   171. ʔée wá ḱapišśní gái ʔai čugúyánətyə.   172.
gaʔánaisdíya taaʔacikuya náanú gáispizáadyáaní ḱéesi nêeʔeyuuceetiuʔumá
gaʔâama ʔéesi.

   173. ʔée wá ʔuṣâaçə dyś zúućaaťání, máamé téeʔe dyś zúuci,
gaʔánaisdíya ʔée dâaʔáminaatikuya ʔée hawée zíi daʔáwáasêeʔestaaní.
174. máamé gái zíi tibêeťaukuyánətyə, záa ʔai háadí zíi ḱáusa
niʔîuçaaciumáńiši níýa.   175. wâaṣu háusi zéedyúpi ʔai gaʔâama gái
ʔuṣâaçəmśəti dyúutuuní guwáa wée ćêeyiši.   176. ʔée wá gái wéemée
ḱámaskuméəti meýú wée dyśýasə wée ťeeyá.   177. ṣuwée wá ʔai dápaci
diḱánə dâaʔapənaiʔi.   178. ṣuwée ʔuṣâaçə dídyá nábáastu ʔísgáýa ṣuwée
ḱámaskuméəti ṣuwée ḱée síńə tidúutya.   179. ṣuwée gái ṣúýati
gaʔánaisdíýa taaʔacikuya ṣuwée gái ʔémí ʔée ʔée ńîiçaańəťyúuʔu guwáa
zaʔáyanikuyaniši.   180. ʔétyu záazíi gái ṣúýati dyúutuunímətyəəka guwáa
haćśma ćêeyiši.

   181. ṣuwée wá ʔai ḱámaskuḱúuyá gâama háuṣu gáaʔaćíní ťúu ṣuwée
ʔéeṣu ḱéesi dyáapə.   182. ṣuwée gái diʔîunáma guwáa ḱée zâaʔapənaimiši
ʔée gaʔánaisdíya gûukačánətyəəciši, ṣuwée gái zíi ʔai ṣuwée ʔai
ʔámúuṁadîuçaaníityə ṣuwée ťeeyu.

   183. ṣuwée wá ʔai gaʔâama háusi gáaʔaćíní gáabáabáa ʔée gaʔánâaya
ʔai gái dâaʔayuuḱami dyəəçəṣa.   184. dínáizáńiṣatyə zíi héḱudá téeʔe
káyawaańətyəəciši, zíi mûuḱaiça zâaʔapeetiši.   185. gái wée
dâaʔáýaipaatikuyańáaťa, záazíi háadí dâaʔáýaińawaatya.   186. záazíi
gaʔánâaya diʔíwîitawanu, máamé háçəcaitaaʔa ʔée guʔúmśədâwá háusi
dyâaʔáci, ʔée zíka gáabáabáa záazíi dîuhimaaku ʔée wá ʔai gaʔánaisdíya
gâama gâaʔaćíniši.   187. ṣuwée wá gái ṣúýati čúuwíišáńətyə gaʔáw agśńi
ṣuwée wéenə dîipaçudyáńətyə, záazíi háma ťúu hámapədá dúwa
piʔíuwáḱətiuʔumáńu, míi mâamé háma hawée zíuʔucibśti.   188. ṣuwée wá
ťúu zíkaná háupədá háńuméesi čúwagśńətyə, ṣuwée wá ṣuwée ʔaisi yúuku
dyâaʔa ʔai háńu díka hawée háusi čúudáašáńətyə.

166. All the while Spider Youth told them not to be afraid.   167. Their father made them a kind of hat that hung down behind their head.   168. He made cornmeal pouches that he wanted them always to have with them. 169. They had hunting charms in them and for this reason he wanted them always to have them with them.   170. He blessed them (saying), "With this it can be done; I made all these now for you for courage and strength." 171. They stayed there that night.   172. Their father told them that the next day at dawn he would take them back home.

173. When the sun was going up, when it went far up, their father kept talking to them, and he showed them where things (were). 174. They asked many questions so it would not be hard anywhere in their doing things.   175. As they were arriving at their house, Sun Youth knew how they had come (that is, with Spider Youth).   176. Spider Youth was still climbing (up with the Sun).   177. He put them (the boys) in the basket.   178. The Sun held the web from one side, and Spider Youth hung it on down.   179. The boy's father told them to do the way that he had asked.   180. The boys did not know how far they had gone.

181. When they got to Spider Woman's house they just went right in. 182. They thanked her for sending them through to see their father, and they prayed for her and left.

183. When they got back home, their grandmother and mother had been waiting for them all this time.   184. They thought that they were lost somewhere far away (or) that mountain lions had eaten them. 185. They had been looking for them, and they could not find them anywhere.   186. Their mother did not recognize them, (because) they were very manly and they returned handsome, and also their grandmother could not believe that they had reached their father's house.   187. The boys took off their clothes and hung them up, as they didn't want to wear them just any time, only when it was necessary.   188. Then once more they dressed like ordinary people, and from then on they lived among the people and joined in (with their daily life).